ISBN 978-1-331-69489-2
PIBN 10222560

1 MONTH OF
FREE
READING

at

www.ForgottenBooks.com

By purchasing this book you are eligible for one month membership to ForgottenBooks.com, giving you unlimited access to our entire collection of over 700,000 titles via our web site and mobile apps.

To claim your free month visit:

www.forgottenbooks.com/free222560

English
Français
Deutsche
Italiano
Español
Português

www.forgottenbooks.com

Mythology Photography **Fiction**
Fishing Christianity **Art** Cooking
Essays Buddhism Freemasonry
Medicine **Biology** Music **Ancient**
Egypt Evolution Carpentry Physics
Dance Geology **Mathematics** Fitness
Shakespeare **Folklore** Yoga Marketing
Confidence Immortality Biographies
Poetry **Psychology** Witchcraft
Electronics Chemistry History **Law**
Accounting **Philosophy** Anthropology
Alchemy Drama Quantum Mechanics
Atheism Sexual Health **Ancient History**
Entrepreneurship Languages Sport
Paleontology Needlework Islam
Metaphysics Investment Archaeology
Parenting Statistics Criminology
Motivational

"The Angel of the Battle Field"
Clara Barton at the period of the Civil War.

THE LIFE OF
CLARA BARTON

BY

PERCY H. EPLER

New York
THE MACMILLAN COMPANY
1915

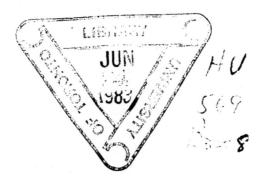

Norwood Press
J. S. Cushing Co. — Berwick & Smith Co.
Norwood, Mass., U.S.A.

To

FOREWORD

"IT is fully within bounds to say that there is no surviving American of either sex whose autobiography, if fully given, would constitute so thrilling and so fascinating a narrative as that of Miss Clara Barton." [1]

Twenty years ago American public opinion was thus expressed in a representative editorial. Though Miss Barton's life had even then reached its meridian and had made history enough for several biographies, none had been written and none has appeared up to this time.

At the present moment unusual interest would seem to be attached to her life story. Amid the terrible catastrophes of the nations that now confront us, the biography of the Angel of the Battle Field cannot but afford a mighty stimulant. It is an inspiration for the relief of suffering, an encouragement to pity and mercy. These are the human emotions which it must inevitably prompt. While such feelings may not always be able to prevent war, they can and do help us prepare a table of relief in the midst of titanic foes of destruction.

Clara Barton's mission was not to glorify war. "Men have worshiped war," she declared, "till it has cost a million times more than the whole world is worth, poured out the best blood and crushed the fairest forms the good God has ever created. — Deck it as you will, war is — 'Hell.' . . . The war side of war could never have called me to the field. All through and through, thought and act, body and soul — I hate it. . . . Only the desire to soften some of its hardships and allay some of its miseries ever induced me, and I presume all other women who have taken similar steps, to dare its pestilent and unholy breath."

Her "work and words," she insisted, "were for the individual soldier — what he does, sees, feels or thinks in these dread hours of leaden rain and iron hail."

[1] *Review of Reviews*, April, 1894.

vii

"If I were to speak of war," she further says, "it would not be to show you the glories of conquering armies but the mischief and misery they strew in their track; and how, while they march on with tread of iron and plumes proudly tossing in the breeze, some one must follow closely in their steps, crouching to the earth, toiling in the rain and darkness, shelterless like themselves, with no thought of pride or glory, fame or praise, or reward; hearts breaking with pity, faces bathed in tears and hands in blood. This is the side which history never shows."

In all this we see her standing for exactly that which expresses America's conviction to-day, — a conviction to which indeed we have been lately lifted again by our standard-bearer, the President; namely, humanity. In her own words, true for all time, but once for all expressed at the Sea Island disaster, it is this: "We cannot desert our great, poor charge of humanity but must stay and suffer with them if need be."

And this is the side which the author has tried to show in this book through the agency of Miss Barton's life, in so far as possible through her own eyes and with the understanding of her own heart. He has searched out her words, scattered in unpublished manuscripts as they mostly are. Here he has found that in her hands war is weighed in new scales, not with the balances of a heartless, obsessed militarism, but with those of humanity.

Great as was Clara Barton's actual contribution to the world, the contribution of herself, her life — greater yet was the moral effect on her race which in America saw through her the uplift of organs of relief hitherto undreamt of. If evil came, unblinded by smoke and carnage, free from hysteria, with perfect self-control, she showed mankind the way out, proved that civilization was not dead, and demonstrated triumph amid apparent defeat. The crown of this leadership of humanity was the foundation in America of the American National Red Cross.

The estimate of humanity is always significant. "Our greatest national heroine and the equal of any soldier or statesman of the Civil War." In these words the *Literary Digest*[1] condensed the verdict of press and public. Long ago Charles Sumner described her as one who possessed "the talent of a statesman, the command of a general

[1] April, 1912.

and the heart and hand of a woman." To-day General Nelson A. Miles holds that she was "the greatest humanitarian the world has ever known," while Jane Addams, emphasizing her importance as an Internationalist and as an inspirer of the social conscience, has said: "No, I shall not attempt to choose twenty from the scores of women I deem worthy of immortality, but the passing of America's grand old lady leaves her foremost in my affections."

Miss Barton was primarily a "doer" "of the word," not a writer. "Persons who use their brains, tongues and pens for the improvement of their kind are those of whom biographies may profitably be written," she says. "The grand things their tongues and pens have said are accessible and form a living inspiration to others, but I, — I know nothing remarkable I have done. The humdrum work of my everyday life seems to me quite without incident."

Thus by her own words does she stand convicted of greatness. So commonplace had become her heroic rôle in the world's theaters of conflict that it was actually to her mind quite without incident — not because incidents were few but because they were countless. This is the principal reason for her failure to write her autobiography. She could not bring it to a focus. Intrusting the story of her life to others to write, she left behind her much valuable and informing material for her biographer. While her childhood is touched upon in a winsome sketch from her pen entitled *The Story of My Childhood*, this would cover less than one full chapter of this book and does not contribute facts of great central importance.

Her unpublished war diaries and letters upon which I have spent long research, together with her conversations, and observations by eye-witnesses, are my chief original sources. For the period after 1877 the published record of the Red Cross administration and its detailed official history have all been consulted and have been found of much value. While fully conscious of many limitations it has been the aim, with all these sources at our command, that the book should come forth with the force of an autobiography.

AUTHOR'S ACKNOWLEDGMENT

THE author wishes to express his sense of deep obligation to the following who have helped him in the preparation of this book: Miss Barton's nephew and executor, Mr. Stephen E. Barton; her nieces, Mrs. Mamie Barton Stafford, Mrs. Fannie M. Vassall; her grand-niece and nephew, Miss Saidee and Mr. Herman P. Riccius, and to her cousin, William E. Barton, D.D., LL.D.; to Dr. Julian B. Hubbell, Mrs. J. Sewall Reed, Mrs. Marion B. Bullock, Mr. Charles Sumner Young; to Mrs. James Bolton (daughter of Judge Joseph Sheldon); to the editor, B. F. Tillinghast; to Mr. Edgar Reed, a captain of industry and a patron of historical research; to the veterans, J. Brainerd Hall and A. S. Roe; to Rev. Dr. Schoppe, Miss Barton's former pastor; to such publications as "The Red Cross" and "A Story of the Red Cross," together with many magazine articles for the past fifty years; to the fellow members of the committee on the biography, a majority of whom I have reached and who have shown marked courtesy as to the present volume; also to Mrs. Lewis G. Fairchild for much stenographic assistance.

PERCY H. EPLER.

INTRODUCTION AND AUTHORIZATION

By WILLIAM E. BARTON, D.D., LL.D.[1]

CLARA BARTON'S life touches the life of her nation at so many vital points that its record can hardly be less than a chapter in our national and international history. In consenting to prepare an introduction to Mr. Epler's book, I am moved in part by a desire to say to the readers of the volume that it is published with the consent and assistance of Miss Barton's relations and literary executors. It is, and for a number of years will be, the only authorized life of Clara Barton. Miss Barton's literary effects were left to her beloved and trusted nephew, Mr. Stephen E. Barton of Boston, who had long been associated with her in the work of the Red Cross. According to him, this biography of Mr. Epler's includes much of "the pith and cream" of her private and unpublished papers and diaries. Miss Barton provided in her will that with Stephen should be associated a small group of relations and friends whom she designated and to whom she intrusted the custody and ultimate distribution of her papers. Always methodical, she had preserved a very large mass of papers, consisting of diaries, letter books, correspondence and miscellaneous documents which she expected would ultimately be used in the preparation of her biography.

Ten years or more from the present time it is confidently expected that the relations and executors will carry out Miss Barton's expectation, but the many boxes of letters and correspondence will involve a work of sifting and sorting material which must occupy several years, and other years will have to be given to the preparation of the larger Life and Letters, — at least ten in all. Such a work as is con-

[1] Rev. William E. Barton, one of the finest and ablest representatives of the Barton stock to-day, was a deeply esteemed cousin of Clara Barton, and speaks here for the Barton family as authorized by the executor, Stephen E. Barton.

templated will be a life of Clara Barton and much more — as the volumes will include masses of letters yet unexamined.

Meantime, there is at present, demand for a comprehensive life of Clara Barton. It is a satisfaction to her relatives and literary executors that this biography has been prepared by Mr. Epler. He knew her well, and she respected and trusted him. He had at hand a considerable body of unpublished material for the preparation of such a work, and Mr. Stephen E. Barton has placed at his disposal such other chief sources as are available. Speaking, therefore, for those who have best reason to be interested in the publication of such a work, I express not only the satisfaction but the pleasure of her family and intimate friends in the present volume.

Perhaps I may be permitted to add a few paragraphs concerning the personality of Clara Barton. First of all I should like to say that she never grew old. Her years numbered seventy, eighty, ninety, and more, but she kept the soul of youth. There was hardly a gray hair in her head. She sat and stood as erect as an Indian maiden, erect not with the rigidity of age, but with the freedom and grace of youth. Her voice, her eye, her step, all had in them those qualities which distinguish youth from age rather than age from youth.

She kept a sunny disposition and a cheerful face. Burdened as she often was by the sorrows, calamities, and atrocities of human life, suffering as she was called to suffer from serious and protracted illness, deeply sensitive in her inmost soul to criticism or injustice, she trod her path serenely down the long vista of the years, and her heart made music and her face radiated sunshine.

Hers was no cheap and unthinking optimism. Her faith in God and man was not that of the superficial or unfeeling observer; she saw life sanely and she saw it whole, and she kept her courage and her faith.

She was by nature a timid woman. Her courage was not the effervescence of mere animal life; it was the triumph of soul over instinctive shrinking from the presence of danger and the sight of pain. If she learned to look on suffering without tears it was not because she grew unfeeling, but because she accomplished a supreme self-mastery at the stern behest of duty. There is a courage which does not reckon with danger, nor stop to consider pain. Not of this sort was Clara Barton. It was her heroic soul and her deep human sympathy that made her strong and brave.

She combined in unusual degree the qualities of modesty and self-confidence. She did not know what it was to indulge in self-praise, and she felt something of constraint and embarrassment when others praised her. I have seen her blush like a schoolgirl at a compliment, and stand before an audience in momentary confusion over a generous word spoken in her introduction. But modest as she was and un-assuming to a high degree, she had also a just and accurate estimate of her own power to master a situation. It was only in things relating to herself that she ever showed embarrassment or lack of self-confidence. Face to face with a great emergency, whether flood, or fire, or pestilence, or the slaughter of battle, she completely forgot herself in the presence of the need confronting her. She knew what needed to be done, and she knew that she knew. Open to advice, she placed strong reliance upon her own judgment, and she moved with no uncertainty toward the ends which she realized needed to be at-tained.

These qualities in her inspired confidence in others. He would have been a brave man who disputed her authority when she had determined upon a given course as right. In stature and in frame she was not a large woman. Her voice was gentle and she seldom raised it, but she issued her quiet directions and they carried with them the authority of her gentle and forceful personality. She was forceful as truly as she was gentle. Incapable of unkindness, she could be stern; gentle and tender and sympathetic, she had in her an element of inflexibility. These qualities possessed by her in no wise neutral-ized each other. Men and women realized the force of her calm judg-ment, the purity of her motives, her power of accomplishment; they believed in her, responded gladly to her leadership, and were safe in so doing.

There is one thing more I should like to say of her, and that is, that in every fiber of her being she was womanly. In her young womanhood she was a teacher, a salaried clerk in Washington, and the matron of a penal institution. Then she was thrown among rough men, and into the midst of rough scenes; she looked upon hatred, murder and every unholy passion. Not only did she keep her soul unsoiled from contact with the world's sin, but she preserved every womanly grace and feminine trait as completely as if she had led a sheltered life. She had no sympathy with mannish women.

She exalted womanliness, honored motherhood, and cherished in her own heart those virtues which are distinctively feminine. I have often wondered how it could be that a woman who had witnessed what she had witnessed, and heard what she had heard, and known what she had to know, and done what for duty's sake she was gladly compelled to do, could have seen and heard and known and done all that she did and experienced no coarsening of the fiber of her soul. Throughout her whole long and varied life she was a true, genuine, Christian lady.

It was not her need of earning a livelihood that first sent her out into the world, but the joy of service. It was not to earn her daily bread or to add to her sufficient means that she continued to give her life to the welfare of humanity. There was that in her being which compelled her to give the best she had unstintedly to human service. No task was too humble for her to perform; no peril was great enough to daunt her. She poured out the rich treasure of her life like Mary of Bethany; she broke her alabaster box over the head of her Lord, and the whole house is still fragrant with the memory of her good deeds.

OAK PARK, ILLINOIS,
        September 29, 1915.

CONTENTS

CHAPTER   PAGE

    I. BIRTH AND BIRTHRIGHTS 1

   II. HER FATHER AND MOTHER? 5

  III. HER TEACHERS 9

  IV. A NURSE AT ELEVEN 12

   V. "I REMEMBER NOTHING BUT FEAR" 14

  VI. EIGHTEEN YEARS OF TEACHING 18

 VII. FIVE YEARS IN WASHINGTON BEFORE THE WAR 24

VIII. THE BEGINNING OF THE CIVIL WAR 28

  IX. TO THE FIRING LINE 33

   X. SECOND BULL RUN AND CHANTILLY 36

  XI. HARPER'S FERRY AND SOUTH MOUNTAIN 48

 XII. ANTIETAM 54

XIII. ON THE MARCH THROUGH MARYLAND AND VIRGINIA 60

XIV. THE WINTER CAMPAIGN BEFORE FREDERICKSBURG . 64

 XV. EIGHT MONTHS AT FORTS WAGNER, SUMTER, AND GREGG IN THE CAMPAIGN BEFORE CHARLESTON 76

XVI. STEPHEN BARTON AT 15 ENTERS THE WAR 86

XVII. THE WILDERNESS AND SPOTTSYLVANIA 89

XVIII. AT THE SIEGE OF PETERSBURG, VIRGINIA 99

XIX. THE "AMEN" OF THE WAR — BEFORE RICHMOND 102

XX. FOUR YEARS' SEARCH FOR MISSING MEN 110

XXI. AT THE OUTBREAK OF THE FRANCO-PRUSSIAN WAR . . . 123

XXII. THE CALL TO BEAR THE RED CROSS TO THE PRUSSIAN FIRING LINE 137

XXIII. "TURN BACK! TURN BACK! THE PRUSSIANS ARE COMING!" 142

XXIV. STRASSBURG 150

CHAPTER		PAGE
XXV.	THE SURRENDER OF METZ, SEDAN, AND STRASSBURG	156
XXVI.	AT THE SIEGE OF PARIS AND THE COMMUNE	164
XXVII.	ADVENT AND CHRISTMAS WITH THE WAR-TORN POOR	176
XXVIII.	TOURS IN ITALY AND THE ISLE OF WIGHT	190
XXIX.	NERVOUS PROSTRATION IN ENGLAND	203
XXX.	CONTINUED NERVOUS PROSTRATION IN AMERICA	211
XXXI.	THE FOUNDATION OF THE RED CROSS IN AMERICA	226
XXXII.	CLARA BARTON AND THE AMERICAN NATIONAL RED CROSS IN NATIONAL AND INTERNATIONAL DISASTERS	235
XXXIII.	CLARA BARTON IN CUBA AND THE SPANISH WAR	282
XXXIV.	THE GALVESTON FLOOD, 1900 — RETIREMENT, 1904 — MEXICO — PRESIDENT FIRST AID TO THE INJURED	319
XXXV.	CLARA BARTON AS INTERNATIONALIST AND PUBLICIST	341
XXXVI.	CLARA BARTON IN HER HOMES	352
XXXVII.	SOCIAL TRAITS	377
XXXVIII.	CLARA BARTON ON WAR	397
XXXIX.	THE RELIGION OF CLARA BARTON	410
XL.	"LET ME GO! LET ME GO!"	423

LIST OF ILLUSTRATIONS

"Angel of the Battle Field" . . . . *Frontispiece*

FACING PAGE

Birthplace of Clara Barton 3
Sarah Stone Barton 5
Captain Stephen Barton 5
Clara Barton's Second Homestead 9
The Third Homestead 13
The Old Barton Mill Site 19
Clara Barton in her Twenties 23
Sally Barton 23
Stephen E. Barton — To-day 87
Minnie Kupfer 145
Antoinette Margot 145
Clara Barton in her Workrooms after the Siege of Strassburg 159
Clara Barton in 1879 221
Clara Barton as Founder of the American National Red Cross, 1882 . 233
First Red Cross Headquarters — 1882–1892. 1915 Vermont Avenue, Washington, D. C. 241
The General Grant Mansion 17th and F Streets, Washington, D. C. — Red Cross Headquarters and Home (1892–1897) 261
Dr. Julian B. Hubbell 279
"Red Cross" at Glen Echo, Md. 369
Clara Barton's Summer Home in Oxford, 1884–1911 373
At 87 387
"As the Leaves Fall" 423
Burial Place of Clara Barton at North Oxford 433

xvii

THE LIFE OF CLARA BARTON

CHAPTER I

BIRTH AND BIRTHRIGHTS

CHRISTMAS DAY, December 25, 1821, Clara Barton was born in an unpretentious farmhouse on the flattened brow of one of the hill crests of North Oxford in central Massachusetts.

Her given name was Clarissa Harlowe, but it was as Clara Barton that she always signed herself, and it is by this simpler name, into which she was immortally christened by baptisms of fire and blood, that she will be remembered.

In Europe the name Barton first appears in England in 1086 A.D. in the "Domesday Book" of William the Conqueror, where it is spelled "Barton" or "Bartun." For fidelity to its country and king the Barton family was early given a manor in Lancashire, where for centuries the old stock was rooted. Upon its coat of arms rested the armorial red, and down through the Wars of the Roses till to-day red has been the Barton color — symbolic of sacrifice. Clara Barton herself seldom appeared without a touch of it upon her costume. "It is my color," she would explain.

In this country the Barton line may be traced back to 1640, by which time Edward Barton had come from England and had settled in the coast town of Salem. A little later he was at Portsmouth, New Hampshire, and in 1671 he had a 300-acre plantation at Cape Porpoise, Maine. In that year, owing to Indian outbreaks, he was forced to flee with his family to Salem, where he died in 1673. His son Mathew, sailor, shipbuilder, and farmer, then returned to Cape Porpoise with his son Samuel. It was Samuel Barton, born in 1664, who founded the Barton family of Oxford, from which Clara Barton is descended.

Samuel, as well as his father and grandfather, lived in the mad era of Salem witchcraft. His grandmother, drawn into one of the

B   I

trials, hotly discredited the craze as "a fantasy," and at twenty-eight years of age Samuel defended at his own peril witches brought under accusation by the fanatic, Mercy Lewis. Indeed, in 1690 he married Hannah Bridges, daughter of Sarah Towne, who was sister of Rebecca Nourse, hanged on Salem Hill for witchcraft in 1692. The year following that tragedy Samuel with his family and the Townes shook the dust of Salem from their feet and moved to Framingham. Here they lived for twenty-three years. In 1716, selling a farm in "upland, swampland and meadow" at Framingham, they moved to Oxford.

Oxford itself had its Red Letter days in early American annals. Just east of Oxford Center was "Fort Hill," whose cliffs were chosen by Huguenot settlers in 1686 as a settlement, rendezvous, and refuge. There they erected factories and mills, the stones of which remain in place to-day. Eastwardly, beneath sidings of sheer rock, gardens were planted in such a spot as only Frenchmen could choose, where late into the frosty fall they were warmed by the sun's reflections against the abutting palisades. But Nipmuc Indians drove the Huguenots from these charming plantations. In the summer of 1694 they butchered a girl and captured two children, and two years later they massacred the Johnson family, dashing out the brains of the three children on the great stone of the fireplace now set up as a monument in front of Town Hall, Oxford. Notwithstanding this bloody history, thirty English colonists, with Colonel Ebenezer Learned at the head, settled at Oxford in 1713 and gave the town its name.

Samuel Barton bought one thirtieth of the colony when he located there in 1716, and soon acquired a quarter interest in all the saw mills and corn mills. In 1720 he became a signer of the covenant and a founder of the Oxford Congregational Church, "moved by obligations to promote the Kingdom of their Lord and Saviour, Jesus Christ — after prayer and conference." He was a man of strong Christian faith.

His youngest son, Edmund Barton, a soldier in the French wars, married Anna Flint of Salem and settled at Sutton. Among his children was Stephen Barton, born June 10, 1740.

Stephen Barton was a physician. His generosity forbade him to present his bills to patients, and though a good practitioner, he was unable to make a living from the profession. In 1764 he settled at Oxford Center, and engaged in trading, becoming in time the landlord of the old Tavern. In 1776 he removed to Windsor, Maine, with his

BIRTHPLACE OF CLARA BARTON

The arrow marks the little room where she was born.

sons, but returned to Oxford in 1790 and established a mechanical shop. He died in Maine in 1805.[1]

One of his sons was Stephen Barton, born August 18, 1774. This was the father of Clara Barton.

Even as a very young man, Stephen showed the Barton spirit. In 1793 the campaign was on against the Indians and the English in Michigan, Indiana, and Ohio, and Stephen could not resist the call.

Of his enlistment and the experiences of the three years that followed, Miss Barton said in 1886: "At twenty-one Stephen joined a body of troops, recruits for the wars of the western frontiers, then menaced by the Indians. They marched on foot, from Boston via Philadelphia, capital of the nation, to Michigan, then the extreme western frontier, a wilderness full of Indians. The main army lay at Detroit under the command of Mad Anthony Wayne, whose worshipful soldier young Stephen became, serving under untold hardships for three years, as a non-commissioned officer, side by side with William Henry Harrison, 'Old Tippecanoe,' and Richard M. Johnson, then lieutenants and later president and vice-president of the United States. He was present at the slaying of Tecumseh, which broke the Indian ranks, and at the Treaty of Peace. At the disbanding he marched home again on foot with other officers, taking their way along the line of the upper Ohio and central New York, both wildernesses. But upon striking the Genesee and Mohawk valleys they were so charmed by the country that they selected and purchased large tracts of government land, as nearly as I can learn, located somewhere in the vicinity of Rochester. I could sincerely wish it had been a few miles farther south and he had reserved it for his children, but it was later sold as so remote from civilization as to be considered useless property."

In the manuscript of a lecture prepared just after the Civil War Miss Barton further said of her father:

"When a little child upon his knee he told me that as he lay helpless in the tangled marshes of Michigan the muddy water oozed up

---

[1] A diary of Stephen Barton, now in the possession of Mrs. E. H. Mosher of Augusta, Maine, goes into the early history of the Barton family in England in considerable detail. It gives an interesting account of the Maine pilgrimages of Stephen Barton, making clear the remarkable versatility of the man — he could shoe an ox, shingle a barn, keep a store, prescribe for the sick, or make a coffin. It also details his love of adventure and the great outdoors.

from the track of an officer's horse and saved him from death by thirst. And that a mouthful of a lean dog that had followed the march saved him from starvation. When he told me how the feathered arrow quivered in the flesh and the tomahawk swung over the white man's head, he told me also with tears of honest pride of the great and beautiful country that had sprung up from those wild scenes of suffering and danger. How he loved these new States for which he gave the strength of his youth!"

SARAH STONE BARTON   CAPTAIN STEPHEN BARTON

Clara Barton's parents.

CHAPTER II

Her Father and Mother

In 1796 "Captain" Barton, as Stephen was known, returned to Massachusetts and eight years later he was married to Sarah Stone. They started housekeeping west of Oxford near Charlton and then moved to a section north of Ben Learned Hill where a new home was built. It was here that Clara was born.

In one of her own delightful recollections Miss Barton says:

"The family grew and prospered and at the end of twelve or thirteen years another little waif was added to it, and this time it was I, — on one bright Christmas day, — and I am told that the family jubilation upon the occasion was so great that the entire dinner and tea sets had to be changed for the serving of the noble guests who gathered. I have also been told that I was a very good child, strong, healthy, happy, making few complaints, although I suspect there was no lack of family grit if it were called for."

The birthplace [1] still stands to-day, a witness to the simple tastes of her people. Though Stephen had by this time a well-tilled farm and had risen to a position of some importance in the community, having served as a moderator and selectman and having been elected a legislator in the General Court of the State, there was yet nothing of the pretentious about his home, a small building of a story and a half. Inside nearly everything was homemade — even the crib in which the Christmas baby was cradled (which may now be seen in the rooms of the Worcester Society of Antiquity). Outside, the flat flagstone in front of the door was marked by the hand tools of the father. It led through lilac bushes to a green dooryard, where, when Clara learned to walk, she was allowed to play alone.

---

[1] The house is about a mile from the main street on a road running at right angles with the electric car line which plies between Worcester and Webster. The point at which to leave the car is Bartlett's Upper Mill, where a weather-beaten sign shows the way "To Clara Barton's Birthplace."

Her oldest sister was Dorothy, seventeen years her senior; her oldest brother, Stephen, was fifteen when she was born. Besides these, there were David, thirteen, and Sally, ten.

From the first, the father found in Clara a pet, a playmate, and, beyond his dreams, a sharer of patriotism and deeds of daring. In later years she often referred to the joy of this comradeship, when, perched upon her father's knee, she imbibed a passion for her country and cultivated "a taste for early history."

"His military habits and tastes never left him," says Miss Barton in " The Story of My Childhood." "Those were also strong political days — Andrew Jackson Days — and very naturally my father became my instructor in military and political lore. I listened breathlessly to his war stories. Illustrations were called for and we made battles and fought them. Every shade of military etiquette was regarded. Colonels, captains, and sergeants were given their proper place and rank. So with the political world; the president, cabinet, and leading officers of the Government were learned by heart, and nothing gratified the keen humor of my father more than the parrotlike readiness with which I lisped these difficult names. I thought the president might be as large as the meeting house, and the vice-president perhaps the size of the schoolhouse. And yet, when later, I, like all the rest of our country's people, was suddenly thrust into the mysteries of war, and had to find and take my place and part in it, I found myself far less a stranger to the conditions than most women, or even ordinary men for that matter. I never addressed a colonel as captain, got my cavalry on foot, or mounted my infantry!"

The drill and discipline of war that thus sank unconsciously into her mind were similar to other training that put iron into her blood.

"A fire in a church would have been sacrilege in those days," she wrote in 1904 in a letter to an Oxford friend — "and I can just remember being taken home one bitter cold Sunday with frozen feet. I had not dared complain and fell in the pew when they set me down."

At this time there were in Oxford no matches to light a fire. The flint, snapped by the lock, was the only method.

"A long way back this memory of mine travels — almost timidly it seems so far away," she wrote to the author in the fall of 1910. "It heard the snap of the first flint lock that kindled a fire on the hearth; and gazed in wonderment at the blaze that came from nothing as the first match lit up the world."

These were character-making days for Clara Barton — the impression that they left upon her was deep and lasting. That in later years she appreciated to the full the great importance of the home in the child's early life is shown by a remark that she made after twenty-five years of teaching. "Show me a child," she said, "well disciplined, perfectly governed at home, and I will show you a child that never breaks the rule of school. A silken thread will bind that child."

Liberalizing their creed to the Universalist communion, the Bartons ordained Hosea Ballou as first pastor, and built the first Universalist Church in existence — the meeting house in Oxford. Yet her father and mother, however liberal in their creed, never relaxed from the deepest habits of all that was best in Pilgrim and Puritan. No matter how snowy, no matter how the winds hurtled over the hilltops — the Barton family not only drove five miles to church every Sunday, but maintained, during the other six days of the week, the deeper fundamentals of conscience and honor peculiar to their forefathers' faith.

Sarah Stone, the mother of Clara Barton, is described as having been a beautiful girl. She was only seventeen when she married Stephen and before she was out of her twenties she had borne him four children. Mrs. Barton was preëminently the housewife — practical and full of common-sense, a fact which partly accounts for the marvelous balance of Clara's whole life. As in the mother of George Bancroft, the historian, and Clara Barton's contemporary in Worcester County, these elements in Sarah Barton brought the unusual in her child down to earth and kept her from the eccentricities of genius. The mother was not a teacher in the book sense, but what Clara learned of her even in the details of cooking — and all the rest — was never lost.

"My mother, as good mothers will, endeavored to interest me in the ways and mysteries of housekeeping, but complained," Clara is quoted as having said, "that among them all she had a poor chance, although it is my belief that her efforts have been as lasting and as much honored by me as any."

In many little ways her mother's training helped her — when she had to be mother to an army and little sister to the soldier. For example, once, after Antietam, a dying soldier asked for a custard pie — to remind him of home, — "one crinkly around the edges, please, and with just the marks of the finger prints." Her eyes swam, but in a few moments Clara Barton herself in the crude commissary made a pie "crinkly at the edges" and scalloped with "finger prints."

A level head was what Sarah Barton sought to give her daughter. Her matter-of-fact face, firm, penetrating with determination, bears out the part she played. Possibly she may have been too severe. No dolls were allowed her little girl, but, as time went on, garden and flower beds, sewing, especially for the poor, and the care of pets about the barn and dooryard, became her pastimes. Should she share her candies or cake and forget a piece for herself, her mother, when one of the company offered to give his back, insisted that Clara must not be an "Indian Giver," and so taught her daughter to be "a good loser," a trait which she was to need sorely when apparent defeats were again and again to discourage her before a final victory.

Other circumstances show that Mrs. Barton's looks did not belie a spirited determination. When a girl she had loved to ride mettlesome horses and had frequently been thrown and hurt but persevered until she gained the mastery. Her fine saddle she kept until Clara's day, and gave it to her in 1835. Sarah Barton's father was a patriot and faced death at the Battle of Bennington. In many ways the mother inherited his spirit.

"Far and beyond it all," Clara Barton once wrote of her mother, "as the years sped on and the hands were still, shone the gleam of the far-sighted mother's watchfulness that neither toil could obscure nor mirth relax."

CLARA BARTON'S SECOND HOMESTEAD
The Learned House.

CHAPTER III

Her Teachers

THE atmosphere of Clara Barton's home was favorable to an early education. Her two sisters, Dorothy and Sally, were teachers, as was Stephen her brother. It is not surprising, then, that before she was over three years old Clara had learned to read. As in the case of Edward Everett Hale, she was unable to remember when she could not read a story for herself. In spelling, arithmetic, and geography, she had also made some progress.

"I had no playmates," she once said, "but in effect six fathers and mothers. They were a family of school teachers. All took charge of me, all educated me, each according to personal taste. My two sisters were scholars and artistic and strove in that direction. My brothers were strong, ruddy, daring young men, full of life and business."

In the winter of 1824 Clara was hoisted on Stephen's strong shoulders and carried a mile and a half to the school taught by Colonel Richard C. Stone. He was the first of a number of fine-grained personalities to come into her life and to leave a strong impress upon it. Her schooling continued under him until 1829 when the fame of his teaching led him to establish the Oxford High School, in which Clara later enrolled. He was succeeded in the district school by Clara's brother, Stephen, in the winter, and by her sisters in the summer.

By the time Clara was eight years old her father had moved his family down the long hill to a 300-acre farm at its foot, extending "from Peaked Hill to Jim Brown's across the flowed swamp." The brook-like French River threaded the broad meadows. Between the intervale and the house, which was none other than the old Ebenezer Learned house, stood three barns and in these Clara climbed and jumped from the great beams, and played at hide and seek in the hay. To this new home came the four children of Captain Barton's nephew who had died, but Clara's sisters remained with

9

her two brothers, who took charge of the little hillside farms about her birthplace — buying them for their own.

This new home on the highway in North Oxford afforded opportunities for exciting outdoor games and feats of daring. Here the woman who later was to cross the pontoon bridge at Fredericksburg under fire and with skirt shot away, learned to cross the little winding French River on teetering logs at its most dangerous depths. Later, when this sport had become tame, she would go to the saw mill and ride out on the saw carriage twenty feet above the stream and be pulled back on the returning log. These, and other water sports, were new and fascinating and were enjoyed the year round.

In summer the "circular" pond was the home of a beautiful flock of ducks, which by the first fall had so increased that wild "divers and dippers" paused in their southward migration to swoop down on the pond's calm surface. Hens, turkeys, dogs, geese, and cats were added to Clara's stock of pets and later three or four of the sleekest heifers, which she learned to milk. This was an art which she never forgot and which she used to good advantage when food failed and she rode with the foragers in the Civil War.

The old house which Captain Barton renovated, and which stands to-day much as it did then, claimed its share of the little daughter's attention. She learned to grind and mix paints and apply them as well as the painter; also to match, trim, and hang paper; and she had a hand in brightening the walls of every room. Further down the street, on the southeast corner, her father later built a smaller house which, however, failed to equal the big Learned house in her affections.

By 1832 her brothers had been so successful that they, too, sold their hill farms and followed their father to the French River at the foot of the mile-long hill where they eventually erected homes across the street from the Learned house. David, with Stephen, bought the saw mill, and erected new dams and a new grain mill. Stephen married, as also did Sally, and both settled in the neighborhood. Dorothy remained single.

The schools that Clara now attended were imperfect. She missed the fine instruction of Colonel Stone, and Dorothy, who had tutored her in days gone by, was unable, through ill health, to help her. Sally was her one instructor, but self-education was still the prime note of the Barton household.

Captain Barton, through "Black Stallion," the king of the stable, had introduced blooded stock on his large grassy farm lands. Nervous, high-bred "Highlander, Virginian, and Morgan" colts raced about the fields. They added a new verve to farm life.

"David," Clara Barton wrote in "The Story of My Childhood," "was the Buffalo Bill of the surrounding country. It was his delight to take me, a little girl five years old, to the field, seize a couple of those beautiful grazing creatures, broken only to the halter and bit, and gathering the reins of both bridles in one hand, throw me upon the back of one colt, spring upon the other himself, and catching me by one foot, and bidding me 'cling fast to the mane,' gallop away over field and fen, in and out among other colts, in wild glee like ourselves. They were merry rides we took. This was my riding school. I never had any other, but it served me well. To this day my seat on a saddle or on the back of a horse is as secure and tireless as in a rocking chair and far more pleasurable. Sometimes in later years when I found myself on a strange horse, in a trooper's saddle, flying for life or liberty in front of pursuit, I blessed the baby lessons of the wild gallops among the beautiful colts." "At five years old I rode wild horses like a little Mexican" she said in another retrospect.

With three teachers of books in the persons of her two sisters and one brother it was well David followed his mother's practical mindedness and became his youngest sister's companion, racing her around in out-of-door sports till she could run and ride like a boy.

Thus the little frame toughened and she laid away energy to meet many sicknesses, among them an almost fatal attack of bloody dysentery and convulsions, which came the very year that she began to ride.

CHAPTER IV

A Nurse at Eleven

1832–1833

In 1832, when Clara was eleven, her schooling was interrupted by an accident that approached the tragic in its consequences though it disclosed the talent that later was to make her the greatest of war nurses and the founder of the Red Cross in America.

In the group of new buildings on the 300-acre farm occurred a barn raising. The high rafters had to be fixed to the ridge pole. David, the athlete of the community, and unexcelled in taking a dare, climbed to the peak. A board broke under his feet, precipitating him to the ground, where his body struck heavy timbers. Seriously injured by a blow on his head, he lingered between life and death for two years. Leeches, setons, counter-irritating blisters, and blood letting failed to allay the fever. Clara felt herself chained to him by an unspeakable and uncontrollable impulse to nurse. She became so skilled that her small fingers were chosen by the doctor to apply the leeches and the plasters, and to give the prescribed medicines, hour after hour.

The mental effect on the patient of her faith and unfailing presence was miraculous. "In his nervous wretchedness he clung to me. I could not be taken away from him except by compulsion," she later remarked. Yet he remained a "sleepless, nervous, cold dyspeptic — the mere wreck of his former self." Bending over him, hurrying to obey his every impulse, Clara locked herself up with the patient for two years.

Referring to this period Miss Barton once said: "For two years I only left his bedside for one half day. I almost forgot that there was an outside to the house."

In 1834 David was given the new system of treatment of steam baths which in time proved successful. Under it he completely re-

THE THIRD HOMESTE D

covered. It was almost, however, at the sacrifice of Clara's life. The serious strain of the long confinement and the continuous care of the patient seriously impaired her health and it was some time before she regained her normal strength. But the experience had brought out the gift that was in her; it was almost prophetic of things to come.

CHAPTER V

"I Remember Nothing but Fear"

"In the earlier years of my life, I remember nothing but fear," Miss Barton confessed in 1907.

Fear would seem to be a most impossible characteristic of one destined to play the part that Miss Barton later did on the firing lines of human tragedy. Had it not been for her mother's training and her father's and brother's interest in her out of doors, Clara would doubtless have drooped away, for, however paradoxical it may seem, fear never ceased to haunt her in one way or another. The courage that she later attained was due not to its absence, but to the fact that she had overcome it.

She had a too vivid imagination. At four years old it peopled the clouds with angry rams and once when she was left alone it threw her screaming in hysterics to the floor. In 1824 to face her first teacher alone overcame her with a convulsion of fear that the teacher relieved with difficulty. But with wise personal care her delicate sensibilities and her fears and embarrassments were thoughtfully shielded.

Yet her supersensitiveness did not leave her. So tender-hearted was she that even when she was ten the butchering of an ox made her faint and gave her a distaste for eating meat that stayed with her all her life. Extreme fear and " chicken-heartedness" — seemingly impossible endowments for a soul that was to face more bloody battle-fields than any of her sex since the world began — instead of decreasing, grew upon her.

Silence was another sign of her panic of fear. Often rather than speak she suffered silently. She early betrayed such bashfulness before strangers and such shrinking timidity that it was painful to herself and to others. "To this day," she said in 1907, "I would rather stand behind the lines of artillery at Antietam or cross the pontoon bridge under fire at Fredericksburg than be expected to preside at a public meeting."

From eleven to thirteen, while she was buried in her nursing, her family forgot the physical effects upon her until, at David's recovery, they woke to find her growth arrested at what should have been the growing age. "So little!" This was the epithet applied to her. She had not grown an inch in two years nor increased a pound! She was but five feet three inches tall — nor was she ever taller.

David's recovery left her without enough to do. The seclusion had made her a hermit — more unused to society than ever — "afraid," she admitted, "of giving trouble by letting my wants be known, thereby giving the very pain I sought to avoid." Even the loss of a pair of gloves she concealed in silence, preferring to suffer and stay home rather than to speak.

Sally, to divert her sister's mind from herself, turned her attention to Scotch and English poetry — particularly Scott's romantic poems. The love of poetry, thus early fostered, had a great effect upon her throughout her life. Her brothers and father wisely continued her interest in horseback riding. In 1831 her heart was overjoyed at the present of a fine horse, a brown Morgan named Billy. His slim legs and curly mane and tail made him a much admired animal. He could change from single foot to a rock, pace, or trot. She could ride so fast that she outdistanced every boy in the neighborhood. With two girls, each on high steppers, the three covered the stretches in the beautiful hill country to Worcester and back in short time. They ended the year in a dashing runaway on Thanksgiving Day in a blinding snowstorm, through which, however, they all kept their saddles.

With the hope of curing her of sensitiveness and bashfulness before strangers, Captain Barton sent Clara in 1829 to the boarding school conducted by her former teacher, Colonel Stone. But she soon became homesick in the huge halls of the academy and among the one hundred and fifty strange girls, and finally her health suffered to such a degree that she had to be taken home. Colonel Stone was kind and thoughtful to the timid, lisping girl, but it was of no avail.

"My timid sensitiveness," Miss Barton said in recalling these days, "must have given great annoyance to my friends. If I could have gotten over it, it would have given far less annoyance and trouble to myself all through life."

This supersensitiveness that threatened to undo her extended to her conscience. Skating was denied girls. But one clear starlit Sunday morning the spirit of an adventurer came upon her and in response to a whistle of the boys she climbed out of the window dressed for a lark on the ice. She was drawn about at the end of a comforter. Then there came rough ice and a fall. She was dragged cruelly and scraped her knee till it bled profusely. She secreted it for two days till, alleging a pretext of tumbling and falling, she told of the hurt member and had it dressed. But she confessed: "My mental suffering far exceeded my physical. I hated myself and failed to sleep and eat."

Her mother, always the balance wheel of the family, upon seeing that her three weeks of mental suffering were far out of proportion to the fault, told her soothingly that she did not think it the worst thing that could have been done; that other little girls had done as badly. She recalled, in fact, that she herself had disobeyed when she rode the wild colt and was thrown and hurt.

"But God will punish me awfully," Clara cried.

"It is not so much God that punishes us, my child," said Stephen Barton, taking her on his knee. "We punish ourselves."

This lesson Clara Barton never forgot, relating it in September, 1909, as freshly as if it had all happened yesterday.

Stephen, her brother-teacher, taught her mathematics, and with this home instruction, even after all the time lost in nursing, she was far ahead of many of the schools of the vicinity. In 1834 Lucian Burleigh, who taught near by and was a man of superior ability, became her tutor, giving her the personal attention which made the education of the day of crude externals so effective. History, language, composition, and English literature were studied.

In 1835 an even more able teacher, Jonathan Dana, took the school of sixty pupils to the south of North Oxford. Clara at once enrolled under him. Philosophy, chemistry, and Latin were the more advanced studies which she now took up.

After school closed there asserted itself the practical mindedness of her nature which refused to let her remain idle. Idleness was torture to her then and forever after, and meant worry and ultimate breakdown. With work and sacrifice present she could live. Without them life was consumed by that oversensitiveness with which it was so charged.

During vacation it was her ambition to weave cloth in the satinet mills of her two brothers. But Clara's mother objected, and had it not been for Stephen, who saw more clearly Clara's need of a vent for her restlessness and pent-up energies, it is probable she would not have been permitted this outlet. In answer to his mother he said: "I wonder if we are not drawing the lines too tightly on my little sister? A few years ago she wanted to learn to dance; this was denied as frivolous and improper; now she asks to work. She took up a work herself and did it two years, a work that no child would be expected to do, and did it well. She is certainly a properly behaved little girl, and I cannot understand why we should trouble ourselves or her so much concerning the proprieties of her life. For my part I am willing to arrange a pair of looms for her and let her try."

Stephen and Clara had their way. On a raised platform before a loom, not because she had to but because she loved it, "like a queen whose foot presses the throne," she mastered the flying shuttle.

It seems worth while here, perhaps, to correct a misconception. It has been said that from her earnings in the mill Clara paid off the mortgage on her father's farm. This is not so. In the first place, there had never been a mortgage on it, and in the second place, Clara had only worked about two weeks in the mills when they burned down.

Once in commenting on the report that for years she had been employed in a cloth factory Miss Barton said: "Nothing to-day could gratify me more than to know that I had been one of those self-reliant intelligent American girls like our sweet poetess, Lucy Larcom, and had stood like her before the power looms in the early progress of the manufactures of our great and matchless country."

Nevertheless, despite the short duration of her stay, it was in these factories housing the second spindle and power looms in America that were set at work those influences which were to take her out of herself and to uproot her sensitiveness. Here concern for others, absorption in a worthy task, and control under pressure began to govern her life.

CHAPTER VI

EIGHTEEN YEARS OF TEACHING

AFTER the terms of advanced preparatory study under Jonathan Dana, and the summer experience in the factory, came the winter of 1836. The mother of Clara Barton faced the question that puzzles every parent: What shall the child do?

She asked this question of the phrenologist, L. W. Fowler, who was then staying at the Barton home, where the latchstring was always out for visiting lecturers, literary men, and clergymen. The matter-of-fact mother, overheard by Clara, who was sick with the mumps and lying on a lounge listening to it all, detailed her faults of timidity, bashfulness, and aggravating silence which sometimes ended, when she was questioned, in a burst of tears.

"The sensitive nature will always remain," declared the wise student of child life, who was really a psychologist. "She will never assert herself for herself; she will suffer wrong first. But for others she will be perfectly fearless. Throw responsibility upon her, give her a school to teach."

This advice was at once followed. At fifteen she took the family rôle and became a teacher. For nearly twenty years her sensitive nature was subjected to the discipline of that profession and her energies controlled by it. District No. 9, up in "Texas village," a mile or so away from her former home in North Oxford, was her first school. It was in May, 1836, that, after passing the teachers' examination with a mark of excellent, she "put down her skirts and put up her hair," and walked to the little schoolhouse.

In 1914 I visited one of the forty pupils of this first school of Clara's — Mrs. Shumway Davis, who still lives near the Barton homestead. Mrs. Davis, who is eighty-four, was only nine years younger than her teacher. She recalls how Clara Barton at once won her class by taking them into her confidence and drawing them out. Even in the

18

THE OLD BARTON MILL SITE

To the left the office where Clara kept books for her brother Stephen.

opening Scripture, in place of the Puritan dictatorial sternness, she broke the pedagogic ice by having the children read in turn. Then she asked them what the Saviour meant in the verses in the Sermon on the Mount.

Social, friendly, and human, she joined with them in the playground till her athletic prowess amazed the four "roughies" of the school, who at once gave her their right hand of fellowship. Instead of being locked out as the previous teacher had been, she "locked" herself "in" the hearts of every boy and girl. It made not only men and women of them, but more — it made them patriots. "Their blood crimsoned the hardest fields," Miss Barton once said, recalling how many of this first class had served their country in time of crisis.

"They respected me because I was as strong as they were," the child teacher wrote in a school diary. Child that she was, she lately reflected she did not know that the severest test of discipline is its absence.

All this time her constitution was gradually changing from that of a weak girl to that of a robust young woman with tremendous powers of endurance. The bracing New England climate, the out-door activities — riding in summer, the gardens, and the hay fields, sleighing and coasting in winter — engaged her attention when not in the schoolroom, and made her glow with health. As an indication of her strength it is rumored that she could swing a keg of sweet cider to her shoulder as easily as any youth.

Her success with her first school led to a call to "Millward" — a Charlton school — the next summer. Then followed sixteen years of continuous teaching both summer and winter, ten of which were spent in a school which she founded in North Oxford. Speaking of this interesting experience Miss Barton said in 1886:

"North Oxford, where my brothers lived, had become by this time a prosperous little place. The humming factories confined, and the quick toned bells set free, hundreds of children and young people every day, and I was requested to plan and draft a schoolhouse, and take charge of the schooling of these operatives. I did so, and for ten consecutive years I stood with them in the crowded schoolroom, summer and winter, without change or relaxation. I saw my little lisping boys become overseers, and my stalwart overseers become business men and themselves owners of mills. My little girls grew to be teachers and mothers of families."

In addition to teaching Clara found time to act as Stephen's book-keeper in the mill and to read and study extensively.

In 1852 her teaching and her own independent study had so well trained her in the more advanced courses that she decided to complete her education by enrolling in Clinton Liberal Institute in New York. "I broke away from my long shackles," she said in 1886, recalling this important change in her life, "came to Clinton, Oneida County, and entered a seminary as a pupil for graduation. There were then no colleges for girls. Glorious Susan Anthony, Cady Stanton, Lucy Stone, and Elizabeth Blackwell had not labored and succeeded as they have now. Every girl should bless these pioneer women in her daily prayers. I got all the institute could give me. While there my mother passed to the better land. My grand old father was claimed by his married children, and I was free to take my course in the world, and seek its work."

At Clinton Liberal Institute she met Mary Norton. Miss Norton recognized her friend's genius for teaching and in 1853 prevailed upon her to accept a post in the New Jersey village of Hightstown.

Some ten miles or so away was Bordentown. Rumors of the extraordinary ability of the little woman to conquer schools where strong men had been driven out by unruly pupils radiated wherever Clara Barton went. From Hightstown news of her power came to Bordentown.

Prejudices existed there against public schools. Some were too denominational in religion to be broad enough to desire them; others too proud to send their children to the public school which had often been styled "free schools for paupers."

Whenever the public school system had been tried among a people divided by sectarian quarrels, the citizens themselves split over the question, while the children, catching their lack of respect for a school system, broke up the sessions and ran wild on the streets.

Miss Barton saw the need in Bordentown and she went to meet it.

"A public school is impossible," she was told. "It has failed every time."

"Give me three months and I will teach free," was her challenge.

Never was there a campaign against odds but Clara Barton an-swered it with this argument of action. She did not demand that something should be done; she demonstrated that it could be.

She took a tumble-down unoccupied building with six pupils. In five weeks the building was too small. Each of the six pupils had become a living advertisement. Emerson has said that it is not the school that educates — it is the schoolmate. Clara Barton recognized this truth and sought to reach out through these first pupils. She studied each child individually even as Fowler had studied her. In this was the magic of her success.

Something of the way in which she was regarded is shown by the following letter from a member of this first class — George Ferguson, now of Brazil, Indiana. "My memories of Miss Barton are certainly the most pleasant. She was kind to her students, pleasant in her work, gentle in disposition and took an interest in us all. We loved her almost as much as we loved our mothers, and it was not without pangs of regret that we saw her give up her pupils and school work on account of failing health. She taught school for several years in Bordentown and showed her charitable spirit by giving up her private school to establish the first public school in the state. I don't think she ever had a pupil but that loved her. Bad boys interested her as much as the good ones. The first letter I ever wrote in my life I wrote to Miss Barton. When she went away on her vacation she asked her students to write to her. We all did, and she answered all with personal letters. I can remember myself writing that letter as if it were only yesterday, and I was mighty proud of the answer I received. Since then I have been corresponding with her and have letters from her which I prize highly."

At the end of five weeks her personality had built up the school so that it was rapidly increasing to six hundred, each scholar having brought on an average one hundred others. A regular salary was now offered and Miss Barton engaged as teacher with Miss Fannie Childs as associate.[1]

By 1855 the citizens of Bordentown had completely changed their minds about public schools. They had erected a new building with eight rooms in it and boasted continually of the well-disciplined system inaugurated by Miss Barton out of nothing but opposition and

[1] Now Mrs. Vassall of Worcester, daughter-in-law of Clara Barton's sister, Sally Barton Vassall. Mrs. Vassall was near Miss Barton in Washington during the war period, and the many letters in her possession, growing out of her early and long acquaintance with her, compose one of the most important commentaries on Miss Barton's life in existence.

rowdyism. Even the "first families" sent their children to the once much condemned public school, preferring the superior teachers there to those of doubtful ability in the private institutions. There exists in Miss Barton's own words a description of this Bordentown chapter of her life that is at once so interesting and vivid that it warrants reproduction here.

"Something drew me to the state of New Jersey. I was a teacher dyed in the wool, and soon discovered that this good state had no public school, that a part of its children were in private schools, the remainder in the streets. The people said they were not paupers, and would not have their children schooled at public expense, would not send them to 'pauper schools.' I considered this state of things and decided to take upon me the opening of public schools generally in that state as well as the eyes of the people. I went to Bordentown, found two hundred children in school, four hundred on the street. They had public school laws, but not enforced; perfectly inoperative. All seemed afraid to undertake it. Friends, I believe every law once made should either be enforced and made operative, or annulled and be no longer a law. The respect of laws, the welfare of the community and the safety of people and property demanded this.

"I found the trustees were nominal officials, arranged with them, apprehensive as they were, and had them officially announce the opening of a public school in the village of Bordentown to be taught by a lady at her own expense, if preferred. A house was found and opened, and one bright morning I found myself there with six bright renegade boys (not a girl could be trusted with me) and the public school was commenced. I understood boys, and school teaching was my trade. We got on well and at the end of twelve months I stood in a new schoolhouse building, which had been built for me at the cost of $4000 and my six pupils had grown to six hundred, a bright, loving, faithful phalanx among whom never a punishment had been administered. At length, broken in strength, with a complete loss of voice, I was compelled to leave them. That, too, was a hard good-by to make. A few years later I found them all over the southern fields standing firmly behind their muskets or lying in their blood; but every one remembered. They remember to-day, those pupils; gray-haired men of business all over the land and seas, their letters come faithfully to my table."

SALLY BARTON
Clara Barton's sister

CLARA BARTON IN HER TWENTIES

Despite Miss Barton's great success in Bordentown the old prejudice against a woman principal was strong there and in consequence a male principal was installed against the wishes of the pupils. Miss Barton's work was through life primarily that of a founder. When that which she had founded had become firmly established her interest in it was never as keen and she was apt to look for new worlds to conquer. And yet, while at Bordentown she ended her career as a teacher, she never ceased to feel a personal sympathy with teacher, pupil, and parent.

"Remembering that fully one-fifth of my life has been passed as a teacher of schools," she remarked twenty years after, "it is not strange that I should feel some interest in the cause of education, some sympathy with those who labor in it as its teachers, some affiliation with the parents and people who bear its expenses, and secure its benefits, and some interest in the children and youth who receive them."

At the end of 1855, leaving the perfected public school system of Bordentown, Miss Barton felt the reaction of the superlative test of strength to which she had been put in establishing it. As in every successful campaign when it was over — but never until then —it deënergized her. Finally the physical weariness manifested itself in a complete breakdown of her voice. For recuperation she retired to Washington.

CHAPTER VII

FIVE YEARS IN WASHINGTON BEFORE THE WAR

1855-1860

THE capital of the country was now to be Miss Barton's residence and the center of her activities for a large part of the next sixty years.

As it was evident that she could no longer teach, she was again confronted with the old question of what she should do. At the Oxford mill she had perfected a "copper plate" style of handwriting. She decided finally to make use of this talent and accepted a position as a clerk in Washington, little dreaming to what International achievements this would later lead her.

She was already fascinated, however, by the national questions around which, consciously or unconsciously, her mind more and more revolved. An apparent defeat in life had become the impulse of a new decision. Were her voice and vocation gone? Her hands remained!

"She laid her hands upon my shoulder," Eleanor Ames recalled three years ago (she had beautiful hands, long and slim and firm), and said [in reply to Miss Ames, who had expressed the wish that opportunities for doing good existed now]: "'My dear, we all tumble over opportunities for being brave and doing good at every step we take. Life is just made of such opportunities. Not nearly all the sick and crippled are on the battlefield, nor is all the danger there either.'"

For such a spirit, work, and interesting work, is never absent.

"I met her often during those years as I have since," writes a friend, as to what she did at this time, "and rarely saw her without some pet scheme of benevolence which she pursued with an enthusiasm that was quite heroic and sometimes amusing. The roll of those she helped or tried to help with her purse, her personal influence, or her counsel would be a long one. Orphan children, deserted wives, destitute women, sick or unsuccessful relatives, men who had failed in business, all who were in want or in trouble, and could claim the slightest acquaintance, came to her for aid, and they were never repulsed. For means for all this she must work and earn a salary."

A weakness in the public service attracted her attention. In the Patent Office secret inventions were being copied and stolen by dishonest clerks. Especially did the child of a county of such inventive genius as Worcester resent such a theft as this.

During the administration of President Pierce, in 1854, at the request of the representative from Massachusetts, she received the appointment she had asked for. The old records of the Department of the Interior, which was established in 1849, disclose her there by 1855 and show that she was one of the first Government clerks of her sex, if indeed not the first.

In 1903 the Commissioner of Patents in a letter of November 12 stated that "no Miss Barton was found on the rolls of the Patent Office from January 1, 1853, to date." But further research on the part of the commissioner brought forth the following letter, written September 22, 1855, by the Hon. Alexander Dewitt, a member of Congress from Oxford to the Secretary of the Interior, Robert Mc-Clelland:

"Having understood the Department had decided to remove the ladies employed in the Patent Office on the 1st of October, I have taken the liberty to address a line in behalf of Miss Clara Barton, a native of my town and district, who has been employed the past year in the Patent Office, and I trust to the entire satisfaction of the Commissioner."

A sentence in a letter to the head of the Department, written by Miss Barton in 1876, offers further proof of her early service. It declares: "Having been the first woman ever appointed independently to a clerkship in the department over which you preside, and trodden among the thorny paths of earlier days, I ought to know what should be required to constitute a good and suitable clerk."

Referring to this matter in 1886, Miss Barton again said : "After some rest I was requested by the commissioner of patents to take charge of a confidential desk, with which he had found difficulty. The secrecy of its papers had not been carefully guarded. I accepted and thus became as I believe the first woman who entered a public office in the Departments of Washington in her own name drawing the salary over her own signature. I was placed equal with the male clerks at $1400 per year. This called for some criticism and no little denunciation on the part of those who foresaw dangerous precedents."

Jealousy, suspicion, and hatred were engendered. The huge building under the Superintendent of Patents, Mr. Charles Mason, was filled with men only. They loafed in the corridors. They whiffed smoke in her face. They spat on the floor before her. Insulting remarks, whistles, and catcalls increased in number and maliciousness. And yet, so excellent was she as a copyist that with an increase of salary she was advanced over her detractors to expert work on original prints, patent abridgments, and caveats. Her opponents, beaten at open opposition, whispered slander. Convicted of untruthfulness, the slanderers — among them some of the guilty patent thieves who were afraid of her — were removed from office by Mr. Mason.

Miss Barton remained in her position till after 1856, when President Buchanan was elected. Then arose the cry of "black republicanism" against all who held antislavery sympathies, and every one connected with the abolition movement felt the whip of the administration. Miss Barton was no exception. In 1857, when she was dismissed, she returned to Oxford, where she stayed for nearly two years. But so tangled were the records and so expert had she become that she was recalled towards the end of Buchanan's administration. At the earnest solicitation of her father, with whom the old ties of confidence had never been broken, she accepted.

Even now war clouds thickened and signs of conflict were overshadowing everything in Washington. Slavery sentiments swayed the Government, the army, the navy, the President, the Cabinet, the statesmen, the Capitol, and even the Treasury, whose loot seemed imminent. To do the work of two disloyal clerks, receive the salary of one, and give the other to the Treasury, was the plan that possessed her.

"Money is where the shoe pinches"   "Money talks" — these are very common axioms, but true, and when it comes to actual giving, the enthusiasm of many patriots is apt to lessen. It was not so with Miss Barton. When a cause or a public *service* was the issue, money was with her the first thing to be sacrificed. In this, which runs so contrary to the common conception of "Yankee shrewdness," she passed the acid test. Her one reply to all who quarreled with her for wanting to give up her money, was "*What is money without a country?*"

In Washington, where the reins of power and the whole vehicle of Government were proslavery, the patriotism of her position stands out all the more strikingly. Buchanan wished to pacify every one, especially the dominant statesmen of the South, with the result that he satisfied none. As the awful possibilities of fratricidal war grew nearer, however, it is little wonder that millions of honest men hesitated between two opinions.

There was no question which side Clara Barton was on. Her mind was made up.

On May 19–20, 1856, she heard Charles Sumner in the Senate. His powerful speech — "The Crime Against Kansas" — in which he voiced the principle that "Freedom is national, slavery is sectional" — held her fascinated until after one o'clock in the morning.

"I heard Sumner's midnight speech," she said to me in 1911. "It was an oration of greater power than any I ever knew. It was upon this very point of the extension of slavery, and it settled it. It was the night before he was struck down. I have often said that *that night war began!* It began not at Sumter but at Sumner." Further on, in a conversation that turned on the Civil War, Miss Barton was asked if it would not have been better if it had never been. Her reply was instant:

"Could the great issue of slavery ever have been settled any other way? If the mere buying of the slaves would have solved the problem, the young men in the field would have dug potatoes till they could have bought every slave.

"But buying the slaves would not have settled it, because the question to be settled was whether new territory such as Kansas and Nebraska, should be slave or free territory. If slave territory, and all other new states slave territory, the South would have had preponderance and could have outvoted the North. Slavery would have been entrenched, forever, the question eternally settled, and *a slave pen would have been set up on Bunker Hill! To prevent that meant war!*"

CHAPTER VIII

The Beginning of the Civil War

"I HAPPENED to see Clara Barton a day or two after Fort Sumter was fired on," says a contemporary of Miss Barton. He then gives this interesting word picture of her:

"She was confident, even enthusiastic. She had feared that the Southern aristocracy, by their close combination and superior political training, might succeed in gradually subjugating the whole country; but of that there was no longer any danger. The war might be long and bloody, but the rebels had abandoned a policy on which the odds were in favor of their ultimate success, for one in which they had no chance at all. For herself, she had saved a little in time of peace, and she intended to devote it and herself to the service of her country and humanity. If war must be, she neither expected nor desired to come out of it with a dollar. If she survived, she could no doubt earn a living. And if she died, it was no matter."

Then "the first great blow of organized war fell, and the nation woke from its dream of peace at the thunder of wave-washed Sumter" — to use Miss Barton's own words. Beyond recall, she presented herself, she knew not then just how, as a living sacrifice upon her country's altar. Death seemed to her the probable cost, but she determined to suffer it.

Something of her enthusiasm and patriotism are reflected in a sentence in a private letter to her niece, Mrs. Vassall, written from Washington:

"I think," she says, "the city will be attacked within the next sixty days. If it must be, let it come, and when there is no longer a soldier's arm to raise the Stars and Stripes above our Capitol, may God give strength to mine."

While she was never called upon to perform this task, it was not long before she had an opportunity for heroic service, and, as was to be expected, she grasped it.

On April 15, Massachusetts responded to Lincoln's call for 75,000 troops with four regiments. One of these, the 6th, under the late Colonel Jones, set out at once for Washington, taking nothing with them but uniforms and guns. Passing through Baltimore, they were murderously assaulted by a mob of ten thousand infuriated opponeuts who choke the streets. Four were killed or mortally wounded, leaving thirty others who suffered lighter wounds. Nevertheless they fought their way through to the station on to Washington.

When they arrived, President Lincoln told them that if they had not come that night, Washington would have been in the hands of the rebels before the morning.

It was no wonder Clara Barton was proud of the 6th Massachusetts, and when the men detrained in Washington's streets, she was there to receive them. Now for the first time she dressed war wounds, and saw blood shed in combat. "Among the soldiers," she wrote, "I recognized my own early associates." Many, including Sergeant J. Stewart Brown and Joseph M. Dyson, were from Worcester. "We bound their wounds," she continued, "and fed them."[1]

When their supply of handkerchiefs was exhausted, Miss Barton, with the other volunteer nurses, rushed home and tore up her sheets for the bandages. But the next day, with five husky negroes as porters, carrying as many hampers and boxes, she led a procession through Washington streets among amazed churchgoers, and distributed necessities to the sick and wounded.

In her services to those who had been injured, Miss Barton did not forget the uninjured soldiers who had gathered in the senate chamber. Here she spread a feast before them and, from the desk of the President of the Senate, read to them from the Worcester *Spy*.

In a letter written six days later, she interestingly reviews the incidents leading up to and following the Baltimore clash:

"WASHINGTON, Apr. 25th, 1861.

"MY DEAR WILL,

"As you will perceive I wrote you on the 19th but have not found it perfectly convenient to send it until now, but we trust that naviga-

[1] Some questions having arisen as to the place of her feeding the men of the 6th Regiment, I quote a paragraph of a personal letter to me describing her first public appearance. "It was the senate chamber where my little feast was held, and the desk of the President of the Senate where I made my first literary effort" (Sept. 16, 1909).

tion is open now for a little.   As yet we have had no cause for alarm, if indeed we were disposed to feel any.   The city is filling up with troops.   The Mass. regiment is quartered in the Capitol and the 7th Penn. arrived at noon.   Almost a week in getting from N. Y. here, they looked tired and worn, but sturdy and brave.   Oh! but you should hear them praise the Mass. troops who were with them, Butler's Brigade.   They say the Mass. Boys are equal to anything they undertake — that they have constructed a R.R. laid the track and built an engine since they entered Maryland.   The wounded at the Infirmary are all improving — some of them recovered and joined the regiment.   We visited the regiment yesterday at the Capitol and found some old friends and acquaintances from Worcester.   Their baggage was all seized and they have *nothing* but their heavy woolen clothes — not a cotton shirt — and many of them not even a pocket handkerchief.   We of course emptied our pockets and came home to tear up old sheets for towels and handkerchiefs, and have filled a large box with all manner of serving utensils, thread, needles, thimbles, scissors, pins, buttons, strings, salves, tallow, etc., etc., — have filled the largest market basket in the house and it will go to them in the next hour.

"But don't tell us they are not determined — just fighting mad — They had just one Worcester *Spy* of the 22d and all were so anxious to know the contents that they begged me to read it aloud to them, which I did.   You would have smiled to see *me* and my *audience* in the Senate Chamber of the U. S.   Oh! but it was better attention than I have been accustomed to see there in the old times.   Ber writes his mother that Oxford is raising a company.   God bless her and the noble fellows who may leave their quiet happy homes to come at the call of their country.   So far as our poor efforts can reach they shall never lack a kindly hand or a sister's sympathy if they come."

About this time, it occurred to Miss Barton to send advertisements to the columns of the Worcester *Spy* asking for stores, supplies and money for the wounded and needy of the 6th regiment.   She stated that she would receive all shipments and disperse them personally.   The city of Worcester was the first to send assistance.   Surrounding towns and cities in Massachusetts followed its example.   So great was the response that Miss Barton's room overflowed, and she was obliged to secure space in a warehouse, near 7th Street and Pennsylvania Avenue.

Henceforth she was a new creature, for she felt she had attached her energies to a coming cause.   The reservoirs of unmastered and too restless energy so long repressed were at last unlocked, and given a field of action big enough.   Therefore, all things had become new. She was a new being.   The sensitiveness, bashfulness, timidity, and self-consciousness were swallowed up.   Pestering fears which she had never known to be absent were cast out.   At the age when other women leaped to new life with their love for one man, she awoke to an affection for wounded humanity, experiencing at the same time the fact that "Perfect love casteth out fear."   With this smart of a country's opening wounds upon her, pressure was given at last sufficient to give control, a task great enough to engulf self, and concern for others mighty enough to release the passion for service.

The following weeks and months began the Peninsular Campaign. For this, she refused to be simply a disperser at the warehouse.   Going down to the docks, she met the wounded soldiers returning on the transports from the swamps of the Chickahominy.   She saw blood and clay had caked on their sore wounds till they were like the hard shells of turtles.   With warm water, lotions, dressings, and restoratives she bent over them, and amid filth and suppurating sores and odors, under the torrid sun of Washington, she washed their neglected wounds. Seeing them back to the hospitals, she remounted the ambulances, and trip after trip rode back to be the first to reach each coming boatload of human freight.

But the question arose — could she not *prevent* the neglect?   Deaths occurred by the hundred because of it.   But it happened days before they reached the docks.   Relief could only be done on the field.   Why should she not go and administer it there instead of waiting helplessly for the transports where so often she was too late?

Miss Barton's own feeling on this matter is shown us in the record of a conference which she had with her friends in 1886

"I was strong and thought I might go to the rescue of the men who fell.   The first regiment of troops, the old 6th Mass. that fought its way through Baltimore, brought my playmates and neighbors, the partakers of my childhood; the brigades of New Jersey brought scores of my brave boys, the same solid phalanx; and the strongest legions from old Herkimer brought the associates of my seminary days. They formed and crowded around me.   What could I do but go with them, or work for them and my country? The patriot blood of my father was warm in my veins. The country which he had fought for, I might at least work for, and I had offered my service to the government in the capacity of a double clerkship at twice $1400 a year, upon discharge of two disloyal clerks from its employ, — the salary never to be given to me, but to be turned back into the U. S. Treasury then poor to beggary, with no currency, no credit. But there was no law for this, and it could not be done and I would not draw salary from our government in such peril, so I resigned and went into direct service of the sick and wounded troops wherever found.

"But I struggled long and hard with my sense of propriety —with the appalling fact that I was only a woman whispering in one ear, and thundering in the other the groans of suffering men dying like dogs — unfed and unsheltered, for the life of every institution which had protected and educated me!

"I said that I struggled with my sense of propriety and I say it with humiliation and shame. I am ashamed that I thought of such a thing."

Society forbade women at the front. Almost the only camp followers of her sex were women of loose life. Would humanity be scandalized and her reputation gone if she tried it? Tradition absolutely forbade a good woman to go unprotected among rough soldiers. And, as a further barrier against it, were ironclad army regulations.

CHAPTER IX

To the Firing Line

July 21, 1861, the Union forces were routed at Bull Run, and Miss Barton, then in her 40th year, saw the flight back to Washington of the disorganized regiments. With some of her friends, and other New England women, she mingled with the panic-stricken multitudes. In the autumn, Mrs. Howe was inspired to write "The Battle Hymn of the Republic." Miss Barton was impelled by an equally great prompting to the great decision of her life. She could not, she would not, write. But she could and she would nurse the bleeding and the dying.

The total Union losses at Bull Run were 2952 — 481 killed, 1011 wounded, 1460 missing. Miss Barton was one of the first to seek the wounded and out of their piteous tales came an even stronger decision to do something to alleviate the suffering and go to the firing line herself.

On October 21, 1861, occurred the slaughter of Ball's Bluff in which the 15th, 19th, and 20th Massachusetts engaged. Many of these soldiers were Miss Barton's acquaintances from Worcester County. General Devens, under the command of General Baker, was a lawyer and later an honored judge in Worcester. Among the many driven over the 100-foot bluff and either shot, or forced into the river to drown, were Worcester men and boys. Willie Grout, who was shot while swimming, was one of these. He was immortalized in the song, "The Vacant Chair," written in his memory by Henry S. Washburn, a Worcester admirer of young Grout.

At the height of this passion to go to the front, late in 1861 news came to Miss Barton that her father was desperately ill at North Oxford. She at once hastened to his bedside and again the beautiful old confidence sprang up between them.

She told him of her secret determination.

D
33

"Go, if it is your duty to go," replied the old patriot, raising him-self on his pillows. "I know soldiers, and they will respect you and your errand."

That settled it. In March, 1862, following the death of her father, she returned to Washington, determined to break conventions and override the red tape of the army rules.

By the late spring she was, therefore, back at her old station. From her dispensaries and warehouses she with redoubled energy relieved transports crowded with wounded and sick who came to her from the opening battlefields of the Army of the Potomac.

May 31 and June 1, 1862, was fought the bloody battle at Fair Oaks, Virginia, with losses approximating 6000 on each side!

There followed the seven days retreat under McClellan with 1,734 killed and 8,062 wounded. From all these Clara Barton heard heart-rending stories. August 9, 1862, came the battle of Cedar Mountain, with 314 killed on the Union side, 1465 wounded, and 622 missing. This battle field was Clara Barton's first. Not only had no woman gone to the firing line, but it was before organized aid had come to the relief of the soldier, before the two great and noble commissions, with which she was never connected, had found their way directly to the front.

She knew by heart the point-blank refusals that would be made to her requests to go. But appearing one day before Dr. Coolidge, Medical Inspector, she obtained through him a pass from Surgeon-General Hammond. This led her to Asst. Quartermaster-General Rucker. He was one of the greathearts of the army. Tears welled up in his eyes as he heard the plea of the little figure.

"I have no fear of the battle field," she told him. "I have large stores but no way to reach the troops."

She described the treatment of the soldiers who arrived often too late. After they reached Washington they were now well enough cared for in hospitals and through private generosity, she explained, but at the front all was neglect. She had looked around to see if other women had broken through the lines. But then there were none. She her-self must go first to the battle front, where the men lay uncared for. When, after the rebuffs of months, Quartermaster Rucker showed sympathy and insight enough to grant her the passports, she burst into tears — then hurriedly departing, she immediately loaded her supplies upon a railroad car and started.

"When our armies fought on Cedar Mountain, I broke the shackles and went to the field " — is the brief way in which she punctuates her terse comment on this significant step.

She arrived the day after the battle of Cedar Mountain — and there was much work for her to do.   Her own paragraph in explanation of it is as vivid and forceful as it is modest and unassuming:

"Five days and nights with three hours sleep — a narrow escape from capture — and some days of getting the wounded into hospitals at Washington brought Saturday, August 30.   And if you chance to feel, that the positions I occupied were rough and unseemly for a *woman* — I can only reply that they were rough and unseemly for *men*. But under all, lay the life of the nation.   I had inherited the rich blessing of health and strength of constitution — such as are seldom given to woman — and I felt that some return was due from me and that I ought to be there."

CHAPTER X

SECOND BULL RUN AND CHANTILLY

CLOSE on Cedar Mountain came the engagement, August 29, at Groveton, Virginia, with 7000 killed, wounded, and missing, followed by the action on the 30th at Manassas, employing Porter's 5th corps, the 1st corps under Major General Sigel, Reynolds' division, army of the Potomac, the third under Major General McDowell's army of Virginia, and Hooker's and Kearney's division, and the 9th corps under General Reno.

That same afternoon (the 30th) word came that another battle was being fought by General Pope on the old Bull Run field. Eight thousand,[1] according to the report, had already been killed, and the battle was still on.

At once Miss Barton made preparations to go to the scene. Haply, we have her own story of the journey — and of what followed:

"Our coaches were not elegant or commodious; they had no windows, no seats, no platforms, no steps, a slide door on the side was the only entrance, and this higher than my head. For my manner of attaining my elevated position, I must beg of you to draw on your own imaginations and spare me the labor of reproducing the boxes, barrels, boards, and rails, which in those days, seemed to help me up and on in the world. We did not criticize the unsightly helpers and were only too thankful that the stiff springs did not quite jostle us out. This description need not be limited to this particular trip or train, but will suffice for all that I have known in Army life. This is the kind of conveyance by which your tons of generous gifts have reached the field with the precious freights. These trains through day and night, sunshine and rain, heat and cold, have thundered over heights, across plains, through ravines, and over hastily built army bridges 90 feet across the rocky stream beneath.

[1] The casualties as later reported were 800 killed, 4000 wounded, 3000 captured or missing.

36

"At 10 o'clock Sunday (August 31) our train drew up at Fairfax Station. The ground, for acres, was a thinly wooded slope — and among the trees on the leaves and grass, were laid the wounded who were pouring in by scores of wagon loads, as picked up on the field under the flag of truce. All day they came and the whole hillside was covered. Bales of hay were broken open and scattered over the ground like littering for cattle, and the sore, famishing men were laid upon it.

"And when the night shut in, in the mist and darkness about us, we knew that standing apart from the world of anxious hearts, throbbing over the whole country, we were a little band of almost empty handed workers literally by ourselves in the wild woods of Virginia, with 3000 suffering men crowded upon the few acres within our reach.

"After gathering up every available implement or convenience for our work, our domestic inventory stood 2 water buckets, 5 tin cups, 1 camp kettle, 1 stewpan, 2 lanterns, 4 bread knives, 3 plates, and a 2-quart tin dish, and 3000 guests to serve.

"You will perceive by this, that I had not yet learned to equip myself, for I was no Pallas, ready armed, but grew into my work by hard thinking and sad experience. It may serve to relieve your apprehension for the future of my labors if I assure you that I was never caught so again.

"You have read of adverse winds. To realize this in its full sense you have only to build a camp fire and attempt to cook something on it.

"There is not a soldier within the sound of my voice, but will sustain me in the assertion that go whichsoever side of it you will, wind will blow the smoke and flame directly in your face. Notwithstanding these difficulties, within fifteen minutes from the time of our arrival we were preparing food, and dressing wounds. You wonder what, and how prepared, and how administered without dishes.

"You generous thoughtful mothers and wives have not forgotten the tons of preserves and fruits with which you filled our hands. Huge boxes of these stood beside that railway track. Every can, jar, bucket, bowl, cup or tumbler, when emptied, that instant became a vehicle of mercy to convey some preparation of mingled bread and wine or soup or coffee to some helpless famishing sufferer who partook of it with the tears rolling down his bronzed cheeks and divided his blessings between the hands that fed him and his God. I never realized until that day how little a human being could be grateful for and that day's experience also taught me the utter worthlessness of that which could not be made to contribute directly to our necessities. The bit of bread which would rest on the surface of a gold eagle was worth more than the coin itself.

"But the most fearful scene was reserved for the night. I have said that the ground was littered with dry hay and that we had only two lanterns, but there were plenty of candles. The wounded were laid so close that it was impossible to move about in the dark. The slightest misstep brought a torrent of groans from some poor mangled fellow in your path.

"Consequently here were seen persons of all grades from the careful man of God who walked with a prayer upon his lips to the careless driver hunting for his lost whip, — each wandering about among this hay with an open flaming candle in his hand.

"The slightest accident, the mere dropping of a light could have enveloped in flames this whole mass of helpless men.

"How we watched and pleaded and cautioned as we worked and wept that night! How we put socks and slippers upon their cold, damp feet, wrapped your blankets and quilts about them, and when we had no longer these to give, how we covered them in the hay and left them to their rest!"

"On Monday (September 1) the enemy's cavalry appeared in the wood opposite and a raid was hourly expected. In the afternoon all the wounded men were sent off and the danger became so imminent that Mrs. Fales thought best to leave, although she only went for stores. I begged to be excused from accompanying her as the ambulances were up to the fields for more and I knew I should never leave a wounded man there if I were taken prisoner forty times. At 6 o'clock it commenced to thunder and lightning and all at once the artillery began to play, joined by the musketry about two miles distant. We sat down in our tent and waited to see them break in, but Reno's forces held them back. The old Twenty-first Massachusetts lay between us and the enemy and they could not pass. God only knows who was lost, I do not, for the next day all fell back. Poor Kearney, Stevens and Webster were brought in and in the afternoon Kearney's and Heintzelman's divisions fell back through our camp on their way to Alexandria. We knew this was the last. We put the thousand wounded men we then had into the train. I took one carload of them and Mrs. M. another. The men took to the horses. We steamed off and two hours later there was no Fairfax Station. We reached Alexandria at 10 o'clock at night, and, oh, the repast which met those poor men at the train. The people of the island are the most noble I ever saw or heard of. I stood in my car and fed the men till they could eat no more. Then the people would take us home and feed us, and after that we came home. I had slept one and one-half hours since Saturday night and I am well and strong and wait to go again if I have need." [1]

Among many other experiences on the field of second Bull Run and Chantilly, Miss Barton recalled incident after incident:

"The slight, naked chest of a fair-haired lad caught my eye," she once recalled, "and dropping down beside him, I bent low to draw the remnant of his torn blouse about him, when with a quick cry he threw his left arm across my neck and, burying his face in the folds of my dress, wept like a child at his mother's knee. I took his head in my hands and held it until his great burst of grief passed away. 'And do you know me?' he asked at length, 'I am Charley Hamilton, who used to carry your satchel home from school!' My faithful pupil, poor Charley. That mangled right arm would never carry a satchel again.

"About three o'clock in the morning I observed a surgeon with his little flickering candle in hand approaching me with cautious step far up in the wood. 'Lady,' he said as he drew near, 'will you go with me? Out on the hills is a poor distressed lad, mortally wounded and dying. His piteous cries for his sister have touched all our hearts and none of us can relieve him but rather seem to distress him by our presence.'

"By this time I was following him back over the bloody track, with great beseeching eyes of anguish on every side looking up into our faces, saying so plainly, 'Don't step on us.'

"'He can't last half an hour longer,' said the surgeon as we toiled on. 'He is already quite cold, shot through the abdomen, a terrible wound.' By this time the cries became plainly audible to me.

[1] Miss Barton kept always with her the letter describing the above incidents which she wrote to a personal friend at the time. "Let me go upstairs and get it and read it to you," she said to me in September, 1908, suiting her action to her word.

"'Mary, Mary, sister Mary, come,—O come, I am wounded, Mary!
I am shot. I am dying — Oh come to me — I have called you so long
and my strength is almost gone — Don't let me die here alone. O
Mary, Mary, come!'

"Of all the tones of entreaty to which I have listened, and certainly
I have had some experience of sorrow, I think these sounding through
that dismal night, the most heart-rending. As we drew near some
twenty persons attracted by his cries had gathered around and stood
with moistened eyes and helpless hands waiting the change which
would relieve them all. And in the midst, stretched upon the ground,
lay, scarcely full grown, a young man with a graceful head of hair,
tangled and matted, thrown back from a forehead and a face of livid
whiteness. His throat was bare. His hands, bloody, clasped his
breast, his large, bewildered eyes turning anxiously in every direction.
And ever from between his ashen lips pealed that piteous cry of 'Mary!
Mary! Come.'

"I approached him unobserved, and motioning the lights away,
I knelt by him alone in the darkness. Shall I confess that I intended
if possible to cheat him out of his terrible death agony? But my lips
were truer than my heart, and would not speak the word 'Brother,' I
had willed them to do. So I placed my hands upon his neck, kissed
his cold forehead and laid my cheek against his.

"The illusion was complete; the act had done the falsehood my
lips refused to speak. I can never forget that cry of joy. 'Oh Mary!
Mary! You have come? I knew you would come if I called you and I
have called you so long. I could not die without you, Mary. Don't
cry, darling, I am not afraid to die now that you have come to me. Oh,
bless you. Bless you, Mary.' And he ran his cold, blood-wet hands
about my neck, passed them over my face, and twined them in my
hair, which by this time had freed itself from fastenings and was
hanging damp and heavy upon my shoulders. He gathered the loose
locks in his stiffened fingers and holding them to his lips continued to
whisper through them 'Bless you, bless you, Mary!' And I felt the
hot tears of joy trickling from the eyes I had thought stony in death.
This encouraged me, and wrapping his feet closely in blankets and
giving him such stimulants as he could take I seated myself on the
ground and lifted him on my lap, and drawing the shawl on my own
shoulders also about his I bade him rest.

"I listened till his blessings grew fainter and in ten minutes with them on his lips he fell asleep. So the gray morning found us. My precious charge had grown warm, and was comfortable.

"Of course the morning light would reveal his mistake. But he had grown calm and was refreshed and able to endure it, and when finally he woke, he seemed puzzled for a moment but then he smiled and said: — 'I knew before I opened my eyes that this couldn't be Mary. I know now that she couldn't get here but it is almost as good. You've made me so happy. Who is it?'

"I said it was simply a lady, who hearing that he was wounded, had come to care for him. He wanted the name, and with childlike simplicity he spelled it letter by letter to know if he were right. 'In my pocket,' he said, ' you will find mother's last letter, please get it and write your name upon it, for I want both names by me when I die.'

"'Will they take away the wounded?' he asked. 'Yes,' I replied, ' the first train for Washington is nearly ready now.' 'I must go,' he said quickly. 'Are you able?' I asked. 'I must go if I die on the way. I'll tell you why. I am poor mother's only son, and when she consented that I go to the war, I promised her faithfully that if I were not killed outright, but wounded, I would try every means in my power to be taken home to her dead or alive. If I die on the train, they will not throw me off, and if I were buried in Washington, she can get me. But out here in the Virginia woods in the hands of the enemy, never. I *must* go!'"

"I sent for the surgeon in charge of the train and requested that my boy be taken.

"'Oh impossible! Madam, he is mortally wounded and will never reach the hospital. We must take those who have a hope of life.' 'But you must take him.' 'I cannot.' — 'Can you, Doctor, guarantee the lives of all you have on that train?' 'I wish I could,' said he sadly. 'They are the worst cases, nearly fifty per cent must die eventually of their wounds and hardships.'

"'Then give this lad a chance with them. He can only die and he has given good and sufficient reasons why he must go — and a woman's word for it, Doctor. You take him. Send your men for him.' Whether yielding to argument or entreaty, I neither knew nor cared so long as he did yield nobly and kindly. And they gathered up the fragments of the poor, torn boy and laid him carefully on a blanket on the crowded train and with stimulants and food and a kind hearted attendant, pledged to take him alive or dead to Armory Square Hospital and tell them he was Hugh Johnson of New York, and to mark his grave.

"Although three hours of my time had been devoted to one sufferer among thousands, it must not be inferred that our general work had been suspended or that my assistants had been equally inefficient. They had seen how I was engaged and nobly redoubled their exertions to make amends for my deficiencies.

"Probably not a man was laid upon those cars who did not receive some personal attention at their hands, some little kindness, if it were only to help lift him more tenderly.

"This finds us shortly after daylight Monday morning. Train after train of cars were rushing on for the wounded and hundreds of wagons were bringing them in from the field still held by the enemy, where some poor sufferers had lain three days with no visible means of sustenance. If immediately placed upon the trains and not detained, at least twenty-four hours must elapse before they could be in the hospital and properly nourished. They were already famishing, weak and sinking from loss of blood and they could ill afford a further fast of twenty-four hours. I felt confident that unless nourished at once, all the weaker portion must be past recovery before reaching the hospitals of Washington. If once taken from the wagons and laid with those already cared for, they would be overlooked and perish on the way. Something must be done to meet this fearful emergency. I sought the various officers on the grounds, explained the case to them and asked permission to feed all the men as they arrived before they should be taken from the wagons. It was well for the poor sufferers of that field that it was controlled by noble-hearted, generous officers, quick to feel and prompt to act.

"They at once saw the propriety of my request and gave orders that all wagons would be stayed at a certain point and only moved on when every one had been seen and fed. This point secured, I commenced my day's work of climbing from the wheel to the brake of every wagon and speaking to and feeding with my own hands each soldier until he expressed himself satisfied.

"Still there were bright spots along the darkened lines. Early in the morning the Provost Marshal came to ask me if I could use fifty men. He had that number, who for some slight breach of military discipline were under guard and useless, unless I could use them. I only regretted there were not five hundred. They came, — strong willing men, — and these, added to our original force and what we had gained incidentally, made our number something over eighty, and believe me, eighty men and three women, acting with well directed purpose will accomplish a good deal in a day. Our fifty prisoners dug graves and gathered and buried the dead, bore mangled men over the rough ground in their arms, loaded cars, built fires, made soup, and administered it. And I failed to discern that their services were less valuable than those of the other men. I had long suspected, and have been since convinced that a private soldier may be placed under guard, courtmartialed, and even be imprisoned without forfeiting his honor or manliness, that the real dishonor is often upon the gold lace rather than the army blue.

"At three o'clock the last train of wounded left. All day we had known that the enemy hung upon the hills and were waiting to break in upon us. . . ."

The Battle of Chantilly came to its climax late in the afternoon of September 1, 1862, and after General Pope had ordered that his forces fall back towards Washington. Pope had reached Centreville, where he was joined by the corps of Franklin and Sumner. At the same time McDowell was ordered to move towards Fairfax Court House; Reno towards Chantilly; Heintzelman to a point between Centreville and Fairfax and in the rear of Reno. General Franklin was sent to the left and rear of McDowell; while Sigel and Porter went to the right of Sumner and the left of Heintzelman.

As General Reno, who was to cover the withdrawal to Centreville, was nearing Chantilly he met Jackson, Ewell, and Hill just as a terrific Virginia thundershower broke over them. Hooker, McDowell, and Kearney came to the support of Reno and the severe fighting was only ended by darkness.

Miss Barton describes the scene:

"At four o'clock the clouds gathered black and murky, and the low growl of distant thunder was heard while lightning continually illuminated the horizon. The still air grew thick and stifled, and the very branches appeared to droop and bow as if in grief at the memory of the terrible scenes so lately enacted and the gallant lives so nobly yielded up beneath their shelter.

"This was the afternoon of Monday. Since Saturday noon I had not thought of tasting food, and we had just drawn around a box for that purpose, when of a sudden, air and earth and all about us shook with one mingled crash of God's and man's artillery. The lightning played and the thunder rolled incessantly and the cannon roared louder and nearer each minute. Chantilly with all its darkness and horrors had opened in the rear.

"The description of this battle I leave to those who saw and moved in it, as it is my purpose to speak only of events in which I was a witness or actor. Although two miles distant, we knew the battle was intended for us, and watched the firing as it neared and receded and waited minute by minute for the rest.

"With what desperation our men fought hour after hour in the rain and darkness! How they were overborne and rallied, how they suffered from mistaken orders, and blundered, and lost themselves in the strange mysterious wood. And how after all, with giant strength and veteran bravery, they checked the foe and held him at bay, is an all proud record of history.

"And the courage of the soldier who braved death in the darkness of Chantilly let no man question.—

"The rain continued to pour in torrents, and the darkness became impenetrable save from the lightning leaping above our heads and the fitful flash of the guns, as volley after volley rang through the stifled air and lighted up the gnarled trunks and dripping branches among which we ever waited and listened.

"In the midst of this, and how guided no man knows, came still another train of wounded men, and a waiting train of cars upon the track received them. This time nearly alone, for my worn-out assistants could work no longer, I continued to administer such food as I had left.

"Do you begin to wonder what it could be. Army crackers put into knapsacks and haversacks and beaten to crumbs between stones, and stirred into a mixture of wine, whiskey and water, and sweetened with coarse brown sugar.

"Not very inviting you will think but I assure you it was always acceptable. But whether it should have been classed as food, or, like the Widow Bedott's cabbage as a delightful beverage it would puzzle an epicure to determine. No matter, so it imparted strength and comfort.

"The departure of this train cleared the grounds of wounded for the night, and as the line of fire from its plunging engines died out in the darkness, a strange sensation of weakness and weariness fell upon me, almost defying my utmost exertion to move one foot before the other.

"A little Sibley tent had been hastily pitched for me in a slight hollow upon the hillside. Your imaginations will not fail to picture its condition. Rivulets of water had rushed through it during the last three hours. Still I attempted to reach it, as its white surface, in the darkness, was a protection from the wheels of wagons and trampling of beasts.

"Perhaps I shall never forget the painful effort which the making of those few rods, and the gaining of the tent cost me. How many times I fell from sheer exhaustion, in the darkness and mud of that slippery hillside, I have no knowledge, but at last I grasped the welcome canvas, and a well established brook which washed in on the upper side at the opening that served as door, met me on my entrance. My entire floor was covered with water, not an inch of dry, solid ground.

"One of my lady assistants had previously taken train for Washington and the other worn out by faithful labors, was crouched upon the top of some boxes in one corner fast alseep. No such convenience remained for me, and I had no strength to arrange one. I sought the highest side of my tent which I remembered was grass grown, and ascertaining that the water was not very deep, I sank down. It was no laughing matter then. But the recollection of my position has since afforded me amusement.

"I remember myself sitting on the ground, upheld by my left arm, my head resting on my hand, impelled by an almost uncontrollable desire to lie completely down, and prevented by the certain conviction that if I did, water would flow into my ears.

"How long I balanced between my desires and cautions, I have no positive knowledge, but it is very certain that the former carried the point by the position from which I was aroused at twelve o'clock by the rumbling of more wagons of wounded men. I slept two hours, and oh, what strength I had gained! I may never know two other hours of equal worth. I sprang to my feet dripping wet, covered with ridges of dead grass and leaves, wrung the water from my hair and skirts, and went forth again to my work.

"When I stood again under the sky, the rain had ceased, the clouds were sullenly retiring and the lightning, as if deserted by its boisterous companions, had withdrawn to a distant corner and was playing quietly by itself. For the great volleying thunders of Heaven and Earth had settled down on the fields. Silent? I said so. And it was, save the ceaseless rumbling of the never ending train of army wagons which brought alike the wounded, the dying and the dead.

"And thus the morning of the third day broke upon us, drenched, weary, hungry, sorefooted, sad-hearted, discouraged, and under orders to retreat.

"A little later, the plaintive wail of a single fife, the slow beat of a muffled drum, the steady tramp — tramp — tramp of heavy feet, the gleam of ten thousand bayonets on the hills, and with bowed heads, and speechless lips, poor Kearney's leaderless men came marching through.

"This was the signal for retreat. All day they came, tired, hungry, ragged, defeated, retreating, they knew not whither — they cared not whither.

"The enemy's cavalry skirting the hills, admonished us each moment, that we must soon decide to go from them or with them. But our work must be accomplished, and no wounded men once given into our hands must be left. And with the spirit of desperation, we struggled on.

"At three o'clock an officer galloped up to me, with 'Miss Barton, can you ride?' 'Yes, sir,' I replied.

"'But you have no lady's saddle — could you ride mine?'

"'Yes, sir, or without it, if you have blanket and surcingle.'

"'Then you can risk another hour,' he exclaimed and galloped off.

"At four he returned at a break-neck speed — and leaping from his horse said, 'Now is your time. The enemy is already breaking over the hills, try the train. It will go through, unless they have flanked, and cut the bridge a mile above us. In that case I've a reserve horse for you, and you must take your chances to escape across the country.'

"In two minutes I was on the train. The last wounded man at the station was also on. The conductor stood with a torch which he applied to a pile of combustible material beside the track. And we rounded the curve which took us from view as we saw the station ablaze, and a troop of cavalry dashing down the hill. The bridge was uncut and midnight found us at Washington.

"You have the full record of my sleep — from Friday night till Wednesday morning — two hours. You will not wonder that I slept during the next twenty-four.

"On Friday (the following), I repaired to Armory Square Hospital to learn who of all the hundreds sent, had reached that point.

"I traced the chaplain's record, and there upon the last page freshly written stood the name of Hugh Johnson.

"Turning to Chaplain Jackson, I asked — 'Did that man live until to-day?'

"'He died during the latter part of last night,' he replied. 'His friends reached him some two days ago, and they are now taking his body from the ward to be conveyed to the depot.'

"I looked in the direction his hand indicated, and there, beside a coffin, about to be lifted into a wagon, stood a gentleman, the mother, and sister Mary!

"'Had he his reason?' I asked.

"'Oh, perfectly.'

"'And his mother and sister were with him two days.'

"'Yes.'

"There was no need of me. He had given his own messages, I could add nothing to their knowledge of him, and would fain be spared the scene of thanks. Poor Hugh, thy piteous prayers reached and were answered, and with eyes and heart full, I turned away, and never saw sister Mary.

"These were days of darkness — a darkness that might be felt.

"The shattered bands of Pope and Banks! Burnside's weary legions! Reinforcements from West Virginia — and all that now remained of the once glorious Army of the Peninsula had gathered for shelter beneath the redoubts and guns that girdled Washington."

CHAPTER XI

HARPER'S FERRY AND SOUTH MOUNTAIN

SEPTEMBER, 1862

THOUGH the plan was to place a woman at the rear, the firing line from the first was Clara Barton's objective. Actuated by her tremendous determination, she was able to outflank an army line, ten miles long, to steal a march by it at midnight, and in the morning, to use her phrase, — "follow the cannon!"

On September 12–15 at Harper's Ferry were engaged the 39th, 111th, 115th, 125th, 126th, and 186th New York, 32d, 60th, and 87th Ohio, 9th Vermont, 65th Illinois, 15th Indiana, 1st and 3d Maryland (Howe brigade), 8th New York cavalry, 12th Illinois cavalry, 1st Maryland cavalry, and four batteries of artillery. Here 44 were killed, 173 were wounded, but 12,520 were missing or captured!

The news of this received by wire threw Washington and the North into a panic. That very night the call came to Miss Barton from a source she never has revealed: "Harper's Ferry — not a moment to be lost."

"The long maneuvering and skirmishing," she wrote in her war diary, "had yielded no fruit. Pope had been sacrificed and all the blood shed from Yorktown to Malvern Hill seemed to have been utterly in vain. But the minor keys, upon which I played my infinitesimal note in the great anthem of war and victory which rang through the land when these two fearful forces met and closed, with gun-lock kissing gun-lock across the rocky bed of Antietam, are yet known only to a few. Washington was filled with dismay, and all the North was moved as a tempest stirs a forest.

"Maryland lay temptingly in view, and Lee and Jackson with the flower of the Rebel army marched for its ripening fields. Who it was that whispered hastily on Saturday night, September 13th, — '*Harper's Ferry, not a moment to be lost*,' — I have never dared to name.

48

"In 30 minutes I was waiting the always kindly spoken *'Come in,'* of my patron saint, Major, now Quartermaster-General, Rucker.

"'Major,' I said — 'I want to go to Harper's Ferry, can I go?'

"'Perhaps so,' he replied, with genial, but doubtful expression. 'Perhaps so, do you want a conveyance?'

"'Yes,' I said.

"'But an army wagon is the only vehicle that will reach there with any burden in safety. I can send you one of these to-morrow morning.'

"I said — 'I will be ready.' But here was to begin a new experience for me. I was to ride 80 miles in an army wagon, and straight into battle and danger at that.

"I could take no female companion, no friend, but the stout working men I had use for.

"You, who are accustomed to see a coach, and a pair of fine horses with a well-dressed gentlemanly driver draw up to your door, will scarcely appreciate the sensation with which I watched the approach of the long and high, white covered, tortoise-motioned vehicle, with its string of little frisky long-eared animals — with the broad shouldered driver astride — and the eternal jerk of the single rein by which he navigated his craft up to my door.

"The time, you will remember, was Sunday — the place, 7th Street, just off Pennsylvania Avenue, Washington City.

"Then and there, my vehicle was loaded, with boxes, bags, and parcels, and last of all, I found a place for myself and the four men who were to go with me.

"I took no Saratoga trunk, but remembered, at the last moment, to tie up a few articles in my handkerchief.

"Thus equipped, and seated, my chain of little uneasy animals, commenced to straighten itself, and soon brought us into the center of Pennsylvania Avenue, in full gaze of the whole city in its best attire, and on its way to church.

"Thus all day we rattled on over the stones and dikes, and up and down the hills of Maryland.

"At nightfall we turned into an open field, and dismounting built a camp fire, prepared supper, and retired, I to my nook in my wagon, the men wrapped in their blankets, camping about me.

"All night an indistinct roar of artillery sounded upon our ears, and waking or sleeping, we were conscious of trouble ahead; but it was well

E

for our rest that no messenger came to tell us how death reveled among our brave troops that night.

"Before daybreak, we had breakfasted, and were on our way. You will not infer, that because by ourselves, we were alone upon the road. We were directly in the midst of a train of army wagons, at least ten miles in length, moving in solid column — the government supplies and ammunition, food, and medicine for an army in battle.

"Weary and sick from their late exposures, and hardships, the men were falling by the wayside, faint, pale and often dying.

"I busied myself as I rode on hour by hour in cutting loaves of bread in slices and passing them to the pale, haggard wrecks as they sat by the roadside, or staggered on to avoid capture, and at each little village we entered, I purchased all the bread its inhabitants would sell.

"Horses as well as men had suffered and their dead bodies strewed the wayside.

"My poor words can never describe to you the consternation and horror with which we descended from our wagon, and trod, there in the mountain pass, that field of death.

"There, where we now walked with peaceful feet, twelve hours before the ground had rocked with carnage. There in the darkness, God's angels of wrath and death had swept and, foe facing foe, the souls of men went out. And there, side by side, stark and cold in death mingled the Northern Blue and the Southern Gray.

"To such of you as have stood in the midst, or followed in the track of armies and witnessed the strange and dreadful confusion of recent battle grounds, I need not describe this field. And to you who have not, no description would ever avail.

"The giant rocks, hanging above our heads, seemed to frown upon the scene and the sighing trees which hung lovingly upon their rugged edge drooped low and wept their pitying dews upon the livid brows and ghastly wounds beneath.

"Climbing hills and clambering over ledges we sought in vain for some poor wretch, in whom life had still left the power to suffer. Not one remained, and grateful for this, but shocked and sick of heart, we returned to our waiting conveyance.

"A mammoth drove of cattle designated as rations for our troops, was passing at the moment. The officer in charge of this, attracted by our cheerful fire the night previous had sought our company and been our guest.   Scarcely was I seated in my wagon when this officer rode up and said confidentially : 'Miss Barton, that house on the lower side of the road under the hill has been taken as a Confederate hospital and is full of wounded rebels.   Their surgeons have come out and asked me for meat, saying that their men will die for lack of animal food.   I am a bonded officer, and responsible for the property under my charge.   What can I do?'

"'You can do nothing,' I said, 'but ride on ahead.   I am neither bonded nor responsible.'

"He was wise, and a word was sufficient.   He had a sudden call to the front of his train and dashed forward.   Speaking to two of my men, I pointed out a large white ox slightly strayed from the drove and attempting to graze.

"We had been with Genl. Pope's army enough to learn to live off the country and I directed them to drive him to that house inside the fence which surrounded it, put up the bars and leave him there, asking no questions.   I need not say that it was all performed with wonderful alacrity, and the last I saw of the white ox he had gone completely over to the enemy, and was reveling in the tall grass about the house.

"Our wounded had been taken on to Frederick, where only the day before :

'When Lee marched over the mountain wall, —

Over the Mountains winding down,
Horse and foot into Frederick town,

Up rose old Barbara Frietchie then,
Bowed with her four score years and ten!

She took up the Flag the men hauled down!

In her attic window the staff she set,
To show that one heart was loyal yet.'

"As we passed on the residents began to tell us of a great battle fought, 'last night' — they said, 'a few miles up the mountain,' and a 'general was killed.'

"Hastened by anxiety and excitement, we were urging on, when suddenly, we found our wheels crushing the bodies of unburied slain !

"Unconsciously, and without searching, we found a battle field, for this ragged range rising heavily on our right was South Mountain and that fallen General — !"

Major General Reno was the general to whose death Miss Barton's interjection refers. It occurred Monday, September 15, at Turner's and Crampton's Gap, South Mountain, Maryland. Sunday, September 14, the Union forces in the engagement were Hooker's 1st corps, Major General Franklin's 6th corps and Major General Reno's 9th corps, with 325 men killed, 1403 wounded, and 85 prisoners missing on the Union side.

"The increase of stragglers along the road," Miss Barton recalled, "was alarming, showing that our army was weary and lacked not only physical strength — but confidence and spirit.

"And why should they not? Always defeated! Always on the retreat! I was almost demoralized myself! And I had just commenced.

"I have already spoken of the great length of the army train and that we could no more change our position than one of the planets. Unless we should wait and fall in the rear, we could not advance a single wagon.

"And for the benefit of those who may not understand, I may say that the order of the train was first, ammunition, next food and clothing for well troops, and finally the hospital supplies. Thus in case of the battle the needed stores for the army, according to the slow, cautious movement of such bodies, must be from two to three days in coming up.

"Meanwhile as usual our men must languish and die. Something must be done to gain time. And I resorted to strategy. We found an early resting place, supped by our camp fire, and slept again among the dews and damps.

"At one o'clock when everything was still, we arose, breakfasted, harnessed, and moved on past the whole train, which like ourselves had camped for the night. At daylight we had gained ten miles and were up with the artillery and in advance even of the ammunition.

"All that weary dusty day I followed the cannon, and nightfall brought us up with the great Army of the Potomac, 80,000 men resting upon their arms in the face of a foe equal in number, sullen, straitened and desperate.

"Closely following the guns we drew up where they did, among the smoke of the thousand camp fires, men hastening to and fro, and the atmosphere loaded with noxious vapors, till it seemed the very breath of pestilence.   We were upon the left wing of the army, and this was the last evening's rest of Burnside's men.   To how many hundred it proved the last rest upon the earth, the next day's record shows.

"In all this vast assemblage I saw no other trace of woman kind.   I was faint, but could not eat; weary, but could not sleep; depressed, but could not weep.

"So I climbed into my wagon, tied down the cover, dropped down in the little nook I had occupied so long, and prayed God with all the earnestness of my soul to stay the morrow's strife, or send us victory. And for my poor self that He impart somewhat of wisdom and strength to my heart, nerve to my arm, speed to my feet, and fill my hands for the terrible duties of the coming day.   Heavy and sad I awaited its approach."

CHAPTER XII

ANTIETAM

SEPTEMBER 16–17, 1862

ON the night of September 16 the two armies near Sharpsburg, Maryland, lay face to face. Between them was the Valley of Antietam. The Union and Confederate armies were upon the opposite ridges.

The night air, as Miss Barton had entered camp, was still heavy with fog and the smoke of the camp fires round which 120,000 combatants lay down to rest in preparation for a fiery, fateful to-morrow. Occasionally the sullen stillness was pierced by the reverberation through the valley of a round of shots from Sharpsburg, where Hooker had crossed Antietam Creek.

Over the Blue Ridge Mountains, the morning sun rose on the following Union troops: Major General Hooker's 1st corps; Major General Sumner's 2d corps; Major General Fitz John Porter's 5th corps; Major General Franklin's 6th corps; Major General Burnside's 9th corps; Major General Williams' 12th corps; Couch's 4th corps; Pleasanton's division of cavalry. These were to meet the fate of the Union side 2,108 killed, 9,549 wounded, and 753 missing, with General Mansfield killed and Major Generals Hooker and Richardson and Brigadier Generals Rodman, Webber, Sedgwick, Hartsuff, Dana, and Meagher wounded.

Miss Barton took up her stand by the side of the artillery, the post she had won by flanking the army at midnight.

"Many of you may never hear the bugle notes which call to battle," she related of the moment,

> " 'The keener's breath
> Whose fearful blast would waken death.'

But if, like us, you had heard them this morning as they rang through these valleys and echoed from the hundred hills, waking one camp from sleep to hasten to another they would have lingered in your ears, as they do in mine to-night.

"With my attendants, I sought the hill tops and as the mist cleared away, and the morning sun broke over Maryland Heights, its rays fell upon the dusty forms of 160,000 men.[1]

"The battle commenced on the right and already with the aid of field glasses we saw our own forces, led by fighting Joe, overborne and falling back.

"Burnside commenced to send cavalry and artillery to his aid, and thinking our place might be there, we followed them around eight miles, turning into a cornfield near a house and barn, and stopping in the rear of the last gun, which completed the terrible line of artillery which ranged diagonally in the rear of Hooker's army. That day a garden wall only separated us. The infantry were already driven back two miles, and stood under cover of the guns. The fighting had been fearful. We had met wounded men, walking or borne to the rear, for the last two miles. But around the old barn lay there, too badly wounded to admit of removal, some 300 thus early in the day, for it was scarce ten o'clock.

"We loosened our mules and commenced our work. The corn was so high as to conceal the house, which stood some distance to the right, but, judging that a path which I observed must lead to it, and also that surgeons must be operating there, I took my arms full of stimulants, and bandages and followed the opening.

"Arriving at a little wicker gate, I found the dooryard of a small house, and myself face to face with one of the kindest and noblest surgeons I have ever met, Dr. Dunn of Conneautville, Pa.

"Speechless both, for an instant, he at length threw up his hands with 'God has indeed remembered us, how did you get from Virginia here so soon? And again to supply our necessities! And they are terrible. We have nothing but our instruments and the little chloroform we brought in our pockets. We have torn up the last sheets we could find in this house. We have not a bandage, rag, lint, or string, and all these shell-wounded men bleeding to death.'

"Upon the porch stood four tables, with an etherized patient upon

---

[1] Written so near the time the number of this host is approximate. Union and Confederate records in the War Department show 73,135 Union men in action and 45,527 Confederate, a total of 118,662.

each, a surgeon standing over him with his box of instruments, and a bunch of green corn leaves beside him.

"With what joy I laid my precious burden down among them, and thought that never before had linen looked so white, or wine so red. Oh! be grateful, ladies, that God put it in your hearts to perform the work you did in those days. How doubly sanctified was the sacred old household linen woven by the hands of the sainted mother long gone to her reward. For you, arose the tender blessings of those grateful men, which linger in my memory as faithfully to-night, as do the bugle notes which called them to their doom.

"Thrice that day was the ground in front of us contested, lost and won and twice our men were driven back under cover of that fearful range of guns, and each time brought its hundreds of wounded to our crowded ground.

"A little after noon, the enemy made a desperate attempt to regain what had been lost; Hooker, Sedgwick, Dana, Richardson, Hartsuff and Mansfield had been borne wounded from the field and the command of the right wing devolved upon General Howard.

"The smoke became so dense as to obscure our sight, and the hot sulphurous breath of battle dried our tongues, and parched our lips to bleeding.

"We were in a slight hollow and all shell which did not break our guns in front, came directly among or over us, bursting above our heads or burying themselves in the hills beyond.

"A man lying upon the ground asked for a drink, I stopped to give it, and having raised him with my right hand, was holding him.

"Just at this moment a bullet sped its free and easy way between us, tearing a hole in my sleeve and found its way into his body. He fell back dead. There was no more to be done for him and I left him to his rest. I have never mended that hole in my sleeve. I wonder if a soldier ever does mend a bullet hole in his coat?

"The patient endurance of these men was most astonishing. As many as could be were carried into the barn, as a slight protection against random shot. Just outside the door lay a man wounded in the face, the ball having entered the lower maxillary on the left side, and lodged among the bones of the right cheek. His imploring look drew me to him, when placing his finger upon the sharp protuberance, he said, 'Lady, will you tell me what this is that burns so?' I replied that it must be the ball which had been too far spent to cut its way entirely through.

"'It is terribly painful,' he said. 'Won't you take it out?'

"I said I would go to the tables for a surgeon. 'No! No!' he said, catching my dress. 'They cannot come to me. I must wait my turn, for this is a little wound. You can get the ball. There is a knife in your pocket. Please take the ball out for me.'

"This was a new call. I had never severed the nerves and fibers of human flesh, and I said I could not hurt him so much. He looked up, with as nearly a smile as such a mangled face could assume, saying, 'You cannot hurt me, dear lady, I can endure any pain that your hands can create. Please do it. It will relieve me so much.'

"I could not withstand his entreaty and opening the best blade of my pocket knife, prepared for the operation. Just at his head lay a stalwart orderly sergeant from Illinois, with a face beaming with intelligence and kindness, and who had a bullet directly through the fleshy part of both thighs. He had been watching the scene with great interest and when he saw me commence to raise the poor fellow's head, and no one to support it, with a desperate effort he succeeded in raising himself to a sitting posture, exclaiming as he did so, 'I will help do that.' Shoving himself along the ground he took the wounded head in his hands and held it while I extracted the ball and washed and bandaged the face.

"I do not think a surgeon would have pronounced it a scientific operation, but that it was successful I dared to hope from the gratitude of the patient.

"I assisted the sergeant to lie down again, brave and cheerful as he had risen, and passed on to others.

"Returning in half an hour, I found him weeping, the great tears rolling diligently down his manly cheeks. I thought his effort had been too great for his strength and expressed my fears. 'Oh! No! No! Madam,' he replied. 'It is not for myself. I am very well, but,' pointing to another just brought in, he said, 'This is my comrade and he tells me that our regiment is all cut to pieces, that my captain was the last officer left, and he is dead.'

"Oh! God — what a costly war! This man could laugh at pain, face death without a tremor, and yet weep like a child over the loss of his comrades and his captain.

"At two o'clock my men came to tell me that the last loaf of bread had been cut and the last cracker pounded. We had three boxes of wine still unopened. What should they do?

"'Open the wine and give that,' I said, 'and God help us.'

"The next instant, an ejaculation from Sergeant Field, who had opened the first box, drew my attention, and to my astonished gaze, the wine had been packed in nicely sifted Indian meal.

"If it had been gold dust, it would have seemed poor in comparison. I had no words. No one spoke. In silence the men wiped their eyes, and resumed their work.

"Of 12 boxes of wine which we carried, the first nine, when opened, were found packed in sawdust; the last three, when all else was gone, in Indian meal.

"A woman would not hesitate long under circumstances like these.

"This was an old farmhouse. Six large kettles were picked up, and set over fires, almost as quickly as I can tell it, and I was mixing water and meal for gruel.

"It occurred to us to explore the cellar. The chimney rested on an arch, and forcing the door, we discovered three barrels and a bag. 'They are full,' said the sergeant, and rolling one into the light, found that it bore the mark of Jackson's Army. These three barrels of flour, and a bag of salt, had been stored there by the Rebel army during its upward march.

"I shall never experience such a sensation of wealth, and competency again, from utter poverty to such riches.

"All that night, my thirty men (for my corps of workers had increased to that number during the day), carried buckets of hot gruel for miles down the line to the wounded and dying where they fell.

"This time, profiting by experience, we had lanterns to hang in and around the barn, and having directed it to be done, I went to the house, and found the surgeon in charge, sitting alone, beside a table, upon which he rested his elbow, apparently meditating upon a bit of tallow candle, which flickered in the center.

"Approaching carefully, I said, 'You are tired, Doctor.' He started up with a look almost savage, 'Tired! Yes, I am tired, tired of such heartlessness, such carelessness!' Turning full upon me, he continued: 'Think of the condition of things. Here are at least 1,000 wounded men, terribly wounded, 500 of whom cannot live till daylight, without attention. That two inch of candle is all I have, or can get. What can I do? How can I endure it?'

"I took him by the arm, and leading him to the door, pointed in the direction of the barn where the lanterns glistened like stars among the waving corn.

"'What is that?' he exclaimed.

"'The barn is lighted,' I said, 'and the house will be directly.'

"'Who did it?'

"'I, Doctor.'

"'Where did you get them?'

"'Brought them with me.'

"'How many have you?'

"'All you want — four boxes.'

"He looked at me a moment — as if waking from a dream, turned away without a word, and never alluded to the circumstances, but the deference which he paid me was almost painful."

During a lecture in the West, Miss Barton related this incident, and as she closed a gentleman sprang upon the stage, and addressing the audience, exclaimed: "Ladies and gentlemen, if I never have acknowledged that favor, I will do it now. I am that surgeon."

"Darkness," Miss Barton continues, "brought silence and peace, and respite and rest to our gallant men. As they had risen, regiment by regiment, from their grassy beds in the morning, so at night the fainting remnant again sank down on the trampled blood-stained earth, the weary to sleep, and the wounded to die.

"Through the long starlit night, we wrought and hoped and prayed. But it was only when, in the hush of the following day, as we glanced over that vast Aceldama, that we learned at what a fearful cost the gallant Union army had won the battle of Antietam.

"Antietam! With its eight miles of camping armies, face to face; 160,000 men to spring up at dawn like the old Scot from the heather! Its miles of artillery shaking the earth like a chain of Etnas! Its ten hours of uninterrupted battle! Its thunder and its fire! The sharp unflinching order, — 'Hold the Bridge, boys, — always the Bridge.' At length, the quiet! The pale moonlight on its cooling guns! The weary men, — the dying and the dead! The flag of truce that buried our enemy's slain, and Antietam was fought, and won, and the foe turned back!"

CHAPTER XIII

ON THE MARCH THROUGH MARYLAND AND VIRGINIA

OCTOBER-DECEMBER, 1862

At the Battle of Antietam with its three days fighting, Clara Barton had remained on the battle field till fever came upon her. Even then she did not leave till her stores were exhausted.

Dragging herself back to the train, she was carried to Washington where she remained till the fever left her.

She could not walk. Could she have done so she would have been somewhere in action. When well enough to stand upon her feet, she made her way to Quartermaster-General Rucker.

In the conversation between them she said that if she could have had five wagons she could also have had supplies for all the wounded at Antietam.

At this General Rucker in tears declared: "You shall have enough next time!"

It was not long till "next time."

She tells it in this way:

"South Mountain and Antietam were fought, and I had returned to take breath. Then followed six weeks of rest to the army — and unrest to the country. For in those days, every man felt himself fully competent to comprehend the situation, and dictate, if he were not called to direct.

"Both armies rested in the valleys and their cavalry skirted the blue cliffs of Maryland heights.

"And I too, in my littleness and weakness felt that something more remained for me to do, and asked for three army wagons, to proceed again to Harper's Ferry, where rumor predicted the forces would next engage.

"A private message from —— came to me, which said, 'They will fight again — can you go? What transportation do you want?' I answered, 'Yes I can go, and I want three six-mule army wagons with good drivers.'

"My request was twice granted. They gave me *six* and an ambulance. And in the sun and dust of a dry, hot, October day (October 23, 1862) I superintended the loading of them, and at two o'clock ordered my little train to move out on the same road I had traveled a few weeks earlier to Antietam.

"There may be those present who are curious to know how eight or ten rough, stout men, who knew nothing of me, received the fact that they were to drive their teams under the charge of a lady.

"This question has been so often asked in private that I deem it proper to answer it publicly.

"Well, the various expressions of their faces afforded a study. They were not soldiers, but civilians in Government employ. Drovers, butchers, hucksters, mule-breakers, probably not one of them had ever passed an hour in what could be termed 'Ladies' society,' in his life. But every man had driven through the whole peninsular campaign. Every one of them had taken his team unharmed out of that retreat, and had sworn an oath never to drive another step in Virginia.

"They were brave and skillful, understood their business to perfection, but had no art. They said and looked what they thought; and I understood them at a glance.

"They mounted and followed their leader and I followed them.

"As early as 4 o'clock, they turned into a field, formed a circle, and prepared to camp.

"I sent for the leader and inquired his purpose. With some surplus of English he assured me that : 'He wasn't going to drive in the night.'

"I replied that he could drive till night, and he would find it for his interest to do so, and I said no more.

"By some course of reasoning he seemed to arrive at the same conclusion. For after a few minutes consultation with the men, who stood grouped about their wagons, cracking their long whips, as a kind of safety valve to their indignation, they drew their teams out into the road, and moved on at a speed by no means retarded by their late adventure. And with full measure of human perversity they not only drove till night, but far into it. But as they were moving in the right direction, and working off their surplus energy, I did not interfere with them.

"They evidently wanted to drive a little after they had been told to stop. But I was not disposed to gratify them, and about nine o'clock getting weary of their fun, they halted beside a field, and announced their intention of camping for the night. They had eight days' dry rations of meat and bread in their feed boxes, upon which they expected to subsist cold, and with little cooking.

"While they were busy with their animals, with the aid of my ambulance driver, a fire was kindled, (these were the days when fence rails suffered), and I prepared a supper, which I now think would grace a well spread table. But as I had no table, I spread my cloth upon the ground, poured the coffee, and sent my driver to call the men to supper.

"They came, a little slowly, and not all at once, but as I cordially assigned each to his place, I took my seat with them, and ate and chatted as if nothing had happened.

"They were not talkative but respectful, ate well, and when through, retreated in better order than they came.

"I washed my dishes and was spending the last few moments by the broad bed of coals, for it was chilly, when I saw this whole body of men emerge from the darkness and come towards me.

"As they approached I received them graciously, and invited them all to sit by the fire.

"They halted, reminding one of a band of brigands, with the red glare of the embers lighting up their bare, brown faces, and confronted me in the silence, awaiting their spokesman, George, who was, of course, their leader, and whose coal-black hair and eyes would well befit the chief of banditti. As they waited, I again invited them to sit by the fire.

"'No thank you,' George replied. "We didn't come to warm us, we are used to the cold. But,' — he went on slowly, as if it were a little hard to say, 'but we come to tell you we are ashamed of our selves.'

I thought honest confession good for the soul, and did not interrupt him.

"'The truth is' — he continued — 'in the first place we didn't want to come. There's fighting ahead and we've seen enough of that for men who don't carry muskets, only whips; and then we never seen a train under charge of a woman before and we couldn't understand it, and we didn't like it, and we thought we'd break it up, and we've been mean and contrary all day, and said a good many hard things and you've treated us like gentlemen.

"We hadn't no right to expect that supper from you, a better meal than we've had in two years. And you've been as polite to us as if we'd been the General and his staff, and it makes us ashamed. And we've come to ask your forgiveness. We shan't trouble you no more.'

"My forgiveness was easily obtained. I reminded them, that as men it was their duty to go where the country had need of them. As for my being a woman, they would get accustomed to that. And I assured them that as long as I had any food, I would share it with them. That, when they were hungry and supperless, I should be, that if harm befell them, I should care for them, if sick, I should nurse them, and that under all circumstances, I should treat them like gentlemen.

"They listened silently, and when I saw the rough, woolen coat-sleeves drawing across their faces, it was one of the best moments of my life.

"Bidding me 'good-night' they withdrew, excepting the leader, who went to my ambulance, hung a lighted lantern in the top, arranged the few quilts inside for my bed, assisted me up the steps, buckled the canvas down snugly outside, covered the fire safely for morning, wrapped his blanket around him and lay down a few feet from me on the ground.

"At daylight I became conscious of low voices and stifled sounds, and soon discovered that these men were endeavoring to speak low and feed and harness their teams quietly, not to disturb me.

"On the other side I heard the crackling of blazing chestnut rails and the rattling of dishes, and George came with a bucket of fresh water, to undo my buckle door latches, and announce that breakfast was nearly ready.

"I had cooked my last meal for my drivers. These men remained with me six months through frost and snow and march and camp and battle; and nursed the sick, dressed the wounded, soothed the dying, and buried the dead; and if possible grew kinder and gentler every day.

CHAPTER XIV

The Winter Campaign before Fredericksburg

December, 1862

With her expedition of drivers and teams and supplies, Clara Barton had overtaken the army at Harper's Ferry, as it was crossing the Potomac. It was here that the teamsters refused to cross, anticipating the battle which all had thought imminent.

But Lee had averted the clash, and there took place a remarkable race of the two streams of combatants, the army of the North along the valley of the Blue Ridge, the army of the South following the valley of the Shenandoah.

For three weeks there were engagements every day. At one point the rebel forces surprised a part of the Federal army and captured a number of the supply wagons. So far away was the army of the North that they had no reënforcements and supplies, except such as could be toted over the mountain passes in wagons and ambulances. Miss Barton became, therefore, the main source of support for the sick and was attached to the army corps.

On reaching Harper's Ferry, Lee's army had slipped away and Gen. McClellan had decided to follow them.

"Our army," writes Miss Barton in her diary, "was in the act of crossing a pontoon bridge at Berlin when we came up with it. We joined and crossed with them and I found myself in the endless train of a moving army.

"If time permitted, I should like to tell you of those grand old marches down beside the Virginian mountains following the lead of Pleasanton's cavalry skirmishing ahead, finding the enemy every day. Those bright autumnal days! And at night the blaze of a thousand camp fires lighting up the forest tops, while from 10,000 voices rang out the never ending chorus of the Union army·

'John Brown's body lies a-mold'ring in the grave
As we go marching on.'

64

"And thus, day after day, no one knew whither, till the rich autumn tints whitened in the frosts of an approaching winter, and the merry brooks that laughed and leaped in the noon-day sun snuggled quietly into their beds at night under blankets of crystal."

In a letter of December 3d, 1862, Miss Barton in the midst of a journey with the wounded to Washington, gives information of her place on the march among the sick and disabled : —

"In the latter part of October I left home for the Army then at Harper's Ferry, where a battle was hourly expected, taking with me supplies I had then on hand. The army had crossed the river without a battle. I followed, and, joining the 9th corps for safety from 'raids,' I continued with them, caring for the sick, supplying from my own stores, until we reached Warrenton Junction, when they were sent to Washington, and leaving my teams and assistants to move on with the army, I accompanied the sick."

She herself was sick, but in the growing cold of winter, with an excruciating pain in her hand, she said nothing. "It did not matter." The fact only crept out in a letter explaining why she did not write : —

"A most painful felon disabled my hand from the first of November, from which I got relief and rest only by narcotics and the knife (used on the open field). For what with water and cold and burns and bruises and frosts, my hands complain a little of unaccustomed hardships. Our march up the Maryland hills and down the Virginia mountains was long, broken and uncertain, harassed by the enemy both front and rear."

Miss Barton's work with the sick took her back to the capital but she did not stay long there.

"I remained there, of course, only a little space of time," she writes, "and met the army at Falmouth, *via* Aquia Creek. Then commenced the weary suspense of waiting for a battle, all the while lying under the guns of the enemy. At length it came. I instantly repaired to 'the front,' — the famous 'Lacy House,' within a stone's throw of the Rappahannock, and indeed, of Fredericksburg itself, for the high bluffs narrow the river at this point until I think a strong man might throw a stone across it.

"From the piazza of this house we watched (as you would watch from your own door steps a transaction in your gardens) the attempted

F

laying of the pontoon bridge, its abandonment under the fire of the sharpshooters on the opposite bank concealed in the cellars, and the embarkation of the glorious 7th Michigan.   We listened to the deafening cheers of their comrades on shore, as they rowed and shouted and fell on the landing, — fire and shot above them and blood below, — the hand to hand fight, — the finishing of the bridge and the crossing of the army, until darkness prevented the further labor of our weary eyes, although it brought no rest to our weary army.   The next day the terrible slaughter ensued.   I crossed to Fredericksburg, and remained two days, and then returned to the fearful scene at the 'Lacy House.'   I cannot tell you the number, but some hundreds of the worst wounded men I have ever seen were lying on a little hay on floors or in tents."

In this battle of December 13, the Northern forces were defeated. On the Union side there were 1,284 killed, 9,600 wounded, and 1,769 missing or prisoners.

Only a little while later, while the events were still fresh in her mind, Miss Barton recalled more in detail of the battle of Fredericksburg:

"We found ourselves beside a broad, muddy river, and a little canvas city grew up in a night upon its banks.   And there we sat and waited 'while the world wondered.'   Ay! It did more than wonder! It murmured, it grumbled, it cried shame, to sit there and shiver under the canvas.   'Cross over the river and occupy those brick houses on the other shore!'   The murmurs grew to a clamor!

"Our gallant leader heard them and his gentle heart grew sore as he looked upon his army that he loved as it loved him and looked upon those fearful sights beyond.   Carelessness or incapacity at the capital had baffled his best laid plans till time had made his foes a wall of adamant. Still the country murmured.   You, friends, have not forgotten how, for these were the dark days of old Fredericksburg, and our little canvas city was Falmouth.

"Finally, one soft, hazy winter's day the army prepared for an attack; but there was neither boat nor bridge, and the sluggish tide rolled dark between.

"The men of Hooker and Franklin were right and left, but here in the center came the brave men of the silvery-haired Sumner.

"Drawn up in line they wait in the beautiful grounds of the stately mansion whose owner, Lacy, had long sought the other side, and stood that day aiming engines of destruction at the home of his youth and the graves of his household.

"There on the second portico I stood and watched the engineers as they moved forward to construct a pontoon bridge. It will be remembered that the rebel army occupying the Heights of Fredericksburg previous to the attack was very cautious about revealing the position of its guns.

"A few boats were fastened and the men marched quickly on with timbers and planks. For a few rods it proved a success, and scarcely could the impatient troops be restrained from rending the air with shouts of triumph.

"On marches the little band with brace and plank, but never to be laid by them. A rain of musket balls has swept their ranks and the brave fellows lie level with the bridge or float down the stream.

"No living thing stirs on the opposite bank. No enemy is in sight. Whence comes this rain of death?

"Maddened by the fate of their comrades, others seize the work and march onward to their doom. For now, the balls are hurling thick and fast, not only at the bridge, but over and beyond to the limit of their range — crashing through the trees, the windows and doors of the Lacy House. And ever here and there a man drops in the waiting ranks, silently as a snow flake. And his comrades bear him in for help, or back for a grave.

"There on the lower bank under a slouched hat stands the man of honest heart and genial face that a soldier could love and honor even through defeat, the ever-trusted, gallant Burnside. Hark — that deep-toned order rising above the heads of his men: 'Bring the guns to bear and shell them out.'

"Then rolled the thunder and the fire. For two hong hours the shot and shell hurled through the roofs and levelled the spires of Fredericksburg. Then the little band of engineers resumed its work, but ere ten spaces of the bridge were gained, they fell like grass before the scythe.

"For an instant all stand aghast; then ran the murmurs — 'The cellars are filled with sharp-shooters and our shell will never reach them.'

"But once more over the heads of his men rose that deep-toned order: '*Man the boats.*'

"Into the boats like tigers then spring the 7th Michigan.

"'Row!! Row!! Ply for your lives, boys.' And they do. But mark! They fall, some into the boats, some out. Other hands seize the oars and strain and tug with might and main. Oh! How slow the seconds drag! How long we have held our breath.

"Almost across — under the Bluffs — and out of range! Thank God — they'll land!

"Ah, yes; but not all. Mark the windows and doors of those houses above them. See the men swarming from them armed to the teeth and rushing to the river.

"They've reached the bluffs above the boats. Down point the muskets. Ah! that rain of shot and shell and flame!

"Out of the boats waist deep in the water; straight through the fire. Up, up the bank the boys in blue! Grimly above, that line of gray!

"Down pours the shot. Up, up the blue, till hand to hand like fighting demons they wrestle on the edge.

"Can we breathe yet? No! Still they struggle. Ah! yes, they break, they fly, up through the street and out of sight, pursuer and pursued.

"It were long to tell of that night crossing and the next terrible day of fire and blood. And when the battle broke o'er field and grove, like a resistless flood daylight exposed Fredericksburg with its fourth-day flag of truce, its dead, starving and wounded, frozen to the ground. The wounded were brought to me, frozen, for days after, and our commissions and their supplies at Washington with no effective organization or power to go beyond! The many wounded lay, uncared for, on the cold snow."

Miss Barton moved among them, and had the snow cleared away, finding famished, frozen, bent figures that once were men. She rushed to tear down an old chimney and built fire blocks and soon had thirteen gallon kettles of coffee and gruel steaming.

But fearful as were the great events of those days, among their unwritten history are thousands of incidents existing only in the memories of those who witnessed them but as truly illustrative of the hour, Miss Barton remarked, as the 40 solid shot and mortar shell which poured the lurid light of day and the pale glimmer of the night through a single roof.

A Rebel officer in the skirmish of the day before was wounded and taken prisoner. Stanching his wound and quenching his thirst, the amazed nurse heard the Rebel officer murmur to her that the army on the Fredericksburg side of the Rappahannock had laid a trap for the Northern soldiers, covering every street and lane with the mouths of hidden cannon. Then, as she here relates, came the following call to go across:

"At 10 o'clock of the battle day when the Rebel fire was hottest, the shell rolling down every street, and the bridge under the heavy cannonade, a courier dashed over and rushing up the steps of the Lacy House, placed in my hand a crumpled bloody slip of paper, a request from the lion-hearted old surgeon on the opposite shore, establishing his hospitals in the very jaws of death.

"The uncouth pencilling said: 'Come to me. Your place is here.'

"The faces of the rough men working at my side which eight weeks ago had flushed with indignation at the very thought of being controlled by a woman, grew ashy white as they guessed the nature of the summons, and the lips which had cursed and pouted in disgust trembled as they begged me to send them, but save myself. I could only permit them to go with me if they chose, and in 20 minutes we were rocking across the swaying bridge, the water hissing with shot on either side.

"Over into that city of death, its roofs riddled by shell, its very church a crowded hospital, every street a battle-line — every hill a rampart, every rock a fortress, and every stone wall a blazing line of forts!

"Oh, what a day's work was that! How those long lines of blue, rank upon rank, charged over the open acres, up to the very mouths of those blazing guns, and how like grain before the sickle they fell and melted away.

"An officer stepped to my side to assist me over the débris at the end of the bridge. While our hands were raised in the act of stepping down, a piece of an exploding shell hissed through between us, just below our arms, carrying away a portion of both the skirts of his coat and my dress, rolling along the ground a few rods from us like a harmless pebble in the water.

"The next instant a solid shot thundered over our heads, a noble steed bounded in the air, and with his gallant rider rolled in the dirt, not 30 feet in the rear! Leaving the kind-hearted officer, I passed on

alone to the hospital.   In less than a half hour he was brought to me —
dead.

"I mention these circumstances not as specimens of my own bravery.
Oh, no! I beg you will not place that construction upon them, for
I never professed anything beyond ordinary courage, and a thousand
times preferred safety to danger.

"But I mention them that those of you, who have never seen a
battle, may the better realize the perils through which these brave
men passed, who, for four long years bore their country's bloody
banner in the face of death, and stood, a living wall of flesh and blood,
between the invading traitor and your peaceful homes.

"In the afternoon of Sunday an officer came hurriedly to tell me that
in a church across the way lay one of his men shot in the face the day
before. His wounds were bleeding slowly and, the blood drying and
hardening about his nose and mouth, he was in immediate danger of
suffocation.

"(Friends, this may seem to you repulsive, but I assure you that
many a brave and beautiful soldier has died of this alone.)

"Seizing a basin of water and a sponge, I ran to the church, to find
the report only too true. Among hundreds of comrades lay my
patient. For any human appearance above his head and shoulders,
it might as well have been anything but a man.

"I knelt by him and commenced with fear and trembling lest some
unlucky movement close the last aperture for breath. After some
hour's labor, I began to recognize features. They seemed familiar.
With what impatience I wrought. Finally my hand wiped away the
last obstruction. An eye opened, and there to my gaze was the sexton
of my old home church!

"I have remarked that every house was a hospital. Passing from
one to another during the tumult of Saturday, I waited for a regiment
of infantry to sweep on its way to the heights. Being alone, and the
only woman visible among that moving sea of men, I naturally attracted the attention of the old veteran, Provost Marshal General
Patrick, who, mistaking me for a resident of the city who had remained
in her home until the crashing shot had driven her into the street,
dashed through the waiting ranks to my side, and, bending down from
his saddle, said in his kindliest tones, 'You are alone and in great
danger, Madam. Do you want protection?'

"Amused at his gallant mistake, I humored it by thanking him, as I turned to the ranks, adding that 'I believed myself the best protected woman in the United States.'

"The soldiers near me caught my words, and responding with 'That's so! that's so,' set up a cheer. This in turn was caught by the next line and so on, line after line, till the whole army joined in the shout, no one knowing what he was cheering at, but never doubting there was a victory somewhere. The gallant old General, taking in the situation, bowed low his bared head, saying, as he galloped away, 'I believe you are right, Madam.'

"It would be difficult for persons in ordinary life to realize the troubles arising from want of space merely for wounded men to occupy when gathered together for surgical treatment and care. You may suggest that 'all out of doors' ought to be large and so it would seem, but the fact did not always prove so. Civilized men seek shelter in sickness, and of this there was ever a scarcity.

"Twelve hundred men were crowded into the Lacy House, which contained but twelve rooms. They covered every foot of the floors and porticos and even lay on the stair landings! A man who could find opportunity to lie between the legs of a table thought himself lucky. He was not likely to be stepped on. In a common cupboard, with four shelves, five men lay, and were fed and attended. Three lived to be removed, and two died of their wounds.

"Think of trying to lie still and die quietly, lest you fall out of a bed six feet high!

"Among the wounded of the 7th Michigan was one Faulkner, of Ashtabula County, Ohio, a mere lad, shot through the lungs and to all appearances, dying. When brought in he could swallow nothing, breathed painfully, and it was with great difficulty that he gave me his name and residence. He could not lie down, but sat leaning against the wall in the corner of the room.

"I observed him carefully as I hurried past from one room to another, and finally thought he had ceased to breathe. At this moment another man with a similar wound was taken in on a stretcher by his comrades, who sought in vain for a spot large enough to lay him down, and appealed to me. I could only tell them that when that poor boy in the corner was removed they could set him down in his place. They went to remove him, but to the astonishment of all, he objected, opened his eyes and persisted in retaining his corner, which he did for some two weeks, when, finally, a mere bundle of skin and bones, for he gave small evidence of either flesh or blood, he was wrapped in a blanket and taken away in an ambulance to Washington, with a bottle of milk punch in his blouse, the only nourishment he could take.

"On my return to Washington, three months later, a messenger came from Lincoln Hospital to say that the men of Ward 17 wanted to see me. I returned with him, and as I entered the ward 70 men saluted me, standing such as could, others rising feebly in their beds, and falling back — exhausted with the effort.

"Every man had left his blood in Fredericksburg — every one was from the Lacy House. My hand had dressed every wound — many of them in the first terrible moments of agony. I had prepared their food in the snow and winds of December and fed them like children.

"How dear they had grown to me in their sufferings, and the three great cheers that greeted my entrance into that hospital ward were dearer than the applause. I would not exchange their memory for the wildest hurrahs that ever greeted the ear of Conqueror or King. When the first greetings were over and the agitation had subsided somewhat, a young man walked up to me with no apparent wound, with bright complexion and in good flesh. There was certainly something familiar in his face, but I could not recall him, until, extending his hand with a smile, he said, 'I am Riley Faulkner of the 7th Michigan. I didn't die, and the milk punch lasted all the way to Washington!'"

Among the single instances of heroism which Miss Barton describes in connection with the battle of Fredericksburg is that of Sergeant Plunkett of the 21st who enlisted from West Boylston — Miss Barton's own county of Worcester.

"I remember a patriot hero who bore the flag over the bodies of his fallen comrades, to plant it on the blazing Heights of Fredericksburg until both arms fell useless at his side. And the shoulders received the precious burden the hands could no longer uphold. Planting his foot firmly by the resting staff his clear voice rang out above the shouts of the charging ranks, the hissing of shot, and the shrieking of shell:

"Don't let it fall, boys, don't let it fall!"

"And it did not and while we laid the armless sergeant in his battle hospital bed in the snow clad camp, his colonel wrapped carefully the tattered silken folds, dabbled and dyed in patriot blood, and sent it home to the Government of the State, with the message that the Old Regiment had never lost its colors but it had worn them out and wanted more.

"With its scores of companions grouped around the pillars, it hangs in the State House to-night," Miss Barton once said in an address. "In some noble hall," she continued, "have you your own like treasures gathered, and your hearts have heaved with grateful pride, and your eyes have grown dim with gathering mist as you behold them. Oh, what a consecrated hall! At what a price it has been decorated! What granite could you rear that could speak like this? Could the gold and ivory of Solomon's Temple bear the price like it? Go there often, men and women. Take your children there, and from the tattered rags teach them the worth of their country. Tell them that for every rent they can count, ten brave lives went out, ten mothers mourned for a son, ten orphans walked the streets, ten homes were desolate. And when all this is estimated, tell them that alongside of each tattered remnant there should droop another fringed in black, whose center should bear only the terrible word, — 'Starved.'"

An instance of the unspeakable gratitude and affection felt for Clara Barton at the battle of Fredericksburg lies in this touching recollection:

"As I stood near the eastern entrance, a man was taken in by his comrades, apparently fainting, and laid upon the floor. A piece of shell had struck him near the ankle. At a glance I discovered that an artery was severed, and he was rapidly sinking. The surgeons had nearly all been ordered into the city, and of the few who remained, not one was obtainable. Making a tourniquet of my handkerchief, I succeeded in arresting the flow at the first trial, gave the poor fellow some stimulant and left him to rest and wait for better skill.

"He chanced to lie near the passage leading from one room to another, and in the course of an hour as I passed by, I felt my dress held firmly by some obstruction. Terrified lest it might have caught on the helpless foot of some broken limb, I turned to find this poor fainting man revived, and holding on with all his might to the skirt of my dress. He could not speak aloud, but the tears were sliding quietly down his brown, dust-covered cheeks. As I knelt to learn his wishes, he whispered, faintly, 'You saved my life.' I smoothed back his tangled hair, wiped his face and replied cheerfully that that was no matter. Did he want anything? — 'No.'

"An hour later as I passed, the same thing occurred, and I was again informed in faint whispers that I had saved his life. And so on, day after day, until he was removed, whenever I came within reach of him I could feel my dress slipping gently through his fingers, and as often as he dared, he arrested me with the same four little words, 'You saved my life!' He never seemed to want anything, and never said anything but this.

"In all the confusion, I neither learned his name nor told him mine. He was taken away to the hospital with the others, and the circumstances nearly forgotten. As I sat buried in the mass of accumulated correspondence, I heard a limping foot in my hall, and a rap at my door. I hastened to open it, and there, leaning upon his crutch, stood my hero of the four words, and before I could recover from my surprise sufficiently to speak he broke the silence with — 'You saved my life!'"

Still another glimpse of Miss Barton's day's work at Fredericksburg comes to us in a letter written in 1903 to Mrs. Margaret Hamilton, the President of the Association of Army Nurses of the Civil War. In this letter she refers to the death at Fredericksburg of Lieutenant Newcomb, a Harvard graduate who returned from extensive study in Europe to enlist:

"I see that scene as clearly as on that December day of 1862. That noble, Christian soul passing away; the timid, stricken brother by his side, all of us repeating together the Scriptures and his saying to me, pitifully, before consciousness left him, 'Please stay with me to the end, for Charlie never saw any one die.' When I rose from the side of the couch where I had knelt for hours, until the last breath had faded, I wrung the blood from the bottom of my clothing before I could step, for the weight about my feet. Dreadful days, dear dear sister; — how little those realize to-day, who cavil over the technicalities of field-work;[1] one's heart grows sick to think of it."

Miss Barton dismisses Fredericksburg with the following retrospect:
"The long autumn march down the mountain passes — Falmouth and old Fredericksburg with its pontoon bridge — sharp-shooters —

---

[1] At the point of the factional differences raised by the opposing wing of the red cross.

deserted streets — its rocky brow of frowning forts — the day of bombardment, and the charge! The broad glacis — one vast Aceldama —

> "'Where slaughter strewed the purple plain
> With torture and dismay,
> Till strength seemed weak, and valour vain,
> And grim and ghastly with the slain, full many a hero lay.'

"The falling back — the night retreat — across the Rappahannock — and Fredericksburg was fought and lost!"

Fredericksburg was unspeakably awful to the memory of Clara Barton.[1] Yet afterward, in clear vision, she saw through it a mighty fact — that it was this defeat that wrenched from President Lincoln and the American people the Emancipation Proclamation! By it, not only was the false self-confidence of the North dispelled forever, but there came out of it also the moral courage that was to turn defeat into victory.

"And the white May blossoms of '63 fell over the glad faces — the swarthy brows, the toil-worn hands of 4,000,000 liberated slaves."

"America," writes Miss Barton, "had freed a race."

---

[1] September 22d, 1862, the period after Antietam's Victory, was in some minds the time that pressed from the north the step to emancipation. HoweVer this may haVe been, it was not enacted nor proclaimed till after the Fredericksburg defeat of the North.

CHAPTER XV

EIGHT MONTHS AT FORTS WAGNER, SUMTER AND GREGG IN THE CAMPAIGN BEFORE CHARLESTON

AFTER the winter campaign at Fredericksburg Clara Barton's time was occupied for a while in acknowledging the supplies she had received and in repairing her depleted stores for the new campaign of 1863.

The following letter written in March, 1863, to Mrs. Thomas, a Pennsylvania woman, gives some glimpse of these activities:

"From my heart I wish I could answer one letter which must not perforce commence with an apology for delay, but the truth is, I am buried so 'many deep' in unanswered correspondence that it seems like injustice to those 'gone before' to reply to even one in time. Thus with a poor attempt at justice, I am in constant error. But you will deal mercifully, and finally pardon me, for there is the broad platform upon which we meet, the very groundwork of our faith.

"It is a sisterly kindness which bids you seek me out and essay to fill my hands, which get so often, and sometimes so fearfully, emptied. I hope I may be able some day to show to you that I appreciate your generous solicitude. I am by no means surprised, for I had heard of Mrs. Thomas years ago, in the days when misery lurked only in by places, and faithful charity groped in darkness and squalor to find out and relieve it. Ah! it were some credit to be charitable then, but in these days when giant misery stalks to the very threshold, and raps with bloody hands on one's own door, it were almost a libel upon the good old Christian term, to call it charity that answers it. The door that never creaked a hinge for the timid tap of the feeble child of want, may swing wide at the thundering knock of the Marshal's staff. This fratricide war, not only opens coffers which never oped before, but hearts as well; dark shadows lie upon the hearthstones, but if in contrast the fading embers of humanity and brotherly love glow with a new radiance, it shall not at last have been all in vain.

"It will be no new experience to me to find my failing resources supplied from Pennsylvania. I have long wished myself capable of framing a fitting eulogium upon that noble state. I have watched her throughout this war. Wherever I have met her soldiers, they have been brave and patriotic. When I have come in contact with her surgeons, I have found them gentlemanly and humane, and the timely generous 'aid' which has been constantly finding its way to me from her valleys and hillsides has bespoken a people at home, well worthy their noble representatives in the field."

April 7, 1863, the South Atlantic Squadron under Admiral Du Pont began the siege of Charleston. Sumter, Wagner, and other batteries met the fleet with 3500 shots from 300 guns, 160 a minute. On Folly Island the army joined the navy for a combined attack, the former under the command of General Seymour. By June 2, 18,000 men were sent to form a land army under Major General Gilmore. Admiral Dahlgren replaced Du Pont in July. The operation centered around the attempt to take Fort Wagner, Morris Island and Forts Gregg and Sumter, all in the possession of the South and strongly fortified.

Miss Barton reached Hilton Head shortly after the 7th of April. Some little action had occurred between Sumter and Du Pont's fleet but the expedition returned to Hilton Head, where except for scattering raids, there was a cessation of hostilities. Sumter it was evident could not be taken at once. This, however, did not mean inaction, for they must prepare for the long attack that lay ahead of them.

The casualties in the opening encounters increased in severity. Miss Barton served day and night. On July 11, in an assault from Morris Island on Fort Wagner, forty-nine were killed, one hundred twenty-three wounded, and one hundred sixty-seven captured and missing. The middle of July [1] from Morris Island General Gilmore with five batteries opened a bombardment on Fort Wagner on the same island, Admiral Dahlgren dropping shells from his monitors. One hundred guns assailed the fort. General Strong with Colonel R. G. Shaw's colored troops advanced under the fire of three Confederate forts. Musketry and hand grenades met the closer advance. In the slaughter Strong and Shaw fell, together with masses of the black

---

[1] The great assault at Fort Wagner was July 18, 1863 — losses, killed 246, wounded 880, missing 389.

troops who were the special objects of Confederate hatred. Another brigade under Colonel H. L. Putnam advanced but to meet a like repulse. The Confederates claim they buried 600 Northern men in front of the fort. The engagements during the remaining days in July brought the total number killed up to 1212.

"I remember so well these islands," explained Miss Barton, "when the guns and the gunners, the muskets and musketeers, struggled for place and foothold among the shifting sands. I remember the first swarthy regiments with their unsoldierly tread, and the soldierly bearing and noble brows of the patient philanthropists who volunteered to lead them. I can see again the scarlet flow of blood as it rolled over the black limbs beneath my hands and the great heave of the heart before it grew still. And I remember Wagner and its 600 dead, and the great souled martyr that lay there with them when the charge was ended and the guns were cold." Vividly she went on to describe the siege of Fort Wagner from Morris Island thus: "I saw the bayonets glisten. The 'swamp angel' threw her bursting bombs, the fleet thundered its cannonade and the dark line of blue trailed its way in the dark line of belching walls of Wagner. I saw them on, up and over the parapets into the jaws of death, and heard the clang of the death-dealing sabers as they grappled with the foe. I saw the ambulances laden down with agony and the wounded slowly crawling to me down the tide washed beach, Voris and Cumminger gasping in their blood. And I heard the deafening clatter of the hoofs of 'Old Sam' as Elwell madly galloped up under the walls of the fort for orders. I heard the tender, wailing fife, the muffled drum and the last shots as the pitiful little graves grew thick in the shifting sands."

Colonel J. G. Elwell, who was one of the generals leading in the assault, described the Island as "a graveyard, occupied by the Rebels and then by the Federal forces." "A cup of good water was nowhere to be found," he wrote in a letter which was read at a reunion of the Yates Phalanx.[1] "Wells were shallow and water brackish, almost deadly in character. The siege was in hot weather and the climate malarious. Every fort of the Island could be reached by the guns of Sumter, Wagner, and other forts. Here Miss Barton

[1] An organization founded by the Illinois war Governor, Richard Yates, of the beautiful old college town of Jacksonville, Illinois.

stayed during the night of the assault. She was there to succor the wounded. She soon became dangerously ill in her tent. I appealed to her to return to Port Royal or she would certainly die.

"Her answer was, 'Do you think I would leave here in a bombardment?'"

There was no protection. Morris Island was a stretch of barren sand hills without a tree. It was hard to walk. The feet sank to the ankles in the beach, where they were calloused and blistered in sand that had been baked in the sun for months.

Miss Barton's eyes were blinded till they became bloodshot by constant gales of sand granules. This fact made it more difficult for her to clear away the peppering particles that stung their way into the wounds of many hundreds, clogging the torn flesh, and when wet with blood acting as a cement about each wound.

Floorless dog tents, pitched in the sand, offered the only shelter, and these were not infrequently blown down by constant stiff squalls from the sea.

Miss Barton's station was opposite the fierce fire from all forts, in the shadow of a sand dune. Underneath a tropic sun all day long she was boiling water over a smoking fire. Then she hurried hour after hour to wash the wounds of men tortured not only by the sudden shot, but by the clinging, caking sand. Tea and coffee, milk and eggs, fruit and farina, she served from her ever ready stores.

On the day of the fiercest assault of Wagner — not evacuated till September 7, but which the Union forces had expected to take at once — she was ready for every new tragic emergency. She kept her fires burning all day, her kettles boiling and food ready for use. For she was the objective of broken columns of wounded men crawling down the sand stretches. To a torn ex-slave, blood dyeing his ebony skin, or to a wounded general she gave like attention.

"Follow me, if you will, through these eight months," Miss Barton said shortly afterward. "I remember eight months of weary siege — scorched by the sun, chilled by the waves, rocked by the tempest, buried in the shifting sands, toiling day after day, in the trenches, with the angry fire of five forts hissing through their ranks during every day of those weary months.

"This was when your brave old regiments stood thundering at the gate of proud rebellious Charleston. . . . There, frowning defiance, with Moultrie on her left, Johnson on her right, and Wagner in front, she stood hurling fierce death and destruction full in the faces of the brave band who beleaguered her walls.

"Sumter, the watch-dog, that stood before her door, pierced with shot and torn with shell, lay maimed and bleeding at her feet, the tidal waves lapping his wounds. Still there was danger in his growl and death in his bite." [1]

"One summer afternoon our brave little army was drawn up among the island sands and formed in line of march. For hours we watched. Dim twilight came — then the darkness for which they had waited, while the gloom and stillness of death settled down on the gathered forces of Morris Island. Then we pressed forward and watched again. A long line of phosphorescent light streamed and shot along the waves ever surging on our right.

"A little to the left, mark that long, dark line, moving steadily on, pace by pace, across that broad space of glistening sand.

"On, straight on, toward that black mass, frowning and darkling in the distance.

"Watch — Watch — with pulseless veins, and breathless lips.

"On — On — God speed their steps!

"Flash — flash — flash — flash — Moultrie — Johnson — Sumter — Wagner — Every black pile blazes and the heavens are on fire.

"Boom! Boom! Boom! Answered the old fleet as it circled into line and poured broadside after broadside till the heavens blazed again. On! On! Pressed the little band passing to its doom — but dark no longer. The foe is met. The muskets blaze. The dark line has changed to a trail of fire. Pressing on, scattered now, we watch the flashing of their muskets, as you the fireflies on your meadows.

"The walls are reached, the torpedoes, and the pikes —

"Up — up — over the parapets, into the fort, hand to hand, foot to foot.

"Does any man say that this war showed no bayonet wounds? He did not scale the walls of Wagner.

"Hand to hand and hilt to hilt they wrestle. The great guns of fort and fleet are still, and there in the darkness and mist we wait, they wait, the weary hour.

[1] Smashed by shell as it had been July 24th, it repulsed an assailing party September 8th, killing 200. Sumter was not completely silenced until October 26th.

"There bearing the tall form of his rider plunged the noble steed of Colonel J. J. Elwell, of Cleveland, Chief Quartermaster of the department of the South. Up the beach he came, through the surf, and fire, up, up, under the very walls of the blazing fort. Rising in his saddle, his strong voice went up, 'How goes the fight, boys? What do you want?'

"Begrimed with smoke and scorched with flame on the topmost parapet appeared the form of the intrepid Putnam.

"'Reënforcements, Colonel! in God's name, get us reënforcements. I can hold out fifteen minutes longer.'

"Whirled the steed and rider, back down the beach to headquarters. 'Men, General, more men. Your troops are struggling in the forts.' 'Take them back again.' Through the surf and fire! Up once more with the welcome tidings.

"Up — ha! What is that? The sides of the fort are black with men — are these reënforcements?

"Ah, would to God! Back! Out! Down, over torpedo and pike into moat and wave, sinking, striving, fainting, crawling, dying!

"Slowly down the beach wends the long line of wounded. And one by one they bring their story of disaster.

"The fort was gained, the center reached. Bravely they fought, but all too few. They waited, braving death, for the help that came not. Leader after leader fell. And there side by side with those of fairer hue, lay the tawny hand of Africa, which that night for the first time in the history of all the ages, had been permitted to strike a lawful, organized blow at the fetters which had bound him body and mind and soul.

"That broad, dark, heaving chest, and struggling breath, that great patient eye and gaping wound!

"'Ah, Sam, that's bad for you.' 'Yes, miss, I knows it. Dey's too many for us dis time — I'm a gwine, but thank God my childers free.'

"The charge had failed. The night was lost. Ah, too late the advantage came. Slowly down wend the long line of ambulances, and the sands about our hospital tents grow red with the blood of the wounded and slain.

"Then came the hundreds back. There were the stricken of the brave 63d and 67th Ohio, and as I plodded through the sand, rain,

G

and darkness, many a pale lip moved in prayer as the fading eye grew strangely bright.

"There on the ground among his soldier boys lay Cumminger, delirious in his pain. 'Bury me here, friends, here in the sands. Don't take me away. I've tried to do my duty to my country and my God. Bury me here right where I fell.'

"But God still had something for brave men to do and he saved him.

"There, suffering, brave and faithful, lay the wounded of three as brave regiments as ever trod an enemy's soil or faced a rebel gun, the 6th, 7th and 10th Connecticut.

"A little farther on lay Voris, of the 67th, pale and unconscious, his bright hair dabbling in the sand, while from the dark wound in his side slowly ebbed the red tide of life!"

General Elwell, who declared that both General Voris of Ohio and General Leggett would have died had it not been for Miss Barton's assistance, gives this account of the assault:

"I was shot with an Enfield cartridge within one hundred and fifty yards of the fort and so disabled that I could not go forward. I was in an awful predicament, perfectly exposed to canister from Wagner and shell from Gregg and Sumter in front, and the enfilade from James Island. I tried to dig a trench in the sand with my sabre, into which I might crawl, but the dry sand would fall back in place about as fast as I could scrape it out with my narrow implement. Failing in this, on all fours I crawled toward the lee of the beach, which was but a few yards off. . . . A charge of canister all around me aroused my reverie to thoughts of action. I abandoned the idea of taking the fort and ordered a retreat of myself, which I undertook to execute in a most unmartial manner on my hands and knees spread out like a turtle.

"After working my way for a half hour and making perhaps two hundred yards, two boys of the Sixty-second Ohio found me and carried me to our first parallel, where had been arranged an extempore hospital. After resting a while I was put on the horse of my lieutenant colonel, from which he had been shot that night and started for the lower end of the island one and a half miles off where better hospital arrangements had been prepared. Oh, what an awful ride that was! But I got there at last, by midnight. I had been on duty for forty-two hours without sleep under the most trying circumstances and my soul longed for sleep which I got in this wise: an army blanket was doubled and laid on the soft side of a plank with an overcoat for a pillow, on which I laid my worn out body.

"And such a sleep! I dreamed that I heard the shouts of my boys in victory, that the rebellion was broken, that the Union was saved, and that I was at my old home and that my dear wife was trying to soothe my pain. . . .

"My sleepy emotions awoke me and a dear, blessed woman was bathing my temples and fanning my fevered face. Clara Barton was there, an angel of mercy doing all in mortal power to assuage the miseries of the unfortunate soldiers."

What Miss Barton's position was on the firing line in the smoke of Fort Wagner and Sumter is evidenced by a paragraph in a letter written by her from her post of danger July 14. In this it is seen that with not a thought of personal danger her only consideration was for the safety of others.

"MORRIS ISLAND — HOSPITAL TENT
OR
"U. S. STEAMER 'PHILADELPHIA'
"Tuesday, July 14th, 1863.

"LIEUT. RICHIE, U. S. STR. 'PAWNEE,' FOLLY ISLAND, S. C.

"MY DEAR FRIEND:

"The caption of my sheet will not surprise you as I presume you would be more likely to look for me in the smoke of Fort Sumter than anywhere else in this vicinity.

"My tent is with the advance hospital — Dr. Craven, Med. Purveyor of this department in charge. We are just the other side and in plain sight of the landing at Lighthouse Inlet, perhaps a mile from the old lighthouse. We are so liable to be shelled out that I trust nothing but myself to remain there, keeping my trunks on board the Philadelphia, which makes it a kind of second home. I have my own ambulance, horses and driver and saddle horse, but do not suppose any of these would aid me in an attempt to call upon you, but if you had opportunity I would be most happy to see you at my tent, or upon this boat, if I chanced to be here. . . ."

Yet she herself came very near death as was shown in a letter written to Annie E. Childs from Hilton Head, October 27, 1863. "I watched the first boat near the coast of Morris Island and saw the first man leap out upon its glistening sands. One week later we met the flash of a hundred guns, and ten thousand muskets lit up the darkness of our desert island and the thunders of Wagner and Sumter shook it to its center, and on those bloody parapets freedom and slavery met and wrested, hand to hand; the false flag and the true, swelling in the same breeze, stood face to face, while warriors met and fought, and martyrs died. Through the long, dark terrible hours, we gazed and hoped and prayed, and at length, must I say it, turned back in despair to comfort our wounded and bury the dead — repulsed! Then followed the long hot weeks of toiling siege and the last trench was dug, and our forces with scarce the loss of a man, walked in upon the graves of their six hundred comrades, buried in Wagner.

"I, no longer able to see, was lying weak and helpless as a child, little knowing and less minding towards what goal my way was wending."

Colonel Elwell adds to this the statement that "after a time she was carried away almost by force to a more healthful locality where she was sick for a long time."

On August 17, from useless assaults, Gilmore proceeded to a siege, bringing up a 200-pound Parrott gun — "the swamp angel" — with which to shell Charleston. Sumter was partly reduced on the 24th, by the aid of 12 batteries and Dahlgren's naval attack.

Not until February 17, 1865, was the Union flag raised over Fort Sumter and Charleston vacated by the Confederate army. "For eight months," says Miss Barton, "our ever accumulating fleet rose and fell upon the tide and tossed upon the billows of Port Royal Harbor.

"Merchant ships had changed to men-of-war, and men-of-war to ironclads, and the pretentious little turrets of the *Monitor* had peeped above the wave, till one continuous line of floating batteries circled the coast of Carolina.

"And if ever in the night their thunders ceased the strangeness of the quiet startled the camping soldier from his uncertain slumber and seductive dream of home.

"But had all this conquered Charleston?

"Sumter had crumbled to a shapeless mass of stone and sand, Wagner was ours and the swamp angel hurled fire and destruction through her deserted streets every hour of the day and night.

"Still did she surrender? Was she humbled? Humbled!! Prouder than ever she sat under her palmetto and rattlesnake flag, with her haughty face still turned to the sea.

"While our weary armies fought on month after month, officers and men pouring out their blood like water for the holy cause which must not be abandoned, the great heart cry of the whole country went up. How long, oh, God, how long?

"Suddenly a whole army is missing. A mighty army gone from sight, an army that fought battles above the clouds. Where can it be? Not at Atlanta? Not back at Chattanooga? The country is electrified with alternate hope and fear.

"It may be that Charleston deigns now an anxious glance at armies as well as navies.

"Hark! That strange mingled sound. A heavy tramp! A clashing of steel! And a ringing rap at her western gate! One glance, and the proud dame recoils in horror and indignation, while far across the old time slave wrought fields of Carolina swept the wild march of Sherman's men.

"Did people call them 'Sherman's Boys'? They might have been boys when they left home, but they are men now, warriors, veterans.

"Then when at length the rebel flag no longer waved from the parapets of Wagner, the first to stand within its conquered walls was that grand old regiment whose banner never fell, whose courage was coolest when the fire was hottest, whose step was firmest when the foe was nearest, and whose shout was ever clearest when it rose above the thunder of the enemy's guns, a child of your own raising, your friends and mine, and whose name I ever speak with the pride of a loyal woman and the tenderness of a sister, the 39th Illinois!"

CHAPTER XVI

STEPHEN BARTON AT 15 ENTERS THE WAR

NOVEMBER, 1863

BY March, 1862, Miss Barton's brother, Captain David Barton, had advanced to the post of quartermaster in the army at Hilton Head, South Carolina, near Charleston. About this time, his son Stephen, but 14 years old, demanded to go. To his aunt Clara, he was as dear and near as a child of her own would have been. He had been so from the time when before the sixties in Oxford he had learned to admire and follow her in her wild gallops in the saddle over green pastures and by winding walls of field stone. Little did either dream then of the use to which they would later put their ability to cling to the back of a speeding horse.

In the fall of 1863, after having watched other boys enlist, a patriotic fervor possessed Stephen, which was probably only enhanced by his father's office.

"I must go," he declared.

"But you can't be mustered in at 15 years old, — it is impossible," they told him.

Even after he had vainly tried to enlist as a drummer boy he was not pacified. His father and aunt Clara had offered their services to their country — why not he?

"If you want to go, I don't see why you shouldn't, and you shall," said Clara Barton, who was on a brief visit home at the time. Thereupon she took him with his father (who was on a short furlough), to D. H. Eames, Clothier, then on the site now occupied by the Riker-Jaynes drug store, corner of Front and Main Streets, Worcester. Here they fitted him with a uniform. It was so small that it had to be made for him. It consisted of blue trousers, reënforced cavalry style, and a natty blue jacket, with big brass buttons with eagles on them. A soldier's cap was added and he was a complete soldier, with a cavalry uniform, minus the yellow braid.

STEPHEN E. BARTON — TO-DAY

"Never was I so proud in my life as when I walked out of Eames store with my Aunt Clara, in my new blue uniform," Stephen Barton said to me in 1912.

Hilton Head Island, where Stephen's father was quartermaster, is known now as Port Royal, South Carolina. To find a place in the service before Charleston the boy returned there with his father and aunt in November, 1863, where a post was soon found for him in the Military Telegraph Department, a great and dangerous field for patriotic youths in the war of the Rebellion.

This department of the service at Hilton Head Island was in charge of Captain L. F. Sheldon. Captain Sheldon and Captain Barton were members of an officers' mess, and Captain Sheldon, having seen Stephen riding around on the government horses in the keeping of the quartermaster's department, proposed to Captain Barton that he act as a mounted messenger, an aide then very much needed. The suggestion was at once acted upon and the next day Stephen was in the service, with one horse for forenoons and another for afternoons. In his leisure moments, the young lad learned the art of telegraphing, and in thirty days he was pronounced an operator and sent to Port Royal Ferry, a small picket station on the creek dividing Beaufort island from the mainland. The operator at that point, one Montalvo, had been captured on a raid to tap the Confederate wires at Pocotaligo, S. C. No one else being available, Stephen was sent to take his place.

The Confederate pickets were on the mainland, and the Federal pickets (a company of South Carolina colored troops) on the island. As the first night came on, thick and dark, a fierce storm drove upon the island, with vivid lightning and heavy thunder. Just then the Confederate pickets made a sharp attack under cover of the darkness and the storm. Bullets whistled about and the crack of rifles and the screech of balls added to the tumult. Stephen, however, stood by his post at the telegraph in his tent. But suddenly, there broke upon the "click-click" of the instrument a darkey's frightened voice.

"Bettah get out o' heah, Boss! Heah's de hoss, sah!"

All bridled and saddled, kept ready by the boy's black brother for a moment's notice, the big Kentucky mare was snorting with dread, and pawing the ground. The colored groom, scared to the whites of his rolling eyes, could hardly hold the lunging animal. Without hesitation the boy picked up the instrument and leaped into the saddle. But the mare took the bit in her teeth and ran away!

She ran in the right direction, however. Clattering along she fled from the firing, each shot frightening her headlong like the snap of a rawhide, each rifle ball like the dig of a spur. Stephen's tug at the reins was no more to her than the pull of a ratline to an ocean liner under full steam. She ran a long distance over the muddy roads, through tall groves of live oaks, festooned with moss and dripping with rain, to Beaufort's stockade, and into the sally-port, indeed right into the arms of sentries on guard. Though challenged to "halt," the boy could not stop. Finally, when he and the horse were stopped by the sentries, it was many minutes before he could find his tongue, and give an account of himself and of the attack on the exposed island, where he had taken the post of the captured operator, that very morning.

Through such an initiation as this, Stephen Barton's courage grew stronger, and we find him serving with honor to himself and his country throughout the war. In the summer of 1864 he was transferred from the Department of the South to the Army of the Potomac in the service of the United States Military Telegraph and Railroad. He was at City Point and with the 9th and 6th corps during the last six months of the siege of Petersburg and the final surrender in April, 1865.

CHAPTER XVII

THE WILDERNESS AND SPOTTSYLVANIA

MAY, 1864

By January, 1864, Miss Barton had recovered her strength after the eight months of almost superhuman effort on Morris Island under the guns of Sumter, Gregg, and Fort Wagner. She had taken her post again at Washington to reassemble supplies for the coming crisis. For, by a climacteric movement, it was the intention of the North to strike now the final blow of the Rebellion.

It has sometimes been said that Miss Barton left the front in 1864. But this is not so. She had determined not to leave until the end, however severe the tragedies grew. The motive for this is seen in a letter written February 5, 1864, to "the Noble Lady, Anna Pasteris Cometti, Baroness of Moriondo, Italia."

"Once, I had hoped to visit your beautiful country, now, I scarce dare dream of ever leaving my own. Surely never, while the hand of affliction rests upon us as to-day, while war distracts her councils and desolates her homes, while wives yield up their husbands, and sisters send the playmates and brothers of their childhood and the tender mother brings forth her fair haired son, armed for the field, and with the proud smile that covers the breaking heart, gives him to her Country, and bids him never disgrace the Banner in the shadow of whose folds she leaves him. While all this is transpiring daily in my own loved land, it is only right that I, with neither husband nor son to give to my country, should wait and watch and labor and weep and pray, with those who sacrifice, and those who fall.

"How little thought we that in a few short days, the bugle should sound the shrill war note through our peaceful land, and the valleys should tremble, and the mountains echo to the tread of marching armies. To-day our sun rises and sets upon a million of American people under arms, spread over a million acres of square miles of land,

and thousands of leagues of sea, and every day brings us tidings of both a victory and a repulse. Still are we strong and confident and hopeful, stronger to-day, than on the day which saw the first sword drawn, more confident as our latent strength develops and more hopeful now that we see more to hope for, as we realize that we are fighting the battles of the world, with the armies of freedom."

Miss Barton was now to be officially recognized by appointment to the Army of the James under General Butler. Her department was to be the Department of Nurses, of which she was to have the office of Superintendent under Surgeon McCormack, Chief Director of the Army of the James, stationed at City Point, Virginia.

The government felt that this honor would not only show appreciation for the magnificent success of Miss Barton's field work on the firing lines, but it would also give her sufficient authority to enable her to execute her ideas. Dorothy Dix, another Worcester girl, was already General Superintendent of Nurses in the war and in many ways was a woman of Miss Barton's own kind, though Miss Dix's greater work for the race was the founding of the present system of Insane Retreats in America and Europe.

But gratifying though this official approval of Miss Barton's work doubtless was, it pales into insignificance when set against the work itself, particularly her services on the field.

"Discontent and gloom, with ever lessening ranks even of the recruiting forces," is her description of the winter of 1864. "The blossoms of May, however," she explained, "fell on a world renowned army of veterans with hard, brown faces, sinews of steel, tread of iron, and hearts as soldierly, true and brave as the Old Guard of Napoleon!

"Uniforms still bright? Uniforms!! Heaven knows if you had any. It were well, if you had shoes. But the weary spring brought the great Captain (General Grant) to the east to fight it out on that line, if it took all summer — aye, and all winter too."

She could never be kept from the firing line. All of the appointments to all the offices in the world could not hold her back from personally going to the front.

In May news came of the conflict between Grant and Lee in the wilderness of Virginia. From May 5 to 7 occurred terrific fighting between the Confederate forces under General Lee and the Union troops under Major General George C. Meade, — also, Major General Hancock (2d corps), Major General Warren (5th corps), Major General Burnside (9th), and General Sheridan with the cavalry. On the Union side, 2,246 were killed, 12,037 wounded, and 3,383 reported missing, a total of 17,666.   From May 8 to May 20 there was almost continuous fighting from Alsop's ferry to the Fredericksburg pike.   These engagements are known in history as the battle of Spottsylvania.   Of the Union forces 2,725 were killed, 13,416 wounded, and 2,258 missing, total, 18,399.   By the 18th these terrible losses had reached the total of 36,065 on the Union side alone.

May 8, the day the battle of Spottsylvania began, Miss Barton hastened to the front and took her position on the road ten miles from Fredericksburg.

Conditions may be best realized by taking one experience and multiplying it into the thousands.   Among the too few men alive to-day who remember the scenes of that time vividly is J. Brainerd Hall of the '57th Massachusetts.   "It was at the battle of the Wilderness, May 6, 1864, that I was wounded and reported killed," he says. "On the afternoon of May 6 when General Grant began to fall back towards Chancellorsville, the 2d Corps Field Hospital was left between the lines.   There were no ambulances and among many such groups was one of fifty men of which I was one, left for want of transportation facilities.   All night we lay between the dead and the dying, most of us mortally wounded.   We were kept busy through the night watching the shells as they passed over us, as well as some that did not but exploded near us and nearly buried us out of sight.   Three times I was nearly suffocated and was snatched from a premature burial.

"The next afternoon Captain Barton of the 57th Massachusetts, Clara Barton's cousin, who had been put in charge of the ambulance train, found me.   Three days later, after being three times captured by Moseby's men, we reached Fredericksburg.   As soon as I was made as comfortable as possible on the floor of the Southern M. E. Church, Captain Barton found Miss Barton, told her where I was and that I was thought to be mortally wounded.   My exhausted condition at that time was such that I have only an indistinct recollection of the first aid Miss Barton gave me, but later when my father, who was with the Sanitary Commission arrived, I had many evidences of her watchful care of me.

"Before Miss Barton arrived, another Angel of Mercy at Fredericksburg had tenderly washed my face for the first time in four days. Then when my father could find no bandages, she loosened her underskirt and cut it up for a bandage. Twenty-three years later learning who this good woman was I visited her at her home at the foot of Marie's Heights. It was Mrs. Martha Stevens, better known in Fredericksburg as Grandmother Stevens.

"When Clara Barton came I was, with her help, moved from the crowded church to a private house where I remained until the railroad to Aquia Creek was rebuilt, when Miss Barton secured me transportation. At Washington I was met by an old employee of my grandmother, Senator Henry Wilson; he at once secured me a furlough and I went north on a stretcher hung over the seats in the passenger car."

Thus it was five days before Sergeant Hall, so neglected that maggots filled his wounds, was treated. His report is but a single evidence of thousands whose sufferings were prolonged through lack of means of transportation. But being taken to Fredericksburg did not end the suffering of even those that could go. For these and more recent multitudes waiting at Belle Plain and Aquia Creek came a gigantic blockade.

At Belle Plain on the left river bank Miss Barton faced this army of wounded men stalled in the glue-like mash of red clay covering many acres. Here they could not move, or be moved. She was dumfounded at the deadlock of the stricken host and the utter inability of the Army Hospital corps or the great commissions to cope with the stranded thousands of wounded, dying alone like "unattended dogs." She determined to alarm Washington, for she utterly mistrusted the red tape stupidity of the officials, who were apparently helpless before the colossal multitude mired and literally "stuck in the mud."

With difficulty she made her way out of the military maelstrom and at last reached a little steamer bound for Washington, where she decided to appear in person. Arriving at night, she summoned the Honorable Henry Wilson, Chairman of the Military Committee of the Senate. Alarmed at the fearful deadlock of the army trains and the fate of scores of thousands of wounded left to die, he called together the War Department at ten o'clock that night. The Department doubted. Wilson demanded that they send aid that very night or he would face the Senate of the United States.   He secured the action he wanted.   By two o'clock that night the Quartermaster-General of the United States himself was with his staff galloping down 6th Street to the Belle Plain wharf where he embarked at once.

Immediately upon his arrival the next morning he took charge in the name of the Government and extricated, fed, and housed the thousands of wounded.

Thus the deadlocked wheels of Government were set in motion, a nonplussed War Department was mastered and a host of wounded succored by the work of the intrepid little woman who attributed it all to Henry Wilson.

Miss Barton here discloses the above situation in her war diary:

"The terrible slaughter of the Wilderness and Spottsylvania turned all pitying hearts and helping hands once more to Fredericksburg. And no one who reached it by way of Belle Plain while this latter constituted the base of supplies for General Grant's army can have forgotten the peculiar geographical location, and the consequent fearful condition of the country immediately about the landing, which consisted of a narrow ridge of high land on the left bank of the river.   Along the right extended the river itself.   On the left, the hills towered up almost to a mountain height.

"The same ridge of high land was in front at a quarter of a mile distant, through which a narrow defile formed the road leading out, and on to Fredericksburg, ten miles away, thus leaving a level space or basin of an area of a fourth of a mile, directly in front of the landing.

"Across this small plain all transportation to and from the army must necessarily pass.   The soil was red clay.   The ten thousand wheels and hoofs had ground it to a powder and a sudden rain upon the surrounding hills had converted the entire basin into one vast mortar bed, smooth and glassy as a lake, and much the color of light brick dust.

"The poor, mutilated starving sufferers of the Wilderness were pouring into Fredericksburg by thousands — all to be taken away in army wagons across ten miles of alternate hills, and hollows, stumps, roots and mud!

" The boats from Washington to Belle Plain were loaded down with fresh troops, while the wagons from Fredericksburg to Belle Plain were loaded with wounded men and went back with supplies. The exchange was transacted on this narrow ridge, called the landing.

"I arrived from Washington about noon of the 8th with such supplies as I could take. It was still raining. Some members of the Christian Commission had reached an earlier boat and being unable to obtain transportation to Fredericksburg had erected a tent or two on the ridge and were evidently considering what to do next.

"To nearly or quite all of them the experience and scene were entirely new. Most of them were clergymen, who had left at a day's notice, by request of the distracted fathers and mothers, who could not go to the relief of the dear ones stricken down by thousands, and thus begged those in whom they had the most confidence to go for them. They went, willingly, but it was no easy task they had undertaken. It was hard enough for old workers who commenced early and were inured to the life and its work.

"I shall never forget the scene which met my eye as I stepped from the boat to the top of the ridge. Standing in this plain of mortar-mud were at least 200 six-mule army wagons, crowded full of wounded men waiting to be taken upon the boats for Washington. They had driven from Fredericksburg that morning. Each driver had gotten his wagon as far as he could, for those in front of, and about him, had stopped.

"Of the depth of the mud, the best judgment was formed from the fact that no entire hub of a wheel was in sight, and you saw nothing of any animal below its knees and the mass of mud all settled into place perfectly smooth and glassy.

"As I contemplated the scene, a young intelligent, delicate gentleman, evidently a clergyman, approached me, and said anxiously, but almost timidly: 'Madam, do you think those wagons are filled with wounded men?' I replied that they undoubtedly were, and waiting to be placed on the boats then unloading. 'How long must they wait?' he asked.

"I said that, judging from the capacity of the boats, I thought they could not be ready to leave much before night.

"'What can we do for them?' he asked still more anxiously.

"'They are hungry and must be fed,'" I replied.

"For a moment his countenance brightened, then fell again as he exclaimed: 'What a pity, we have a great deal of clothing and reading matter, but no food in any quantity, excepting crackers.' I told him that I had coffee and that between us I thought we could arrange to give them all hot coffee and crackers.

"'But where shall we make our coffee?' he inquired, gazing wistfully about the bare, wet hillside. I pointed to a little hollow beside a stump. 'There is a good place for a fire,' I explained, 'and any of this loose brush will do.'

"'Just here?' he asked. 'Just here, sir.'

"He gathered the brush manfully and very soon we had some fire and a great deal of smoke, two crotched sticks and a crane, if you please, and presently, a dozen camp kettles of steaming hot coffee. My helper's pale face grew almost as bright as the flames and the smutty brands looked blacker than ever in his slim white fingers.

"Suddenly a new difficulty met him. 'Our crackers are in barrels, and we have neither basket nor box. How can we carry them?'

"I suggested that aprons would be better than either, and getting something as near the size and shape of a common table-cloth as I could find, tied one about him and one about me, fastened all four of the corners to the waist, and pinned the sides, thus leaving one hand for a kettle of coffee and one free, to administer it.

"Thus equipped we moved down the slope. Twenty steps brought us to the abrupt edge which joined the mud, much as the bank of a canal does the black line of water beside it.

"But here came the crowning obstacle of all. So completely had the man been engrossed in his work, so delighted as one difficulty after another vanished and success became more and more apparent, that he entirely lost sight of the distance and difficulties between himself and the objects to be served.

"If you could have seen the expression of consternation and dismay depicted in every feature of his fine face, as he imploringly exclaimed, 'How are we to get to them?'

"'There is no way but to walk,' I answered.

"He gave me one more look as much as to say, 'Are you going to step in there?' I allowed no time for the question, but in spite of all the solemnity of the occasion, and the terribleness of the scene before me, I found myself striving hard to keep the muscles of my face all straight. As it was, the corners of my mouth would draw into wickedness, as with a backward glance I saw the good man tighten his grasp upon his apron and take his first step into military life.

"But thank God, it was not his last.

"I believe it is recorded in Heaven — the faithful work performed by that Christian Commission minister through long weary months of rain and dust and summer suns and winter snows. The sick soldier blessed and the dying prayed for him, as through many a dreadful day he stood fearless and firm amongst fire and smoke (not made of brush), and walked calmly and unquestioningly through something redder and thicker than the mud of Belle Plain.

"No one has forgotten the heart sickness which spread over the entire country as the busy wires flashed the dire tidings of the terrible destitution and suffering of the wounded of the Wilderness whom I attended as they lay in Fredericksburg. But you may never have known how many hundredfold of these ills were augmented by the conduct of improper, heartless, unfaithful officers in the immediate command of the city and upon whose actions and indecisions depended entirely the care, food, shelter, comfort, and lives of that whole city of wounded men. One of the highest officers there has since been convicted a traitor. And another, a little dapper Captain quartered with the owners of one of the finest mansions in the town, boasted that he had changed his opinion since entering the city the day before, — that it was in fact a pretty hard thing for refined people like the people of Fredericksburg to be compelled to open their homes and admit 'these dirty, lousy, common soldiers,' and that he was not going to compel it.

"This I heard him say and waited, until I saw him make his words good — till I saw, crowded into one old sunken hotel, lying helpless upon its bare, wet, bloody floors, 500 fainting men hold up their cold, bloodless, dingy hands, as I passed, and beg me in Heaven's name for a cracker to keep them from starving (and I had none); or to give them a cup that they might have something to drink water from, if they could get it (and I had no cup, and could get none), till I saw 200 six-mule army wagons in a line, ranged down the street to head-quarters, and reaching so far out on the Wilderness road that I never found the end of it; every wagon crowded with wounded men, stopped, standing in the rain and mud, wrenched back and forth by the restless hungry animals all night from four o'clock in the afternoon till eight next morning and how much longer I know not. — The dark spot in the mud under many a wagon, told only too plainly where some poor fellow's life had dripped out in those dreadful hours."

At an earlier moment Sergeant Hall's experience bears evidence of a condition which Miss Barton had all along deplored — an inefficiency and cowardliness on the part of some of the minor officers. When Sergeant Hall was hit by a ball which went through his abdomen and came out laterally, leaving a wound which to this day has never healed, he staggered to the rear, where, among several disloyal officers, he found a skulking superior. Pointing his revolver at him as he lay behind a log, Sergeant Hall addressed a senior officer of his Regiment in substance as follows: " What is the trouble with you ? " The reply was " Sergeant, I am sunstruck and the boys have all left me."

"Yes," said Hall, " you probably are, not seven o'clock in the morning and we in the woods and the smoke so thick you can't see the sun. Get up, you drunken coward. Get up ! Go to the front !" and at the point of his pistol he drove him back to the firing line.

Bleeding profusely Sergeant Hall crossed the Orange plank road and lay down just as Longstreet came up on the left of the Union line.

He called to a New York surgeon who was passing to look at his wound and showed him the abdominal punctures. " You'll be in hell in five minutes," laughed the surgeon, and passed on, Sergeant Hall replying, " Well, I'll take my chances with you, Doctor."

About this time the firing of Longstreet cut off a large limb and it fell on Hall, striking him in the abdomen, but he soon rallied from the shock and made for the rear.

As to the fact that every artery of transit was choked and wounded troops were unable to be moved:

"I remembered one man who would set it right, if he knew it, who possessed the power and who would believe me if I told him," says Miss Barton in describing this experience. " I commanded immediate conveyance back to Belle Plain. With difficulty I obtained it, and four stout horses with a light army wagon took me ten miles at an unbroken gallop, through field and swamp, and stumps and mud to Belle Plain and a steam tug at once to Washington. Landing at dusk I sent for Henry Wilson, Chairman of the Military Committee

H

of the Senate. A messenger brought him at eight, saddened and appalled like every other patriot in that fearful hour, at the weight of woe under which the nation staggered, groaned, and wept.

"He listened to the story of suffering and faithlessness, and hurried from my presence, with lips compressed and face like ashes. At ten he stood in the War Department. They could not credit his report. He must have been deceived by some frightened villain. No official report of unusual suffering had reached them. Nothing had been called for by the military authorities commanding Fredericksburg.

"Mr. Wilson assured them that the officers in trust there were not to be relied upon. They were faithless, overcome by the blandishments of the wily inhabitants. Still the department doubted. It was then that he proved that my confidence in his firmness was not misplaced, as facing his doubters he replies: 'One of two things will have to be done — either you will send someone to-night with the power to investigate and correct the abuses of our wounded men at Fredericksburg — or the Senate will send some one to-morrow.'

"This threat recalled their scattered senses.

"At two o'clock in the morning the Quartermaster-General and staff galloped to the 6th Street wharf under orders; at ten they were in Fredericksburg. At noon the wounded men were fed from the food of the city and the houses were opened to the '*dirty, lousy* soldiers' of the Union Army.

"Both railroad and canal were opened. In three days I returned with carloads of supplies.

"No more jolting in army wagons! And every man who left Fredericksburg by boat or by car owes it to the firm decision of one man that his grating bones were not dragged 10 miles across the country or left to bleach in the sands of that city."

CHAPTER XVIII

AT THE SIEGE OF PETERSBURG, VIRGINIA

1864

THE siege of Petersburg commenced June 15, 1864, and did not end till Petersburg's fall, April 2, 1865.

The troops which began the siege were the 10th and 18th corps, Army of the James, under Major General B. F. Butler, and the 2d, 5th, 6th, and 9th corps, Army of the Potomac, under Major General George C. Meade. Two of the worst of the many engagements before the beleaguered town were those of June 15 and 19, 1864, when 1,688 men were killed, and 9,698 wounded, missing, or captured; and July [1] 1-3, including the days previous at Malvern Hill on the 27th and the mine explosion on the 30th when 504 were killed, 1,881 wounded, and 1,413 missing or taken prisoners.

As in the past, Miss Barton was not so horrified by the terrors of the engagements themselves as by the needless suffering which followed.

"The Petersburg mine with its four thousand dead and wounded and no flag of truce, the wounded broiling in a July sun, the dead bodies putrefying where they fell!" This is her brief but vivid description of the catastrophe.

She was as usual in the midst of the action. The very night the mine exploded she flew to the aid of the injured. In one of the flashes of inspiration that came to her, she recalled to us in Worcester in 1910 her midnight ride through thunder and lightning to Petersburg.

"One night, following the battle of the mine, a party of horsemen rode up to my place. They drew apart and talked among themselves for five minutes. Now and then they looked in my direction, I noticed, but I did not look at them. One of them finally stepped out of the party and approaching me said, 'Miss Barton, I have some bad news.'

---

[1] July 1-29, 2,495 killed and wounded.

99

'What is it?' I said. 'The mine has been blown up,' said he. 'We have lost a great many men and Gardner [a friend of Miss Barton] is among them.'

"'Is he killed?' I asked.

"'Yes,' said he.

"I was asked if I wanted to go to the mine and I said, 'Yes.' The troop of horsemen offered to accompany me there, but I said one would be enough. It was terribly dark. We had no way of keeping one another in sight except for our horses. My horse was black, the other was white. It was a long twenty mile ride. The lightning was terrific; the thunder fearful. When the lightning came we were able to distinguish one another and see where we were going. The rain commenced almost immediately.

"The horses became frightened. They did not run, but they stopped stock still and would not budge an inch. They stayed in one spot for three or four hours, shivering. When the rain subsided and the light came we resumed our way.

"At the mine we found everything in confusion. There were a great many killed there."

Miss Barton was at Petersburg again and again, for whenever the smoldering siege flamed out there were of necessity the wounded to care for.

As illustrating the impractical natures of many of the people which the country sent to aid the army and with whom Miss Barton had continually to cope, she tells the following story:

"I recollect an incident which occurred at Point of Rocks when our army was pressing Petersburg in '64.

"The soldiers had lain in the trenches, soaked with water through half the season, till the burning suns of summer had dried the mud to the hardness of brick. Now they were scorching and baking and blistering through the other half.

"An old veteran, from a western regiment, had obtained leave to come down to the hospital and commission tents, in the hope of making some very obviously necessary additions to his wardrobe.

"I had been making the rounds of the hospital tents and for a moment stepped into the commission quarters when this tall, sunburned, honest-faced soldier stepped in after me and approaching the agent said he should like to get a pair of stockings.

"The agent replied with great kindness that he was very sorry that he could not oblige him, but they were out of stockings, except some very fine ones they had saved for *dead men !*

"If you could have seen the look of puzzled astonishment which spread over the veteran's face, as he strove to comprehend the meaning of the reply! He looked at me, at his own turtle-backed feet, innocent of stockings for months, until finally giving it up, he broke out with, 'Stockings for dead men!' And turning on his heel he stalked out of the tent, no richer and apparently no wiser than when he entered. Doubtless he went back to the camp and trenches in disgust. And the young agent who had been from home only a fortnight, and had never learned by observation that men could lie quietly in their graves without stockings and shirts was just as deeply puzzled to comprehend the astonishment of the soldier and stood gazing after him in silent wonder as he walked away. From their different standpoints neither could get a glimpse of the other's thoughts any more than the good lady could understand how war should increase the price of candles. 'Candles higher!' she exclaimed, 'why, bless me, do they fight by candle light?'"

CHAPTER XIX

THE "AMEN" OF THE WAR — BEFORE RICHMOND

1865

AT the climax of the Civil War, Miss Barton was in Washington keeping in close touch not only with those directing affairs at the capital but with the men on the field. In a letter of March 5, 1865, to Eliza Golay of Geneva, Switzerland, her point of view and her convictions on the great conflict are interestingly set forth.

"I accept with pleasure your expressions of gratitude for any little kindness I may have shown your suffering brother. What could it have been in comparison with what he has done and suffered for my country. Has he not toiled in its trenches, hungered in its necessities, helped to bear back the advancing foe, and, wounded and fainting far from home or kindred, pressed the bloody soil of a stranger's land, and that land my country, that country my home, that home my loved America? Grateful to me! It is I who should be grateful, and I am.

"It would be impossible for me to give you any adequate idea of the vastness and terribleness of our great national struggle, so much space, so many armies, such countless battle fields, such painful marches and such terrible conflicts, and it is my pride and joy that my countrymen have been found equal to the sacrifice — only their patriotism had equaled their bravery. The best blood of America has flowed like water. The proudest of her sons have struggled for the honor of a soldier's name — to-day a son of our chief magistrate, one of our Secretary of State, and one of our highest Senator, stand under the enemy's fire, and on the same sanguinary fields stood and fought and bled your brother, our brother now. Like them he has fought bravely and well, and suffered well; he has given us the best strength of his good right arm — but ours shall be around him in gratitude and love. He shall be kindly cared for, tenderly cherished.

Knowing me first and only of my country women he has come gently to my side and asked to be my younger brother. The place had been always vacant and I have taken him gladly to fill it. I have promised to be his American elder sister, and he is to heed my counsels, but when I promised that I did not realize how much I was to be the gainer, that not only had I found a brother but a lovely and loving sister. Yes, my dear sister, I do love you and I will always love you and fondly hope that it may not be forever ideal, but that some happy day, my arms shall twine about your neck and your cheek rest lovingly against my arm. I have no portrait of myself to-day, and it will be plain, (not like my fair sister's) when I do have it, but such as it is I will send you soon.

"You speak of your parents and tell me that they hold me kindly in their hearts. Tell them of my filial affection and respect and I shall be glad to have them for both my honored father and mother are sleeping peacefully under the green sods of my own native hills far away in the quiet north. Once more assure them of my love, and that I will try to prove it by the faithful care with which I will watch over the footsteps of their dear absent one.

"And now my dear sister, good bye for a little, till you write me again which I hope will be very soon. Write me familiarly and without pains and I will write you the same. Once more good bye and keep me in your heart as you are in the heart of

"Your affectionate sister,
"CLARA BARTON."

Great as had been Miss Barton's sacrifices in the war — she was now called upon to make the greatest one of all. Having eased the death agony of thousands of "younger brothers" as she called those in the service, she was now to see a brother of her own flesh and blood suffer and die.

Clara Barton had not been the only member of her family to wander toward the South. In 1854 her eldest brother Stephen purchased a steam mill in Hertford County, North Carolina, where he built up an industry in a village called, after the name, "Bartonville."

In 1861 at the outbreak of the war the entire product of the lumber mill was "hemmed in" from sale. Store, blacksmith shop, grain, and cattle likewise stood in danger of confiscation by the Confederates.

Immediately he sent twenty of his northern helpers home by way of Miss Barton in Washington with all the ready money he and she could collect. After having been robbed and all but killed, they came to Miss Barton's Washington lodgings, penniless, for help. Later most of them entered the northern army. Stephen Barton, however, had decided to remain and brave the crisis, if possible saving his property. Shortly thereafter a number of the southerners appeared as a Vigilance Committee and ordered him to leave the State. This he refused to do and was knocked down. Stunned and bleeding, he attacked the group of men and "unarmed and single handed" beat them off.

Miss Barton did not accompany General Butler's expedition south which went to the rescue of her brother, deflecting its direction to reach him. He refused to go. But in the summer of 1863 Captain Flusser, commander of the North Carolina fleet, took several gunboats, passed up the Chowan river to the Barton village and mills, and offered to take Stephen Barton north. He again declined to go, being still determined to hold out and protect his property.

When Captain Flusser was a little later killed in action, Miss Barton's last hope of rescuing Stephen died. For he bravely remained at his mills and was not captured by the South but by the *North!* Mistaken either intentionally or unintentionally for a Confederate, lying sick in a wagon, he was robbed and sent a prisoner to Norfolk.

"You know how my last hope died with the gallant Flusser," Miss Barton wrote in a Civil War letter. "One chilly day last Autumn when General Butler's troops were pressing the line of Richmond, we were having unusually sharp work and the poor fellows were dropping back in scores to our flying hospital tents. It was smoky and dreary, and I was out trying to revive and assist them as they were laid down from the stretchers. I saw a Lieutenant who was shot in the lungs. He was lying on his back strangling. I sprang and raised him partly up and asked the boys to remove him to me, as I seated myself on a large coil of tent rope which was lying on the ground, where I could support him upright, till the surgeons could get to him. While I was in this position, with hands and arms bare and bloody to the elbows, an orderly dashed up, and, looking about, seemed to conclude that I was the person sought, (naturally enough as there was no other woman) and dismounting handed me a letter. With one hand and my teeth I tore it open for special news from home boded no good in those days, and I saw this was from my nephew Samuel. It enclosed another addressed to himself, and to my bewildered eyes it was in the handwriting of my brother. The post-mark and date were Norfolk, and he said he was a prisoner there, that six weeks before he had been captured by a raiding party of General Butler's men, while journeying some forty miles from home, his object having been, as I learned later, mainly to obtain medicine and appliances. As you know he had a hernia of long standing. He was ill lying upon a bed in his wagon at the time of his capture. All had been taken from him, teams, bed, necessary clothing, blankets, medicine, and he had been thrown into the fourth story of a crowded prison house, to lie on bare floors with chills and fever, and chronic diarrhea; he could not eat the food, and could purchase none, as they had taken all his money (nearly 3 thousand dollars) and papers from him at the time of his capture, and that these circumstances sufficiently explained the object of his imprisonment, and the hardships imposed upon him, and the positive refusal to allow him to communicate with his friends, and it was evident to all, that unless relieved, he could not live many weeks. This letter he persuaded a negro guard to take out for him.

"I waited till the surgeons sent for my suffering charge, washed my hands, stepped into an ambulance and was driven to General Butler's headquarters, perhaps a mile and a half distant. He was busy of course, but never too busy to attend to the wants of those around him. I gave him the letter, he comprehended all at once, and turning hastily to me, said, 'This is hard, what can I do for you?' I commenced to say that brother was a Union man. He stopped me, with 'Yes, yes, I understand it all, what shall I do?' 'He is very ill, allow me to go to him, General,' I replied.

"'Surely, but cannot we do better? He can come here.'

"'You have shelter for him?' he asked inquiringly. I replied that I had an old negro hut with ground floor but it was shelter when I had time to be in it.

"He rang for a clerk and dictated a dispatch to General Shepley, I think, at Norfolk, to send Mr. Stephen Barton immediately to him with all property and papers found upon him at the time of his arrest and to let no one know of the order. Then turning to me he said kindly, 'Now go and get ready for him. As soon as he comes, I will send him to you.'

"You who know me will understand the fullness of heart and the difficulty with which I saw my way out of that tent. I went back to my post, and that night, the next day, the next night, and the next day I passed without sleep. My man arranged a loft in my cabin, and a straw bunk for the sick man who was to come.

"At 10 o'clock the third night, I sat weary and alone by the cabin fire, when suddenly the door opened, and the bright face of the surgeon in charge appeared. 'Don't be disturbed,' he said, 'we bring you some one.' Six years before I had seen Stephen, strong, muscular, erect, two hundred and twenty pounds, dark, iron gray. He walked into my presence now, pale, tottering, a hundred and thirty, his thin white locks resting upon his shoulders, bent and walking feebly with a cane.

"At seven that evening he had reached General Butler's headquarters and been taken to him. He commenced as I had done, to assure the General that he had never been a rebel, but was cut short by a kind inquiry concerning his journey and how he had endured it, and could he ride a mile or two farther that night? 'Oh, yes, if it is necessary,' he answered, supposing his prison to be that distance away. 'Because,' added the General, 'if you can, you will find your sister there.' 'My sister!' he exclaimed, 'is she a prisoner too?'

"He was pleasantly assured that neither of us were prisoners, put into the General's carriage and taken to me. He remained six weeks, waiting the General's call to examine the case. It came, one crisp, searching winter's morning. I took him in an ambulance, to headquarters. How well I remember wrapping a cloak and shawl about him, as he sat shivering in the ambulance, weak and nervous, waiting his turn to enter the crowded office. That also came, we entered, and were seated by an orderly; my brother at the side of the door. He was immediately removed by the General and reseated directly in front of the door. Two other persons were then called for, Lieut. Budd of a N. Y. Regiment and one Hutchings a detective from Boston. These were the men who had arrested Capt. Barton, and subsequently consigned him to prison. They were evidently ignorant of the cause of their summons to headquarters, and each had known nothing of the presence of the other until they met at the door. On entering they confronted their old white-haired victim, started, glanced at each other, changed color, recovered badly, walked in and were seated. When Stephen had stated the facts the General turned to the others with : 'Gentlemen, this is a true statement; many of the circumstances I know to be true, the rest I believe to be.' He then questioned Budd and Hutchings in reference to their object in making the arrest, asking them why they had done it, why they had taken the money, and why, if they believed Stephen worthy of arrest, they had left him alone, and free, after taking his property, only to throw him into prison when he followed them into Norfolk?

"'Gentlemen, this money must be restored and all of it. I hold you equally responsible. You will divide the responsibility between you, and in case of the failure of either to pay his share, I hold each responsible for the whole amount.' The Lieutenant turned pale, pleaded his poverty, and the necessities of his aged parents. The General could see that this might be hard, but could not see how Capt. Barton should be obliged to support either him or his parents." . .

Stephen Barton never recovered from the shock of the experiences through which he had gone. He left General Butler's tent a dying man. The following days and nights he was tenderly cared for by his sister, who divided her time between the negro cabin where he lay and the city crowded with its wounded.

In a particularly vivid reminiscence Miss Barton describes these first few days of April, 1865, before Richmond:

"The camp fires burned low and red in front of Richmond, while the ceaseless watch fires along the Appomattox and the James threw their pale light athwart the bronzed face of the weary sentinel as he treads his endless beat.

"The 1st day of April? Will your ears ever again thrill with such call of bugles and roll of drums as broke your slumbers on that dawning morn? Will your eyes look ever on such carnage more? Before you, stretching far beyond your gaze, lie the entrenchments of Richmond, glistening with artillery, manned and loaded, and behind them, Lee's veteran army, trained and desperate. Here an open field and your unprotected breast to assault and carry those entrenchments! All day the fight goes on. List the wild shouts of the charging rank. Wright and Ord are driving them in. Gibbon and Parks are forcing

Petersburg. Grant shortens his lines. Night settles down, and you wait in darkness, and gather your dead.

"Morning once more. Once more the bugles, and the drums; once more the thunder of a thousand guns, and the rattle of musketry, like the hail of a tornado. Firm as a rock you are holding the East, while Sheridan like an avenging cloud sweeps in from the West. And the work is done.

"One more night of darkness and death and when the morning of the 3d of April broke upon your weary, war-worn gaze, you had no enemy left to fight. Broken and conquered he has fled in confusion."

Of Stephen Miss Barton writes:

"Hearing a voice, I crept softly down my little confiscated stairway and waited in the shadows near Stephen's bedside. He had turned his face partly into his pillow and resting upon his hands was at prayer. The first words which my ear caught distinctly were:

"'Oh God, whose children we all are, look down with thine eye of justice and mercy upon this terrible conflict, and weaken the wrong, and strengthen the right till this unequal contest close. Oh God, save my country. Bless Abraham and his armies!'

"A sob from me revealed my presence. He started, and raising his skeleton form until he rested upon his elbow, he said, 'I thought I was alone,' then turning upon me a look of mingled anxiety, pity, and horror, which I can never describe, he asked hastily:

"'Sister, what are these incessant sounds I hear? The whole atmosphere is filled with them. They seem like the mingled groans of human agony. I have not heard them before, tell me what it is.'

"I could not speak the words that would so shock his sensitive nature, but only stood before him humble and penitent as if I had something to do with it all, — and feel the tears roll over my face. My silence confirmed his secret suspicions and raising himself still higher, he exclaimed: 'Are these the groans of wounded men? Are they so many that my senses cannot take them in? That my ear cannot distinguish them?' And sitting fully upright, clasping his bony hands, he broke forth in tones that will never leave me —

"'Oh our God, in mercy to the poor creatures thou hast called into existence, send down thine angels either in love or wrath to stay this strife and bid it cease. Count the least of these cries as priceless jewels, each drop of blood as ruby gems and let them buy the freedom of the world.

Clothe the feet of thy messengers with the speed of the lightning and bid them proclaim through the sacrifices of the people, a people's freedom, and through the sufferings of a nation, a nation's peace.'

"And there under the guns of Richmond, amid the groans of the dying, in the shadows of the smoky rafters of an old negro hut, by the rude chimney where the dusky form of the bondsman had crouched for years, and on the ground, trodden hard by the foot of the slave, I knelt beside that rough couch of boards, and, to the patriot prayer that rose above, sobbed 'Amen.'

"The stolen money was never restored. Stephen struggled on a few weeks longer, alternating, hoping and despairing, suffering from the physical abuse he had received, crushed in spirit, battling with disease and weakness as only a brave man can, worrying over his unprotected property and his debts in the old home he never reached, watching the war, and praying for the success of the Union Armies, and died without knowing, and God be praised for this, that the reckless torches of that same Union Army would lay in ashes and ruins, the result of the hard labor of his own worn out life and wreck the fortunes of his only child.

"Although doubting and fearing, we had never despaired of his recovery, until the morning when he commenced to sink and we saw him rapidly passing away. He was at once aware of his condition and spoke of his business, desiring that, first of all, when his property could be reached, his debts should be faithfully paid. A few little minutes more and there lay before us, still and pitiful, all that remained to tell of that hard life's struggle and battle, which had failed most of all through a great-hearted love for humanity, his faithfulness to what he conceived to be his duty, and his readiness to do more for mankind than it was willing to do for itself."

CHAPTER XX

FOUR YEARS' SEARCH FOR MISSING MEN

1865–1869

THE close of the long hard struggle between the North and the South opened up a new line of service for Miss Barton.

Every great battle of the Civil War records thousands of "missing" men. They may have been alive or they may have been prisoners; or they may have been on the roll of the "unknown dead." The Quartermaster of the Federal Army reported 359,528 deaths among the Northern troops during the war and 315,555 graves. Of these only 172,400 were identified. This means that 143,155 lay in graves unidentified and unknown.

Added to this, the thousands of missing still alive and the many thousands of unlocated prisoners rolled up a list unspeakably appalling. What had become of these men was a source of inquiry of tens of thousands of grief-stricken relatives.

The matter lay heavy on Clara Barton's heart. She notes it here:

"The white spring blossoms fall again, and still on marching armies, but with steps reversed, arms at rest, and the faces no longer toward the foe! And they fall again on the bowed heads, and the sorrowing hearts of the widows and orphans of the old Northern homes! On an army worn out, on sick and wounded men from hospital and barrack! On an army of skeletons dragged from prisons of which it shames humanity to tell! On the graves of an army of martyrs and on one solitary bier, flag draped, borne reverently through the land, with a mourning nation weeping in its train!

"Yes, it is over. The calls are answered. The marches are ended, the nation saved. And with the glory of gladness in her eyes, the shekinah of victory on her brow, she covers her tear-stained face, and with grief-bowed head sits humbly in the ashes of her woe, to mourn her lost, to weep for her dead!

"Victory, yes! but oh, the cost! The desolation, the woe, and the want, that spread over the whole land. 13,000 dead in one prison! 300,000 dead in one year! Dead everywhere! On every battle field they lie! In the crowded yards of every prison ground! In the dark ravines of the tangled forest! In the miry prison swamps, where the slimy serpent crawls by day, and the will-o'-the-wisp dances at night! In the beds of the mighty rivers! Under the waves of the salt sea! In the drifting sands of the desert-islands! On the lonely picket line! And by the roadside, where the weary soldier lay down with his knapsack, and his gun, and his march of life was ended! There, in the strange beds they sleep, till the morning of the great reveille!

"Facing the frowning battlements of Petersburg, Richmond and Charleston, and the flower of the Rebel Army, there I saw them fight and die. And there, with their Eastern comrades, their bones whiten in the sand. The fields of Virginia are rich with their blood."

The fact the dear ones did not come home — this was still all their families knew. Heart-breaking appeals from all over the nation kept flowing into Washington. Finally, early in March, President Lincoln, unable longer to stand the strain of this correspondence without doing anything, summoned Miss Barton. For over four awful years she had ministered to the soldiers' needs on the battle field. Now, as if that were not enough, the President and the country fell back on her to locate over 80,000 men. Of the gigantic task which confronted her, Miss Barton writes:

"The heart-broken friends appealed to me for help, and by the aid of surviving comrades, I gained intelligence of the fate of nearly one-half the number of soldiers; I greatly fear there are some whose names stand to-day on the rolls against the dark word — Deserter — who were never faithless to their trust, who fell in the stern path of duty on the lonely picket line, perhaps, or wounded, and left in some tangled ravine to perish alone, under the waters in some dark night, or, crazed with fever, to lie in some tent or hut, or by the wayside, unknowing and unknown, with none to tell his fate, or save his honor. 'Alone with his tarnished name he sleeps — quiet and sweet.'

"This may not be a fact, but I have stronger grounds for fear than those who have never searched the fate of soldiers on the field, or looked after the losses of an army, and in justice to our men, I am glad of every opportunity to name my apprehensions, for it has long been my honest belief that, in spite of the best efforts, our army records show a larger number of deserters than we ever really had.

"The very nature of the grounds over which our armies fought, their wildness, ruggedness, the unparalleled extent of territory and the great duration of time, all conspired to render it one of the most difficult of wars, of which to keep accurate and positive record."

With the assassination of President Lincoln on the 14th of April, Miss Barton was left to face the great problem of the missing men alone. Not disheartened, however, she conceived a plan of action which she outlined for Congress as follows:

"During the last year of the War, I became aware from letters received from various parts of the country, that a very large number of our soldiers had disappeared from view without leaving behind them any visible trace or record. Whether they had fallen in battle, were lingering in rebel prisons, or perished in some other way, was only to be conjectured.

"In the then painfully excited state of the public mind any information respecting them would have afforded the most grateful relief to their families.

"These considerations induced me in the spring of 1865 to endeavor to gather from our returning armies such information as individual soldiers could furnish of the fate of their missing comrades.

"I assumed that where official records existed the officers of the Government would willingly furnish all the information required, and I, therefore, sought only to glean these barren fields which would be overlooked, from the scantiness of the return they would yield.

"The fresh memory of each surviving veteran, and of every citizen who had watched the last hours of a dying soldier were the records I sought to consult. But, as army after army and one regiment after another became disbanded and returned to their homes, it became impossible to hold communication with them except by an extended and complex system of correspondence.

"In conducting this I caused printed lists of all missing soldiers who had come to my knowledge, to be posted in conspicuous places, in all the towns and considerable villages in the country, requesting information from all who might be able to furnish any."

On the 11th of March, Miss Barton had taken her station at Annapolis — the depot of the reception of thousands of exchanged prisoners from Andersonville and other Southern prisons. This she had done at the suggestion of President Lincoln, who had issued a letter advising the friends of missing soldiers to communicate with her there. And yet, notwithstanding this, it was May before the War Department delegated to her the proper authority to proceed — making two months of heart-rending delay.

Several bushels of letters from despairing, broken-hearted friends of missing men and unknown dead were waiting to be opened. She struck out a path for herself, although the Government then allowed her but the use of a tent, furniture, and a moderate supply of postage stamps. The War Office denominated her "General Correspondent for the Friends of Paroled Prisoners."

In many respects the records at Annapolis were a tangled maze and most incomplete. Prisoners sent home by thousands had not been recorded. It was not known, therefore, what prisoners were left, and what were not. Large numbers had been discharged without record.

To remedy these colossal omissions, an entire register had to be devised, and Miss Barton had to organize it.

As usual when Miss Barton found a deadlock, she took the initiative. She was conscious that the bureau for missing men was not meeting the issue and that thousands of wives, children, and parents were still in heart-rending anxiety. She felt buried under the distracting appeals which she continued to receive and which harried her beyond human endurance. While the Government's hands were tied and weeks and months elapsed, should she give it up? No. She would organize a department herself. She, therefore, found a central office, hired a force of twelve men, and opened for use what remained of her private bank account. As the months flew by, it was costing her thousands of dollars to maintain the bureau. She searched the burial records and prison records in States, hospitals, and even on the desolate battle fields themselves. This involved rebel stockades, Wilmington, Salisbury, Florence, and Charleston prisons, and most of all, Andersonville.

May 15, 1865, found a mass of unanswered letters in her hands with new ones coming in at the rate of 100 a day. Miss Barton's strategic and never-losing stroke was now an appeal to the country. This plea to the people, like every other she made, was eminently success-

I

ful. The country responded to her requests for information with a pathetic eagerness. All types and conditions of men sent information to her.

But the most remarkable reply came from one man — a discharged Andersonville prisoner, Dorrence Atwater. He had been detailed while himself a living skeleton, yet a man with a clear mind, to keep an official list of the dead and their burial. In his coat lining he secreted a duplicate copy with location of graves. Brought to a Washington hospital, he offered to the Government these 13,000 names. He urged action before the graves be lost sight of forever. The Government blindly hesitated and delayed. Just at this opportune time, Clara Barton's bulletins of request for information came before his eyes; Atwater acted immediately and wrote Miss Barton of his remarkable secret. He had the key to these nearly thirteen thousands of graves of those soldiers who died in Andersonville.

His story made a deep impression upon Miss Barton's mind.

"Among the many private soldiers, who by some gallant deed, or worthy act, have won for themselves a place in the historic record of their country, perhaps there is not one," she writes, "to whom so many thousand hearts, throughout the entire land, would so gratefully accord the page, and so lovingly embellish it with immortelles, glistening with tear-drops of sad and tender memories, as the young soldier, Dorrence Atwater.

"At the age of sixteen, he enlisted in the Connecticut squadron which helped to form the famous regiment of Harris Light Cavalry, commanded by Colonel, afterward General, Kilpatrick. A soldier from choice, a bold rider, and knowing little of fear, it is natural to conclude that Atwater was never happier than when dashing into Richmond with Kilpatrick on his brilliant raid of May, 1862. But there was destined to come a day when he would enter the Rebel capital under circumstances less exhilarating, as a few days subsequent to the Battle of Gettysburg, while bearing despatches to his General, with the last home letter in his pocket which brought the intelligence of the sudden death of his mother, he was captured and taken prisoner to Richmond and Belle Isle. This was the beginning of misfortunes, the shadow of which, up to the present moment, has never quite lifted from his pathway.

"After five months of suffering and illness in Belle Isle, at the intercession of the Adjutant of his regiment, also captive in Richmond, and whose regimental clerk Atwater had been, he was taken to Richmond, and detailed to take account of the supplies sent by the U. S. Government to its own men suffering in Rebel Prisons.

"In February, 1864, while holding this position for some weeks, he was sent with the first detachment of prisoners to Andersonville,

from the shelterless 'stockade' in midwinter, to the scarcely better protected 'old hospital' outside; three months more of fever, scurvy, and starvation, — and again he was detailed to the Rebel Surgeon's Office and set to keep the daily death record of his comrades, the Union prisoners, as score by score they perished by his side. He was now nineteen — and though wasted to a skeleton, naturally active and faithful, a clerk of no ordinary skill and experience. Rendered thoughtful by suffering, tender by afflictions, it would seem that he had been providentially fitted for the great work given him to do.

"With a degree of judgment and forethought, which would have done credit to a man twice his years, he appears to have measured his task and comprehended its importance at the outset, and directed every energy of both mind and body to its faithful accomplishment. Day by day he watched the long trenches fill with the naked skeletons of the once sturdy Union Blue, — the pride of the American Armies, — and day by day, he traced on the great brown pages of his Confederate sheet record, the last, and all that was ever to be known of the brave dead sleepers in their crowded, coffinless beds, — the name, company, regiment, disease, date of death, and number of grave.

"Five more weary months of this, and in September, he found himself registering a hundred names a day, and saw seven tenths of them followed by the word 'scorbute.' For, although midsummer in a country teeming with vegetation, no green thing had been permitted to find its way inside that deadly palisade. Atwater then came to the conclusion that a record which told so fearful a tale of willful cruelty or design against the perpetrators would never be permitted to exist and pass into history. That, in any case, whichsoever side might ultimately succeed, Southern pride would compel the destruction of that record, and with it must pass forever from the page of the earth the last authentic information — in a majority of instances the last trace — of the fate of every man who perished in 'Andersonville,' leaving only anxiety, distress, the agony of suspense, and the darkness of oblivion to the thousands upon thousands of waiting mourners throughout the North. The loving memories of his own mother, whose last words had been of her soldier boys, clung tenderly about his heart, and his soul yearned for some means by which to save the thousands of other mothers from this needless agony of uncertainty worse than death, and he decided upon commencing a duplicate of his own record, upon separate sheets of paper which he managed to abstract, even going back of himself and gleaning all that he could of the first three months while he lay in stockade and hospital.

"Bringing his duplicate up to date in October, and concealing it from all eyes, both friend and foe, from that time he kept both his secret and his double record as he had at first kept the one, with little expectation of living to bring it away himself, but hoping that he might be enabled to pass it into the hands of some stronger comrade who could get it through our lines.

"In February, 1865, it was decided to remove the prisoners from Andersonville to the region of Columbia, South Carolina, and Atwater, with a guard, was ordered to precede the main body, and make ready his papers and records for the registry of the incoming dead. He left Andersonville on the 20th of February with his duplicate record concealed about his person, but before the journey was completed they were met by the news of the capture of Columbia by General Sherman, the destination was changed, and Atwater was hurried away to Salisbury. Two days after his arrival came the earliest order for exchange and he chanced to be among the first ten thousand paroled at Wilmington. The middle of March, 1865, found our boy captive of twenty-two months a paroled prisoner at Annapolis, with his record of the 13,000 dead of Andersonville, while as many thousand homes were shrouded in darkness, as many thousand families waited in agonized suspense for the unveiling of its fearful mysteries.

"So far, the boy's prophecies were proven, and his sad dream realized. He had not miscalculated the terrible anxiety of the public, and chafed under his parole for liberty to forward his record to the people for whom he had kept it."

As soon as Miss Barton learned of the existence of Atwater's records, she consulted the Secretary of War and upon his orders, together with Mr. Atwater went to Andersonville, with Assistant Quartermaster

James, and forty painters and joiners. It was then midsummer and it was necessary before fall to reinter the dead who had been packed in shallow trenches. In the boiling feverish sun, sapped as was her strength, Miss Barton kept on day after day with the work — retiring to the tent for the night, only to begin again next morning till the number of 12,800 bodies which they located were reinterred with Christian burial in graves 4 feet deep. Four hundred Confederates also were as tenderly buried. Following this task in the horrible aftermath of war, she did not cease her hunt for the unidentified till 700 more were later found.

"When all was finished I pulled the rope which raised the stars and stripes above the place for the first time and I have never seen Andersonville since," is her characteristically modest comment.

It had, however, left an impression on her mind never to be effaced. Later she was to see the "packed cities of Europe, reeling with starvation after the worst sieges of the Franco-Prussian War" — but the sight was to be to her one of "joy and peace" as compared with the death-laden boats that unloaded the victims of Andersonville at Annapolis — human wrecks covered with sores and scarce able to breathe. "To speak of Andersonville is but reasonable," she said, "knowing that I have looked upon its terrible face. But not in the same breath in which I would speak of anything else, would I speak of it. It classes with, and was equaled by nothing but the regions below.

"I have looked over its twenty-five acres of pitiless stockade, its burrows in the earth, its stinted stream, its turfless hillside, shadeless in summer and shelterless in winter; its well, and tunnels and graves; its seven forts of death; its ball and chains; its stocks and tortures; its kennels for blood-hounds; its sentry boxes and its dead line; my heart went out, and I said, 'Surely this was not the gate of hell, but hell itself,' and for comfort, I turned away to the nine acres of crowded graves, and I said that here at last was rest, and this to them was the gate of Heaven."

"Then I saw the little graves marked, blessed them for the heart-broken mother in the old Northern home, raised over them the flag they loved, and died for, and left them to their rest.

"And there they lie to-night, apart from all they loved, but mighty in their silence, teaching the world a lesson of human cruelty it had never learned, and writing a page in the world's history so black that it might call upon the horrors of the Inquisition to light it up.

"They starved in Andersonville. There, side by side, we found their graves, and marked the spot for you. There, so far away, so pitiful and alone, I laid my hand softly on the sacred earth, and almost felt the mother's great heart beating underneath, for I knew, though the blood of her own veins still forced its valves, she had buried it there, in that little grave, a holocaust to love and freedom."

At last Congress was moved to action — impelled perhaps by the sight of Miss Barton bearing the heavy burden of the search alone.

The governmental probe was led by her never failing friend, Senator (afterwards Vice President) Henry Wilson of Massachusetts. He was still chairman of the National Committee of Military Affairs. With him were Congressman Colfax of Indiana, Speaker of the House, the Senators from Iowa and Ohio, and a circle of accompanying representatives and senators.

They reported that they had found Miss Barton surrounded by thousands of letters and records, conducting the work according to her own simple but accurate system. They learned that she had already expended $8000 of her own money and had not yet reached the end of her great undertaking.

The dignified committee of investigators, realizing her tremendous sacrifices, could not keep back the tears or control their emotions. Why should the awful responsibility rest on her?

The outcome of the deliberations of this committee is shown in a resolution which was later presented to the 37th Congress on March 10, 1866, and which eventually became a bill.

"Whereas Miss Clara Barton has expended from her own resources large sums of money in endeavoring to discover missing soldiers of the United States army and in communicating intelligence to their relatives : —

"*Resolved* by the Senate and House of Representatives that the sum of $15,000 be appropriated to reimburse Miss Barton and to aid in the further prosecution of the search, and that the printing necessary for the furtherance of this object shall be done by the Public Printer."

This appropriation was in no sense pay for Miss Barton's work but simply a reimbursement of funds of her own which she had used. Her time she gave without charge as well as many dollars never restored.

Miss Barton's labors, we have seen, did not cease with the close of the war in the spring of '65· She realized that the hardest battles were yet to be fought by the people — and she was determined to stand by them until something like peace and comfort had been once more established in their hearts and homes.

"Our war closed in the spring of '65," she recalled, "but for four years longer, in an awful aftermath, I worked among the débris, gathering up the wrecks, and sometimes during the lecture-season, telling a few simple war stories to the people over the country in their halls and churches."

Her motive she expressed in these words:

"If I have been privileged to stand by your loved ones when the trial hour came, and their brave lives went out amid the din and smoke of battle, or when they lingered pining in distant hospitals or by the way-side, and their last look was turned upon my face instead of upon yours, their last words addressed to me, when they would have been gold and precious stones to you, the secret is not mine when it is demanded of me. I must give it up. If it has been my lot to look over those great burial places of our country's dead with their acres of skeleton-filled graves, and witness for myself the terrible circumstances among which death was welcomed, neither is this knowledge mine. It belongs to you, to all my countrymen if they demand it. I am by the very circumstances the servant of the people who have sacrificed so much."

Miss Barton was regarded as a sister to the soldier from Maine to Virginia. As a miracle of mercy, her name was a household word throughout the length and breadth of the land. She used the impulse of this popular fame, however, as but a further aid to prosecute her search and extend her task of comfort and mercy as is evidenced in the following story told by her:

"I recall an incident which might serve as a type of all those days:

"Having occasion to pass through a somewhat western city in the winter of '65 and '66, my attention was one day suddenly arrested by the figure of a singularly attired, weird looking little boy, with a basket on his arm standing in front of a bakery.

"A soldier's cap and pantaloons in which his tiny form seemed nearly lost and the faded light blue cape of a storm beaten over-coat reaching to his knees, with the once bright buttons still striving to adorn its tattered edge, comprised the uniform of the little shivering hero.

"He stood perfectly motionless, evidently unconscious of any presence save the large, warm, nut-brown loaves within the window. As I could not pass such a picture, I stopped, and asked if he were hungry! 'Not very,' he said, hesitatingly, 'not very, but Annie is.' 'Who is Annie?' I asked. 'My little sister.' 'Have you no father and mother?' 'Father was killed at Chattanooga, and ma's sick.' His voice trembled a little. 'No brothers?' I asked. 'I had three brothers,' and his little voice grew smaller and trembled more, 'but they all went to the War. Willie was shot in the woods when they were all on fire' (he meant the wilderness) 'and Charlie, he starved to death in Andersonville, and Jamie, he was next to me, and he went for a Drummer Boy, and died in the Hospital. And then there was only Ma and me and Annie. Annie was a baby when they went away, and Ma's grown sick and Annie's often hungry and cold and I can't always get enough for her. I pick up chips and wood, but Ma doesn't like me to ask for food, she says it's a bad habit for little boys to learn,' and the tears slid quietly down his child cheeks, wan and care-worn.

"I went home with him — far on the outskirts of the city, long beyond the reach of sidewalks, through alternate frost and mud, — a cheerless room, and as we entered a thin hectic woman partly rose from her bed to greet me. Her story was only a confirmation of what I had heard. Her boys enlisted first and early, and the father, partly to be near them, and partly through dread of the draft which he could not meet, followed them.

"One by one they had met their fate.

"One by one her idols broken.

One by one her hopes had died.

"Till with bleeding feet, and breaking heart she had trodden the wine press alone.

"As she talked on quietly and tearfully, Baby Annie stole out of her hiding place, and peered wistfully into the basket. And the little military guardian drew up to my side with simple, childlike confidence, as he said, 'This was Jamie's cap and cloak. They sent them home from the hospital when he was dead. But they didn't send Jamie home. Nor Willie, nor Charlie.' I said 'No!' 'Nor Papa. There's only Ma and me and Annie, — that's all!'

"And these were more than there would be long, poor child, for already the pale messenger waits at the gate, and his weird shadow falleth ever nearer."

In response to the demand of these thousands who wanted to know the facts of the war, Miss Barton arranged to deliver three hundred lectures in different parts of the country. The proceeds of these addresses were to enable her to continue her work of binding up the bitter wounds of these whose loved ones had never returned.

As a public speaker Miss Barton seems to have been singularly successful — due no doubt in part at least to the fact that she had a big message and one in which countless numbers were interested. John B. Gough, regarded at the time as one of the greatest orators in America, said that he had never heard anything more touching, more thrilling, in his life than these talks given by Miss Barton to ease the public heart. "I want everyone to hear her," he declared. The *Times* of Syracuse concluded its report of a lecture with: "Few eyes but were dim; few hearts but were saddened."

These war lectures, first given throughout the East, were also given in the West where the country's sad soul melted before Miss Barton and a tear-stained multitude thronged everywhere to hear her. The report of the *Transcript*, of Peoria, Illinois, for December 6, 1867, is typical: "Miss Barton is a lady of under medium height, with a broad forehead, a deep eye, and an earnest enthusiasm in manner. She was modestly dressed in black silk, and on being introduced came forward to the stand and in a clear, ringing voice spoke in an animated conversational tone that transported the imagination of the hearer to the scenes she so vividly described. Peoria has seen no more successful speaker."

But the strain of lectures following so close on her other superhuman efforts ultimately proved too much for Miss Barton's strength. The occasion of her breakdown she describes herself:

"One early winter evening in '68, I stood on the platform of one of the finest new opera houses in the East, filled to repletion with, it seemed to me, the most charming attendance I had ever beheld, plumed and jeweled ladies, stalwart youths, reverend white-haired men, and gradually to my horror I felt my voice giving out, leaving me. The next moment I opened my mouth but no sound followed. Again and again I attempted it, with no result. It was finished! Nervous prostration had declared itself. I went to my home in Washington, lay helpless all winter, and was finally ordered to Europe by my physician."

It was hard for Miss Barton to go. She wished to stay in America and continue her deeds of mercy. But it was impossible.

"How gladly would I lay my right arm beside yours, so strong and ready," she wrote to Mrs. Cady Stanton and Susan B. Anthony, "but its strength is gone. The years of unsheltered days and nights, the sun and storm, the dews and damps have done their work and now with bitter tears, I turn my face away from the land I have loved so well and seek in a foreign clime, perchance a little of the good strength once lent me here.

"If ever any of it return and I can serve your noble cause abroad you will tell me. If strong enough I must sail from New York for Europe in a few weeks."

CHAPTER XXI

AT THE OUTBREAK OF THE FRANCO-PRUSSIAN WAR

1869–1870

IT was not until the fall of 1869 that Miss Barton had recovered sufficiently to undertake the trip abroad. "Three years of absolute rest," the doctor had prescribed, and at last in September we find her sailing for England doubtless fully determined to follow orders. But circumstances and her great love for humanity were destined to interfere with this determination.

Landing in Liverpool there followed — she writes in a manuscript journal of the time — "two weeks in bonny Scotland among its bloom and heather, its lakes and mountains, its classic old cities, its towers and its castles; one night of thundering over a British railway as if shot from a cannon and here is London; a few days with its miles of gray granite walls, its atmosphere of smoke, its beautiful parks, its matchless thoroughfares, its millions of living breathing life, its towers, its St. Paul's, its Parliament, its inconceivable charities, its untold wealth, its thieves and its beggars; a dismal night across the channel and marvelously you have bade adieu to a possession you have always had, born with you, a friend that has served your every need, and which you never thought before to lose — your mother tongue!

"*Bonjour — Madame a votre service.* (I hope you like it better than I do.) A day or two in Imperial Paris with all the splendor of the Empire, its regal Empress the pattern of the world, a happy wife and mother. A few hours with my old time, treasured war friend, E. B. Washburn, then our minister to France. A little talk on the 'situation,' a few doubts of the plan of reconstruction and on to the Southeast through happy France, her second crops ripening for the winter and her vineyards purpling in the sunshine. On through the valleys of thrift and beauty, with now and then a glimpse of Alpine ranges in the dim distance, till once more your lungs expand with the atmosphere of a

Republic; for the terminus of this is Switzerland, cosmopolitan Geneva, and here, friends, tired with our rushing journey, let us rest. For we have come to stay three years — so they told us at home, when they sent us away. Oh! yes! Time to admire this loveliest of cities, resting on the bosom of its clear blue lake! Time to return the salutation of the great hoary-headed king, Mont Blanc, as he nods from his distant throne of perpetual snows. Time to make acquaintance with the old residences and labor places of John Calvin, Voltaire, Rousseau, Neckar and Madam de Staël at lovely Copet."

But a month after Miss Barton's arrival in Geneva she was visited by the president and members of the "International Committee for the Relief of the Wounded in War." They called to learn why the United States had declined to sign the treaty of Geneva providing for the relief of sick and wounded soldiers. "Our position," explained Miss Barton, "was incomprehensible to them. If the treaty had originated with a monarchial government they could see some ground for hesitancy. But it originated in a Republic older than our own. To what did America object, and how could these objections be overcome? They had twice formally presented it to the government at Washington, once in 1864, through our Minister Plenipotentiary at Berne, who was present at the convention; again in 1868, through Rev. Dr. Henry W. Bellows, the great head of war relief in America. They had failed in both instances. No satisfactory or adequate reason had ever been given by the nation for the course pursued. They had thought the people of America, with their grand sanitary record, would be the first to appreciate and accept it. I listened in silent wonder to all this recital, and when I did reply it was to say that I had never heard of the Convention of Geneva nor of the treaty, and was sure that as a country America did not know she had declined; that she would be the last to withhold recognition of a humane movement; that it had doubtless been referred to and declined by some one department of the government, or some one official, and had never been submitted to the people; and as its literature was in languages foreign to our English-speaking population, it had no way of reaching us.

"You will naturally infer that I examined it. I became all the more deeply impressed with the wisdom of its principles, the good practical sense of its details, and its extreme usefulness in practice. Humane intelligence had devised its provisions and peculiarly adapted it to win popular favor. The absurdity of our own position in relation to it was simply marvelous. As I counted up its roll of twenty-two nations, not a civilized people in the world but ourselves missing, and saw Greece, Spain, and Turkey there, I began to fear that in the eyes of the rest of mankind we could not be far from barbarians. This reflection did not furnish a stimulating food for national pride. I grew more and more ashamed.

"Although the gradual growth of the idea of something like humanity in war, stimulated by the ignorant and insane horrors of India and the Crimea, and soothed and instructed by the sensible and practical work of Florence Nightingale, had slowly but surely led up to the conditions which made such a movement possible, it was not until the remarkable campaign of Napoleon III in Northern Italy again woke the slumbering sympathies of the world that any definite steps revealed themselves."

The International Red Cross thus explained and revealed to Clara Barton made a deep impression upon her mind. Of this impression and the uppermost facts in it she further said:

"It was to the direct influence of the work by Monsieur Henry Dunant, entitled *Un Souvenir de Solferino* as well as to the personal exertions of that gentleman that the movement which led to the International Congress of 1864 and its results were immediately due.

"Monsieur Dunant, a Swiss gentleman, was traveling in Italy on his own account in the year 1859, and was in the neighborhood of Solferino the day of the great battle of the 24th of June. The aspect of the battle field, the suffering of the vast numbers of wounded scattered over it, the occurrences which he afterwards observed, and the hospitals, where he remained some days assisting as a volunteer in attending upon the wounded, deeply impressed him.

"Notwithstanding the liberal provisions which had been made by the French army surgeons, means of transport, surgical stores, and dietary, and in addition, the aid afforded by the inhabitants of the places to which the wounded were first brought, Monsieur Dunant said that owing to the vastness of their numbers, the wounded were left for days without attention or proper surgical relief, and he was led to consider whether there were any means by which this superadded suffering in time of war might be obviated. This led to the publication of the *Souvenir de Solferino* in 1862, containing descriptions of what he had observed in the battle field and in hospitals, as well as numerous arguments in favor of a proposition for founding in every country, societies for the relief of the wounded.

"The work created a great sensation and was quickly translated into several European languages, and the Genevese Society of Public Utility appointed a committee of which General Dufor, the General in Chief of the Swiss Confederation, accepted the presidency, for the purpose of supporting and encouraging the dissemination of the proposals of Mr. Dunant."

February 9th, 1863, Dr. Louis Appia seconded the appeal of the founder, Monsieur Dunant, before the courts of Europe, to whom he had appealed in a Congress at Berlin. The Grand Duke of Baden was the first donor. The International Conference at Geneva that followed early in 1864 was attended by delegates from sixteen governments, including Great Britain, France, Spain, Prussia, Austria, and Italy.

"This conference sat four days, framed important resolutions and resulted in the calling of an International Congress, known as the International Convention of Geneva of 1864 for the purpose of considering the question of neutralization of the sick and wounded soldiers of belligerent armies.

"This congress was assembled from the Supreme Federal Council of Switzerland. The invitation was accepted by sixteen powers and the congress opened on the 8th of August, 1864, at the Hôtel de Ville, Geneva, provided for the occasion by the Federal Government.

"There were present twenty-five members of the Diplomatic, Military and Medical staffs of various nations and armies.

"The deliberations lasted nearly a fortnight, and resulted in a code of Nine Articles agreed upon by the convention and signed on the 22d of August by the representatives of those governments which had previously accredited their delegates with sufficient power for signing a treaty. There were submitted ten articles of agreement to the main document known as 'The Treaty of Geneva for the Relief of Sick and Wounded Soldiers.'

"Twelve governments affixed their signatures. The President elected was Gustave Moynier.

"This is considered," stated Miss Barton as she reflected upon the results of the founder, Monsieur Dunant, "a most remarkable instance of a general treaty brought about by the exertion of an individual in private life.

"It will be borne in mind that the aim of the Congress of 1864 was to obtain the neutralization of the wounded in belligerent armies, and of the persons and material necessary for their care and treatment — and to determine whether the humane principles which had from time to time been applied exceptionally might not under certain limitations be rendered consistent with military necessities on all occasions, and be established as a rule.

"The conference of 1863, less official in character, had aimed at the foundation of a system of Relief Societies for all countries and its resolutions are to this end.

"A word in regard to the character of the Nine Articles, of the Treaty formed by the congress of the convention of 1864, may not be out of place.

"The 1st naturally provides for the security of the hospitals in which the wounded might happen to be collected, that they shall be held neutral, and be respected by belligerents and that the sick or wounded remain in them.

"Articles 2 and 3 provide for the neutrality and safety of all persons employed in the care of the wounded in hospitals, surgeons, chaplains, nurses, attendants, even after the enemy has gained the ground; but when no longer required for the wounded, they shall be promptly conducted under escort to the outposts of the enemy to rejoin the corps to which they belong, thus preventing all opportunity to roam free and make observations under cover of neutrality.

"Article 4 settles the terms on which the material of hospitals, field and general, shall be regarded, that field hospitals shall not be subject to capture.

"Article 5, with the view of quieting the fears of the inhabitants in the vicinity of a battle, who often flee in terror, as well as to secure their assistance, and the comfort of their homes for the care of the wounded, offers military protection and certain exemptions to all who shall entertain and care for the wounded, in their houses.

"Article 6 binds the parties contracting the Treaty not only to give the requisite care and treatment to all sick and wounded who fall into their hands, but that their misfortunes shall not be aggravated by the prospect of banishment or imprisonment. They shall not be retained as prisoners of war, but if circumstances admit, may be given up immediately after the action to be cared for by their own army, or if retained until recovered and found disabled for service, they shall be safely returned to their own country and friends, and that all convoys of sick and wounded shall be protected by absolute neutrality.

"In order to secure the neutralization of hospitals and materials, and nurses engaged in the services of the wounded, it was necessary to fix upon some common sign by which they could be recognized by all parties and all nations uniting in the Treaty. Thus Article 7 provides for hospital and convoys — an arm badge for persons. The design proposed was a red cross upon a white ground."

Thus proceeded the Articles of the Red Cross Convention to which Miss Barton's attention had been drawn.

"The question naturally arises in every mind," Miss Barton continued in further explanation, 'why were we not a party to the Treaty and why had we no societies?'

"Although the fact seems not only singular, but painful, I think the reasons can be made obvious.

"It will be remembered that the conference and congress of Geneva was held during the years 1863 and 1864. The United States, having been invited with all other nations to send delegates, was officially represented at the latter by Mr. Bowles, then residing in Paris, and by him the Resolutions and articles of both assemblies were officially transmitted to our government for action.

"It was not unnatural that our renowned Secretary of State, William H. Seward, should have declined on the officially stated ground that we already were in the midst of a relentless and barbarous war.

"Some years later, another convention, known as the convention of 1868, was held in Paris, and another set of articles dealing with the wounded in maritime warfare, as well as the land forces, was submitted to the nations.

"In this convention, the United States was most fitly represented by its noble and world-renowned philanthropist, Rev. Dr. Henry W. Bellows, who was appointed its representative in this country. By that honored gentleman, the articles of the original Treaty, including the additions of 1868, were again presented to the U. S. Government and were again declined, most likely for the reason they had once before been declined. But through the faithful endeavors of Dr. Bellows, a society was actually formed during that year, though the subject, as well as its literature, was foreign to our people, who knowing little of it, felt no interest, and still further, a society formed for the purpose of International Relief in War, lacking any International Treaty to that end, and lacking all the privileges and powers to be conferred by the Treaty, was simply Hamlet with Hamlet left out, and like a sapling planted without a root, it naturally withered away.

"It is not singular that the International Committee of Geneva became perplexed by the repeated declinations and apathy of a nation which had given to the world the examples of a sanitary and Christian commission, and sought explanation."

All that winter of 1869–70, Geneva was the centre of Miss Barton's residence where she made her home mostly at the Consulate, with U. S. Consul Upton and Mrs. Upton. She felt the sting of the cold, however, and sought the Island of Corsica. But she found that the climate induced conditions resembling the malarial attacks in Carolina in the War, when much quinine had to be "pumped" into her system. She returned in March to Switzerland, and went again to the home of the Uptons. On the 26th of May she set out for Berne, "in quest of strength among its mountain views and baths."

A few days after her arrival there she wrote to her brother David and interestingly set forth her impressions of the place

"I am not certain if I have waited a little too long or not quite long enough between writing. It seems to me to have been quite a good while, and yet if I were to wait a few days longer, I could tell you more about the portion of country to which I have just come.

"I left Geneva last Wednesday (this is Monday), for this city — Berne, the Capital of Switzerland, and much more in the heart of the country than I have ever been before, Geneva being almost on the line of France, and much more resembling it in manners and customs than other parts of Switzerland.

"I came here for the benefit of some excellent Turkish baths which are at the establishment where I am — two or three miles outside of the city of Berne. I find everything in excellent order and thus far, very pleasant. I have only taken two baths yet, my second this morning and cannot yet judge how they will agree with me, but anticipate

x

good results. They are something like the old time 'steam bath' which you will remember, only that hot air is substituted for steam. You are in rooms instead of a box — go from one to another for various degrees of heat, have the cold water at the last and come out refreshed.

"The climate of Switzerland has been pretty hard for me.[1] I have had three or four very severe catarrhal colds. The last I took some four weeks ago and it remained so long and settled so heavily on my chest, if not my lungs, that I decided to come to the baths. The climate of Europe may be a good specific for my malarial difficulty — and I presume is — but sometimes I cannot help thinking, with Ben Bond, that the 'ditheathe is wuth than the dithorder.'

"The country is very beautiful here now; it is the custom to cut all grass fields twice and the first cutting is being done now, the field just in front of my windows is being mowed to-day. Of course, the grass is not, like your clover, three feet tall, but it is good height and seems not to be clear and of one kind like our hay fields at home, but mixed and full of all manner of flowers, all colors, some very pretty, but it seems to me as if the clear grass would be better. This first cutting is for the horses, the next, which will take place in August and September, will be for the cows, — finer and not so full of flowers and bitter weeds. The cows are all out spending their summer vacation now on the sides of the mountains with the dairymen and women and the shepherds. The butter is churned there every day and brought fresh (not a particle of salt) to town every morning and evening. When cheese is made, it is generally done in large manufactories. I find no mules and little donkeys here as in Geneva and I have not seen cows at work in yoke and harness here, but all is done by horses, real horses, of the size of the Boston drays. Berne is an agricultural district and little jackasses and cows can't do the business.

"There must be a lot of fruit here by the promise of the trees, and it must be as early or earlier than Washington. I should like to be able to tell you about the great mountains, and little lakes and seas of ice and waterfalls that must be so near me here, but I must wait till I have seen them. I am only fifteen miles from the chain of Bernese Alps, the peaks of which are always white with snow. They are in

[1] "Switzerland has pretty days and her snow capped peaks are grand, but even in a July evening they remind you of their power to bite and pierce," Miss Barton wrote on another occasion.

plain sight from my windows when there is not an Indian summer haze over everything. Just now, I am at present boarding at the baths, but am expecting, this week, the arrival of my friends (the Sheldons) from New Haven (from London now), who have been almost or quite a year attempting to get to me.

"I suppose they left London day before yesterday, and if so, and they reach me, we shall probably make a home for ourselves for the summer and make journeys out from it as we find most agreeable. Then I shall hope to be able to tell you about the mountains, lakes and snow and ice. How I wish you could be here to go with me this summer. I never see a lovely piece of country that I do not wish you could be here to see it too, the land and productions and cattle would interest you so much. I am sure you would want to take home some specimens of stock and perhaps grain, but I like the looks of your grass much the best, and I think your potatoes are by far the superior of anything I have seen of the kind abroad ; yet I like the fresh mountain butter very much, and when the grapes come, they are well worth the eating, although I think America will yet raise more and finer grapes than Europe. I believe the flavor will be better. This is not a grape section. Whenever attention is given to raising grapes and making wine, there is little or no farming done. Geneva makes wine but Berne raises wheat and rye and hay. The two cities are only some sixty miles apart, six hours by rail. I have not heard of your having any sickness this spring. I do hope you escaped it. I had a dear good letter from Steve some weeks ago. He is a darling boy and tells me he is coming home. I was rejoiced to get his letter. How well he has done.

"I have forgotten where I last wrote you from, whether it was before I went to Corsica or after my arrival there, but I might repeat if need be that I did not find that climate beneficial and it took a great deal of quinine to work Corsica out of my system. It was a good specimen of Carolina for me. Since my return to Switzerland, I have spent almost two months with Mr. and Mrs. Upton, our Consul at Geneva, who have been very dear friends ever since I reached Europe, and always, when not at Papa Golay's, the consulate has been my home. In coming to Berne, Mr. Rublee, the American Minister of all Switzerland and Mrs. Rublee hold the same relation to me that the Uptons do in Geneva. They invited me and were very anxious that I should spend the winter with them, last winter, but I declined, thinking Berne too cold, and near the mountains. But they have selected the Baths for me now and come or send daily to look after me. No one could have found kinder or better friends than I have in a strange country. It burdens me just as it does in America to think how I shall ever repay so much kindness and attention.

"I wonder if you have any photographs of yourself. I have one or two but they are in my albums in Washington. Sometimes I wish very much to look at your square face and grizzly beard.

"I must write Steve immediately or he will not get it before leaving for home. How is Julia's lameness? I hope it is better, if not all gone. Please give much love to her and tell her I should like to have her share my Turkish Baths. I think they might be good for her.

"Papa Golay talks a great deal about 'Little Nettie' but thinks he shall never see her. He is the best Papa in the world. Now dear Dave, don't work too hard this summer; hire an extra man in haying to save yourself. It will be cheaper in the end, and don't worry or fret about anything. No matter what comes, take it easy. It doesn't make much difference. Life is so short at best. And it isn't best to worry and grieve it away; when this is done there is a new one for us where we shall forget all the ills and annoyances of this and perhaps have an opportunity to do better. So, whatever comes, keep up cheerful and happy and hope for the best. Eat well, sleep well, watch your hay and potatoes grow, and be the halest and happiest old 'gray beard' in town.

"Your loving sis,
"CLARA."

On the 15th of July, while she was at her villa at Berne, came the shocking tidings of Napoleon's declaration of war against King William of Germany.

The cause of the Franco-Prussian War Miss Barton studied carefully. Residing in the neutral territory of Switzerland and being conversant with many savants, scholars, and reformers, she was in a position to formulate a just opinion on the conflict.

In a letter of July 21st, she diagnoses the situation, a situation in which seeds are sown for the war forty-four years after, the International crisis of 1914-15:

"It is scarcely possible to conceive of anything more precipitous than the business of this little week of time, which has thrown the great nations into the attitude of war, and put to the test of decision the courts or people of every country in Europe.

"A week ago she thought herself at peace. True, she had heard a day or two before of a few hasty words between France and Prussia, but no one deemed it to mean more than words until the wires of the 15th flashed Napoleon's declaration of war. All Europe stood aghast. What did it mean? What was it all about?

"No one could believe it meant war in reality, and the nations held their breath.

"Even the Prussian press said it 'could not be,' it was '*zu dumm!*' But the reader of history has yet to learn that nothing can be 'too foolish,' and no pretext too slight, where personal interest, royal dignity, ambition, or pride are injured or threatened.

"But in which of these, in the present instance, lies the tenderest nerve, it is difficult, at this early moment of confusion and consternation, to decide.

"Spain, which appears to have given, most innocently, the first provocation, holds no place in the quarrel, and has less to say and do about it than any other country.

"Her crime consists in that her poor crown goes a begging, and she offered it to one, and another, until at length the young German Prince Leopold of Hohenzollern, having neither a crown nor the prospect of one, accepted it. But when France, anxious to preserve the national balance of power, and fearing to see her rival, and old enemy, Germany, ruling on two sides, holding the keys to both the Baltic and Mediterranean, objected, he declined it. But when for still further security, France insisted upon demanding of the King of Prussia that in case of a pretender, neither the Prince of Hohenzollern nor any other subject of his, should ever accept it, the king refused to confer with the messenger. This insults the dignity of France, and she replies in one word — 'War,' and her populace, wild with enthusiasm, shouts — '*Vive la guerre!*'

"The decision passes over to Prussia. The old king listens in profound silence while Bismarck reads to him the declaration, and starts with visible astonishment at the passage in M. Ollivier's statement, in which he says that France 'accepts the war' and 'throws upon Prussia the responsibility.'

"When all is finished, he turns to his son, the Prince Royal, embraces him tenderly, steps a little to one side, and after a moment's hesitation, replies for Prussia in scarce more words than Napoleon has for France: 'War! Prepare for War!' And thus it is commenced.

"It were long to tell, and will be the work of later days to gather up and report, the various opinions and actions of the surrounding nations of Europe.

"To-day it is enough to know that all France and Prussia with both Northern and Southern Germany, are armed and marching to the Rhine; that at any moment we may hear that her blue waters are purpled with the flowing tide of human life; that the flying wheels of the artillery are plowing her golden fields, already bending low for the harvest, and the crushing hoof of the cavalry trampling out her unripened vintage.

"It may, however, be interesting, or at least amusing, some time after this, if the war continues, when the nations shall have settled themselves and taken position, to refer to these first impressions and decisions, before policy, strategy, or power have wholly entered into the warp and woof of what may yet become a vast political web, enveloping the entire continent of Europe, and with this view I gather a few of the most important.

"We are assured that nothing could exceed the outburst of patriotic enthusiasm manifested by the French people at the moment of the declaration, and the troops were with difficulty restrained.

"'To the Rhine! To the Rhine!' rang out on every side.

"This is balanced by an enthusiasm equally strong, perhaps a trifle more calm, on the part of the Prussians, the business men of Dresden immediately offering a prize to him who should capture the first French cannon. Baden, Würtemberg and Bavaria at once proffer money and troops.

"Hanover was a little slow to come in at first, and partly turned to France, but overpowered by the stream of public opinion, she wheels into line.

"Netherlands takes a decided stand and maintains an armed neutrality under the Prince of Orange.

"Italy attempted some demonstration in favor of Prussia and against Rome, but this was immediately put down, and the people gave their verdict as follows: 'We shall neither French nor Prussians be, but Italians!' Poor Italy has nothing to spare for her neighbors' quarrels; she will need all her military power for the arrest of her own revolutionary element.

"Austria at once announced her neutrality, and the Emperor so wrote Napoleon with his own hand.

"Denmark, like the Netherlands, hesitated. She remembered bitterly the loss of Schleswig-Holstein by the Prussian Aggression, and naturally turns away. There is exultation in the thought of a blockade of the Baltic at such a moment for Prussia. Revenge is sweet; but this endangers amicable relations with England, Russia, and North America, and perhaps she cannot afford to indulge her resentment, however gratifying it might be. So, *via* Hamburg, at last comes rumor of her declaration of neutrality.

"The intelligence from Russia is vague and uncertain. England attempted to act the mediator, but failed, and announces a 'strict neutrality' although she had previously declared her sympathies to be with Prussia. If one be not mistaken, Napoleon will need patience, faith, and a good appetite to relish the neutral dish England will serve up for him under these conditions. Her style of neutrality is something wonderful. Its acts — Lo: Are they not written in the book of the heart of every soldier who fought in the armies of Abraham?

"And last comes little Switzerland bright as a diamond in her rough mountain setting, proclaiming a neutrality which she means; with no policy but truth, no strategy but honesty, no diplomatism in this matter, but to preserve inviolate, and at all hazards, her own national independence and God-given liberty. Hers is an armed neutrality in which one has faith. Down all her mountain sides, and through all her valleys, and over her fields, come one, and two, and three, her sturdy brown cheeked mountain farmers in their neat uniforms of blue, with knapsack, and cartridge-box, grasping the ready musket with hands long calloused by the plow, the sickle, and the scythe.

"Since twenty-four hours from the declaration of war, there has been pouring across her green, peaceful bosom, this strange, steady stream of soldier-life, till one fancies the fiery torch of Duncraggan must have been sped over the hills.

"Forty thousand troops to-day line her borders; the entire length of her frontiers from Basle to Lake Leman and the Boden-see glistens with bayonets and darkens with men.

"Switzerland means nothing but honest neutrality and the preservation of her liberties at any cost, and when she tells you that she needs help, you may believe it and know that she deserves it."

In this long letter Miss Barton shows how closely she has been following the events of the International crisis which was to open up for her a new field of service. Though since 1864 there had occurred the war between Napoleon and Italy, and the war between Prussia and Austria in 1866, both of which offered a kind of trial of the International Red Cross, the real and major test was reserved for the impending conflict between France and Germany. Miss Barton was therefore "on the ground" at the psychological moment to see just how the association worked and to participate in its ultimate triumph.

At this crisis there broke one day upon the keen clear air of her Swiss home, the distant sounds of a royal party hastening back from a tour of the Alps. To Miss Barton's amazement it came in the direction of her villa. Finally flashed the scarlet and gold of the liveries of the Grand Duke of Baden. After the outriders came the splendid coach of the Grand Duchess, the daughter of King Wilhelm of Prussia, so soon to be Emperor Wilhelm I of Germany. In it rode the Grand Duchess herself. After presenting her card through the footman she personally alighted and clasped Miss Barton's hand. She hailed her in the name of humanity and said she already knew her through what she had done in the Civil War.

Holding her hand-clasp the more firmly she plead with Miss Barton to go with her and consecrate this knowledge to fields of relief in the opening war. Thus came a motive to discount ill health and proceed to the Franco-Prussian front. Mrs. James R. Bolton, daughter of Judge Sheldon, was in the chalet which the Sheldons had entered June 4th, 1870. "I remember perfectly well," said Mrs. Bolton, then six years old, "when the Grand Duchess of Baden came to our chalet." The wheels of her cortège had rumbled along the highway when suddenly her large retinue appeared in royal livery. The Grand Duchess alighted and met Miss Barton. She stated that the fame of Clara Barton's heroism in the American Civil War had captured Europe and especially Germany. She asked if she would not come to Strassburg, await the siege at Carlsruhe, and when it lifted organize relief."

CHAPTER XXII

THE CALL TO BEAR THE RED CROSS TO THE PRUSSIAN FIRING LINE

ON July 19, 1870, nearly a year after their first visit to her and following the declaration of war, the officers of the International Red Cross of Europe came to Clara Barton a second time. Their purpose, like that of the Grand Duchess, was to enlist her help. They reiterated what they had heard of her leadership in deeds of mercy in the American Civil War just closed — Indeed her fame, far more than she realized, had become International. The committee appealed to her therefore to lead with them a great systematic plan of relief at the front in the sure crisis between France and Prussia.

In reply Miss Barton told them that she was an invalid and that her exertions were limited to the baths at Berne. She explained how for months before she left America she had been confined to her bed and that the physicians had decided that her only hope of life lay in securing absolute rest and freedom from care for at least three years. And yet in spite of all this she could not say "no." [1]

In the past when Miss Barton saw the need of service she was given the necessary strength to perform it, and so it was now. It would almost seem as though once again the call for help, the picture of suffering and distress to come drawn by the Grand Duchess of Baden and the Red Cross officers, tapped new and fresh reservoirs of energy. In the face of consequences which in the opinion of her medical advisers would probably prove fatal to herself she decided to answer

---

[1] On another occasion, referring to her inability to accompany Dr. Appia and his commission Miss Barton said: "Do you think the knowledge of my exhausted powers of endurance that would not let me dare, and compelled me to decline, lay heavy on my soul? Do you think I bore a cross that day? If you do not you indeed know me little. But the courtesy and the honors were all the same. I accepted these and promised to follow by myself and do what I could, and if I broke down alone I should be no hindrance to other workers, and the same week I followed them to Basle."

the irresistible and compelling cry of humanity. Of the invitation and of her subsequent journey to Basle, the Swiss Headquarters of the Red Cross Society, and really the International Headquarters as well, she says:

"On the fifteenth of July, 1870, France declared war against Prussia. Within three days, a band of agents from the International Committee of Geneva, headed by Dr. Louis Appia (one of the prime movers of the convention), equipped for work and *en route* for the seat of war, stood at the door of my villa inviting me to go with them and take such part as I had taken in our own war. I had not strength to trust for that, and declined with thanks, promising to follow in my own time and way and I did follow within a week. No shot had been fired — no man had fallen. Yet this organized, powerful commission was on its way, with its skilled agents, ready to receive, direct and dispense the charities and accumulations which the generous sympathies of twenty-two nations, if applied to, might place at its disposal. These men had treaty power to go directly on to any field, and work unmolested in full coöperation with the military and commanders-in-chief; their supplies held sacred and their efforts recognized and seconded in every direction by either belligerent army. Not a man could lie uncared for nor unfed. I thought of the Peninsula in McClellan's campaign, of Pittsburg Landing, Cedar Mountain and second Bull Run, Antietam, Old Fredericksburg with its acres of snow-covered and gun-covered glacis, and its fourth-day flag of truce; of its dead, and starving wounded, frozen to the ground, and our commission and their supplies in Washington, with no effective organization to get beyond; of the Petersburg mine, with its four thousand dead and wounded and no flag of truce, the wounded broiling in a July sun, dying and rotting where they fell. I remembered our prisons, crowded with starving men whom all the powers and pities of the world could not reach even with a bit of bread. I thought of the widows' weeds still fresh and dark through all the land, north and south, from the pine to the palm; the shadows on the hearths and hearts over all my country. Sore, broken hearts, ruined, desolate homes! Was this a people to decline a humanity in war? Was this a country to reject a treaty for the help of wounded soldiers? Were these the women and men to stand aloof and consider? I believed if these people knew that the last cloud of war had forever passed from their horizon, the tender, painful, deathless memories of what had been, would bring them in with a force no power could resist. They needed only to know."

Right here, therefore, in addition to her decision to go to the Franco-Prussian front was born Clara Barton's second decision, the decision to introduce the Red Cross into America.

"As I journeyed on and saw the work of these Red Cross societies in the field, accomplishing in four months under their systematic organization what we failed to accomplish in four years without it — no mistakes, no needless suffering, no starving, no lack of care, no waste, no confusion, but order, plenty, cleanliness and comfort wherever that little flag made its way — a whole continent marshaled under the banner of the Red Cross — as I saw all this, and joined and worked in it, you will not wonder that I said to myself 'if I live to return to my country I will try to make my people understand the Red Cross and that treaty.' But I did more than resolve, I promised other nations I would do it, and other reasons pressed me to remember my promise. The Franco-Prussian war and the war of the Commune were both enormous in the extent of their operations and in the suffering of individuals. This great modern International impulse of charity went out everywhere to meet and alleviate its miseries. The small, poor countries gave of their poverty and the rich nations poured out abundantly of their vast resources. The contributions of those under the Red Cross went quietly, promptly, through International responsible channels, were thoughtfully and carefully distributed through well-known agents; returns, accurate to a franc, were made and duly published to the credit of the contributing nations, and the object aimed at was accomplished."

It was always a source of pleasure to Miss Barton to remember that she saw the Red Cross put to the test, participated in its first great triumph and had a vision of its future usefulness. Little wonder that she was unable to withstand its mighty "pull"; little wonder that she felt a return of strength as she saw "Dr. Appia with his trained corps of assistants, fine, sturdy men, on their way to the front" and realized that "not a drop of blood could flow before they would be there to staunch it, not a soldier fall before practiced and well provided hands would be there to gather him up."

"France, Germany and Switzerland," Miss Barton explains, "had been in the International compact for years past, all organized, every town and city with its Red Cross Relief Committee, its well filled workrooms like our relief societies in our war, but all prepared in times of peace and plenty, awaiting the emergency.

"The Swiss headquarters were at Basle, bordering on both France and Germany; and there all the supplies were to be sent and held on call from the hundreds of workers at the fields, for the use of the sick and wounded of either side indiscriminately wherever the need was found greatest. The belligerent nations had each its own headquarters; that of Germany at Berlin, with the Empress Augusta at its head; that of France at Paris, under the auspices of its lovely Empress.

"But you will understand that the International feature of this requires that all contributions from other nations be sent through the International headquarters, hence, no people within the compact except the belligerents, could send direct to either France or Germany, but must correspond with the Central Committee at Geneva, and learn from it the place of greatest need and the proper agents on the spot to whom the consignment should be made. This wise provision both marked and sustained their neutrality.

"Up to this moment, no point beyond Basle had been reached. This was, then, the great central depot of the International Red Cross and it was worth something to have seen it as I saw it in less than two weeks after the sudden declaration, a declaration as unexpected, as if some nation should declare war against us to-morrow.

"My first steps were to the storehouses, and to my amazement, I found there a larger supply than I had ever seen at any one time in readiness for the field at our own sanitary commission rooms in Washington, even in the fourth year of the war; and the trains were loaded with boxes and barrels pouring in from every city, town and hamlet in Switzerland, even from Austria and Northern Italy, and the trained, educated nurses stood awaiting their appointments, each with this badge upon the arm or breast, and every box, package or barrel with a broad bright scarlet cross, which rendered it as safe and sacred from molestation (one might almost say) as the bread and wine before the altar.

"You will conclude that quiet old historic Basle was, by this time, a busy city. It was frightened out of its senses. Bordering on both France and Germany, it lay directly on the possible march of either army on its way to the other; and the moment she shall allow this crossing, her neutrality will be declared broken, and not only Basle, but all Switzerland, will be held in a state of actual war and become common battleground for both.

"I passed a week in that city among this work, to learn it more thoroughly, to be able to judge it in its practical bearings, its merits and demerits, so far as I could, before giving my qualifications and endorsement. You will not wonder that Basle felt her responsibility and trembled for both her own safety and the safety of the State!"

CHAPTER XXIII

"Turn Back! Turn Back! The Prussians are Coming!"

Miss Barton's diary of this time describes the tide of refugees which she encountered at Basle — men and women and children driven from their homes and fleeing the terrors of war. And yet terrible as was this procession — a procession with whose woes Europe has run red and with whose tears it has been bathed from the earliest times till to-day, "it was not," she writes, "too terrifying to one having a good stock of memories!"

"For the last three days," her diary continues, "we have had only news of battles lost by the French. The Prince Royal of Prussia has won a battle at Weissenburg and Saarbrücken, and followed the flying French troops up the Rhine. Yesterday came the news that the Prussians would cross the river. Basle is frightened and sinks powder under her bridge, the old bridge of half stone and half wood, once graced by the clock which ran out an ugly red tongue at Germany at every stroke of its pendulum. The Prussians have destroyed the railroad between Basle and Carlsruhe, thus closing all public conveyance on the German side.

"A dispatch has just been received from the International Committee of the Red Cross at Mülhausen, France, inviting me to come there. Dr. Appia and his noble band of pioneers had evidently passed that way. This would be in a direct line to Strassburg, and the field of Weissenburg, and I have decided to leave by the earliest train next morning.

"As good fortune would have it, there comes to me at this moment a kind featured, gentle-toned, intelligent Swiss girl, who had left the *Canton de Vaud* to go alone to care for the wounded. The society introduced her to me.

"Perhaps it would be well to anticipate so far as to speak of this young lady more fully, for all through you will know her as my faithful

Antoinette — Antoinette Margot,[1] Swiss by birth, French by cultivation, education and habit. The two national characteristics met and joined in her. The enthusiasm of the one, the fidelity of the other, were so perfectly blended and balanced in her, that one could never determine which prevailed. No matter, as both were unquenchable, unconquerable. She was raised in the city of Lyons, France, an only daughter, and at that age, an artist of great note, even in the schools of artistic France. Fairhaired, playful, bright and confiding, she spoke English as learned from books, and selected her forms of expression by inference. One day she made the remark that something was 'unpretty.' Observing a smile on my face, she asked if that were not correct? I replied that we do not say unpretty in English. 'No. But you say unwise, unselfish, unkind and ungrateful, — why not unpretty?' 'I do not know,' I answered. I didn't either.

"There was something in that face to be drawn to 'at sight,' and to her astonishment and delight I told her she might accompany me.

"Scarce was this arrangement completed when breathless messengers rushed to tell us that the French still fled before the troops of the Prince Royal, that the Prussians were marching direct upon the Rhine, if indeed it were not already crossed, and that the French have destroyed their railroad to Strassburg, that the rolling-stock of the road has been run off to save it, and that even the station was closed.

"This was after dark — the news was not of a nature to favor delay. Instead of five o'clock by train next morning, I would start at daybreak by private carriage.

"At length a cocher was found who would undertake the journey — the task of driving to Mülhausen for a consideration which, under the circumstances, it was quite possible for him to obtain. At the appointed hour with some small satchels, the requisite supply of shawls and waterproofs, with my quiet, sensible young companion, I set off once more, shall I say — for 'the front'? That expression was very strange after a lapse of five years, and I had thought never to hear it again in connection with myself.

[1] "In less than one year I fell into the path of the great Franco-German war, and with its brave and beneficent Red Cross went through this. This slender little lady at my right, Mlle. Antoinette Margot, fourteen years younger than now, went with me every step; over broken ranks, through fire and blood, and both came out alive. God knows how. And now, in this year, she has left her beloved France to come and be with me." Miss Barton's tribute to Miss Margot in 1886.

"A mile from Basle, we met the pickets, but passed without serious interruption for the first six miles, when the detentions became longer, and the road lined with fugitives fleeing to Switzerland, entire families, carrying such articles as were possible.

"The better classes in family and public carriages; the next, in farmer and peasant wagons, drawn by horses, oxen, cows, and often the animals of the family accompanying the wagon which contained the most useful articles for an emergency, — kettles, beds and clothing.

"Those who could not afford this style of removal, were wearily but hastily trudging along on foot, carrying in their arms such as their strength would allow, and the tired children plodding along on behind, or drawn in little carts, with bundles of clothing, and bits of bread.

"Sometimes a family was fortunate to have a cow or a goat with them when they had no wagon. Sometimes, after the Bernese custom, a large dog drew the wagon of luggage. But in some manner, all were making on, often in tears, and always with grief in their faces. All day we saw but two carriages going in our direction. But all whom we met looked at us in astonishment. 'The Prussians are coming,' or, — 'There has been a terrible battle and everybody is being killed. *Turn back, turn back !*'

"Sometimes one would be so earnest as to come to the heads of our horses, to urge us to return, and it was not always easy to keep our driver in heart.

"At —— we were met and stopped by a large body of people, the mayor at the head, and our destination inquired, and at the same time, informed that it was exceedingly hazardous to proceed, as great battles were going on at a short distance from Mülhausen, and that the Prussians were crossing the Rhine in great force. But when to all this we replied that we were aware of the state of things, and that was the reason of our going, that we went to care for the wounded of the battles, they all cried with one voice, 'Mon Dieu — God bless you,' and the old white haired mayor led the way to the side of our carriage, to take our hands, exclaiming, 'God preserve and be with you, my children, and He is with you, or you would not be here on this mission.' And the crowd that jostled in the street one after another, followed his example with the tears falling over their faces, even to the little children to whom we reached down our hands to reach theirs, or to touch them as they were held up to us.

MINNIE KUPFER   ANTOINETE MARGOT

Miss Barton's faithful companions in the Franco-Prussian War, as pictured in later life.

"No wonder they wept! Their fathers, sons and brothers would be in the bloody carnage so soon to follow. Already they had bade to, God only knows how many, the last farewell.

"At length, they let go our bridles and we passed on, and with such scenes every moment in some form occurring, we performed the remainder of our journey to Mülhausen.

"We made our way directly to the President of the International Committee of the Red Cross of Mülhausen, Monsieur August Dolfus."

But Miss Barton and her party found no suffering to relieve — no need of their services — Therefore, "on to Strassburg" they cried. This was a journey they were to make against great odds. There was not a vehicle to take them and no driver willing to go towards the awful theater of war, whence came the mad hum and tide of fugitives, with tales of suffering, torture, and death.

Finally a driver did appear — but Miss Barton would not engage him. Her reasons she explains in the following passage:

"In company with our lovely hostess, Madame Dolfus, we went in search of a carriage, but met only the same response. 'There is not a carriage to be had in Mülhausen. Everything has gone to Basle with the fugitives.' At length a man appeared who said he would call a carriage from the country, and start with us at three o'clock next morning. He at first stated his terms by the day, which seemed proper enough, but when asked how much time would be required to perform the journey, he named some four or five days, and when asked his price for the journey, and care for himself and horses, it was something tremendous. This was evidently done with the intention of compelling us back to his proposition by the day and once having us in his power, detain us on the road at pleasure. In every line of his face was written villainy. That low, flat, broad head, projecting chin, greasy, chocolate colored face and the snaky eye boded no good, and great as was my anxiety to proceed, and impossible as it seemed under the circumstances, in a cold drizzling rain, to find another opportunity, this was not to be accepted. Instinctively putting my hand to my throat as in the presence of a murderer, I informed our proposed coachman that I did not desire his services. At first he seemed astonished, next angry, but seeing that neither produced the desired result, he lowered his terms. But getting no response, he fell again, and when I informed him that I did not wish his services at any price, he went outside and waited, certain I should repent and send for him. He reckoned without his host. I may have been mistaken, but I have never been able to rid myself of the conviction that it would have proved our last journey, if that escort had been accepted. He knew we could not be without money, and in all the panic then reigning there would be none to question. He need not even wait to conceal his victims. When discovered, it would only add one more to the tale of murder by the Prussian troops, and probably be just as true as the others."

Just as Miss Barton had about given up hope of securing transportation, she received an offer that seemed almost too good to be true. A well-known man of Mülhausen came to her and explained that he must attempt at whatever risk to take a woman friend to Strassburg the next day. This woman's family needed her. She had become separated from her children by the war and she must get to them. She would like Miss Barton's company.

"Love is braver than war, truer than steel, stronger than fear or danger of death, and while others fled in thousands, this woman turned to face them all in a walled and fortified city, certain of siege," Miss Barton writes.

"This proposition was welcome, and at five o'clock next morning we drove out of Mülhausen with cards and letters to all the world, but nothing sealed.

"Our journey this day was a repetition of the day previous, only less pleasant. The rain fell fitfully all day, the sky was leaden, and the fugitives looked darker and more distressed than ever, not a man at work in his fields. All was consternation and terror. The most terrifying reports were continually poured into our ears. We were told that the Prussian troops had cut off the hands of a French vender who was captured carrying water to the soldiers, that they had cut the throats of the peasants as they passed, and that they slew all the wounded prisoners, that they set fire to the houses, and shot and bayoneted the inhabitants as they rushed out, and scores of other things equally preposterous.

"It is all the time to be borne in mind, that with the exception of a few scouts, and here and there a mounted guard, there were yet no Prussians on the French side of the river Rhine. All this vast talk of the army having crossed over was purely imaginary, existing only in their excited terrors, but it was useless to expostulate. In their fright and ignorance, they neither could nor would be convinced and on they rushed.

"To the enthusiastic Frenchman, France is the world, and to the illiterate peasantry, all places outside of France must be very near it. They are a home staying as well as a home loving people.

"We hastened to our rendezvous, and found a carriage had really been obtained for the next station of importance, Schlettstadt, a distance of some twenty miles.

"This journey, like the other, was performed in the rain, and without the appearance of any enemy. But at each place, we found it difficult to convince the inhabitants that every other town was not in a great state of defense, and determined to resist the Prussians at all hazards, each believing itself to be the only unguarded, unarmed and unresisting city in all the land, all confident of the entire success of France, that she could not be overcome, and that any reverses she might meet, were simply intentional, places not worth retaining; but that somewhere the armies of France were, or would be, in a day or two, astonishing the world with their marvelous victories. And yet each particular village or city thought it would perhaps be just as well off belonging to the German states, as to France.

"It was a study of people never to be forgotten, and never to be as well learned, perhaps, in any other way, or under any other circumstances than by this slow travel making one's way through the country at a time like this.

"The peasants stopped to speak to us on the way and each spoke from his heart. The ideas associated with war in the minds of these people are something beyond description.

"At half past three, we found ourselves driven into the town of Schlettstadt, and alighted at the door of an inn. Ah, what a babel was that entrance room. About twenty men sat around their beer tables and discussed the situation. I tried in my confused mind to estimate how much more talking twenty women would have done. It was impossible to distinguish our own voices. We did not try, but simply waited. At length the landlord appeared and hastily withdrew us into a portion of the house, and here again we waited, and asked the probability of the passage of any train of cars, as we knew this town lay on the Paris and Strassburg Railroad.

"Oh, no, that was not possible. The Prussian army lay between there and Strassburg. It would be quite impossible for us to reach there by any conveyance; we could only go about twenty miles further, when we should be stopped. But having heard this every twenty miles all the way from Basle, it was growing an old story, to which we paid little heed, and stepping out into the street to look about us, we heard a familiar whistle in the distance. Holding our breaths, it repeated itself, nearer and nearer till we could not be mistaken.

"It was the train for Strassburg!

"We rushed to the station and saw it come in. Surely enough we were not mistaken. Here was a long train coming up from the central portion of France, and bound to Strassburg, not a regular but a wild train! None had preceded it and none was to follow it! It would unload and return directly. It had most probably supplies for the garrison, but no one asked any questions except if we could go on it. A hasty 'Oui, oui,' and in two minutes our satchels and selves were transferred from our noisy inn, to a seat in a rough train, which moved on as if it had no time to lose. Every one may know how it seems to be overtaken by a train. But this seemed like being overtaken by a railroad! Two hours of this speed accomplished as much for us, as all the day before it, and at six o'clock we drew cautiously before the iron track and closed gates of the citadel of Strassburg.

"Still drizzling rain, mud half over shoes, and a crowd of people, carriages, carts, milk women by the hundred, loads of wood, peasants, wagons piled high with vegetables and fruit for the supplying of a city of 80,000 all huddled and waiting in a line, at least a half a mile in length, which only foot passengers could pass.

"Wearily waiting in mist and rain; wearily watching in doubt and pain; leaving our train with satchels in hand, we became foot passengers, and walked, or rather waded on to the head of this motley line, up to the gates, under the ramparts, beyond which no one might pass till the commandant of the garrison ordered that these massive gates turn on their hinges. And here we waited, watching the measured tread of the sentinel upon the heights above, where the old grim ramparts, bare and brown, kept faithful guard over the frightened town — waiting, waiting till the middle of the second hour, when there came a rush of horsemen and a clang of steel up to the other side of the gates.

"The ponderous bolts withdrew and with a heavy creak they fell back and the crowd commenced to surge through, across the moat filled to the brim, over the drawbridge, through the stone archway at least forty rods, winding and dark. At length out into the day, among soldiers and citizens, foot and horse, vehicles of all kinds, bayonets and bugles, in all the confusion of an armed city awaiting siege.

"It was time for a hotel, supper and sleep, and it was something astonishing the journey we had performed that day under all its difficulties, changing carriages every few miles, riding against the report of the enemy all the way, intercepted at every little village and cross road, detained for hours at a time for conveyance, and yet we had made our way from Mülhausen to Strassburg, a distance of seventy-two miles, in time for supper!

CHAPTER XXIV

STRASSBURG

"I SENT my card to the American Consulate, saying I would call the next morning at 12 o'clock," continues Miss Barton.

"This was my first sight of historic old Strassburg, and you will not think me too derelict in my duty, if on my way to the American Consulate next morning, I linger a little longer in the principal streets for a view of the quaint, queer buildings, go some squares out of my way for a glance at the grand old cathedral monument 1000 years old when our nation was born; its fine red sandstone elaborately carved to the very top of its dome, 495 feet from the pavement; its famous clock; its stained glass windows of the middle-ages before the art was lost; and the meditative storks perched upon the chimneys with their rude nests built roughly upon the tops, and their young training themselves for their long first journey to Africa for the winter.

"During all this walk the rain fell continually, often in torrents, and we stood in the long covered arches to escape it. Take cold, did you say? Oh yes! But those were the days when colds didn't count.

"To my surprise I found the American Consulate profusely decorated with U. S. flags, in honor of my visit, and the residence of both the consul and the vice-consul were the same.

"An exclamation of surprise drew from them the fact that both were soldiers of the Union, although both Germans."

Miss Barton's story of her departure from Strassburg is interestingly told in her diary:

"Battles and rumors of battles had filled our ears for the last two weeks. But at length we received a report from a source which could be trusted. A messenger from the Red Cross Committee came to say that the Germans were over in force, that the troops of Frederick, Prince Royal of Prussia, have met the French at Hagenau, and they are fighting like demons.

"The obliging consul offered himself as an escort if we could get out of the city, which we decided to attempt at half past four next morning, this being one of the two times in twenty-four hours in which the gates were opened. There were great numbers of German-Americans in the city, summer visitors and travelers — wild at the thought of being shut up and bombarded, and who besieged the consulate in the name of the Americans for help to get out of Alsace. The consul would attempt to take out a large omnibus full to the German lines that morning. We left the consulate, in a pouring rain as usual, at four o'clock.

"It was a question if the Prussian lines could be passed, but this proved to be only a secondary question, for a drive of five minutes brought us up to the eternal gates of Strassburg. Here were French lines to pass first, and a waiting crowd of persons scarce inferior to that we had seen on the other side at our entrance, and our omnibus constantly filling.

"We wait an hour, two hours; it is six o'clock. Such crying of children! Such groaning of persons not naturally compressible! We drive to another gate and wait another hour, always in the rain. Five ladies leave. We scarcely miss them. Almost as dense as before! We drive back again, and wait another hour. It is eight o'clock.

"The consul, to make more room and to be free, had mounted a young and almost untrained horse, evidently not a society animal, manifesting a most marked distrust of men and things, and was prancing about in a kind of anxious disgust, and the vice-consul, too kindly gallant to leave us, followed us about from gate to gate with bread and coffee. The consul had been a surgeon, the vice-consul a chaplain in our war. The latter had dressed himself in his uniform of army blue which he had made new at the close of the war to take home with him.

"There was something in all these unexpected surroundings that carried me back to the brave loyal old days, and set me to wondering if I could ever love other days, and honor other wars as I did those.

"The military situation of the city deserves a passing notice. Three days previous a detachment of Prussian Cavalry had appeared before the gates, and demanded the surrender of the city, and had met the refusal with the assurance that the city would be bombarded in twenty-four hours. This naturally filled the inhabitants with terror. The attempts of the military to quiet the fears of the people were most ludicrous. They placed at all the street corners, printed placards to the effect that no one need fear as the city was strongly defended, and the troops would fight till the last loaf was gone, and the last soldier slain.

"This was the thing most of all to be dreaded by the inhabitants. It really mattered little to them, individually, in whose hands they were, so long as they were at peace and out of danger. But it did matter much, if a few thousand troops, well protected and bomb proof, could close the gates, retire behind their entrenchments, having permitted the enemy to approach within easy range, and hold the city under bombardment while its defenseless inhabitants had nowhere to retire for safety, except, perhaps, to their cellars while their houses burned down over their heads, consuming them in the flame and burying them in the ashes.

"The tone of these military assurances was not consoling to the people of Strassburg, who went on saying bitterly: 'A fine protection indeed. In times of peace we were never burdened with less than a garrison of 40,000 troops, and compelled to suffer all the annoyance growing out of it. But now, in war, and active danger, we are left with not more than five to six thousand men, just enough to draw the fire of the enemy, and place us in all the attitude of war and its accompanying perils, with none of its protections.' The military claimed as many as 11,000 troops within the defenses of Strassburg, but the people were confident that the withdrawal of half that number would leave their fortress bare and guns unmanned, and from the bottom of their honest and terror-stricken hearts, they wished the withdrawal could be effected.

"As was suspected, our delay in getting out was occasioned by the density of the fog and mist, the military hesitating to open the gates lest the Prussian force might be massed near, concealed by the fog, waiting to rush in.

"At length the clouds lifted, and partially dispelled the fears as well.

"The crowd commenced, like 'poor Joe' to 'move on,' and we along with it, finally out of the confines of Strassburg and on our way to the lines of the enemy."

Strassburg did not need Miss Barton now. She could return there when famine and suffering came, but for the present her place was at the front. Hagenau was her objective point, the storm center of a terrific and deadly struggle.

"We had the United States flag at our front," Miss Barton's narrative proceeds, "and the first sentry halted us to learn what it was. When informed, he promptly disputed it. He had been in Mexico, and Guatemala and Australia and the Sandwich Islands, and it was not the American flag at all. Reference to a chart of flags convinced him, and we passed. But this made us aware of a great mistake we had committed.

"In our hurry of getting off in the rain and darkness of the early morning, we had forgotten our International Red Cross Flag, and all our insignia. There was no return, — as well seek to go back through the gates of death. We must trust to luck."

At the demand for the Red Cross insignia by the keen acute sentry, Miss Barton retired, seized the bow of red ribbon, without which color she was seldom seen, and twisted it into a red cross which with the thread and needle taken from her pocket she sewed upon her arm.

"The next sentinel, about a league from Strassburg, recognized our flag, saluted it, and did not even halt us. A mile farther, more pickets, a little more detention, but permitted to pass. Evidently, they all realized that there was a net beyond, fine enough to catch and strong enough to hold us, which we also suspected.

"Three miles farther on, we came into it, a full German camp! Troops without number, horses and wagons at rest, tents pitched, and the scarlet and gold of Baden floating gracefully on the breeze! These were the forces of the Grand Duke and here the bayonets were crossed in the center of the road before us.

"The troops were drilling in a broad field at the right, and just at this particular juncture, the band sounded the Long Roll. If you could have seen the Consul's horse! John Gilpin was not to be spoken of after that.

"This stroke of diplomacy left us quite alone in our dilemma. The numerous occupants of the omnibus talked much German to the sentry to little purpose. We were ordered back. Somebody must do something, and I asked for the 'Colonel commanding.' He came, a princely man with a fine Saxon face. He advanced, struck an attitude, and stood before me in perfect silence.

"'You speak English, I presume, Colonel?'

"'A little, madame,' evidently a trifle flattered by the presumption. I explained our desires. He replied with dignified courtesy that he respected my mission, and regarded the wishes of the other persons, but the orders were most strict. 'No person could pass and repass the lines.'

"'We are an army entire, madame, and proceed to the bombardment of Strassburg. You are free to return but not to advance, save on one condition.'

"'What may that be, Colonel?'

"'Capture, madame! You can pass our lines, but you will be a prisoner from that moment.'

"'Do you mean by this, Colonel, that we shall be thrown into confinement and held there?'

"'Oh, no, madame,' he answered, returning my incredulous smile. "'Oh, no, you will be prisoners of war, free within our lines, but not to pass out of them till the close of the war.'

"'The wounded will be within your lines?'

"'We hope so, madame, as we intend to lose no fields.'

"'And your lines extend from Belgium to Switzerland?'

"'Yes, — and from Berlin surely to here?'

"'Certainly.'

"'That is space enough for me, Colonel. Let me in.'

"'You accept the conditions, then?'

"'Fully, Colonel, and for us all.'

"The bayonets were withdrawn, our horses moved on, and for the first time in my life, I was a prisoner.

"Just at the juncture the consul hove in sight with his awkward colt, shying sidelong, crossfooting, giving the impression of six or seven legs in place of four. His official position took him through — the consul I mean — not the colt. *He* didn't appear to hold any position.

"And here were we, almost in sound of the guns of the Prince Royal at Hagenau!"

Miss Barton was to make Carlsruhe, three hours distant from Strassburg, where there was a huge depot for the wounded, her central station, going out from it in all directions on her errands of mercy to the wounded. The Duchess of Baden, the wife of the Grand Duke of Baden, the friend and first great donor of the International Red

Cross, was also at Carlsruhe, where one saw "the beautiful new standard of the Red Cross and the scarlet and gold of Baden floating together in the sky."

"The beloved Grand Duchess Louise of Baden, was the only daughter of the Prussian King and coming Emperor. She was untiring," Miss Barton declared, "in the conduct of the noble society she had already formed and patronized. Her many and beautiful castles, with their magnificent grounds, throughout all Baden, were transformed into military hospitals, and her entire court with herself at its head, formed into a committee of superintendence and organization for relief.

"I have seen a wounded Arab from the French armies, who knew no word of any language but his own, stretch out his arms to her in adoration and blessings as she passed his bed.

"Switzerland which received the entire fleeing fugitives from Alsace-Lorraine, and the outcome of Strassburg after bombardment, and into which Bourbaki threw his whole army in defeat, not only nourished these, but she gave of her money and material as from a bottomless well; there was no end of her bounty."

While at Carlsruhe, Miss Barton was asked to stay at the palace of the Duchess, but except for visits there she declined, preferring to be with the poor and in the besieged cities or on the field with the wounded. "I stood with the besieging armies of the Grand Duke of Baden," she explained, "while they bombarded Strassburg for 100 days and nights, and the ground on which that splendid besieging army was camped, was level as a lawn, and fertile as a well kept garden. And poor Strassburg, shattered and scathed as it was!" She spent many days in the society of the Grand Duchess, who, as she later wrote, conceived "great affection and admiration" for Miss Barton. "How shall I forget," she says in a letter written in 1912, "what she has been to us here in the year 1870, helping us in such a wonderful way during the time of war we had to go through with then! She was one of those who understood fully the meaning of the Red Cross and who knew full well how to put in action the great and beautiful, though difficult, duties the Red Cross involved in itself. Next to this, my personal relations with dear Miss Clara Barton have been most particular ones."

CHAPTER XXV

The Surrender of Metz, Sedan, and Strassburg

To all Europe Clara Barton was the impersonation of American mercy in the Civil War and her name was widely revered for the work she had done. The wonderful development of the Sanitary Commission, the perfected system of ambulances, the nursing, — in all of these the court circles were much interested. The Duke of Baden, whose invitation to the palace at Carlsruhe she had at length for a time accepted, discussed these topics with her eagerly. The work of the Red Cross in Germany was also doubtless discussed, inasmuch as they had an excellent opportunity to watch its progress at Carlsruhe. Already it was evident that the Society was becoming deeply rooted in German soil — a fact clearly shown by the operations at Berlin, the great center of the movement from which the supplies were sent out. Here they had 200 salaried persons employed, to say nothing of the hundreds who gladly gave their services free.

But discussion and "talk," interesting as they might be, were not for Miss Barton when there was work to be done, and on August 6, 1870, we find her again following the cannon on the battle fields of Hagenau and Wörth. "I saw the Prussian army hurled upon the French at Hagenau and Wörth, till the soft earth for miles, was ploughed with cannon and planted with slain," she says.

After the battle of Saarbrücken, the French, defeated on both wings, retreated, losing six thousand prisoners. On August 18 came Gravelotte, where two hundred and eighty thousand Germans were pitted against one hundred and sixty thousand Frenchmen who were driven back to Metz. This main French army, outmarched, was thus cut off from its base and fell back to the Metz fortress. By September 1, the major part of the French forces had been bottled up in the fort.

August 30 began a decisive defeat for Marshal MacMahon. The Germans surprised the army at night while circling about the sleeping French soldiers and planted cannon which at daybreak belched forth, and eighty thousand capitulated.

The second French army, cut off from Paris, had subsequently been surrounded and drawn into the fortress of Sedan. A furious onslaught followed, the fortress finally surrendering. After this battle of September 1, when the entire fortress was captured, Clara Barton was upon the field in person, ministering to the thousands of wounded and mangled.

At length, September 28, Strassburg itself gave in. Returning from one of the battle fields in front of another sieged town in Alsace-Lorraine, Miss Barton was as always urged to stay with the Grand Duchess of Baden in the ducal castle. The September afternoon of the surrender of Strassburg to the Grand Duchess's husband, the Grand Duke of Baden, Miss Barton was sitting in a balcony chatting with the Grand Duchess. The heat was intense. Both were in the shade of the palace walls. Suddenly in a whirl of dust appeared a breathless courier from the siege line. "Strassburg has fallen" was all he could cry — then he fell upon his knees at the foot of the balcony, overcome from running in the heat. All along Miss Barton, pained by the distress of the beleaguered city, had determined to go back and enter Strassburg and relieve the besieged French citizens in their starvation, nakedness, and wounds. And so, when Strassburg threw open its gates to the Grand Duke of Baden, she at once put this determination into effect, crossing the Rhine and entering with the German army.

A slight, delicate figure in a plain dark dress, she made her way through shattered streets into the bombarded homes. In cellars where they were hidden, in the damp and mold, her eye found out twenty thousand starving, half-naked women and children and aged men. Many were sick and wounded from shot and shell. The city numbered among its victims many mothers with their breasts shot off, many little children maimed. It swarmed with twenty thousand of them crawling forth from dark holes more like skeletons than human forms of flesh and blood. Fathers and sons and husbands had been to a man in the conscript ranks of the French army and were dead on the field or in German prisons. It was estimated that many thousands of the inhabitants of Strassburg were without the shadow of a roof over their heads, an ounce of food or an article of clothing save that which they had rescued from burning buildings, and all were without either work or pay.

As one means of practically helping them help themselves, Miss Barton drew upon her own resources, purchased materials, and set two hundred and fifty poor women to work making articles of clothing. There was no building to use as warehouse or workroom. But this made no difference. She noted a huge rock and established first headquarters there. For eight months, 1500 garments a week were turned out, a large workroom being finally obtained. When finally a workroom was procured in a spacious structure so rushing was the distribution of garments to sew that the expert men cutters, up to their knees the first day in the masses of cut-out cloth, found their feet clear the morning of the next day and all the cloth taken by the mothers of Strassburg as fast as they could cut it.[1]

An eyewitness's view of Miss Barton at Strassburg has been preserved in a partly finished painting by Antoinette Margot, who had been, as Miss Barton noted, a French artist of merit, before she took her with her to the German sieges. Miss Margot knew Clara Barton's work from day to day for three years, and thus perpetuated her station at her daily round of duty in Strassburg as the siege lifted. She caught her in this picture with her head turned away to a baby in a woman's arms. Women lean forward toward her to catch her words. Children are clinging to her skirts. One little orphan boy, half afraid, was lifting a corner of her gown to his lips. Her dress in this picture is green — a favorite color of Miss Barton at the time. Indeed it was often in her early life. "When Clara goes to town to buy a brown dress," Miss Barton's grandniece Myrtis has related (quoting her grandaunt Sally), "I know she will get it, for Clara always does what she says, but one way or another, that dress always changes to green, before she can get home."

To Miss Barton, a wounded Frenchman was the same as a wounded German. Her charity, like her Christianity, was wide. Herself a Protestant, the ministering of veiled Sisters of Mercy engaged in their work of rescue she saw with joy. But one hundred days and nights are a long time to endure the terrors of a siege, and before the German army entered, the Sisters of Mercy had long passed the limit

[1] Told Mrs. Marion Balcom Bullock in 1875, at North Grafton, upon Miss Barton's return from the Franco-Prussian War.

From original picture of Marion Balcom Bullock

CLARA BARTON IN HER WORKROOMS AFTER THE SIEGE OF STRASSBURG

of human aid. Even horses and animals that had not been eaten had died, fodder long ago having been exhausted and the poor beasts left chewing at one another's tails and hides.

"Saturday at 2 P.M. we all started for Strassburg and reached there — that ruined city at 5 o'clock." Thus begins a paragraph of an interesting letter. "We saw the work rooms used by Clara. We saw also garments that had been cut and made there — We lunched with Mr. Kruger and family and then rode two hours among the awfully destroyed portions of the bombarded city. — I could not help an ugly feeling toward the Prussians — How merciless they had been — Acres and acres were wholly in ruins in this city of 80,000 people — not a house fully uninjured. In Mr. Kruger's house we saw several balls lodged in the walls and doors —The people's hatred of their conquerors was very universal, we are told." [1]

Hit by the many thousands of shells dropped in Strassburg in the hundred-day siege, Miss Barton saw, as she entered, building after building but a heap of ruins. She must begin to rehabilitate and reclothe the thousands crawling torn and tattered from their mole-like holes in cellars over which most of the houses were riddled or burned. This was why no house or hall was possible when on a big flat rock she established headquarters and gave out supplies to the crowding victims of the siege.

Miss Barton worked along with Miss Margot for some forty days. She then returned across the Rhine to tell the story to the Grand Duchess. So impressed was the Duchess that she followed Miss Barton back to the distressed city with innumerable boxes of supplies, groups of noble women assistants, and more money than could be used.

As practical as she was heroic, Miss Barton at once saw that unless a system was devised, the twenty thousand poor would be pauperized and supported in idleness. So after a time she boldly wrote the Grand Duchess: "You are making paupers of all Strassburg with your generosity: send me materials rather than clothing that I may hire them to be made up here and thus create an industry for my people. They were not beggars as French, and we must not make them so as Germans."

She, therefore, asked for cloth for thirty thousand garments to give

---

[1] Personal account of Mrs. Joseph Sheldon.

the people work. The work would mean wages. The wages would
mean self-support and self-respect. The Grand Duchess, with her
usual keenness of judgment, responded, and Miss Barton helped lead
the city back into a state of industry, society, and order.

The type of constructive work in making these thousands of garments is well described in a letter written later by Miss Barton (August
20, 1871) to Miss Annie Childs of Worcester. In it after a playful
apology she gives a cheery, vivid personal sketch of herself in the
midst of the poverty-stricken sewing women of shattered Strassburg.

"Lyons, France, August 20, 1871.
"My dear Annie:
"If I were to make an apology as long as my offence, I could write
nothing else, but I don't like apologies. You don't either, do you?

"Then let me hasten to proclaim myself an idle, lazy, procrastinating,
miserable do nothing, and good for nothing — if that isn't enough I
leave the sentence open for you to finish, and I sign it squarely when
you have done, and call it 'quits'! But really it has been too bad I
have neglected everybody in general, not you in particular. I thought
I was too busy to write. I don't suppose I was, only that I didn't
employ my time well. I know this is often so, and perhaps always.
I wish I had been better educated in this regard as well as every other.
If you are ever married, as you doubtless will be, and have a family
of 8 or 10 children, I beg you will make it a specialty in their several
educations that they be taught to do things in the proper time. You
will do me the favor to remember this as one of my efforts for the good
of humanity.

"I wanted all last winter to tell you about my 'dressmaking' and
describe to you my 'shop.' I knew it would interest you if no one else.
Now wasn't that the last thing you would have thought of, that I should
come to Europe and set up dressmaking and French dressmaking at
that. I knew the fact would be a little surprise to most of my old
friends who knew me best, but to you I imagine it a matter of bewilder-
ing astonishment. Well you should have seen the patterns! 'Did I
have patterns?' Didn't I? And didn't I cut them myself? And
didn't I direct all the making until I had imparted my wonderful art
to others. And you think my garments were fearfully and wonderfully
made? Well, that opinion comes of your being an 'old maid' and so

particular. I assure you, Miss Anna Childs, that they were nice garments, and prettily cut, and well made and I found them in excellent demand. Everybody wanted them. And never a word of complaint of the price; everybody seemed to be perfectly convinced that they were cheap enough at my first offer. I had ten young girls (like your dressmakers) and from one to three men tailors, who worked twelve hours a day, but only with the shears, never an hour's sewing, and no one sewed at my 'shop' only those who must be taught to take something out and do it over. And we made dresses and sacques, and petticoats and chemises and aprons and hoods, mittens and pantaloons, vests, blouses, shirts, sacks of all kinds of material, and all sizes that ever the tiniest baby grew to, and yes, such lots of things for babies, little dresses, little bonnets, cloaks, blankets, 2000 garments every week. I don't think they were gored and flounced and frilled as much as yours, Miss Annie Childs, but they were strong and warm and handsome. It is true all my seamstresses had not such nimble delicate fingers as one might desire for the finest work. They wore very large thimbles, sometimes, but there were plenty of small fingers in the family. They came very gladly twice a week to see me, and showed me with great pride their successful efforts. Always the work came home in the market basket and always that same basket would be loaded the other way with bread, and a little meat if it were possible. It was such a comfort to see them week by week grow better clothed, themselves and the children, till by and by a woman and a baby came to look only like a big and little bundle of the same clothing she carried in her basket. And all the working people of the city came to look like walking bundles of the same clothing. To be sure it took away something from the picturesque style of the city as I first saw it, when at least 10,000 human beings were perfectly arrayed for models for the painter and the sculptor. I admit that it was highly artistic, but I thought it a *peu trop* for the season, considering that the earliest snows had commenced to fall. Ah, but don't you wish now that you had come and worked at the head of my 'shop.' Don't I wish it? More than once I sighed in my inmost soul for you. How rich I should have been with you at my side — just think of it.

"I shall write to Fannie [1] some time when 'I hain't told all the news'

<hr />

[1] Mrs. Fannie Childs Vassall, who in Worcester has preserved many such precious unpublished letters.

M

to you. Please hand her this if she looks patient and strong enough to stand it."

While thus employed in giving new courage, and material blessings as well, to the people of Strassburg, Miss Barton kept her eye on other localities about to suffer as Strassburg had. For example there was Metz, besieged by the army of the king and Moltke.

Very soon, on October 27, came the surrender of Metz, before which Miss Barton had been with the wounded in the fierce mad fighting of the August dog-days and to which she now went again. "I saw the whole city reeling from hunger," she says, "I saw General Changarnier bear a flag of truce to Prince Frederick and say to him in a broken voice, 'I hope you may never see the misery and suffering which I have seen in Metz."

From Metz, Miss Barton returned to Strassburg to continue her reconstruction of society there. With the coming of winter, intense cold was added to the other discomforts of the people. For years the weather had not been so severe as it was that winter. It is significant to see how the little woman who had come to Europe for rest, supposedly an invalid, loses all thought of herself in her "passion for humanity," and arctic-like though the atmosphere is, does not cease her activities in the interests of "her people."

Belfort,[1] the last French fortress, had held out bravely, never surrendering until Bourbaki's army, one hundred thousand strong, after suffering horribly, had taken every able-bodied man and escaped over the mountains. To Belfort Miss Barton went, bringing relief to its citizens as she had taken relief into the wrecks of the other cities of the war. But by Christmas of 1870 she had returned to Strassburg and was once more overseeing the women's workroom where thousands of garments were made.

During all these campaigns there was evidenced Miss Barton's remarkable power of mind and spirit over weak nerves and body. But occasionally the body so broken in the Civil War would intrude itself. At one time for example she speaks of her inability to sleep. "The greatest obstacle I meet in the way of a full restoration to health," she says in a letter home, "is my utter inability to get sleep. An average of five hours is the maximum. When I was stronger, this would do me. I could run my machine at full speed upon this

[1] See pages 176–177.

power and did it for years, but now the belts are slack and the wheels slip and I lose so much power that my pond is all drawn off."

"But there are many bright spots," she confides to Mrs. Vassall in a letter describing the holiday season in Strassburg. "It was Christmas eve, 5 o'clock, cold as Greenland! I had sent my assistants home the day before to enjoy a few days of leisure with their friends. I was writing at this farthest end of my large room from which only white curtains separate and inclose me in my little country room. The postman's rap at my door caused me to look up, and through the curtains, I could discern a glimmer of myriad of lights like stars but moving from point to point as if the firmament was not satisfied with its arrangement of its luminaries and sought an opportunity to rearrange them.

"Startled at first, I rose from my seat to rush out, but suddenly remembering the evening and the occasion, it occurred to me that my presence at that special instant would not be desired.

"The walking out revealed a Christmas tree in full blaze all for myself. It had been arranged and left by my good ladies before their departure and with instructions to the domestics to produce and light it at five o'clock in the evening. It abounded in fruit, flowers and mosses and some nice little things which their good hearts had dictated for my comfort; and so in the delicate shadows, falling like tracery upon the white cover, spread beneath its branches, I sat down and read your letter. I could not truly say that my hand did not sometimes brush across my eyes."

CHAPTER XXVI

AT THE SIEGE OF PARIS AND THE COMMUNE

EARLY in January, 1871, news reached Miss Barton of another sphere of suffering and pain. As far back as September, 1870, the Germans had begun the siege of Paris. This lasted for more than four months, but finally, on January 28, Paris capitulated — though peace was not declared until May 10.

With the victorious Prussian legions Clara Barton entered Paris afoot and alone except for her faithful friend, Anna Zimmerman. Her name was now a household word among the Germans and she was given everywhere the right of way. But she could not well ride, as all the horses in the environs had long since been eaten by the starving citizens.

The first thing with which she was impressed was the fact that the survivors were terribly in need of clothes. The winter had been the severest the people had known for a quarter of a century, and the suffering was widespread. She therefore made her way through the wretched streets to the Mayor, who had been reinstated to his office.

"Mayor, I have come," she said bravely, "to help you. I have forty thousand garments outside the city and plenty of money." The garments were those made by the starving women of Strassburg.

The United States not being a party to the Genevan Convention of the Red Cross, the American ship from Boston, with its great cargo sent by the American Republic, had been consigned to no agency able to care for it at once. But at Montbèliard, Miss Barton had finally opened a channel for distribution of these supplies. Now it was available and its generous stores were at her hand.

By September 4, 1870, at the news of the defeat of the French, the third Republic had been founded, and against the Republic on the 18th of March, 1871, the Commune broke forth. By May, the Commune had only just been put down. Buildings were still smoking from its fires. Hundreds were yet waiting in prison to be shot. The mobs of Paris were still so eager for bread and clothes, that they overcame the police. It was into such chaos as this Miss Barton, friend of the populace, appeared with her usual supplies. The minds of those among whom she walked were changed. "God! It is an angel," was the exclamation with which they broke forth.

"I saw Paris,' wrote Miss Barton, "when the Commune fell and the army of Versailles shot down its victims on the streets by the ghastly glare of blazing palaces, and I thanked God that there was never anything in America with which this could be compared."

Miss Barton's work of reconstruction and mercy in Paris was all done through the channels of the Red Cross, which she had come to prize deeply. Writing of this she said: "When the Siege of Paris was at hand, the Committee threw a commission into Brussels, charged with the direction and help of flying hospitals. Nine committees were established in the provinces with power to act for the central committee, and to write the people for help. Meanwhile the Red Cross in Paris did its utmost to investigate the distress there, and to prepare for the result of the siege. History has recorded the sufferings, the horrors of misery, that accompanied and followed that siege, but history can never relate what wretchedness was averted, what agonies were alleviated, what multitudes of lives were saved by the friends and effort of the relief societies. What the State of France must have been without the merciful help of the Red Cross, imagination does not picture. After the armistice was signed, there were removed from Paris, under the auspices of the relief societies, ten thousand wounded men, who otherwise must have lingered in agony, or died from want of care; and there were brought back by them to French soil, nine thousand more who had been cared for in German hospitals."

Miss Barton stayed in Paris until late in the summer of 1871, when she made a trip to Lyons from which, on August 20, she wrote to Miss Annie Childs. In this letter one sees her lack of sympathy with certain superficialities of the French nature — though at the same time it is evident that she feels no less keenly for them in the suffering which they have endured in the war:

"When I left Strassburg, I went to Paris and after six weeks there, distributing clothing and money, I left and came to Lyons to visit a family of one of the young ladies who have aided me twice since the war commenced and I have remained here about as long as I was in Paris. But am ready to leave and shall go again this week to Paris for a day or two to meet some parties of Americans who will be there on their way home and from there I am to go as I have been once into the central eastern portion of France to :ee the places and peoples who have been much destroyed by the war and sieges. I have no idea how much time I shall consume there. I must judge this by the condition I find the people in. I am almost tired of France and long for Germany or something which is solid and Saxon. There is no truth, no fixedness of purpose, nothing reliable, nothing sensible in France, and it only disgusts one that they have always claimed the leadership of the world and that so stupidly it has been conceded to them. I do hope the German bayonets have punched a hole in that bubble large enough to burst it. It is certainly time. If they were even *neat*, I would not complain so much of them, but they are such a dirty race of people — dirty, but fashionable. One gets tired of this. Now you will see from this that it is a real merit in me to work for the French. I do it out of pity and charity towards suffering humanity — because they needed it and not because I gratify my love or my taste by it. I do neither. I think it right to do so or I would not touch it, I˙do assure you."

Again in a second letter to Miss Childs, written but a few weeks later, Miss Barton gives further impressions of the French people:

"I am well aware that in the expressions of my opinion I shall sadly cross swords with all fashionable travelers of my country, and even those who have resided for years in the fine cities of France. They will feel an honest indignation at my assertions (if they were ever to know them) and I can understand that perfectly well and respect them for it, but we have not seen the country under the same phases. They, as all others who are in a country or a family to be *entertained*, have seen the elegant and best side, the side made to be shown and seen. Paris is lovely, nowhere on the face of the earth perhaps can one find richer appointments or perhaps be so well served; all this is lovely, beautiful. It is not with this that I differ. But I speak of the whole people; when one shall lay off the robes of the pleasure seeker and traveler and work among the people, see them in their homes from North to South and from East to West of the country, see them crushed down by the bayonets of their own Government, driven by its taxes into hovels which must not admit air and light, for the tax on doors and windows, devoured by vermin and find seventy out of every hundred, who can neither read nor write the name they bear, one cannot help question, if there be not some other standard by which to estimate France than by the Hotels and Boulevards of Paris; another class of people than its polished gentry and its well trained supple servants whose business it is to make you so perfectly comfortable that you forget everything but *them*, and *your own* luxurious comfort.   One questions if an honest-hearted American could desire longer to blind the eyes and follow the old infatuation of aping France as a nation and a people in all we do and say and think.   It is this 'bubble' that I am glad has burst in the eyes of our own people, for their good, not that I love France less, and rejoice in its calamities, but that I love America more, and rejoice in its escape for which I pray."

Paris on September 17, 1871, is described by Miss Barton in a letter to her sister Sally.   Between its lines we hear the last shots of the Commune.   We also are made to realize to what a degree Miss Barton's health must have improved.   We learn that an American friend has been wounded and her studio blown up during an explosion of 50,000 pounds of powder — and yet Miss Barton is not planning a retreat to rest and quiet, but rather she is considering giving herself to the service in northern France, devastated by the war. She looks again askance at southern France and betrays a bit of prejudice perhaps against the people there, a feeling due no doubt to her long German residence.

"Nine years ago this very hour I was making gruel at Antietam and the days are not unlike, bright and clear, but that day had some things which this has not, thank God; although I am in the heart of Paris, there is less smoke and noise.   Ah, yes, and less of blood and death.   Still it is not all peace and happiness here, and many wait to die.   The powers that be still claim their victims, and one by one, and ten by ten, they will march before the guns, and sink to graves as bloody and less honored than the little mounds of Antietam.   How long that seems and what armies and how much of war I have seen since, what thousands of marching troops, what fields of slain, what prisons, what hospitals, what ruins, what cities in ashes, what hunger and nakedness, what orphanage, what widowhood, what wrongs and what vengeance. And yet one lives and laughs as if nothing had happened and thanks good fortune that it is as well as it is.

"And especially am I thankful that I have at last got a living line, a real flesh and blood word from you, you who have been only a memory, a myth to me for almost eight months and all I could learn was that everybody was 'glad' you had good care. Well this was consoling, I admit, but at the same time I confess it was a trifle puzzling —

"Now indeed I am glad that you had good care and I know that you did if you had Fannie and Ber to look after you and I hope some one will take care of them if ever they need it, 'which, Oh Lord' I hope they won't. By this time I think of you in Washington, the hot weather passing by and some little indications of returning life through the city. I am not certain if I have sent you a line since I have been in Paris this time, but I think so. I have made a practice of crowding a little slip into all the letters I have sent home of late and I think one went in Annie's, but I am not sure, so I will tell you again that I am here seeing some Americans and indeed any Americans who happen to be here. This is the season in which they most do congregate in Paris to get their fineries and cross over to England ready to sail for home before the bad weather.

"All the American world seems to be passing here, some days I can do nothing but see them. I had a splendid visit with Laura Curtis Bullard; the Daggetts of Chicago are here now, and I see sights with them. Mary Safford walked in upon me one morning some ten days ago; she has gone to England and will sail the 26th; to my joy and astonishment who should usher themselves into my parlor one evening last week but Miss Robinson and Mrs. Gardner. Miss Robinson is married to a Mr. Newell of Virginia who is now in Washington. They are painting, doing some of the finest work which is done in Paris, most of which goes to America at high prices, and indeed is in splendid pieces nearly the size of the panels in the rotunda and I expect finer execution, all historical. Miss Robinson is now painting Miles Standish's first encounter with the Indians. She had it two-thirds finished and it was blown to pieces by the Commune. She herself was wounded in the face, slight wounds. Their house was blown to atoms and they in it. It stood beside the powder magazine in which were exploded 50,000 pounds of powder. It lifted their house from its foundation, parted the timbers and it all fell in. I have been to see them, and went again to dine. There is a great deal of American life here, and one feels nearly at home among it. I am to go this evening to a social gathering of Americans at Mrs. Demming's, an American lady who has resided in Paris twenty years. They meet in her parlors Sunday evenings and talk and sing old fashioned church tunes, and Sabbath school hymns from American singing books. I'll tell you more of it after I have been if there should be anything to tell. This week I received letters from Joseph and Abby Sheldon who were just to start again from New Haven for London. They must be there by this time, and I have written them at London. They come to stay six months or a year in England, and want me to spend as much time with them as I can. They have left their children with Mr. Sheldon's father in Syracuse. They will enjoy their trip and stay in Europe much better for this; they will be able to travel some now, if the time comes to them. I wonder what could have given you such a throat difficulty? Had you been taking severe colds, or had you lived in too hot rooms during the winter and weakened the breathing tubes by too relaxing atmosphere, or had the coal gas done this for you? There was some cause which should be avoided another season. I can understand how Vester's sudden cold should settle somewhere and make him sick, but yours I do not understand as clearly to my own mind, you must watch for the cause.

"It is so long since I wrote you the letter in which I said I was not quite as strong as I was in the winter, that the facts have entirely changed. I am much stronger now, than I have been at any time since I left home. Indeed, I think I am well and I sleep as much as is necessary for any one to do. It is true I did work hard last winter, but that was for an emergency and one may as well not exist as not to be able to meet a little exigency when it occurs. I have rested well since and hope to keep on resting if it does not make me too indolent. My digestion has been excellent for me all summer. It has refused nothing of late but lobster and that it always did. I only tried a thimble full by special request, but found it much more potent than the Atlantic Ocean.

"I am sorry about Rosa, but I always had some fears for her bark after she should cut her moorings and hoist her anchor entirely — but children must learn. It was not a present that I sent you and Rosa by Dorr, just a bit of cotton gingham if I remember rightly like the clothes which were being made in my work rooms to show you the kind. I could not send a present because of the duty. It would be woman's material in a man's trunk and he could not account for it satisfactorily, and I expected he would have trouble with it there, but if he did and lost it, it was worth nothing, no one would care. I should have been glad to send something worth sending, but Dorr dared not take it.

"I have forgotten where Falmouth is, if I ever knew. I remember the old Falmouth opposite Fredericksburg where I lived one winter in a wagon, but this Falmouth must be in Massachusetts and my geography is at fault. That must be because I could not make Sall wake up soon enough to tell me when I used to get up in the bed to study in my night gown by candle light. I can remember it 'berry well, berry snowy day.'

"I read all our women are saying and doing with great interest. Elizabeth Stuart Phelps and Gail Hamilton, side by side in the Independent, interest me exceedingly. I had a letter from Mrs. Haskell recently which was a treat, especially to know how well she had become. I never thought so much for her. Miss Antoinette Margot is with us. She is one of the best lady artists of Lyons, or of Switzerland. She sits a little way from me at this moment painting one of the most delightful cats one ever saw and laughing till she cries to see him getting ready to spring at me. She can change his tone and temper at every touch of her brush; his eyes grow greener and greener, and she says he has commenced to swear at me already.

"Fannie Atwater tells me she is well now and speaks in the most grateful terms of you and Annie. She thanks me for giving her such friends, and I in turn must thank you with all my heart for having extended so much care to the poor little girl who I am sure needed it at that time. Dorr will be home in March. I should like to see him, but I suppose he will come and go as far on the other side of me, and I shall not see him.

"I think it was Annie who told me that Sumner Barton was about to be remarried, and so it has really taken place. No please, don't send me the cards, keep them if you will with yours. I want to speak of your Thanksgiving, but it pains me. I thought of it on the day and knew you would be at Oxford. I knew also how sharp a pang there was for each heart and how each would strive to hide the wound from the rest, and that each would succeed pretty well and yet that all would see — Oh! what a great faithful woman [1] left the stage in one short sharp hour; how often the long drawn breath comes to me, and only then I realize that I had been thinking of her, good and kind and just; how often one wonders about the other side; do they know each other there?

"I hope you will go to Washington this winter. How we would like to see one of its good bright, cloudless days; nowhere else have I found so good, light skies, such changeless days. It is not pretty, oh, no, no, not pretty, oftentimes not even passable and yet I like it. Switzerland has pretty days and her snow capped cliffs are grand, but even in a July evening, they remind you of their power to bite and pierce. Little sea girt Corsica was weird, wild, soft and bewitching, strange, unique, but she slew while she charmed and she had so much that one wearied of. The south of France is better, but there is a trail over them all. They, the people, are ignorant, idle and filthy, loafing and slouching about with packed jackasses, spoiled by travelers till they charge you double and double that, for every little thing they do for you, or sell to you, and beg of you at the end. You cannot avoid the feeling that you ought to hurry and die as quick as possible to let them have your old clothes.

"Do you think the suffrage cause is gaining ground in America? Or as rapidly as one might wish and think — it argues well for it that it has some sturdy opponents.

"The —— gives a doleful account of the attempted union of New York and Boston, at the Annual Meeting at Cleveland and declares that both parties are nearly destroyed. The 'Nation' says their political efforts are intriguing, that their arrangements in Massachusetts were a 'perfect puzzle,' and that altogether they could not 'have made a worse show of capacity for politics.'

"The 'Times' (N. Y.) criticizes. Of course the 'Independent' is hopeful and the 'Revolution' sanguine. The English papers many of them say we are scarcely gaining any ground in America. Still, I suspect the wheels are rolling on, being so much greater in circumference than formerly they do not appear to roll so fast, but one hears

[1] Mrs. Louisa Fitts, at whose Oxford home the Vassall relatives and Bartons often gathered, as she was very much beloved.

always the whole tribe of Mark Twain's and Josh Billings' barking at their heels — this is a pretty sure evidence that they move enough. Then she adds: — "just now an artist has stepped in, implements in hand, and announced his desire to take my rooms.   I replied 'yes' of course, 'if they would do him any good,' but he didn't know whether this meant he *mought* or *mought* not, so I said *oui monsieur* — Pretty soon he wanted to 'make my face' and just to bring the features into good position, I said 'ja,' this time, and he proceeded to proceed. And in the style of the pathetic ballad of Sally Salter and Charley Church, I should say, that

> The rooms that he wanted to take, then he took,
> The face that he wanted to make, then he mook,
> While we at our tables kept working, and work.

"I came very near placing quotations at the commencement of that 'stanza,' but I bethought me in time to rule out before they were dry, and I now truly declare (who perhaps should not declare it) to you, (who probably would not suspect it) that the entire verse of poetry writ above is original and impromptu —

"How are all my dear cousins in Worcester.   I never hear, perhaps because of my perversity in never writing, which I always think I am going to do *next week sure.*

"The last I heard of Cousins Bacon and Starr they were both lame but I trust that is all over now, and that they are both able to *skate* by this time.   I can remember when Cousin Pamelia was splendid at sliding down hill.   It seems to me that I can hear her laugh now, as she rolled over in the snow.   And do you ever see dear Cousin Maria? How often I think of her with her hands all free of tasks and care, and wonder if they do not seem to her to be too free, too empty?   How I should like to see her to-day.   And my cousin Jerry.   Never a word about him, although I have no doubt that he is just as good and handsome as ever, and goes on prospering and to prosper, 'so mote it be.'

"Are the Dennys well?   Do you ever hear of Cousin Lydia Grout, or George and that family of charming cousins.   I am glad you spoke of Nancy.   I wanted to hear from her, I think she and Uncle John are a little lonely — love to them — and love to all that care for it.   They are dearer to me here alone than I am to them among so many.   I think of them oftener than they of me, but that is natural and right. There are kisses for you, dear Fannie, and one, just one for that naughty fellow that lies on the lounge. Please give my love to Cousin Ned when you meet him."

In a letter of September 18, 1871, to Mrs. Vassall, following a few personal paragraphs, Miss Barton volunteers a number of interesting social comments:

"I am spending some fine days in Paris, just what I most desired. I wanted to see some American people. It had been so long; and indeed there is no lack of them here. All Paris swarms with them as I suppose it always does, and all grades. Some I am proud of, and some I am ashamed of; some speak remarkably well and some cannot utter a proper sentence. Generally they are well dressed as the world goes, but to my eye overrigged as a sailor would say, but always much better than the English who are the most fearful dressers in all Christendom. English women are solid and sensible, learned and self-possessed, and all the world respects them. But the art of selecting and putting clothes on to themselves is something quite beyond their line of vision, not that they do not wear enough — O, Heavens no, not that! There is always enough and to spare, but there is no calculating what portion a member of the body corporate it will be found dangling from and Joseph's coat bore no comparison. Still they are splendid women and handsome, 50 per cent more beautiful than the French. The French declare that the Germans cannot dress in decent manner, but I have seen much good, comfortable looking dressing in Germany and I liked it rather. I don't know what has induced me to write so much upon the silly matter of dress unless that some of my 'sisterin' abroad annoy me a little with theirs. I can see how busy Ber must be with his large family and congratulate both him and his children upon the relationship. I imagine him to be a most sensible and paternal of parents. I shall be only too glad when you can really take your legitimate place in the work. I can see an equal call for your services. Go and look after the little girls, they may not like to tell all their troubles to their State Papa, but would rejoice to reveal some things to a mama. Go with Ber. I think that is one of your rights — it is at least your privilege, and you know it is very well said that until women get their *rights* — they must keep their privileges.

"I also have something of a family in Europe, some hundreds of state children, but of my own *immediate* family, I have two delightful girls. They are as fully grown and developed as my two boys in America were, rather more, and about as nearly alike, but charming girls, both good as they could be, and be human live girls; one is all gentleness, the other all strength, but both so loving, so obedient, so true. The elder is Miss Margot (Antoinette). She is a thorough artiste, and is with me at present painting and visiting Louvre and the Luxemburg and comparing notes with the Parisian painters. She is at this moment painting an American flag and looking back over her shoulder, to say to me, ' *elle est très jolie.*' Miss Zimmerman (Anna) is at her home in Carlsruhe looking after the thousand wants of a clergyman's house — keeping the big brothers in order for the Universities they are plodding through — obeying her papa and mamma who tell her she is too independent and ambitious — writing at odd moments as she can pick them, reading Carlyle, Dickens, Goethe, Schiller as she can steal the minutes, pining that she must be held in just such bondage of body and soul, praying for the day when she may come and live with me a little more and beginning a long, strong, logical letter once in a while with 'To the devil with the housework — Why must I fritter away all the best years of my own life and starve my brain to cram my brothers who already have been taught twenty times more than they can apply?' And she is right. But my sheet will be full and I shall have said nothing at all, but I have just written your marm and I think perhaps that will find its way to you, and you must just have had a surfeit through Annie. I am glad she went on a vacation. I wonder what they do at Falmouth. When I come home, can't we go? I am not at all certain where I shall pass the Winter. It may be I shall think I must work in France. I cannot tell how they will present themselves by winter or I may think it well to quarter myself here in Paris and wait, and I have half a mind to go to Spain. This is perhaps the most sensible use I could make of the time. I must wait a little the turning of events. I can tell better after a month more in the East of France. I am glad you have had a visit from Georgie. It was nice of her to send me a line. Is not Alice with you now? Has she turned to ashes? Very possible, human nature can as well as wood or coal. Write me when you have time and don't let Ber abuse you.   CLARA.

"To Ber:

    "I am first rate, how are you!   Clara.

    "for particulars, see   ————.

"My regards and commiserations to Willis for his state of widowhood. I have been thinking I should have to write him a special letter all to himself not upon that subject, however."

CHAPTER XXVII

Advent and Christmas with the War-torn Poor

In October, 1871, Miss Barton left Paris for the still suffering towns of northern France. The shooting of the Paris Communists had but died away. The struggle was just over and the Republic in command. It would seem now as if she might have found a little of that rest and freedom from care which she had come to Europe to gain. Surely after the ten-year strain amid the horrors of war and its wreckage, she was entitled to it.

But to Miss Barton the time for rest was the time for collapse. It was such a collapse to which the superhuman strain had seemed to doom her after the American Civil War, — a collapse which she postponed by her search for missing men. In 1869, when her work was done and rest came, there came with it the inevitable breakdown. But the Prussian field of 1870 recalled her to strength. Now with that war and the Commune over she does not think of herself, but of those who have suffered through the war. Rest is again put from her as she decides to give herself to the task of reconstruction in the more devastated sections of the country.

Writing to her sister in 1871, beginning with Belfort, where she worked till October 27, she reviews the progress of her task in this second year of relief.

"I don't know when I wrote you last nor when I received a letter from you, but I do know that both have been 'ower lang.' I am certain that I must have written from Paris probably some time before leaving for Belfort. I did leave for there one day and passing down over the old war track along the line of Dijon where I made my first stop, went on to Besançon and calling upon the Prefect made the best investigation I could into the condition of the poor of the vicinity.

From here I journeyed to Montbèliard and from there to Belfort at which point I made the commencement of my work.

"I asked of the authorities to designate the manner in which they would like to have something done for the comfort of their destitute people. They conferred and informed me that if they were not ashamed to ask of any one so hard a task as to meet their poor personally and give them what I desired them to have with my own hands, they should beg me to do that. The moral and mental effect would be so much better than to receive it from them. I said I would do it and the administration of the town arranged his own house for the purpose and with the concurrence of the Mayors of the town and all the surrounding villages, they called out the distressed and those who had suffered most by the war and siege and sent them to me day by day to tell their stories of suffering and receive what I had to give them. Some days a hundred families came, but generally about half that number. They waited at the door and were admitted by policemen, a family at a time.

"What a history their stories would make; what a commentary upon war. But still, what a state of morals or rather immorals I found here, for all being straight Catholics felt themselves bound to confess to me, a mark of respect and confidence which I certainly was far from demanding and deserving of them, but, if it was good for their souls, I could not refuse it. Often I took them up from their knees, where they would get in spite of me. I could not always be quick enough to catch and prevent them.

"The fortifications of Belfort are something immense and built in the wild hills — the castle half cut in the rock like Stirling and Dumbarton and so high above the town which nestles like a basket of kittens beneath its line of rock turrets. And here these poor creatures lived for months with the shot pouring over their heads like a hail storm, in cellars till they were blind. Many told me of members of their family who starved, too timid to come out and face the shot; others did face it and were killed or maimed for life; others went through safely and bravely and bless God that they never surrendered. They successfully guarded and defended one gate so they were never out of food and say they could have defended themselves five years and would have done so if France had not made their terms of peace. This information they received three times before they could believe it, and thinking it a ruse of the enemy answered each time with double shot and they were only about five thousand garrisoned troops and never reënforced."

Before going on through the siege belt of ruined cities Miss Barton visited Carlsruhe, where from the poor she is plunged into the presence of royalty. The Grand Duchess never "let go her hand till it is time to go." Tuesday she goes with the royal party to the Legislative Hall where the Grand Duke opens the assembly.

"So you see," she concluded of Belfort, "these people cannot have been left very rich and prosperous. I remained here until about the 27th of October and having nearly closed my work, I came up to Carlsruhe to rest and arrange my papers, and see what was wanted of me. I had been sent for so many times and could not go. This you know is the home of Miss Zimmerman who was with me at Strassburg. Her father is a clergyman and she is now at home. She is always homesick for me to come, and I like to gratify her if I can. Miss Margot is with me and will probably remain in Carlsruhe this winter at her profession (painting). For me, I shall find it necessary to return to Montbèliard and close my work and after that I am not certain whether I shall return to Carlsruhe to stay a little or not. For my good girls and for the Grand Duchess, I like to remain here, but I presume there are much pleasanter places in which to pass a winter. I think it must be a little cold, but it is said to be exceedingly dry. The Grand Duchess (who is now Her *Imperial* Highness since her old papa is no longer king, but Emperor) had not returned from her summer retreat on Lake Constance when I arrived. But Mlle. Sternberg, her 1st maid of Honor was here and sent for me immediately to come to the Castle where I found her very ill, doubtful if she ever recovers. The next day Princess Wilhelm returned (she had been with the Grand Duchess) and sent for me to come to her. I spent what time I could with her till she left to visit her mother and sister at Frankfort. She is cousin of Prince Alexis, the son of the Czar of Russia, now traveling in America, and a most charming person. She brought messages from the Grand Duchess to wait if I could for her to return and I did. They came only in time to open the Parliament (or Congress, or whatever name an English speaking person might give it). They arrived in the night (I think to avoid parade of troops and town) and the next day, Sunday, she sent for me to spend the evening with her. I went at five and remained till long after all was still. We were alone on a cozy little sofa by a light fire, and never did she let go both my hands at once till it was time to go. It may be only once in a life time that one finds combined a heart so pure and large and loving and a brain so clear and active and tireless as one meets in this sweet gentlewoman.

"On Tuesday at twelve, the Grand Duke would open the 'Chambers' by a speech. I would go, of course, and at eleven we went to get and retain our seats.

"When the Royal Party left the castle for the Hall, the bells rang out right merrily and soon all the mass of decorated gold lace gathered in the body of the house below us. The Legislative body and dignitaries Home and Foreign rose up from their seats and shouted three times most lustily as the Grand Duchess followed by three children stepped lightly to her seat in the galleries, bowing three graceful bows in her pretty white hat and blue and white silk dress, and immediately again three other shouts and the Grand Duke followed by his princely brothers walked up the aisle below, stopped at the foot of the throne and bowed, first to the Grand Duchess who had risen in her gallery (box) to welcome him, then to his ministers, then to the Assembly, then seated himself upon his crimson throne, and after prayers read his short speech in a most beautiful manner, clear, slowly and audible with long pauses and clear accent. Then all the members one at a time raised the right hand and said 'Ich schware' which seemed unpardonably wicked of them to swear so *much*, and then it was finished and we came home."

The assembly suggests political comments which led her further to comment on Germany's institutionalism. She then reverts to institutionalism in the state church and its tendency to deaden progress.

"Germany is naturally well satisfied and perhaps a little proud," she continued, "of the closing up of her military difficulties and the consolidation of her states. She likes to feel herself an Empire, but still there is a large and strong Republican party here and year by year the Government makes concessions to them. The empire gives far more liberty to the masses than they had before. The tendency of all Europe is towards more liberal government. Step by step it is demanded and yielded. If only once they can come to cut asunder

their church and state notions and have some reasonable liberty of
conscience, it will check in a great measure their rapid march toward
infidelity and atheism. They are asked to believe so much that they
find it extremely difficult to believe anything. One is taught from
childhood, here, that his own natural thoughts and ideas are all
carnal and not one must be accepted or retained; every natural scion
of the original tree must be cut away or torn off and the whole be
engrafted upon the church or rather a slip from the indoctrinated and
holy tree of the established church, and so in the end the entire stalk
shall bear holy flowers and fruit.

"Poor Anna Zimmerman, walking my room back and forth yesterday like a chafing lion with her hot, red cheeks and great black eyes
full of life and fire throws her arms above her head as she advances
towards me exclaiming: 'They tell me that my own thoughts are
wicked — of the Devil, and I must not follow them. — My God, if
I don't think my own thoughts whose thoughts shall I think!' I
thought her question reasonable enough, but she in her earnestness
couldn't comprehend what I found to laugh at."

Turning towards home, the Chicago fire leads her to speak of
Germany's spirit of relief and to note the sympathy evoked.

"It is something wonderful, the intense interest and sympathy
which has been shown in Germany for Chicago," she pointed out.
"Every little village raises money for it, concerts and entertainments
and sermons, and in all the little shops of a well established character
one sees the placard, 'Funds accepted here for the sufferers of Chicago,'
but no one can understand us. Being a city of forty years old, they
ask me if it had any large buildings."

The horror of the Chicago fire, much as she laments its terrible
destructiveness, leads her to see East and West being fused through
affliction.

"To my mind," she explained, "this unprecedented calamity seems
physically a loss and a scourge, but morally it may have been a necessity and a blessing. One may learn his friends in affliction, and if the
growing West re-learn from this, the facts she was fast forgetting, that
she is really a child of the East, that nestled in those old despised New
England homes are hearts beating with true parental love, and not
burning with jealousy, as they have fancied, and that the hands grown
hard with toil among the rocks and gravel knolls, closing firm over

tiny gains, can open quick and wide at the bidding of human sympathies and that whoever is to be 'left out,' the old parent East does not propose that it shall be her western children in their distress — if they can really read and learn this lesson, it may be worth more to them in the future of the great family, than all that has gone up in the smoke and flame.

"For years, no feature of our nation has troubled me so much or so far filled my soul with apprehensions of future danger as the general and persistent misjudgment of the East by the West. I have long read in it a steadily growing disrespect and hatred, division, dissension and civil war with no basis which the world could know, or Heaven could tolerate. Whatever may have a tendency to help unlearn a lesson so sad and so fatal, at any cost should perhaps scarcely be reckoned a calamity."

Taking up relief work again in the middle of December, as the holidays began for others, she thus describes it to her sister Sally:[1]

"If I have not written you since the 25th of November when I remember to have done so, I have not told you anything of my going to give something to the poor people who had suffered so much by the war. I went from Carlsruhe about the middle of December in the coldest time we have had in all the winter. It was fearfully cold. Miss Margot went with me. It was a day and a half's travel, and some of the way it was so cold in the train I dared not let Miss Margot fall asleep. I knew she was exceedingly cold and I kept her awake through precaution. We spent the first night at Mülhausen with Mr. and Mrs. Dollfres, French people of literary note, whom I have known during all the war. Next day we went to Belfort, and passed the night and Sunday with the administration, Monsieur Leblue, and arranged some trunks I had left there in October, and Monday morning we went to Montbèliard and called on the Prefect (a Jew) to whom I had previously made a donation of money and informed him that I wanted to make the next donation in person. I wished to see the poor myself.

"He was very amiable and agreed to arrange it and I left him to do it while I went on to Besançon to see the Prefect of Doubs. Here it was so cold and cheerless I could not sleep at night and returned next day. I was made the guest of the noble families of the Town, for

---

[1] In a letter written the January following, in 1872.

Montbèliard was an old court town and the Grandmother of the
Czar of Russia was a princess of Montbèliard, so that there are still
relics of royalty there, and a pretty old castle.   I found excellent
arrangements for taking care of the poor, the best I have seen in all
France.   They have committees for both gentlemen and ladies and
the president of the ladies' committee is Mrs. Morell, a person so much
like Mrs. Griffin that I feel that I have really seen Mrs. Griffin and
worked with her a few days this winter.

"These committees assembled in the Hall, and called their poor
there, and they came in hundreds and walked in a long line or in two
long lines reaching from the door and through the yard and down the
snowy street.   At the suggestion of Mrs. Morell I gave them orders
for wood and rent, so that the husbands could not compel the women
to give up the money to them to get drink on and deprive the family.
We wrote hundreds of orders.   I signed them and then we went to
the hall and received the women.   They were my own then.   I admitted them and gave them the orders and took in the rest and so
day after day till all was done.   The orders were drawn immediately
and when I left just before Christmas, all the poor had wood for two
months and rent paid till the 1st of April.   They looked so poor, but
were so happy at such an unexpected fortune, and I was so glad to
have been able to do it.   It was Boston that did this good little thing.
I have written a long letter to the committee about it.   I thought
they would be glad to know it while the fires were still burning.

"Then I came back [to Carlsruhe] and I wanted to go to Strassburg
and give something to my old working women there.   They would
not be so poor as the women of Montbèliard for much had been done
for them, but I wanted to see and remember them and so I said I
would go.   I wanted Miss Zimmerman to go with me as she helped
me to organize the Strassburg work last year.   I said I would not give
anything in charity to the women.   I had not permitted them to
beg.   They had always worked for me and been paid.   I would give
them a Christmas fête and invite them like other people.   So we
bought two splendid pine trees fresh from the Black Forest and I
knew all my women, so I had only to count the heads and give purses.
I purchased three hundred good strong morocco purses with steel
clasps, prettily lined, and pretty things for the children and to orna-
ment the trees; many dozens of little wax candles with holders to

light the trees. I had stopped at Strassburg on my way back from Montbèliard and hired the best hall in town for Saturday night, Dec. 30th. On Wednesday night we went to Strassburg, had our invitations printed and sent to the women by post. Then I ordered 20 cakes and 500 rolls at a good bakery. I cannot tell you how long and high each cake was but one would cut from twenty to twenty-five slices, big slices. I engaged a caterer I knew there to furnish chocolate and coffee. The hall had a fine kitchen and dining room. I asked the banks to change my money into the last coinage of French silver, newly issued, and they did. The best ladies of the city came to help us. The trees were set, the purses filled, the hall arrayed, and the tables spread and set, so white and clean. And oh the trees were so pretty — on a long platform along all one end of the hall in front of two enormous mirrors and the floor spread with moss all scattered full of fine cut white paper and isin-glass which made perfect snow and ice, and brightened with hundreds of little scarlet winter berries. The hall was so brilliant with chandeliers and mirrors that one could read the finest print in its most distant corner. I describe the scene so particularly because I think it was the prettiest thing I ever saw. Don't say it was that that made my eyes sore, it wasn't.

"The hour was seven. At six thirty the women began to arrive. M. Kruger, the vice-consul, received and seated them in the anteroom till it was time to light the trees. I had not seen them yet and did not know that so many were there, but when we went through the room on our way to welcome the wounded children, hundreds of women rose before us like an army, not a word, still, like so many soldiers, and stood for us to pass. At seven the trees were lighted, the doors opened and all this regiment of women walked in and took seats.

"A fine parlor organ stood under the trees, a Christmas hymn was started and these poor women in the fullness of their hearts joined in a burst of song such as I never heard before. They sang as if they meant God should know how glad they were and how grateful.

And then there was prayer and an address of welcome (I wouldn't have them instructed) and then Mr. Kruger and your sister went under the trees upon the platform where all the purses hung. There were elegant ladies to take them down from the trees and hand them to me while Mr. Kruger called each woman's name and she came up and gave her hand to me and I put in it the purse of silver with her name on a pretty buff card attached to it; then the ladies took her round to see the trees and to sign her name at a table presided over by the Misses Rausche of Strassburg Boarding school, and then they were taken to the refreshment room and the clergymen's daughters of the city with Miss Zimmerman at the head received and served them to chocolate and all the good things and then they did talk and laugh and cry for joy.   And such a time — some hundreds of poor women almost beggars!   It was worth going a mile to see.'

"All this while Mr. Kruger and I were giving the gifts, but when it was done I went and ate with them.   Then I came back and gave the gifts to my eleven cutters, ten pretty girls, and one father.   I gave them work boxes and portfolios, etc., and then the Comte de Lecours had arranged a little surprise for me which the women enjoyed exceedingly.   Then Mr. Bergman, my esteemed friend, the President of the Syndicate of Alsace, addressed the women and they all crowded up around the front of the platform to listen to him like so many children.   He told them among other things that Miss Barton had said she wished they would all keep the money in the purses as a keepsake and make it the beginning of a sum for the savings bank which would reopen next week, and having told them this, he said to them so pleasantly and familiarly, 'I think we ought to make her this promise, eh?'   You should have heard the storm of 'yes, yes, we will' that filled the room.   This finished the evening except for their goodbyes to me which each one insisted on making for herself.   This occupied almost an hour till the last one was gone and then it was almost twelve and we went home to our hotel and to bed.   But all the time I knew I had seen a very pretty thing.

"There were about sixty women who did not get their invitations. It was no wonder.   They had never had a letter before in their lives and the letter carriers never heard of them, and they lived in such old alleys, and garrets and cellars.   The next day I made a list of all those not to be found, and a list of all there, and put it in all the papers of the city and it was told to them and they came to our work rooms a few days after and we gave them the purses and then it was all done and we came back to Carlsruhe on one of the first days of January and I have been here ever since.

"I had a good deal of writing to do and I suppose I have used my eyes a little too much. I was going over to London directly after leaving Strassburg to stay with Abby and Joseph Sheldon who are continually writing me to come to them. I meant to have been there now, but I received letters on my return from Strassburg from the head of the Boston Committee saying that they had held a meeting after hearing something from me and decided to beg me to take charge of their business yet unfinished in France. They saw that it was wrong and begged me to take it in hand, if I could not do anything personally to take the overlook of it, and I replied to them and will wait for their answers. I thought then it would be nonsense to cross the Channel if I must recross to France in a few weeks so I decided to remain here until I could finish up on the Continent, and go to England free. I do long to be free of work once more for a little while. I have been rather busy. I have a little home in Carlsruhe, — I got tired of a hotel and took some small rooms, a little apartment and furnished it to suit me (rented) and have a little German girl. She was the private waiting maid of Madame de Mertzingin and I knew her; so I live as independently as I please. I can arrange my living to suit me better. I can have a beefsteak and baked potatoes for breakfast and not be driven to a choice between a crust of dry bread or a gallon of coffee and I can have my dinner at four and not be forced to eat at eight o'clock at night as is done here."

For a moment the hearthstone causes old-time longings to flame up, after which she compares a girl's training in America with that in Germany, repeating a talk with the Grand Duchess.

"I am sure you have had a great deal of trouble with my things," she interjected, "and so has Lieut. Westfall. I am sorry but cannot help it. I want to write to the Lieut. but dare not send one of my blind letters. I must wait till I can use my eyes again. I am glad you went and visited 'all the world of Massachusetts.' I want to see our old brother Dave more than I can tell and I think I shall some time. I don't understand if Ida has left the Treasury for all time, or a rest. Is she not well? I am sorry you wandered about waiting for some one to carry you from pillar to post; wait a little, Sall, and we will have a coach and one, and ride when we please. I will have it sent over to you every day to take a ride on condition that you will promise to come and take tea with me every time and you shan't wait to be carried somewhere. It was all vexatious and heart-aching. I know it all by experience so old that it seems to me it must have been a part of another existence, but it wasn't. It was only the first end of this old patched and tangled web. What a good soul-stirring time you had at the convention, didn't you? That was splendid. Shall I ever see something like that I wonder? What a meeting. How I want to see and know Mrs. Livermore. I don't suppose I ever shall, but I knew her so long ago. What beautiful things she wrote when she must have been so young. No wonder she can speak well.

"I speak very much of these things with the Grand Duchess. She sent for me about a week ago to spend a morning and she spoke of little else than the progress of woman and schools for girls in America. She had evidently been reading something — I presume some German criticism upon the too-liberal spirit of America — and wished to compare notes I think. I told her all as it was, and I said I believed in special training for all kinds of life but that I thought it possible to train too much till the original spirit was crushed out and ashes left in the place of coals and there was danger of Germany's doing this with her great respect for discipline. I said too, that I thought them too strict and that they cramped their people by rules and regulations and hurt many good original minds. This was plain speech for a woman in a plain black gown without even a ring on her hands to address to a Princess and sovereign, but when I am asked, I answer — let it be what it will. I guess it didn't offend, for she sent me a very pretty letter next morning.

"I can't think what the dress is that you speak of having made up and washed. I can just recall that I sent something but it could not have been anything but a piece from something from my shelves when we cut for the women. I can't think if it was calico or cotton gingham. I knew I wanted to send something good, but Dorr was afraid to take it lest he have trouble at the Custom House and they trouble him about his own things. I know we packed his baggage in terrible haste one night after midnight and I can't think of anything more about him. This was the day but one before I closed up in Strassburg and started for Paris — and it was not quite a sure thing if we would get there very safely and so difficult was it that it took three days to do the traveling of one day of ordinary times. But it is all better now. This winter is easier than the last was. I have made some friends and am not a stranger in Europe any longer. And I have warm friends in Strassburg, even if I do say it.   Last week Mr. & Mrs. Bergman came to Carlsruhe to visit us, that is, Miss Zimmerman and me.   They had been to tea with me twice (they were at a hotel) in my house and I arranged a visit for them at court.

"This is, I expect, the first social exchange of visits between a leading French Officer and a German court since the war; gentlemen may have visited, but not the ladies.   But Mrs. Bergman and the Grand Duchess visited, and better still, the poor women came on to Germany to visit me.   I have made some peace between them if they won't fight again and spoil it all.   I will enclose in this one of my invitations to the women's fête and Christmas tree.   Your German letter carrier will read it to you.   Now I think in mercy to *your* eyes, I must stop.   Don't be troubled about me, my eyes will be all right soon.   I will be very careful."

"I thought I could not write any more, but I find it so funny to write with my eyes shut as if I were playing blind man's buff, that I think I must do another sheet.   I was afraid to commence to tell you how nice I thought your picture gallery was — indeed I think it was splendid.   How could you think of it at all, how did you get up your ideas?   I laughed till I cried again and again, indeed I am not sure but that hurt my eyes some — I wish you had told me more about it.   I wanted all the pictures.   I related it one evening at tea at Madame General de Freystedt's and you should have seen the merriment of their German court ladies.   They have a good deal of fun in their heads.   They were particularly amused at the old hoop and line, especially as I explained to them our beloved President swinging around the circle to gain popularity.   Miss Margot has not been invited into the mystery of your gallery yet, as she is at Lyons with her people, but is expected to return any day now to renew her studies here.   I will make her full explanations as soon as she is back.   She criticises me sometimes to her great amusement. She would not be bad help for you on such an account and she would be in the 7th Heaven if she could do it.

"No, I did not think of the 11th of September as being the day of Lake City, but how well, I remember that day and how anxious a day it was, but after all not unhappy.   We felt that we had gained so much, our experiment had not failed, and it did not fail in the end. It accomplished just what you say it did. Our dear boy lived to feel that he had done his work and was ready to go — a little life it was and had in it much more than many another of four score and ten.

"I had not heard of Lizzy Learned's last affliction, can this be so? Where did Lizzy get such a complication of maladies? And is there anything in the new remedy. I have not heard of it. The Grand Duchess asked me about it. Her 1st maid of Honor, Mlle. de Stern-berg, of whom you must have heard me make mention, is supposed to be dying of a cancer. But she also seems to have a multitude of illnesses. I called on her a few weeks ago. She was a mere skeleton and is too sick now to see any but her nurses.

"Does Nancy do the work at home and is her Uncle John all there is? I cannot think how it can seem there without 'Bamma,' poor dear, honest, faithful, Christian, guileless 'Bamma' who worked faith-fully up to the last day without complaint and lay down bravely with the harness of life about her without a murmur —

"Do you have much fruit this year? I am out of patience with Europe — I never find fruit here. It is always a 'scarce year.' They say indeed there was none in all the Rhine valley. Little measley apples are two and three cents apiece. Prunes which are only the plums which grow here, dried, are 50¢ a pound. And I have searched the town over without success for a little dried apple. All oranges here are either sour or bitter always. I have nearly forgotten, but it seems to me that we had better fruit arrangements at home. You see by this, that I am pretty hungry, don't you? Or I shouldn't write of it. Now I think I have finished by this time."

The request of the Boston Committee concerning the American relief cargo came counter to the request of her American friends, the Sheldons, that she at once stop writing 'blind' letters, leave relief fields and save her own declining health by crossing to London where she could rest.

Between the two she chose as usual the sphere of service and hoped to remain on the continent in the winter "to take charge of the busi-ness yet unfinished in France."

Till the spring of 1872, Miss Barton is at Carlsruhe. But she re-mains blinded! Her eyes, bloodshot by the stinging cannon smoke of the American and Franco-German campaigns, have at last succumbed, and she has to sit with them bandaged day after day. Yet even when so afflicted she insists on being active and learns to write while sightless, "blind letters" like the one above which was written to her sister in January, 1872.

Concerning her eyes she further said in another letter,[1] "I passed some very dull weeks, very green and shady with exceedingly long nights, although after the greater pain and nervous excitement was over, I wrote a great deal with them closely bandaged." As to this January letter she commented : —

"I believe I can write you a readable letter without looking on at all. I have used my eyes pretty much of late and they complain so sadly of my bad treatment that I have decided to give them a rest and not write any more at present, but as I don't know how long the rest must continue, I don't want you to wait without news of me for an indefinite period. I want to tell you that I did receive your good long letters and was exceedingly glad of them. It had been a little age that I had not heard of you. I must write without a reference to your letter for I could not read it to-day. My poor eyes ache too badly for that."

[1] Written from England July 5, after her tours.

CHAPTER XXVIII

Tours in Italy and the Isle of Wight

April–September, 1872

In March of the early spring of 1872 Miss Barton decided to go to Italy. Writing of her improved health she said to her sister Sally, "I was infinitely better by this time. Still must not put any close strain upon my eyes."

Looking back upon the stages of her journey she retraced it thus, as we find it, in two letters, one written on the trip in an opera house, in April, and a later one after the tour's end, July 5, from England:

"Perhaps while I sit crowded into this dark corner listening to a perfect deluge of opera music,[1] I may be able to steal out the opportunity to scribble a few rough lines to tell you where I am and how I came here. About two weeks ago, Mr. and Mrs. Sheldon wrote me from London that they were out of patience that I should stay alone in Germany and write blind letters, and had determined to submit to nothing more of the kind and should leave London in three days to come for me and take me with them to London. They thought that their position both as friends and Americans demanded that they see personally what my condition was. Very obediently, I made arrangements to accompany them and in due season they made their appearance *via* the Rhine. After a visit of two days, I bade good-by to the little band of dear ones in Carlsruhe, among them were both Miss Margot and Miss Zimmerman, the latter sick in bed, and started for London through Strassburg, which city they were anxious to see.

"We spent Sunday there, and I had all the world to bid good-by to once more and get off Sunday night at six o'clock with my heart tender and sore with all the ordeals of the last two days. We came on to Paris that night, and met a family of Americans from London,

---

[1] Clara Barton could never be said to have an ear for music. For years, she would not allow a piano in the house as it distracted her. Finally, however, one was smuggled in.

intimate friends of Mr. and Mrs. Sheldon whom they had promised to meet there on their way to Italy for a trip of sight seeing of six weeks. The family was composed of four persons, Mr. and Mrs. Holmes, their daughter and son-in-law, Mr. and Mrs. Taylor, all of whom had resided in London and Paris some eight years, Mr. Holmes having been the American Commissioner to the Paris Exhibition in 1862, I think it was. They are among the most intelligent and excellent people I have had the pleasure to meet. Although I had never known them, I seemed to have been an old acquaintance of theirs and they at once insisted that I make one of their party on the trip. Mr. and Mrs. Sheldon saw how good an opportunity it was for me and with many tears poor Abby turned against all her own desires and interests, she said, and ordered me to accept the proposition. It was, of course, as late as one ought to start on a trip to Rome and Naples and if I would see them this year, it was my time. They [the Holmes party] were fine travellers. Italy was a familiar route to them, and it entered their heads to attach me to their party. I felt it to be a great piece of temerity on my part to think of dropping 'sans ceremonie' plump into the middle of an elegant family party arranged for a private travel, and I said so, and said all I could, but all was over ruled, and even Mrs. Sheldon said 'go' — it was too good an opportunity to lose, she said, and added at the end of her advice

'What a fool I am. I always did give up what I wanted most.' And so we separated in the streets of Paris, March 28th, 5 o'clock in the afternoon, she for London and I for Italy. I had my little hand satchel, having stored all my European luggage with my Paris Bankers till my return.

"I set out with my new found party for Italy. They had all been over the ground before and the route was arranged as follows: First down the Lyons road to Macon (not Lyons), on to Turin, Milan, Venice, Rome, Naples, back to Rome, to Leghorn, Pisa, Nice, Marseilles, Lyons, Paris and London with all intervening points of interest, traveling leisurely and homelike and seeing all one wanted to see. Our first day took us to Macon near Geneva which was an old route to me and to us all, or we should not have made it in the night, all the night traveling, as we used to do on the entire journey.

"We passed on to Culoz and at 4.00 P.M., came up to the Italian line and were overhauled for a foreign country. Having neither

tobacco nor liquors in our satchels, we were permitted to enter the
domain of his Majesty, King Victor Emanuel, and after a railway
dinner, we proceeded and at five came up to the famous Mont Cenis
tunnel under the Alps — 8 miles in length and in some places 8000 feet
below the surface of the earth.   The track is double and the solid rock
is cut smooth on all sides, having been bored by machinery.   There are
14 strong lights a kilometre apart and numbered like the glass box of
a street lamp so that as one passes, the distance is clearly ascertained.
There is no smoke like ordinary tunnels; an immense apparatus
erected at one opening rushes the air through the entire length of the
tunnel and it is as fresh as a spring morning.   The cars are so strongly
lighted that a dim glimpse of the track beside the train is all the time
possible.   It is an immense and beautiful work.

"You remember that it was over Mont Cenis that Napoleon first
constructed a road to march his armies into Italy.   At 10 o'clock at
night we were at Turin.   By this time I was conscious of being tired,
and altogether I was not very strong and just for variety I had a chill
in the night and of course decided to abandon my journey and return.
But as Turin was one of the cities to be visited, and naturally two or
more days were to be given to it, I could afford to wait and watch
further developments.   My chill did not recur, although I continued
weak for some time but kept on the journey.

"Turin is a charming city, by far the most modern in appearance of
any of them in Italy; well laid out, fine broad streets, choice, excellent
markets abounding in fruit, clean and entirely free from beggary.   It
seems also to have no poor quarter — the general practice being for
every wealthy family to take into its service and care, one, two or
more poor families entire, lodging them in tenements fitted in the
attic stories of their own residences, rather than below in the streets,
thus at the same time holding surveillance and compelling respecta-
bility.   I liked the plan.   I don't know if it were one of Victor Emanuel's ideas.   You know that Turin was always his Capital residence
till a few years ago when he established himself at Florence, which
now is in turn abandoned for Rome.   It has one hundred churches,
very rich in jewels and antiquities.   I remember in the Metropolitan
church to have seen the marble figure, sitting, like life, of Marie
Adelaide, the wife of Victor Emanuel and mother of Princess Clotilde
of France, and the private jewels of the church were shown us (for a

consideration, everything in Italy is displayed for a consideration) but for no consideration could I undertake to describe them; images of solid silver, men and women weighing several hundred pounds and covered with jewels one of which in some instances was of greater value than the massive silver image it adorned. The Royal Palace was most magnificent. The rooms were all shown; here in this gilded saloon, where their busts stand, were married Princess Clotilde and the Queen of Portugal. The plate glass mirrors are 20 feet high, and everything accords with them.

"The Armory contains an entire gallery of Mounted Knights in armor, full dress, horses like life, armed to the teeth and among them lies the sword that Napoleon used at Marengo. Above the city is a fine old Monastery to which we climbed for a view of Mont Blanc, Mont Rosa and all the chain of southern Alps, snow white and dazzling, stretching away into the eternal blue.

"On the second of April, Tuesday, we took train for Milan riding for hours in the bright spring sunshine of Northern Italy, the Alps behind us, and the Apennines before, the wheat waving in all the freshness of early green, and the trees just bursting into leaf. Here at Milan, we were met by a young lady protégé of Mr. Holmes, a young American girl who is to come out soon as a prima donna. She is finishing her musical studies in Milan, and while we were installed at an excellent hotel, our dinners were always with Mlle. Katrina.

"The great sight of Milan is its Cathedral, the second in size and magnificence in Europe. This also I could not justly describe. It is built entirely of marble commenced in the 13th century and like all these old massive structures, never finished. It covers many acres, and seems to be one sea of turrets rising at irregular heights towards the clouds. Although the comparison would be most inelegant, I will say that it reminded me of a shipping yard, the marble turrets and statues being replaced by thousands of masts. Indeed if my memory serve me well, it has 135 spires, and 1923 statues on the outside from the ground to the top and 700 inside. There is in one of the roofs which you pass as you ascend (far above to the top) an entire flower garden in marble, hundreds of flowers forming minarets and no two carved alike or representing the same flower. It was a long way to the top which at length was gained after many times of sitting and (for me) even of lying down to rest on the various roofs passed in

o

leading from one flight of stairs to another; roofs of pure white marble, polished and glistening in the sunshine like the crust of the snow banks in the New England hills on the bright winter days, (I wonder if I ever see them again); and here again, we saw marvelous jewels, 'gold, silver and precious stones.' The tomb of Carle who 'stayed the plague' is in a chapel beneath, the coffin and even the roof of the chapel of solid silver.   Mass is held here each morning and on certain days of the year miracles are wrought.   There are many sacred relics in the Cathedral, as several nails from the Cross, the Virgin is showed, and a seamless coat of the Lord Jesus Christ, etc. etc.   The picture galleries were especially fine, containing many celebrated originals among which is Leonardo da Vinci's Last Supper of the Master and Disciples in the original fresco.   And the celebrated 'Ambrosian Library' so old and rare; its volumes were indeed a curiosity, illustrated volumes of the 4th century.   And the Royal Palace, erected on the site of the old palace of the early Dukes of Lombardy — — where Attila thundered about in his destruction.   Later this palace, like nearly all in Italy, had been at some time or another occupied by Napoleon 1st.   Here was his bed chamber, unchanged, decorated in scarlet and gold — heavy velvet curtains richly wrought in flowers of pure fine gold thread.   Then the celebrated Theatre 'La Scala' the largest in the world; its stage is 100 feet in depth and wide in proportion and not including the recesses.   The pit alone holds 1100 people and there are six rows of galleries, 100 musicians in the orchestra. The principal boxes are purchased by the nobility for the season — a single box from 400 to 500 dollars (the season).   I name all these particulars for Vester's benefit; he may be interested in the facts. Our young prima donna stepped upon the stage (as our visit was in the day time) and sang to us.   She had sung there before to an audience of 5000, but I think she took just as much pains for us and I am sure we were not less enthusiastic.   I expect some day to hear her sing when she is famous, but it will never afford me greater pleasure than when she sang to her audience of five in the great 'Scala' of Milan.

"One little incident happening not long before was so pretty I am tempted to tell it to you.   'Katrina' (who is of German parents, but was born and has always lived in New York) had only led before the public once, *i.e.* last winter she was the 'Leading Lady' of the first

Opera in Turin and on the evening of the close of the engagement, she was 'called out' to sing a little national air in which she had been exceedingly popular — When she stepped before the curtain, she found the entire house a blaze of light, which at first 'upset her,' but gathering up, she went through her air, to the last strain, when four men entered and placed at her feet an enormous bouquet of the choicest flowers, nearly four feet across. She managed to accept it, but attached to it was a note which requested her when it should be faded, before throwing it away to open it with care at the end of the week. This was done, and hidden among the flowers were found a magnificent gold watch and chain, pins, necklaces of coral, turquoises and pearls, bracelets, and rings which I could not enumerate. It had been ordered and arranged in Geneva and sent all the way through the mountain passes to her. I thought this was a pretty success for the début of a little American girl studying in a strange land with little money. As a child she used to sing in New York with Patti. But you must be tired of Milan and wish I would hasten on if I am going. Well I will.

"And so imagine this to be Saturday, the 6th of April, 9 o'clock A.M., and I just taking the train eastward. The day was so lovely, so full of the spring time, the grass and grain so green, the swinging vines swaying over all the fields, the birds literally bursting their little throats, the fields filled with peasants in gay dress working to merry tunes, and when you could draw your eyes away from their near scenes, they fell to the northward, first upon a line of dim hazy blue; but over this, skirting the horizon again the whole chain, peak after peak of ranging Alps, such an unbroken line of glittering snow. Here on the South only four miles away lies the field of Solferino where France lost 1000 officers in a day. At 4 P.M. we were at 'Verona' wondering if we should see its 'gentlemen' and giving certainly more than our usual interest to this subject and at 5 we halted at a singular depot, with no rattle of cabs or hacks, no tramping of horses, still as death, all about us, and as we walked out there lay waiting us hundreds of gondolas, black as a pall, some covered, some open, all drawn up to the side of the canal to take us weary travelers to our hotels. This was indeed novel, but we selected our carriage, stepped in, without baggage sat down, and leaning lazily back left it to our gondolier to pick his way through the watery streets, some wide, some narrow, leading into and out of each other, like veritable city streets and lanes. The ways on each side lined perfectly thick with old palaces and majestic buildings of centuries ago, their fronts to the sea and their magnificient stone steps leading directly into the water and when one would pay a call, the gondolier had only to bring his boat along side and you stepped out as from another carriage to the steps of a mansion. We were taken to 'Hotel Victoria' made as comfortable as a first class Italian hotel can make one and after supper commenced upon the sights. Ah, but there was so much to see, not that it is a city of enterprise, a flourishing mart of trade, or business, oh, no, far from it. Venice only exists upon the record of its former greatness. Take all this away, and the travelers upon it and I believe twelve months would find a famine there, but there is little danger of this while Byron and Shakespeare remain bright in English literature.

"There, as everywhere in Italy, one must commence with the Cathedral and having gone through this, and some scores of churches, the Campo Santo and the Bell Tower, one is at liberty to enter upon the palaces, gardens and theaters. But Venice, offers some deviations from this general rule — most cities have prisons, but they have not all the dungeons of St. Marc. All have bridges, but all have not a 'Rialto,' nor a Bridge of Sighs. I suspect I do not need to remind you of many old historical facts; you who are always digging into the past will have them all 'papered and labeled' and stored away ready for use. But I might mention the 72 little islands upon which Venice was built — which were only a part of the Adriatic, and not reckoned as land at all, and it was only that a set of not warlike people from here and there in the vicinity, grown weary and afraid of their fighting and troublesome neighbors, mostly from Austria, determined to place themselves in a position more difficult to attack, so they came far over the sea to these little islands and commenced a city, and gave a general invitation to all war-pestered, peace-loving citizens of the world to come and join them; from time to time they united their islands, built their houses for dwelling and trade upon the streets laid down upon the piles, with one side opening upon the street of earth and the opposite upon the sea, as I have before described.

"But, the depravity of human nature!! No sooner were they a little strong and comfortable themselves, than they sent out ships to prey upon and plunder their neighbors, and well nigh ravaged the cities of the earth. They decorated their palaces with the spoils of other nations, married the sea, and declared themselves Omnipotent and Divine.

"Among other things their religion and church must have a hero, and they sent afar and got (as they said) the body of St. Mark, brought it and great numbers of relics belonging to him, buried him with the divinest honors in their principal church, and named it St. Mark, San Marco. This was as early as the 9th century. It is a large but not handsome edifice, facing a paved court or 'piazza' some 500 feet in length, surrounded by palaces now used for public purposes, stores, etc. All the world of Venice walks in the Piazza of St. Mark. The pigeon was esteemed a sacred bird with them, and he is still cherished here and treated with great honor. One of the curiosities to be seen are the pigeons of St. Mark. I cannot at this moment recall it definitely enough to state to you how many hundreds are supposed to reside in the immediate vicinity, but their dinner hour is 2 o'clock P.M. The great bell of this clock strikes $\frac{3}{4}$ past and they commence wheeling and circling into the court. They cover the fronts of all the buildings, sit as thickly as possible upon every window seat, hang in all the cornices, and stand in full platoons in every foot of spare pavement for a number of rods around the especial corner where their dinner is served. A young man (it was formerly a young girl) is appointed by the Government as feeder of the pigeons. It is not necessary to say that he is punctual with his repast, he could not live with his tumultuous boarders if he were not. As the bell strikes two, he pours the grain.

"In one way or another I imagine you must have become aware of me in England," [1] she writes home from London at the end of her tour, thus indicating her place of return.

The year to which Miss Barton came back on her return from Italy proved a trying one. Her health was none too good. The inevitable recoil of nature had begun to set in before she went away, as evidenced first of all by her trouble with her eyes, and the almost unremitting strain of the last twelve years of war and war relief were telling upon her.

The question before her now was — where should she spend the

[1] July 5, 1872.

approaching winter? Writing from England to Mrs. Vassall she debates this matter.

"Of course, I must add my little 'confidential' if I hadn't a private word to say, and indeed I haven't done anything privately for so long, that I feel entirely public. My chief thought is how to dispose of my 'radiant' and amiable self in the next four or five months — one would like to roll up and sleep till they are over, and the sun and soft air came back again. One can't go where the winters are mild, for the people make no provision for the little winter they do have, and one is really most uncomfortable of all, in such a country. The Sheldons are in London, and I should enjoy a visit with them, but go to London in the winter!!! and walk about the streets at 2 o'clock P.M. with a lantern!! Every one besets me to remain here, or to return here from France, and indeed I have a little home here, some small pretty rooms in which are Miss Margot and myself, and in which she will doubtless keep old maid's hall and paint—but I always question if I shall stay — You should see us at breakfast — indeed you should come and breakfast with us — nice home — French coffee, rolls, fresh butter and fruit, etc. etc. Miss Margot asks me a great deal about you, and thinks it would be a wonderful thing to see you. She asked me yesterday if she could not send you something in my letter, some little 'nothing' just that you might know there was such a person. After a moment's reflection, I told her that as she was skillful with her pencil, I thought perhaps she could interest you by a sketch of the pattern of our new set of crockery for our table, and from which we were that moment breakfasting. She immediately took the design and sends it to you with a kiss from a little blue-eyed lady who one day hopes to see 'Aunt Sally.' She hopes you will like the design of the set, which was of her own selection, and purchasing.

"Can you tell me about Rosa, and how they get along this winter, how about their house, do they keep it, and does Jared 'own' Rosa 'still'? Please give a great deal of love to Rosa when you see her, and tell her I should like her to *fix me up every day.*

"Now it is late, Miss Margot has been in bed a long time, and I must go too. Write me as usual to Berne, for the next time, but if I come to Carlsruhe for the winter, I will give you my address here. Germany is a good place to correspond from, the weight of letters is the same as ours, and the postage very small; especially with America.

It costs the same to send a letter from there to England or France, that it will to send this to you, with the exception of half a penny for changing it in London, but if I sent by German steamer just the same as to England — about 7 cents — (or 9 kreuzers). This same sent from France would cost 62 cents. I only mention this to show you how behind the progress of the times that poor deluded nation is, thinking to enrich her treasury by taxing intelligence. She does this to raise and support a great standing army, to eat out her body and soul.[1] Good night and a kiss."

Miss Barton, already in London lodgings, decides not to winter at Carlsruhe but at London.

In August she left the metropolis for a bracing sea change on the Isle of Wight.

Of this delightful five weeks' holiday — one of the few real holidays of her life — she writes to Sally as follows

"Only a word to thank you for your letter of the 30th of August. I am rejoiced to know you are better and settled in your new home. You ask for a little news of me in my present life; it is not filled with any very astounding incidents but such as they are you are welcome to. Since my return from my last spring journey I have not left London until three weeks ago, when I came with Mrs. Taylor, one of the traveling party, and who broke down under its fatigues, to this pretty little seaside town, on the southeast coast of the Isle of Wight to pass a month. Our party consists of four, Mrs. Taylor and myself, Miss Antoinette Margot, who had also become ill at her painting in Germany and came to me to get recruited, and a *femme de chambre* to keep all in order. We sent her ahead to secure a house and she was a marvel of success. She found the prettiest little home, all in good order, so neat and well furnished, close to the sea. And when we came on the evening following, our home was all waiting for us and our nice supper waiting on the table. We have a pretty parlor, sitting and dining room, nice chambers for each — good kitchen, large halls, all so new and nice. The beach is fine and handsome and covered with people. The country round about is most charming; it is one of the loveliest islands in the world. A few miles below us is a winter resort, and a favorite place for the Queen and Royal family. We can walk

---

[1] Miss Barton forgets again the colossal indemnity France has to pay Germany — whence the tax.

on the beach to the most charming villages on either side of us and all
the world bathes in the surf — I too —.   We are a merry house full, I
do assure you, and say a great many funny things in the course of the
twenty-four hours.   Some of the Taylors or Holmes come down from
London to spend Sunday each week, the more the merrier for we are a
hospitable crew and it is wonderful to see how fast Mrs. Taylor and
Miss Margot gain in strength.   We shall remain till the 28th of Sept.,
i.e. nearly two weeks longer and then return to London.   I am not
certain if I shall pass all the winter in London.   I must wait and see
how it looks.   I suppose it is a dark, dismal, foggy place in winter, but
it still has its advantages.   It has good warm houses, good fires, great
facilities for general information and to crown all, speaks the good,
Queen's English which is always welcome to my ears in spite of
everything.   But if it proves too dismal or damp, I shall take to my
old tricks and 'put out.'"

September 28, 1872, she returned to London and thus describes her
lodgings and friends:

"In London I am thus far in 'Lodgings,' which I like exceedingly.
My landlady is so much of a lady, and has such good common sense,
and clear appreciation of all that is witty or ridiculous, that I have
enjoyed her house exceedingly and am left almost as free as if it were
all my own.   Mrs. Rowse has thorough London habits, and is never
in bed till after one o'clock at night, or rather morning and consequently not up till between 9 and 10; while I go to bed in good
Christian time, and am up as I have been all my life at 5 o'clock in the
morning.   So there are $4\frac{1}{2}$ hours that no one in the house stirs but me,
and I range about, open doors and windows, and enjoy myself generally in my housekeeping — so that anything that goes wrong about
the house, I declare to have been done after I was in bed the night
before — while all that Mrs. Rowse finds wrong she declares was done
by the 'other housekeeper' before she was up.   But on the whole, it
runs pretty straight and I fancy that no one but the two housekeepers
discern anything out of the way.   Mr. Holmes' people are all the time
wanting me to come and make one of their family and want even to
change to a finer and larger house as an inducement, but I like to be
head of my own family you know, even if it is small.   I have kept house
more than two thirds of the time since I have been in Europe and it
is never any trouble for me to do it.

"The Fowlers (L. M.) and I have found each other out in London. We have spent some evenings together and he has visited me. They want me to become their neighbor and have also attempted in a recent removal they have made to place themselves in a locality which they thought I should like. They are now lecturing in the North of England and invite me to Manchester to attend a course of lectures. I fear I cannot, but I shall hope to see more of them when they return to London. He is the same gentle, kind man he used to be so many years ago, gray now, stoops a little, but is wise, considerate and gentlemanly as he always must be. Mrs. Fowler is younger, dark complexion, fine head, black curly hair, and full of life and vivacity. She is a charming lady. They have three daughters. Of all the people in England I was most glad to find them. Mr. Fowler recollected father, and gave me directly his traits of character, even to minute characteristics. Told me how averse he was to unmeaning ceremonies and how impatient it made him.

"They have done a most excellent work in England. Have been worth so much to the middle classes, given instruction as they would never get from other sources. I was so glad of all you told me about Oxford, that you saw Ruth. I hope she will have a comfortable winter. And I am so glad that Nancy came to stay with you when you were sick. I know what it is to have her come into the house when all is not well. She is such a good nurse, but she is always acceptable to me, sick or well — few people in the world seem so near to me as Nancy; we were such early friends. I don't know why I don't find a moment some time to tell her. It is not because I don't want to. Is Uncle John pretty well? You did not say how Chester was."

Stanley, the explorer, was now in England. How he broke through the crust of English conservatism to a royal English loyalty she interestingly describes·

"Speaking of lectures, I see to-day that you are to have a course from Mr. Stanley. I am glad of it — he has done so splendidly in England; he has both deserved respect and commanded it. The poor Geographical Society is used up. There are none so poor as to do them reverence. England tried every way to kill Stanley's reputation after they found they could not appropriate him by making him a Welshman or some other obscure Britisher dug up for the occasion, but she has given it up and finished by doing him all the honor she can heap upon him. But it is true we Yankees held our breath the night after his fracas at Brighton. Mrs. Taylor and I argued and fought for him against fearful odds till after midnight. All the world saw he had so ruined himself that he might as well leave England after such a demonstration as that — 'No one would ever again consider him enough of a gentleman to try to associate with him.' But we said if the claims to the position of gentleman in England consisted on standing up like a dunce before a pack of bullies to be badgered in public, occasionally smiling a sickly grin of complacency, then we were glad our blunt countryman disclaimed the title and stood for an honest boor with some grains of self-respect and a little spirit which on his side of the water was called 'spunk.'

"But it did require many days to bring over opponents to our side and even the hottest would jump at the chance of getting a good sneeze out of Stanley's snuff box. I hope you'll hear and see him.

"I haven't and I ought to and want to answer Fanny's nice note to me. I was so thankful to her for it, and I shall write soon, I hope, but I must wait till I can make it a little more legible than this. The truth is I have just been rowing a heavy boat and I went so far out in the channel that both wind and tide were strong and it took such heavy strokes to pull into shore that my muscles are not quite firm in their motion. I hope you can read it. Same address to me as usual at London and with love to all, I am your loving sis,

CLARA.

"I think this bright purple paper calls for *Yellow* ink, but I don't happen to have any. It's a very funny fancy."

CHAPTER XXIX

NERVOUS PROSTRATION IN ENGLAND

1872–1873

MISS BARTON'S winter in London, unhappily, proved a disappointment. Nervous prostration and trouble with her throat and chest kept her shut in for many months.

This long invalidism, beginning in September, 1872, had by July, 1873, robbed her of her strength and ability to bear "the little burdens" as she called them, with composure. She complained that it was never bright in London and that this had had its due influence on her system.

Her rooms and trunks were a confused mass of woolens, clothes such as she had used in the wars, and which she had not gone over for months. Her chest, always weak, would now not admit of the least labor of the arms.

Her health seemed permanently gone. At times, death, she felt, was imminent. She kept yearning for sunshine which would help her "face the dark river with a stouter heart." At one time she declared she expected never to leave London and that the sky was as immovable as a sheet of zinc. She felt already "in a metallic coffin" with the screws "turned down."

In a letter at the end of this long siege of sickness she goes over the long painful experience to her niece, Mrs. Vassall of Worcester.

"LONDON, July 11, 1873.
"EASTON ROAD.

"DEAREST FANNIE:

"Your dear good letter and that of your 'Bear' came a few days ago. It is funny to be 'interviewed' at this distance, and I am glad that you got no worse reports than you did. I don't think I am so homesick as it would seem, but I am weak and little things seem such a burden to me, that it hinders me from doing many things that would

make me more at ease if they could be done. But one must be patient.
There is not a month that I was not in my bed most of the time, and
now I can go about town and even once out of town, but not for a
long trip.

"It is kind of you all to offer to come to help me, but I believe I
shall be able to get over my difficulties without giving so much trouble
to any one. By 'getting over them' I mean measurably over them.
I cannot say that I even hope to be strong again as I was before the
last illness. I cannot tell, but it would be a wonder to me if ever the
nervous strength returns to any degree of real usefulness. The
greatest trouble I meet now is to bear the little burdens, the persons
and things around me, and not show too plainly that I have not the
strength and composure to bear them calmly, in short to 'hold my
horses.' You, dear Fannie, will know what that means and how to
the weak the grasshopper becomes a burden. I am glad you have
found a physician who has some strength for you if it is really so,
but I must confess that my previously small share of confidence in
medical aid and wisdom has not increased by the last year's experience.
I hear of you in the most trying heat at home; it is just as warm in
England some days, but to-day, for instance, ladies are clothed in
wool suits and a shawl generally. I went out just now a few moments
with Mamie while our rooms were put in order, but came back because I was too cool, and it is never very bright in London. I suppose
this has its due influence on one's nervous system and I would have
been glad at any time within the last month to be made ready and
go over to France or Germany. I think it would be better, but I
could not get strong enough to get ready to go. You wonder what
'getting ready' means. It seems to you that it requires little preparation to put up a bag or small trunk of things and cross the Channel,
and so it does, but it is summer and I have several trunks of mainly
woolen things as this cool climate and my little strength since I have
been in Europe have made it necessary to have. All of course are
unpacked and in state of utter confusion as one's trunks must be into
which their own hand could not go for months and months but others
constantly go, and in haste, and the moths in London are like flies in
abundance. It would not mend my nerves to know I had gone off
travelling and left all I have to be devoured and I have been made
worse several times by attempting to get a dress or some little article

from a trunk. My weak chest will not admit of the least labor of the arms yet.

" So I wait for strength as an army waits for Q. M. and Commissary supplies before it can march. I made one little trial or two, to see what I could do. Papa Holmes (with whose family I went to Italy) came one day to ask me if I could go to Liverpool where he was going, and over into Wales and pass a week. It was about the time that Colonel Hinton was going to sail and I thought with so many good friends on the road, I might try it. So I went as far as Stratford on Avon, but I grew so tired I gave out and let the party go on and I came home. It was not much of a journey, only a few hours, but I found it quite sufficient.

"I don't think I am homesick if that is the term they give it, but no one knows only those who have tried it what the depressing atmosphere of London may be to one who is not strong and more especially to one who feels they are never to leave it, as I expected last winter. I think I could have faced the prospect of the dark river with a stouter heart if I had been strengthened by a few glimpses of sunlight sometimes, but I waited such months watching my little window panes for a patch of sky over which one could discern that a cloud moved, but never was the surface light and thin enough for this. It was immovable as a sheet of zinc; one felt themselves already in a metallic coffin, only waiting to be closed in a little snugger, and have the screws turned down. But I have tried to be cheerful and full of life and fun as I could be with so little ability to speak as I have had and it may be that you and your Mamma Sally's sleeping men see deeper and get nearer to the reality than those about me or perhaps than even myself am well aware of. It is possible I have at times succeeded in cheating myself a little — all the better if it is so. I should be glad to be spared the trial of going on to the continent of Europe again. I am so tired of it. I never want to see it again, but it may be best, and then Mamie ought not to leave Europe without going there. I should be sorry to embark her for America having seen only poor smokey old London. If some one of our friends had been coming over with whom I could have sent her to journey some, I should have been very glad of it. I can perhaps arrange it from here, but up to the present moment, I have not been able to find the right opportunity. I thank you very much, dear Fannie, for all your interest and can only hope I may never find a chance to repay it in the same manner.

"I have seen no one who was going to Worcester. And for me, I shall try to get home this autumn. I suppose America will at all events be as well as here, and has greater range of climate and easier travel.

"As for the prospect of a full recovery of my original health (*i.e.* previous to last winter) I cannot decide yet. I may when once out of this climate and atmosphere in which I have fallen recover at once and fully and I may never be able to throw off the effects of such prolonged prostration. My own opinion inclines strongly to the latter. I do not think any one need come to see me home. I should be sorry to give that trouble to any one, and will do mv best to get on by myself.

"And now with a kiss, great love to all and the best wishes to your own dear self, I am

"As ever,
"Yours,
"CLARA."

But even amidst this depression she reaches a conclusion "to be cheerful and full of life and fun."

Here occurred the inevitable conquest of body, by her determination not to let circumstances master her but to master them and through a change of mind pierce "the opaque" till it became "a bright transparency."

A homespun illustration of her method of practicing this mental cure happily survives in this note which she slipped upon the table to be read by her niece, Mamie Barton, who had come over to spend the winter with her:

"Auntie wants to write Mamie a little letter. She is more sorry than she can tell that she has such a stupid illness that forbids her to be company for anyone.

"Auntie does not feel less social for this and although it is hard and painful, she will not feel despondent a moment but hopeful and cheerful for the present and future, if the circumstances immediately about her, do not combine to depress her to a degree which she *cannot* control. If she had a headache or a nervous head which a noise would disturb or make ache, there would be some good reason for all about her to keep quiet, and leave her to her rest and reflections,

but she has nothing of this, and never has. Her head is strong physically. (She will not refer to its mental qualities.) And as she has nothing to do all night but to rest and reflect, she does not need special opportunity for these during the day. If she were all alone, she would not get lonely or nervous on account of the quiet and silence about her. She has had great experiences in this and is accustomed to it. But when she feels herself imposing a dull dead silence on all persons about her, those whom she loves most dearly and for whose hourly comfort and happiness she would sacrifice anything in reason and see her dear little girls gliding about without speaking a sentence, — never sees a laugh or scarce a smile, — it makes her feel herself such a restriction, such a detractor from their happiness and leaves her such a prey to sad reflections and makes her feel the misfortune of her illness so deeply that at times, it seems impossible to bear it. She grows more and more depressed every minute and the poor strained nerves refuse longer control, and, in spite of all her womanly determination, break into tears and groans. This would make me very ill in time. Mamie doesn't want this of all things, Auntie knows, and she writes this poor little letter to explain to her the causes and the results, and tell her how to avoid the one and improve the other.

"Just then throw away the old time, never to be departed from, notion, handed down from nobody knows where, that all ill or ailing persons are to be treated the same, and that mainly like a dead person, surrounded by dumb watchers, and dim tapers, waiting to be buried, and remember that one whose heart is cheery and one whose mind is active, but whose mouth is closed to speech, might like to borrow the use of the mouths of those around them, — might and must want most of all, some one to talk for them, — to say the nonsense and make the fun they cannot say and make for themselves. And that nothing so much as a good funny time a day would so shorten and deaden the pain that must be borne in either case. Now if the two dear good little girls could only bring themselves to have the same chatty day that Auntie knows they would have if they were in their own room by themselves, laughing, singing, doing nonsense, and in short, feeling themselves perfectly free to enjoy themselves as I always know they do when by themselves, Auntie would be more grateful to them than for anything else they could do for her. And she has faith in the good understanding of her dear Mamie, to believe that she still sees the real state of the case as she could *not* see it before. And she knows that once she sees it, that big lump of Benevolence just on the top of her head, will not permit her to do anything but have a good jolly time in spite of her disagreeable old Auntie who can't just now help a bit to make it but who needs it more than ever, and most of all.

"Mamie needn't work on that old puzzling dress unless she *greatly desires* to.

"Now with great love, and great hopes, and sincere commiseration, Auntie closes this her first epistle to the daughter of David and waiting to hear her cry out in a 'loud voice,' she remains as usual
"OLD DOLOROUS."

While Clara Barton was in London, Florence Nightingale, the world's other little sister to the Soldier; invalided also by her war experiences, was seeking the road to recovery.

The place of Florence Nightingale in Miss Barton's affections, we may happily now recount from her own words. She points to Miss Nightingale and her assistants as they started to carry aid to the wounded in the Crimean War in 1854. "Begging leave in the name of humanity to go and render it, they marked," she says, "an era never before reached in the progress of the world; and when two weeks later Miss Nightingale with her forty faithful attendants sailed from the shores of England, it meant more for its future history than all the fleets of armies or navies, cannon and commissary, munitions of war and regiments of men that had sailed before her in that vast campaign!

"This little unarmed pilgrim band of women that day struck a blow not only at the barbarities of war, but they laid the axe deep at the root of war itself.

" The world knows by heart the story of Scutari and the Barrack Hospitals, and how under the intelligent direction and labors of the civil volunteer corps, disease lessened, gangrene disappeared, and pestilence fell away as the moths and mildew and poisonous vapors of night flee before the purifying rays of the morning sun, and how under the strong support of the military head and England's gracious queen, this work went on until the hospitals of the entire British armies in the Crimea, from awful depths of wretchedness, became types."

"Did you see Florence Nightingale, when you wintered in London?" I asked Miss Barton in 1909. "No, I was shut in and so was Miss Nightingale. I think she was in a hospital."

Miss Barton's work at the front in the Civil War had been done in entire ignorance of the great example that Florence Nightingale had set. "But the great example had been given," she said of Miss Nightingale later, "the slow but willing world had learned its lesson at the cost of its teacher. For when Florence Nightingale, covered with the praises and honors of the world, bending under the weight of England's gratitude, again sought her green Island home, it was to seek also a bed to painful invalidism from which she has never risen and probably never will. At such cost is the good work of the world accomplished."

Miss Nightingale in a succeeding ministry found herself misunderstood and lost her Governmental position — suffering much from Governmental heartlessness and neglect.

England, in later Governmental acts, was more appreciative of her war heroine than was the Government of America of hers, a fact unpleasantly reminding one of the platitude that "Republics are ungrateful."

Popular veneration of Miss Nightingale was widespread. Illustrative of the people's love is a story told much at the time. "At the close of the Crimean War," it was said, "a dinner was given in London to a number of the more prominent officers. Talk turned upon the war and the exploits of its heroes. Lord Stratford suggested that it would be interesting to discover who, in the opinion of the company, was the person whose war-time career would longest be remembered in the history of England.

"Each took a slip of paper on which the name of his choice was written and handed the slip to Lord Stratford, who read them and announced the name which had secured a majority of votes. When the little papers were unfolded, a strange thing became manifest — the vote was unanimous. Every man present had written the same name and that not a soldier, though they were loyal admirers of their most famous captains. Each slip bore the two words Florence Nightingale!"

P

But physical nature was to be as kind to Miss Barton in London as human nature was to Florence Nightingale, and England's early Spring revived her drooping spirits. With the warm sunshine and the growing green things and the flowers her spirits and strength rose again. She even, as she wrote, set out to go as far as Shakespeare's home at Stratford-on-Avon.

"I can go about town and even once have been out of town but not for a long trip," she wrote rejoicingly.

Antoinette Margot was still faithfully by her side, and her niece, Mamie Barton, now Mrs. John Stafford of Oxford, the young guest of Miss Barton, who had spent the winter with her.

In October Miss Barton had sufficiently recovered her strength to attempt the passage home and she set sail for the United States during the first week of the month, carrying with her as her deepest hope, "*The founding of the Red Cross in America*."

CHAPTER XXX

CONTINUED NERVOUS PROSTRATION IN AMERICA

1873-1880

THROUGH all her long periods of illness Miss Barton never forgot her resolve to establish the National Red Cross in the United States. Yet while her mind and soul were inspired by the vision of what was to be, her body was weak. The crossing of the ocean proved too much for her, and shortly after her arrival in Washington she was ill again.

By February, 1874, her active spirit planned her propaganda for the establishment of the American National Red Cross, and she aimed at a residence on Capitol Hill — to be near the seat of affairs.

But in the latter half of the following letter she discloses the warning hand of her physician. Beginning with putting herself in another's place as usual, she writes in February to a niece:

"DEAREST POLLY:

"It is so nice to hear that you run about in the snow. Do all you can of such nonsense without getting cold. It cannot harm you in any other way. Just rush out and gallop around, and have a good time generally. What is the use of living in the country if we can't get its freedom of action. Romp around over your back hills — they are splendid, — but tie up the *ears*, don't try to breath through them. You are not a *fish* that you should take air in through your *gills*. I know, my dear little girl, how 'hard it is to forget them' and their troubles, but be kind to them, they will complain less.

"Don't get cold from it more than you can help. Do anything to keep warm, especially the feet. Grandpa Barton used to say he did not believe a person ever took cold while their feet were really thoroughly warm.

"I am so glad to know that your Papa David is a little better, if it only lasts. But you have had another storm since your last, at least *we* have, and the ground is covered to-day. Sleighs are out, but it is bright and warm like May — only for the snow. . . .

"Dr. Thompson came to make his first call, and then I had an opportunity to ask him if I could live on Capitol Hill. You should have heard his decided and determined '*NO*. No, my child, you *cannot!* The thing is not to be thought of for a moment for *you*. Other people of different temperament and in full strength may live there with safety, but *not you*.' So that is settled for all my aspirations. Dr. Thompson wants me to go and visit them in his beautiful home and stay as many weeks as I can content myself. He is as good as a brother — and I think perhaps the most successful physician in Washington — 'What am I going to do with myself now?'

"I neglected to say that the Dr. gave my limits where I could live in the city, viz.: from 7th to 16th sts. & from N. Y. Ave. only. These are my jail limits. . . ."

On May 24th, word reached Miss Barton there that her sister Sally was dying. Ill though she was, Miss Barton left Washington for Worcester in a Pullman car. Heartbroken, she reached Worcester the evening after her sister's death. She felt the wrench of loneliness that comes at the breaking of the home circle. Only David remained. The father and mother and oldest sister Dorothy had been dead some years. Stephen, her oldest brother, she had lost in 1865.

"Worn out, sleepless, wretched and despairing," she wrote in 1886, "news came to me that the last sister, lovely as an angel, named for my mother, was fading in Worcester, Massachusetts. I was taken from my bed and rushed through palace cars to meet her at once. I reached there in the evening. She had gone in the morning. It was too much. Body and soul were stricken. Two years of utter prostration without power to walk or wearily to rise from my bed, or to sleep, eat or to see friends, write or read a letter, taught me deeper sympathy for human suffering than I had known before, or than can be known save by living it."

Miss Barton remained for part of the year with Mrs. Vassall of Worcester and with other relatives nearby, and then, still failing in health, went to a countryside home of the Learned family in "New England Village" — (North Grafton), where Minnie Kupfer, her faithful companion in the Franco-Prussian War, was by her side and in October wrote of her as follows to Mary Barton:

"WORCESTER, October 21, 1874.

'MY DEAR MISS MAMIE:

"I wish I could tell you that your dear Aunty is very much better, but I cannot say as much as that. There are many ups and downs yet, I can only hope and trust that she will grow stronger, perhaps so much the better if the progress to health is slow and sure.

"I send you some little drawings which your dear Aunty made. She takes up now and then the box of pencils which you took down from the upper room and uses them very skillfully as you may see.

"Yours sincerely,

"M. W. KUPFER."

A sketch of her own condition Miss Barton gives in another letter to the same niece:

"DEAREST MAMIE

"They let me see no one at present — I am weak — Night before last I had a chill which lasted ten hours without once letting up. I was cold and wet as a fish every minute of the time.

"Give great love to all.   "BYAS."

In another note she added

"Want to see Dave and Julia *so, so, so* much. Had an ugly old chill yesterday — wanted them both to come to me *then* — "

These severe chills had now been prostrating her for many weeks, Mrs. Abby Sheldon having written of them as far back as July 28th:

"WORCESTER, July 28, 1874.

"Tues., P.M.

"DEAR MAMIE:

"Aunt Clara gained every day last week until Friday — then she had another chill — slight, but enough to keep her back Saturday and Monday. Yesterday she felt remarkably well, but this morning she had another touch of chill — lighter than before, but a decided hindrance. If the Dr. could only manage these chills, I am sure she would very soon be on her feet.

"I can see that she is better in many ways than she was a week ago, but she is still a sick woman.

"Very sincerely yours,

"ABBY SHELDON."

That the sunniness of Miss Barton's disposition penetrated even into her sick room is shown in the following plea for company:

"New England Village, Mass., — 1874.

"Dearest Mamie ·

"I have only one minute in which to say pocket your popgun and come on. No one here ain't afraid of ye.

"Bring your pictures and stay your stay.. I meant to have written yesterday, but I did not.

"All so so. Miss K. has a little bilious attack to-day and I ain't firstrate today but it is all the weather. Here is the postman.

"Byas."

On June 30th, 1875, she wrote, nearly a year later:

"Dearest Polly:

"We go on just as usual, no interruptions, nothing to hinder and nothing to help. We are haying to-day, *i.e.* cutting the grass in the orchard and about the house. I don't go out to superintend it.

"School is closed here for 12 weeks, and it is *said* the mills will stop July 1st. I do not know this *surely*. Our roses are in full bloom and cherries getting red.

"This Village is just as nice as ever. Everyone is so kind and polite, and such freedom from gossip. Society has been well led here in the past and low things put down unnoticed, instead of being carried about and retailed and laughed at.

"You must tell me how the revival is getting on. I hope it will do good, and the table-tippings — you must tell me of them.

"Have you noticed so as to make up any aggregate the number of persons who have probably been destroyed by accidents or rather the convulsive overacting of the natural elements these last few months. I have not kept the numbers at all, but it seems to me not less than 60,000 since the commencement of this year. You know the great earthquake of New Granada took from 15 to 20,000. The bursting volcanoes of Iceland nearly as many, the floods in Hungary 5000 or more and now in France from 10,000 to 20,000 and these are only a portion of the great disasters. Add to these the loss of life by fires and steamers and the numbers are appalling — more than equal to a great and devastating war.

"I wonder when they will call in the disagreeing jury on the Beecher case. They evidently will never agree, and perhaps it is best they should not. I think the best ending of it would be to never find a jury that would render a verdict. It would not change anything if they did, and not agreeing will I suppose leave each to pay his own costs (if he can) and certainly neither of them could pay costs for both, and if they have both danced a little perhaps it is right they should join in paying the fiddler, but if those *carpet* men have been lying, I hope they will get their deserts. *That was scoundrelly.*

"It is warm, but such *pretty* weather one likes to look at it. How glad I am that that lying carpet layer who sprang up against Mr. Beecher and Mrs. Tilton is likely to get the worst of it. I hope he will get 10 years in prison. I have seen such devils as that myself."

Again she wrote:

"Your dear note has just come. It was good of you to write me again before I answered you. I haven't written much for a few days. I shall be so glad to see you. You come. You ought to get up and start by 5 o'clock so as to come while it is cool and not get sweaty and hot coming, but it is only two or three miles farther than to Worcester. You will stay all night or a few days, won't you? I am sure your horse wont want to go back at once and our grass is cut now so he can browse in the orchard, and stamp under the trees all he likes.

"What beauty dresses you and Ida have. How nice to be able to wear little dresses, isn't it? I am so glad you have taken *one* lesson. Go on, 'Sing on, pray on, sisters of Emmanuel. You will conquer yet.' We want to see you *so so* much, and both send much love to you and all."

The Friday before New Year's, 1875, she again wrote:

"DEAREST POLLY:

"I am not a bit well today, but shall be better 'morrow day' I hope. We shall send a little package which will go with this and you will have a specimen of my *first worsted work*, which please receive both of you with auntie's best love and wishes for a Happy, Happy New Year.   "BYAS."

Her condition demanded that early in 1876 she go to a rest cure. She chose Dr. Jackson's Sanitarium of Dansville, New York, remaining in the hospital and vicinity for nearly ten years.

"I have *made* a journey," she announced to a friend, "for a very *needed purpose*. And I journey with great labor and trouble and risk. I am come with great pain to see if I can be advised or taught how to get back some of my lost strength. I have come to school, and I am listening and obeying like a faithful pupil. I am here to strive with might and main for the prize which is life, its forfeit death, so don't fear that I shall run away, or rush off to some new scene. I shall stay, and learn, and study, and obey. You know there is no medicine here, one is not cured, but instructed how to get well, if possible, or at least to keep from getting worse. This was my great dread and danger before I came here, that I could not hold myself where I was through the warm season.

"My mind is relieved from care now. I know I am surrounded by those who know a great deal more than I do and at last I can lay down the reins and ride at my ease. I am relieved from the management of my team, and this is such a rest.

"I am not expected to write much but rest a great deal. On days when I take baths I can do nothing else."

In a July letter she describes her life:

"OUR HOME, July 21, 1876.

"DEAREST MAMIE:

"It is a good cool morning. 'Byas' has taken a walk along the cottages out on to the high grounds overlooking the town, come back, taken her little red 'blanket' pencils and paper and come out into the shady corner of one of the wings of the Institute, found a seat with herself in the shade, and her feet and limbs in the sunshine and is going to write Mamie till the gong rings for breakfast. It is just as quiet and lovely all about as it can be, only the birdies and squirrels run around. The leaves are still on the trees, the grass as green as it can be, and full of clover blossoms, and Byas can go right out into it and sit down and write among it all. How do you suppose that seems to her after all these years of imprisonment? No one but Byas can know how it seems, or even have the most distant conception of it. And it is dry here and lets one get off clothing that weak persons must be burdened with in damp climates or places. Byas wears no flannel, neither under nor over, but cotton flannel, then one of her little thin white sheet underskirts, and her linen dress, but it is all made over, has no belt, high boots and short stockings, so as to have no trouble with elastics or supporters. She is dressed just as free and easy as a gentleman with lots of pockets and perambulates around to suit herself. Now she can't say more for the first gong has sounded. The place is in its tramp towards the halls and parlors. All speak to Byas as they pass. Here comes the Chaplain and will stop to say something and so Byas must say good bye till later. After breakfast she will take a bath and so may not get at this again to-day: Bye Bye.

"After breakfast Byas has slipped out of the parlor during the morning devotions and come up to her room till bath time, to get the chance to finish Mamie's letter because she will wait anxiously to get it."

Even here her correspondence Internationally and Nationally grew daily larger — with always as the motive the formation of the Red Cross in America.

"DANSVILLE, N. Y.
"Sunday, Dec. 3, 1876.

"DEAREST MAMIE:

"Your card came yesterday and found me as busy as it left you, but I will get a moment to write more than I could say on a card.

"I have letters from France and Alsace but not from persons you know; they are always in French. This is the birthday of the dear Grand Duchess and I ought to be writing her but I do not feel quite equal to it.

"I hear from M.——. He is still weak from a severe illness of several months overwork, and perplexities and cares of business produced nervous prostration. He is still too ill to see persons, and sleeps very little, remains in his room almost entirely. Still is gaining, lost 70 pounds weight. See what nervous prostration can do to strong men and imagine what it is for already weak women to go through and be careful."

January 1, 1877, in a letter to Marion Bullock we find Miss Barton still under the wise care at Dr. Jackson's Hospital.

"TO MY DARLING MARION:

"The time allowed me to write is so small — Miss Adams will tell you how close the lines are drawn here against overmuch writing — I am better than I used to be." (Referring to her North Grafton prostration in 1874–1875, when Mrs. Bullock, then a young girl, lived next door).

Her recovery, however, was in view.

"I am careful but can do many things."

As at the end of the Civil War when John B. Gough pronounced Miss Barton, his fellow citizen, the most interesting lecturer he had heard, so now upon her return from European battle fields he had been publishing the facts of her triumphs.

Of this she wrote:

"It was very kind of you to write of Mr. Gough and his remarks on me. I thought I had shown you the little 'emblems' and decoration which he spoke of — They are only crosses given to me by the Emperor of Germany, and the Grand Duchess of Baden and her husband the Grand Duke and the 'Red Cross of Geneva.' All presented as testimonials of service performed in the Franco-Prussian War — the Geneva Cross, the Iron Cross of merit, the Gold Cross of remembrance.

"CLARA BARTON."

The same day she wrote her niece:

"DANSVILLE, Jan. 1, 1877.

"MY DEAREST MAMIE:

"I should have written you sooner but I had a hard cold and was not well enough to write, so everyone has waited till the pile of letters is something appalling to behold. I am over my cold now but of course not so strong and able to write as if I had not had it.

"We, too, are having winter. Snow a foot deep. I go sleighing some. It is pretty cold but I like this. I do not cough this winter thus far.

"No, I do not paint any, and am not writing a book. I am doing nothing, and that is all I *can* do.

"They had a famous Christmas tree at the 'Home' in Liberty Hall and 800 presents given from it. I was not well enough to be present.

"Be a good little girl and write sometimes to slack old

"BYAS."

So much did she profit by the treatment that by November she entered a private home she had bought on Leonard Street where she plunged deeper into her Red Cross campaign and also went to housekeeping as her companion describes in the following:

DANSVILLE, Nov. 2.

" She has a good home-woman — who can do *all* there is to be done, and take care of 'Byas' so she can get on with her desk. And Byas has cleared it of letters, and can do other writing now. Her woman is middle-aged, of German descent, married — good about the house as well as in — can do common sewing and has her own machine. She is kind and pleasant and tries to do all she can to make it pleasant and easy."

It is plain that "to get on with her desk" meant but one thing — The Red Cross and The Treaty of Geneva.

By January, 1878, she had commenced her strategic visits to Washington, having in mind the coming hour to strike for the Red Cross.

That she was well received among the nation's notables is apparent in this letter:

"WASHINGTON, D. C., Jan. 4, '78.
"501 C St. South East.

"MY DEAREST MAMIE:

"Your dear letter came about New Years, but I have not had a moment of time since to write you.

"For two days before the 1st, I was busy sending off cards, for I have to make them do all my calling for the holidays and much of my writing and calling for the year.

"Then New Years Day I received with Mrs. Hitz and all the world came from 10 A.M. till P.M. although I left the scene at 8½

"One feature of the occasion was my completed portrait which was that presented to Mrs. John Hitz and hung on the wall for criticism and remarks by the callers. It was favorably judged I believe. It is not a life sized head, but about ⅓ life size, the entire figure, standing in a room with all its accessories as table, bookcase, pictures, etc., about such a size as Antoinette always wanted to paint of me. About the photo all for yourself — you shall have it, my little girl, if I have to make it myself. Yesterday I had a good deal of writing to do, and last evening I spent at the President's, not at a levee, but by invitation in the parlor with only a few friends. I do not think it perhaps worth the while to speak of this as it might seem like vanity, when it is me, but I wanted you to know what a beautiful bright lady I think Mrs. Hayes to be. She is brilliant and beautiful, brunette with abundant jet black hair put back over her ears, and with just such little curls as I used to wear which were such a delight to poor Antoinette, you recollect, just the ends of the hair in a puff curl with a wide comb behind the ear. She is entirely different from the Grand Duchess, and still bright and full of life like her. I have not seen her enough to know if she is as affectionate. Did I tell you of the last letter I had from the Grand Duchess? In it she tells me all about her family and all the people there, — how her children have grown, how old they all are, their ways and characteristics, all about Miss Zimmerman, and that she is Godmother for Anna's little girl and that she inquired most kindly for you, and hopes you are well and happy. I have forgotten if I wrote it all to you or not, it may have come after my last letter from home had been written you, and I forgot it here."

By this year of 1878 Miss Barton is living "full days" again. One finds little indication of the former invalid in the following New Year's letter:

"MY DEAR IDA:

"This comes to wish you a Happy New Year. With a heart full of love, and a soul full of cheer.

"Your dear letter has been waiting too long for a reply, but I had many things to press it aside, and had a hard cold besides which would not let me do anything; so 'all the world' waited if it hasn't 'wondered,' until my desk became a sight to behold. Now I am ploughing through it and like all work poorly done, some of it will have to be done over."

Deep as she was, however, in work, she never talked shop about herself. She transferred herself at once to the position of her friend:

"Do you have lots of sleigh rides? I do, when I am able to take them.

"You recollect writing me of 'Tom' Lamb — well he has trace of me and the jolliest letters you ever saw is the result. One came last night of eight pages. He told me in a former letter of his call at your house and all about 'David' and you all, when I answered and asked him questions of himself and his farm, and if he kept many horses, as if I remembered that ran a little in the blood. I knew this would draw his fire, and his answer came last night, 'Yes, I

CLARA BARTON IN 1879
As she arose from nervous prostration to found the Red Cross in America.

keep seven horses and not David Lamb's old horses either. I have one that can go a mile in three minutes; I wish you were here to ride after it, this good sleighing, it would almost take your breath away, but don't think by this I want to kill you.'

"You will perhaps not understand that allusion to David Lamb, but your father will. Wants me to come and help him milk his cows (30) and go fishing in Lake Ontario with him. He's a jolly fellow, as he was a boy. Thinks all the way I can keep him from coming to see me, is by coming to see him."

By the Fall of 1878 more than ever the all-important theme in Clara Barton's mind was the foundation of the Red Cross. She made a determined effort to reach Congress, with permanent headquarters in Washington. Bending under the herculean attempt, she had to retreat for recovery, as is thus shown:

"DANSVILLE, N. Y., April 27, '79.

"MY DEAR MARION (Mrs. Marion Balcom Bullock):

"Then came other cases more engrossing than before and then I had to return to Washington last fall, but grew ill, and had to come home again, and so am here now. Being unsettled by going to Washington for the early winter, I remained in Miss Kupfer's house the remainder of the winter but on the first of the month I came to my home of year before last, which has been all made up new and is large enough for us all. And so Miss Kupfer came to live in it with me, and is as happy as a bird. Miss —— is still with me, but she spends a portion of her time in study, and I have other help. I was quite weak most of the winter but am better now, and can walk all over my grounds, and shall soon be about as usual.

"How is that precious mother of yours, since I left her I have never found her equal. No face could come into my doorway that would bring with it such a thrill of joy (as if a sister had come) as hers. I don't think she ever quite knew how near she came to me and how deep she got into my heart affection. I live in hopes one day to see her, and you too.

"Please tell your dear mama that I am in better health and strength than she ever thought to see me, and better than she ever will see me unless she comes, I fear, and so I think she had best do it — sometime. . . ."

There is a great deal in Miss Barton's letters in the fall of 1879 concerning horses and riding, recalling vividly her own girlhood when to cling to the back of a racing horse gave her the keenest pleasure. Here for example in a letter to her niece, Mrs. Adolph Riccius, we find her saying:

"I should enjoy some of your rides. I keep no horse and someway don't enjoy riding with other people. My jolly days of riding were, I think, with your mother. I don't believe any two girls and women in that town ever got as much actual fun out of riding and driving about as we have from first to last. I wonder if she does not think so? and I wonder if she rides much now? I can scarcely imagine your father without a horse, and driving about all over town in some kind of a 'caboose' if it were only two rails with a board across."

To Adolph she writes, November 30, 1879, much in the same strain, adding a bit of advice:

"I wouldn't drive a bit hard, and I wouldn't let the horses stand uncovered in the cold winds. I would get home in time so you could put up the team by decent bed time. Better still if I could go with you and Ida for company and all come home together. Indeed I am not sure but I am enjoying that almost as much in imagination as I could the reality. What a power imagination is! I think you have had a little more snow than we have. We have had nothing like sleighing yet, the ground just white for a few hours twice, but the 'cold wave' passed over us a week ago, and caught a great deal of grain and fruit ungathered and came very near freezing my cellar and in that case I don't know but I should have been compelled to call upon Ida for some of her canned fruits and stuff to help me out."

In a letter to Mrs. Riccius, Miss Barton has more to say about these canned fruits and her other housewifely occupations:

"And you put up lots of fruit did you? I wish we could compare notes on that point 'cause' I have a little. I cannot tell you how much work I have done this summer and fall, say in the last four months, and no one could tell you how much I have enjoyed it. I have done much housekeeping and have had it all my own way, and have got it so homelike, i.e. to me (I don't know if it would seem so to any one else or not) that I feel not only happy, but I feel a little proud, not of the success — but of the strength that let me do it. I am quite alone but for a German boy who lives with me. He is accustomed to housework, can cook and keep house generally and will be a baker when he has finished learning his trade, but he needs to go no farther to bake for me.   His bread is unquestionable — think of us two with six great loaves at a baking, and I make the pies, ten at a time, and I don't have a great deal of company and it is all eaten. And big boiled dinners and soups, for I had a large garden, and my cellar is well filled.   I too have a kitty and he is pretty much master of the house.   He is black and white and weighs as much as he can. I have made him a winter house of a large dry goods box and 25 pounds of good hay, — he takes fresh raw steak for breakfast with a saucer of milk then retires to his house and sleeps most of the day. Toward dusk he generally helps himself to a fresh meat lunch with the fur on, from the cellar or barn or field and about seven he comes in for his tea, and it is real tea with a little sugar, and a good deal of milk and a small plate of crackers, nothing else for supper.   He wants to sit in my lap and have me feed him his soaked cracker from my fingers and then be told he is a good pussy for about fifteen minutes.   Then he springs out into the night and the darkness and away into the unlucky game from then till long after midnight.   He is always back in his house in the morning but frequently so tired out that he will not answer the call to breakfast till ten o'clock or after. I need not say that we are not troubled with rats or mice.   Miss Kupfer has had charge of Kitty's education since he was three months old.   He doesn't speak German although I have no doubt he understands it.   But Miss Kupfer has about fifty other pupils that do speak it.   She is Matron and teacher of German and French at the Seminary, and full of work.   I took Thanksgiving dinner there, and this week Friday the entire. Faculty and house pupils will hold their weekly 'sociable' at my house — The members will be only from twelve to twenty I suppose, but nice people, and some very accomplished pupils.   I don't know if I shall succeed in entertaining them well.   I wish you and Mamie were here to assist me.   It is only a 'sociable' and as it is held just after dinner there are no refreshments — so you see it is as your father would say 'all talk and no cider.' "

To no public service was Clara Barton ever deaf.   Dansville Seminary near by interested her, and besides quartering some of the teachers at her home, she plead for it in a public meeting after this manner:

"I am aware that the great question in the present crisis is a financial one, that the present proprietors of the Institution, in their young zeal to make their school all it should be, have incurred debts, which it is at present, and perhaps forever, under existing circumstances, and single handed, impossible for them to liquidate, and the beautiful feature of the case is, that you, the public, — their creditors, have generously met together to find how you can aid them in their perplexed, and praise-worthy efforts.

"I am their nearest neighbor, and during all this year certainly I have looked on with admiration and wonder, at the patient labor I saw there, and the tireless, pains-taking, patient cheerfulness with which it was performed, — the ability and good order with which all was conducted, and the correct high moral tone pervading and illuminating every act, and apparently every thought, and have never ceased to feel how fortunate, beyond almost any village of its size I have known, was this village of *Dansville* in having in its midst, and especially in the absence of any well organized system of Public Schools, this *Seminary*, within the shadow of its home equal in its facilities for both sexes to a college in Dansville."

Haply we have the impression Miss Barton's personality left upon the people of Dansville as they expressed it in the press at an ovation in her honor:

"Miss Barton is a woman somewhat above medium size, of pleasant mobile features; wonderfully expressive. Her dark eyes have liquid depths which seem unfathomable. They have so often looked upon suffering humanity that they seem full of pity, but there is something about them suggesting fire that can blaze upon occasion with righteous indignation at a wrong. Her luxuriant hair, still black as the raven's wings, does not follow fashion's ways, but is dressed like hair in Longfellow's Evangeline, low down on either side of the forehead. On this occasion Miss Barton was attired in a rich black silk. At her throat was suspended a magnificent pansy amethyst presented her by the Grand Duchess of Baden, the finest and largest stone of the kind in this country. At the right she wore her royal arch mason badge which came to her from her father, and just below it the jewel of the American Red Cross. On the left was the Servian decoration of the Red Cross presented by Queen Natalie; just above the Gold Cross of remembrance presented by the Grand Duke and Duchess of

Baden; and just above these two, the iron cross of Merit, for which so many serve a lifetime, the gift of the Emperor and Empress of Germany. And yet with all these proud testimonials of eminent service Miss Barton stood before her friends simply, as their warm-hearted neighbor, their loving sister."

During 1880–'81 she concentrated her every energy to bringing to a climax her campaign of education concerning the Red Cross Treaty of Geneva.

From Dansville, N. Y., January 17, 1881, she wrote:

"I have done a good deal of what would be called Public Writing in the last year, and this, added to my large correspondence, and all the calls I have the time for, has made it a long year, but the good Lord be praised for giving me the strength to be busy once more."

CHAPTER XXXI

THE FOUNDATION OF THE RED CROSS IN AMERICA

To Clara Barton belongs the story of the birth of the Red Cross in America, and we shall rely upon her various manuscripts and printed histories to tell it in so far as it is possible.

First of all we must recall that Miss Barton succeeded where two able statesmanlike reformers had failed. The United States Minister Plenipotentiary to Switzerland had urged the adhesion to the Red Cross Treaty of Geneva during the Civil War as early as 1864. Later, beginning in 1868, the famous Dr. Henry W. Bellows, the genius and force behind the Sanitary Commission of the Civil War, tried for ten years to secure in the United States the recognition and adoption of the Treaty. But even he could not overcome the national apathy. Indeed, he faced a certain antipathy born of a jealous fear lest the International features and the league with monarchical governments might weaken the Republic.

Upon Miss Barton's taking up the treaty that after ten years of effort was apparently a failure so far as the United States was concerned, Dr. Bellows turned to her and said: "I advise you to give it up as hopeless." Later, seeing her determination, he wrote:

"MY DEAR MISS BARTON: It has been a sore disappointment and mortification to those who inaugurated the plan of organized relief by private contributions for sick and wounded soldiers, in our late war, since so largely followed by other nations, that they should still find the United States the only great government that refuses to join in the Treaty framed by the International Convention of

---

[1] The original manuscripts of the addresses of Miss Barton as preserved by her executor, are the sources from which most of the history of these two Red Cross chapters are drawn. Parts of these, later found, have been issued as reports in print in the pages of "*The Red Cross*" and "*The Story of the Red Cross*." To interlard this material, I use personalia, unpublished letters, etc.

Geneva, for neutralizing battle fields, after the battle, and making the persons of surgeons and nurses flying to the relief of the wounded and dying, free from arrest.

"This great international agreement for mitigating the horrors of war, finds its chief defect in the conspicuous refusal of the United States government to join in the Treaty! The importance of our national concurrence with other governments in this noble Treaty, has been urged upon every administration since the war, but has thus far met only the reply that our national policy did not allow us to enter into entangling alliances with other powers. I rejoice to hear from you, that our late President, and his chief official advisers were of a different opinion, and encouraged the hope that in the interests of mercy and humanity, it might be safe to agree by treaty with all the civilized world, that we would soften to non-combatants, the hateful conditions that made relief on battle fields a peril or a forbidden act. I trust you will press this matter upon our present administration with all the weight of your well-earned influence. Having myself somewhat ignominiously failed to get any encouragement for this measure from two administrations, I leave it in your more fortunate hands, hoping that the time is ripe for a less jealous policy than American self isolation in International movements for extending and universalizing mercy towards the victims of war.

"Yours truly,
"H. W. BELLOWS."

"Outwardly the subject slept," Miss Barton explains, "until 1877, when it was again presented, during the administration of President Hayes. After almost five years I was able to go to Washington with a letter from Monsieur Moynier, President of the International Committee of Geneva, to the President of the United States asking once more that our government accept the articles of the Convention. Having been made the official bearer of this letter, I presented it to President Hayes, who received it kindly, referring it to the Secretary of State, Mr. Evarts, who in his turn referred it to his Assistant Secretary as the person who knew all about it and to report his decision."

This letter was as follows:

"GENEVA, 19 August, 1877.

"International Committee for the Relief of Wounded Soldiers:

"To the President of the United States at Washington.

"MR. PRESIDENT:

"The International Committee of the Red Cross desire most earnestly that the United States should be associated with them in their work, and they take the liberty of addressing themselves to you with the hope that you will second their efforts. In order that the functions of the National Society of the Red Cross be faithfully performed, it is indispensable that it should have the sympathy and protection of the Government. It would be irrational to establish an association upon the principles of The Convention of Geneva, without the Association having the assurance that the Army of its own country, of which it should be an auxiliary, would be guided, should the case occur, by the same principles. It would consequently be useless for us to appeal to the people of the country, inasmuch as the United States as a Government has made no declaration of adhering officially to the principles laid down by the Convention of the 22nd of August, 1864.

"Such is, then, Mr. President, the principal object of the present request. We do not doubt but this will meet with a favorable reception from you, for the United States are in advance of Europe upon the subject of war, and the celebrated 'Instructions of the American Army' are a monument which does honor to the United States.

"You are aware, Mr. President, that the Government of the United States, was officially represented at the conference of Geneva in 1864, by two delegates, and this mark of approbation, given to the work which was being accomplished, was then considered by everyone as a precursor of a legal satisfaction. Until the present time, however, this confirmation has not taken place, and we think that this formality, which would have no other bearing than to express publicly the acquiescence of the United States in these humanitarian principles now admitted by all civilized people, has only been retarded because the occasion has not offered itself. We flatter ourselves with the hope that appealing directly to your generous sentiments will determine you to take the necessary measure to put an end to a situation so much to be regretted.

"We only wait such good news, Mr. President, in order to urge the founding of an American Society of the Red Cross.

"We have already an able and devoted assistant in Miss Clara Barton, to whom we confide the care of handing to you this present request.

"It would be very desirable that the projected association should be under your distinguished patronage and we hope that you will not refuse us this favor.

"Receive, Mr. President, the assurance of our highest consideration,
"For the International Committee,
"G. MOYNIER, President."

This letter was shelved — a fact which Miss Barton soon perceived. "I then saw," she noted, "how the fate of The Red Cross depended not alone on the Department but on *one man* who was Assistant Secretary of State in 1864 and in 1868 when the Treaty had on two occasions been presented to our Government. It was a settled thing. There was nothing to hope from that Administration. It would be decided because it had been decided. If I pressed it to a decision, this would outweigh it with a third refusal. I waited. My next thought was to refer it to Congress. That would be irregular and discourteous to the administration. I did not like to take it; still I attempted it, but could not get it considered as it found neither political patronage nor votes.

"The next year I returned to Washington to try Congress again. I published a little pamphlet of two leaves addressed to the members and Senators to be laid upon their desks in the hope they would take the trouble to read so little as that. My strength failed before I could get the bills presented, and I went home again. There then remained but a portion of the administration and I determined to outlive it, hoping another would be more responsive. Meanwhile I wrote, talked and did whatever I could to spread the idea among the people."

During this time a committee was formed by Miss Barton, consisting of four people, three women and one man. This committee called itself the "American National Committee, or Society of the Red Cross for the Relief of Sufferings by war, pestilence, famine, fire, flood and other calamities, so great as to be regarded as national in extent." A small pamphlet was published explaining its objects.

That Miss Barton's zeal for the cause did not lessen with the passing of time is shown by the following quotations from a speech of 1881: "I will not yield the pact of the treaty; for patriotism, for national honor, I will stand by that at all cost. My first and greatest endeavor has been to wipe from the scroll of my country's fame the stain of imputed lack of common humanity; to take her out of the roll of barbarians. In 1869 there were twenty-two nations in the compact. There are now thirty and since that date have been added Roumania, Persia, San Salvador, Montenegro, Servia, Bolivia, Chili, the Argentine Republic and Peru. If the United States of America is diligent and fortunate, she may perhaps come to stand number thirty-two in the roll of civilization and humanity! At present she stands among the barbarians and heathen."

Her deductions in full she formulated in an address and published it in the year 1881 in "An Address to the President, Congress and the People of the United States."

With the election of Garfield to the Presidency it was at once seen that the Red Cross in America was likely to become an established fact. The great soul of Garfield had been touched all along by Miss Barton's conception of the Red Cross for America. She had worked in blood and fire before his eyes. He himself had stood with her under the rain of bullets and shell in the Civil War for their country's cause. Hence the bond of sympathy was strong.

"When President Garfield came, I went again to Washington," Miss Barton says. "The request that the treaty be signed was cordially received by the President and by him referred to Secretary Blaine who considered it himself, conferred fully with me, and finally laid it before the President and Cabinet." [1]

Miss Barton found that the one objection to perpetuating the Red Cross system for relief in war in America, was that we then had no wars and were not likely to have any. This seemed to many an unanswerable argument.

Miss Barton's constructive mind at once pointed to other great national disasters, as fields of relief, recording her convictions thus:

[1] "In his letter of reply of May 20th, 1881, Secretary Blaine promised 'full sympathy,' careful attention and consideration to Miss Barton's presentation. He stated further that he had no doubt but that the administration would recommend to Congress the adoption of the International treaty."

"None is more liable than our own country to great overmastering calamities. Seldom a year passes that the nation from sea to sea is not brought to utter consternation by the shock of some unforeseen disaster and stands shivering like a ship in the gale, powerless, horrified, despairing. Plagues, cholera, fires, floods, famine, all bear upon us with terrible force. Like war these events are entirely out of the common course. Like death, they are sure to come in some form and at some time, and like it, no mortal knows how, or when or where. What have we in readiness to meet these emergencies save the good heart of the people and their impulsive gifts. Certainly no organized system for collection, reception, distribution, no agents, nurses."

The result was the plan later evolved for the extension of the Red Cross to disasters in time of peace of which she wrote:

"The American Committee felt itself sustained in making these important extensions in its field of action by the text of Article 20 of the Berlin Conference of 1886, which recommends that the societies established under the Treaty of Geneva, extend relief in time of peace to public calamities, which require, like war, prompt and well organized help.

She then proceeded to trace the evolution of the whole idea in America and to immortalize the master minds who had caught the vision of the Red Cross.[1]

"The committee of 1877," writes Miss Barton, "devoted itself to the dissemination of a knowledge of the subject among the people, and the creation of a sentiment favorable to the adoption of the Treaty by the government; but, it was not until almost four years later, with the incoming of the administration of Garfield, that any favorable response was made, — and audience gained, — or the slightest echo returned to the faithful and persistent rappings of humanity through seventeen weary years.

"It will not, perhaps, be inappropriate, to name some of the persons no less than the measure, to whose active exertions, and philanthropic natures, the accession of our country to the Treaty of Geneva was at last due.

---

[1] She stated that with the exception of our own, no Red Cross constitution covered more than the field of war. The Congress at Berne accepted, or ratified, her application of the organization to calamities in time of peace, and that phase of the Red Cross became known as " The American Amendment."

"Its first official advocate and tireless friend from the advent of the presentation of 1877, was Hon. Omar D. Conger, now senator from Michigan, then a member of the House. Hon. Secretary Windom, a member of President Garfield's cabinet laid it before the President in cabinet session. It was cordially received, and responded to, by the President and his cabinet. Hon. Secretary of State, James G. Blaine, wrote a cordial letter of approval, and President Garfield promised to recommend in his first annual message to congress, the accession of the United States to the Treaty.

"Upon receipt of this information, the original American Committee of 1877 was reorganized and incorporated, under the name of the American Association of the Red Cross with the same objects as at first." A new and more comprehensive constitution was drafted by the Hon. William Lawrence of Ohio, then First Comptroller of the Treasury of the United States.

"Years of untold labor were now beginning to tell," she continued.

"By advice of President Garfield and three members of his historic cabinet, James G. Blaine, William Windom, and Robert T. Lincoln, it was known as the Association of the American Red Cross, and by desire and nomination of President Garfield, I was made its President and requested to name my officers.

"The Association was formed during the winter of 1880–81 with the view on the part of President Garfield of facilitating the adoption of the Treaty which he would name in his next message, which was never written.

"Scarcely was this accomplished, when the assassin's shot palsied the great heart and strong hand on which the first hopes of the Red Cross had grown. Then followed the weary eighty days of national agony, when hope seemed once more smothered in the pall and the bier.

"But a great-hearted and strong-handed successor came to the rescue, and nobly took up the work where it had been left. The first general message of President Arthur carried out the plan and faithfully performed the promise of his lamented predecessor. This act carried the subject before the Hon. Committee of Foreign Affairs in the Senate and there it again met its original friend, Senator Morgan of Alabama, who had been one of the first to comprehend its true character, and Senator Lapham of New York, who had been its un-

CLARA BARTON AS FOUNDER OF THE AMERICAN NATIONAL
RED CROSS, 1882

tiring friend, and who had given to it his watchful care, and strong legal ability upon all occasions.

"The dark days of the long neglected Treaty began to brighten, and its lines to fall in pleasant places.

"After able discussion the accession of the United States to the Articles of the Conventions of both 1864 and 1868, was agreed upon, and the Treaty received the signature of President Arthur on the 1st of March, 1882.

"It was ratified by the Senate on the 16th of the same month, and the stipulations were exchanged at Berne, Switzerland, on the 9th of June, and on the 26th of July, the Treaty was proclaimed by the President to the people of the United States.

"Thus the first great movement towards the neutralization of nations and International Relief in war became to this country an accomplished fact, and a Law of the Land."

The President of the International Red Cross at the convention at Geneva, September 2, 1882, characterized the birth of the American Red Cross, as follows:

"Its whole history is associated with a name already known to you — that of Miss Clara Barton; without the energy and persever-ance of this remarkable woman, we should not for a long time have had the pleasure of seeing the Red Cross received into the United States."

"I would say," Miss Barton wrote in 1882, "that our adhesion to this treaty has changed our articles of war and our military hospital flag. We have no longer the old faded yellow flag, but a bright red cross at every post and the same sign to be worn by all military surgeons and attendants if the orders of the war department have yet reached them. We are to-day, you will be glad to know, not only in full accord with the International Treaty of Geneva but are considered one of the strongest pledged nations within it.

"All this had been accomplished, by the kindly help of a few per-sonal friends, tireless and unremitting, and while the news of the accession of the Government of the United States to the treaty of Geneva, lit bonfires, that night (for I cabled at their request) in the streets of Switzerland, France, Germany, and Spain, a little four line paragraph in the Congressional doings of the day in the 'Evening Star,' Washington, alone announced to the people of America that an International Treaty had been added to their rolls. No formal distinction had been bestowed, no one honored, no one politically advanced, no money of the Government expended and like other things of like nature, it was left in obscurity to make its own way and live its own hard life."

In all this, though she did the work that founded it in America, Clara Barton never sought the Presidency of the American Red Cross. In fact, she planned in 1881 that President Garfield be President.

She declared that in Europe Kings, Emperors, Princes, and foremost men of State, were the presiding officers. But President Garfield stoutly refused and insisted that Miss Barton, in recognition of her long efforts to introduce the Red Cross Treaty of Geneva to this country, assume the office.

CHAPTER XXXII

CLARA BARTON AND THE AMERICAN NATIONAL RED CROSS IN NATIONAL AND INTERNATIONAL DISASTERS

1882–1897

"THE spring of 1882," Miss Barton relates in the "Story of the Red Cross," "found us a few people tired out and weak with five years of costly service, a treaty gained with no fund, no war, or prospect of any, and no helpful connection with, or acknowledgment by, the Government."

But Miss Barton was never deterred from a great purpose by obstacles which human endeavor could overcome. She had determined to make the Red Cross Society a living organ of personal mercy, and as the first requisite to this end was money, she gave liberally from her own resources.

The enemy was now to be mostly the forces of nature. But she felt that these must be met the same as destructive forces in war, by aggressiveness, describing it thus:

"The foes we had to meet had to be met as they came. They always must if any good is to be accomplished — Until a government and society can control the elements and regulate a spring freshet, a whirlwind or cyclone, they will find that red tape is not strong enough to hold these ravages in check."

"As to the labor of a Red Cross Field of relief, there are twenty in my recollection," she said looking back in later years, "and Galveston (the last great disaster where in 1900 nearly 10,000 lives were lost), was by no means the hardest. They have been lived, but never told. To be called upon to tell the whole story seems a labor scarcely less than to have lived it."

So comparatively recent are these great tragedies, that with the help of interesting reports in "The History of the Red Cross in Peace and War," and "The Story of the Red Cross," and with many unpublished letters which I have found, these pages need but condense the story of human relief.

The Red Cross fields of relief include in the space of twenty-three years:

The Michigan Forest Fires in 1881.
The Mississippi River Floods in 1882.
The Mississippi River Floods in 1883.
The Cyclone in Louisiana and Alabama in 1883.
The Balkan War in 1883.
The Ohio and Mississippi River Floods in 1884.
The Texas Famine in 1885.
The Charleston Earthquake in 1886.
The Mt. Vernon, Ill., Cyclone in 1888.
The Florida Yellow Fever Epidemic in 1888.
The Johnstown Disaster in 1889.
The Russian Famine in 1892.
The Pomeroy, Iowa, Cyclone in 1893.
The South Carolina Islands Hurricane and Tidal Wave in 1893–1894.
The Armenian Massacres, Turkey, Asia Minor, in 1896.
The Cuban Reconcentrado Relief in 1898–1900.
The Spanish-American War in 1898.
The Galveston Storm in 1900.
The Typhoid Fever Epidemic, Butler, Pa., in 1904.

In all of these national disasters, Miss Barton, usually in person, directed the new arm of organized mercy. By specific action, before the eyes of the nation on these colossal fields of suffering, she determined to graft the Red Cross into the body of the Republic.

Five years of her life had previously been devoted to educating the nation and the Government by carrying on a campaign of information. Now she is to give herself for nearly a quarter of a century to the operation of the Red Cross on twenty fields. "On these," she modestly comments, at the end of one of her narratives, "one has a little insight into the labor of a Red Cross Field of Relief."

During this quarter century, Miss Barton made her own home, first in Washington, then in Glen Echo, the Red Cross headquarters of the nation. From 1882, apart from her gifts to the field, she sustained the expenses of these headquarters at a sacrifice of $4000 a year, an expense totalling $76,000 during her Presidency. This did not include many advances she made to aid sudden demands for relief nor deficits afterwards which she cleared by giving from her own purse.

The first national calamity to which Miss Barton directed the new-born Red Cross came, as we have seen, in 1881 — almost a year before the official accession of the United States to the Treaty of Geneva.

This was the forest fire in Michigan in 1881. By offering a field for experiment this calamity operated greatly to the good of the society, for it demonstrated the practical value of its work.

To meet the immediate needs in this instance, Miss Barton placed the sum of three thousand dollars subject to the draft of the Red Cross. Dr. Julian B. Hubbell, then a medical student of the University of Michigan, and a man whom she had met before at Dansville where he was an instructor in the Seminary, was chosen to act as field agent. "Half the State of Michigan on fire" was the report that came to them. Dr. Hubbell reported that hundreds of people had been burned to death by the sweep of the flames and thousands were panic stricken. Nothing but charred stumps were left of the vast forest districts extending across the state.

At Miss Barton's home in Dansville, the white banner and scarlet cross were flung to the breeze. Relief rooms were packed with incoming supplies, boxes were stamped with the Red Cross seal, and Major Bunnell was sent as distributor. Rochester, New York, the second auxiliary center to bestir relief measures, began with a donation of $2500 in money and 250 members. Syracuse rapidly followed with the third local Red Cross. As the days went on material and money were raised and distributed, amounting in all to $80,000.

After this first successful tryout of the Red Cross in America, there followed weeks and months given over to making more generally known the purpose and the ideals of the Society. These months saw the assassination and death of President Garfield and the accession of his successor, who gave his support no less ungrudgingly than had the martyred President. And they were months which also brought with them the second disaster in which the Red Cross was to figure. This was the Mississippi flood in the early spring of 1882, where millions of acres of cotton and sugar plantations were inundated and thousands upon thousands of homes covered in the cataclysm of the waters. As President of the formative organization, Miss Barton dispatched all the funds possible.   This first relief amounted to $8000 in money and seeds.   But New Orleans under Dr. Southmayd asked to form a local Red Cross, which was to be for years to come a right arm of Red Cross work in the South.   Vicksburg and Memphis did the same.   The Red Cross nucleus, not yet Nationally or Internationally received, met to organize relief and chose to work through its New Orleans field agent and so rush aid to the flood areas.

"The recent overflow of the Mississippi," explained Miss Barton, "afforded subject for still further and more extended trial; and it is a pleasure to add, with results equally gratifying and assuring.

"It is a fact worthy of mention that the munificent contribution of one individual through the Rochester Society of $10,000 in seeds for planting the desolated district, was rendered doubly, trebly, valuable by the rapidity and precision with which it was distributed through the organized societies of the Red Cross.

"The slow decline of the water delayed the planting till great haste was necessary in order to secure any return from the land that year.

"A call from the national, to the Rochester Society, to meet this new emergency was promptly responded to and within three days the seed was on its way to the Red Cross Society of Memphis, which society, being notified of its transit, made the necessary provisions for its immediate distribution, and within twenty-four hours after its arrival in Memphis, it was assorted, and reshipped to the proper points in five different states with full instructions for final distribution.

"It is a comfort to-day to know that thousands of acres of that so recently desolated valley are rich with ripening vegetation and that thousands of persons are subsisting upon the results of that one well arranged act of generosity."

Thus was initiated the key to Miss Barton's plan — namely, to work through local Red Cross Branches.   Success attended it from the first.

"The Red Cross Society of Rochester with less than a year of existence," she said, "has contributed over fourteen thousand dollars in material and money to the relief of sufferers by calamities.

"The incipent movement towards the formation of the magnificent society of Rochester, as well as Syracuse, was made entirely by Rev. Dr. Gracey, the noted missionary to India and now Presiding Elder of the Methodist Church of the District of Rochester. So much may the timely efforts of one person accomplish."

The Rochester Society never lost the contagion of the cause inspired by Clara Barton. Just as it came to the help of the South in the case of the Mississippi floods so later in Johnstown did it again respond. This attitude is an indication of that called forth wherever Clara Barton made her magnetic personality felt.

Local Red Cross centers once formed, never in other crises forgot her first plea. Thus without a war department or President of the United States at the head of the Red Cross, she seized the imagination, fired the hearts and won the open hand of the American people. In return, in every national catastrophe when the press flashed her will, this same people poured out money more than she needed.

The growing power and the practical efficiency of the Red Cross as demonstrated a second time, in the Mississippi floods, greatly enthused the whole country and especially drew upon itself the favorable attention of the United States Senate then in session. March 1, 1882, the President signed the treaty of Geneva and transmitted it to the Senate for action. The Senate, impressed as it was then by the Red Cross in action, on the same day, voted favorably upon the treaty. Miss Barton's having put the Red Cross into actual service on the field had been worth more than volumes of argument or days of oratory. So interested had the Senate become that it requested her to write a brief history of the Red Cross at the Government's expense.

Again in the early spring of 1883, the Mississippi floods on which the Red Cross was rising to practical recognition and national fame increased to greater height than the year before. Indications pointed to their exceeding their former limit of destruction. They began with an unprecedented rise in the headwaters of the Ohio. The flood crest in rapid descent raced down over one thousand miles, everywhere submerging grain lands and farms. Dr. Julian B. Hubbell again left Michigan University at the request of Miss Barton and superintended the distribution of relief, including vast stores of seeds for replanting denuded farm lands.

To meet the disaster of a Mississippi and Louisiana cyclone in May the New Orleans Red Cross took the field.

At this period, May, 1883, at the solicitation of General Benjamin F.

Butler, Miss Barton took the superintendency of the woman's reformatory at Sherborn, Massachusetts, doing the work of the preceding
superintendent, and the Secretary and Treasurer for $1500. She re-
tired at the end of the year after a remarkable influence over the
inmates.

As she patrolled the halls, inmates sprang out of bed and stood
behind grated doors.

"What is it?" exclaimed Miss Barton to one of these.

"I heard you coming and just wanted to look at you," was the
reply.

As always she communicated her power by personal touch. It
was the same secret she exerted wherever she was. In the school
personal touch was her method of success. In the battle field it
was the same and again even in the case of criminal women. She
did it by inspiring their confidence in her, and more than all by manifesting her confidence in them.

She had two letter boxes placed in the corridors. "One for their
letters to me," she explained, "so that they may tell me anything
and everything. They often write because they are so lonesome.
The other box is for letters to the commissioners about any complaints they have to make, and nobody may see what they write."

Much in the spirit of Dorothy Dix's work with the insane, a work
which has caused the founding of institutions in thirty-eight states
and in England, Canada, and Scotland, is this work of Clara Barton's
in the Reformatory. "The smelling yeasty mass of human sin,"
she called it. Yet she willed to pass it through the filter of her own
personality.

"Last May I found as I entered its great halls, two hundred and
fifty women convicts," she explained. "It has at present two hundred and seventy-five convicts. With those who so kindly care for
them, they make up a family of something over three hundred. These
convicts I am expected to feed, clothe, work and govern.

" Sherborn Reformatory is classed as a State's prison, and it is thus
squared by the same rule of discipline as ordinary State prisons, and
for the punishment of state crimes. And yet it is to be remembered
that not one-fourth part of these women are guilty of, or convicted
of any real sort of crime — simple offenses, drunkenness and unseemly appearance upon the streets. And yet, these poor, hopeless,

FIRST RED CROSS HEADQUARTERS — 1882–1892. 1915, VERMONT
AVENUE, WASHINGTON, D.C.

misguided, rum-wrecked women and night walking girls are sentenced to the same servitude, subjected to the same code of discipline — and go out with the same brand of shame upon the brow, nay, far deeper than the clear-headed, cool, intelligent, calculating men of Concord, where every inmate is convicted of crime. The sad conviction settles down upon me every day that the sole brains of the crimes of the Commonwealth are in Concord: the wrecks they have made are in Sherborn. And in my dealing with these women, I cannot lose sight of this fact. They are more weak than wicked, often more sinned against than sinning, and this to my mind, invites a parental system of government; and to this they are all amenable; even the most obstinate yields to the rule of kindness, firmly and steadily administered."

But early in 1884 Miss Barton retired from the superintendency of Sherborn Reformatory, her term expiring with that of the appointing Governor, General Butler.

She returned to Washington and arranged to have Dr. Julian H. Hubbell come there also to act as general Field Agent with permanent residence at the headquarters at the capital. Her letters at this time have the following letterhead:

Washington, D. C.

The American Association of the Red Cross organized under the Treaty of Geneva for the Relief of Sufferings of war, pestilence, famine, fires, floods and other Great National Calamities.

Chester A. Arthur — President Board of Consultation.

Executive Officers:

Clara Barton, President,
Walter P. Phillips, General Secretary,
George Kennan, Treasurer.

Trustees:

Charles Folger,
Robert T. Lincoln,
George B. Loring.

In this year of 1884, once again in February the Ohio River with the first thaws of spring broke its banks. It deluged the Ohio River

R

Valley for over 600 miles with a flood of huge proportions. Sensing the fact that the Mississippi, augmented by the swelling flood of the Ohio was soon to submerge thousands of square miles, Miss Barton at once went to Pittsburg to study the crisis at the fountain head. Informing the country through wiring the Associated Press, she hastened down the river. The government had appropriated several thousands of dollars for relief work through the War Department. But there was much more to be done. So great had the flood become that the surging waters even at Cincinnati had climbed the bluffs and possessed the lower town so that large steamers could have been propelled on the streets.

Through Miss Barton the country was made conscious of the need of the flood sufferers, and checks, telegrams for money, and freight receipts for shipments poured in.

It was necessary to rent large warehouses in Cincinnati to accommodate the supplies that a sympathetic nation sent to the stricken section for distribution through its Red Cross leader.

Proceeding down the river Miss Barton formed a second distributing center at Evansville. "Scarcely had we reached there," she narrates briefly in the early pages of "The Red Cross," "when a cyclone struck the river below, and traveling up its entire length, leveled every standing object upon its banks, swept the houses along like cockleshells, uprooted the greatest trees and whirled them down its mighty current — catching here and there its human victims, or leaving them with life only, — houseless, homeless, wringing their hands on a frozen, fireless shore — with every coal-pit filled with water."

She chartered a steamer, "The *Josh V. Throop* with Captain and crew of thirty, at $60 per day." And with the Red Cross flag flying from her mast head she started Saturday, March 8, on her voyage of mercy with the decks hidden under the heavy cargo of bales and bundles of clothing, boxes and barrels of food and holds full of fuel. Patrolling the river she left everywhere supplies of clothing and coal. Reaching Cairo in five days, she reloaded the boat and returned to Evansville. Three weeks of day and night in constant relief activity passed by before her return. All this time Miss Barton kept her boat plying to and fro, ministering to the malarial, the homeless, and the sick. She scattered also among them thousands of dollars' worth of seeds and implements with which they might start life again.

"Ready money for instant relief, no paid officers, no solicited funds, no red tape, instantaneous action" — these were the principles under which she worked. It was this system that allowed Miss Barton to sail down the swollen Ohio in her chartered steamer, to feed the victims at second story windows, and to clothe and give fuel to the sufferers. As from side to side, from village to village, steamed the relief boat, thousands of dollars' worth of supplies left the flood-evicted inhabitants agape with wonder and tear-stained with gratitude.

At the news of this strange craft with its cross of the crusades and the Jesuits of the fifteenth century flying over the prairie rivers in the nineteenth, local societies of the Red Cross sprang up like wildfire throughout the Middle West, centering at St. Louis and Chicago.

In all the newspapers and press reports of the country, it was now evident once for all that in winning Public Opinion she had secured the personal initiative and referendum that is the real force in the American Commonwealth.

To vibrate her will over the land in a moment, the press from this time on laid at her command its power behind the throne. Henceforth its wires flashed her pleas, its papers published her alarms, and its columns put the country behind her.

As Miss Barton had foreseen, the April rise of the Mississippi flowing down from its headwaters was joined by the rise of the Missouri and other large rivers, and when these were augmented by the colossal outpouring of the Ohio, at times thirty miles wide as it neared its junction with the "Father of Waters," it was evident that the stoutest levees were going to break and that even New Orleans was to be in danger. She at once, therefore, chartered a second steamboat at St. Louis, *The Mattie Bell*. General Beckwith, who, as Commissary General, superintended loading her cargoes in the Civil War for Virginia, met her on the levee and oversaw the loading of the new relief boat. Vast quantities of Red Cross supplies had arrived — too many for the *Mattie Bell*. These Miss Barton directed General Beckwith to load on the Government relief boats. "Clothing, corn, oats and salt," she enumerated as among the essentials for her own cargo. April 2d, overloading the boat with these, steering for the lower river, the waters in the broken levees and crevasses roaring all the way before them to New Orleans, she daringly set out "to rescue the drowning and give them emergency relief." But it was a practical work — looking toward the future. Therefore, stock everywhere was saved and carried to safe places. With food and clothing, they also proceeded to discharge farm implements and seed for planting anew. Whenever the decks were cleared, with the funds from the newly aroused national interest in the Red Cross (to be fair to the merchants), they purchased new supplies of the merchants of Mississippi River towns and cities. They worked by night as well as by day. But at night they were in imminent danger because in the dark the steamer constantly poked her flat nose into crevasses. They were threatened by sparks also as the belching smoke stacks dropped their cinders on the combustible cargo. But Miss Barton insisted that the Red Cross banner still wave and that the rescue ship still zigzag its way over the vast flood from shore to shore notwithstanding its deck loads of inflammable hay and foodstuffs and fuel.

That Miss Barton demanded that they stay to the finish and not retire after the first hurry of enthusiasm is shown in the following personal note nearly three months from the time the relief work began:

"EVANSVILLE, IND., May 10, 1884.

"Our Mississippi trip is ended, but not our Mississippi work by any means, as we are constantly sending back to them in their need.

"We have some more to do on the Upper Ohio, and then we can clear our work in the overflows for this year."

Accordingly, after the Mississippi had been traversed to the Gulf, she returned and discharged the steamboat again at St. Louis, only to recharter the Ohio River steamer, the *Josh V. Throop*. Her plan was to reload with timber, heavy supplies for rebuilding, and seeds for replanting, and so reconstruct the farming life that had been everywhere swept away along the devastated Ohio. When necessity pointed, the *Throop* would dock, the carpenters would land, and in a few hours rebuild a home, which the Red Cross party on board would refurnish and replenish.

The gratitude which this relief elicited is well preserved in the words of a first flood sufferer and is but typical of that called forth by the visits of Miss Barton's ship from Cincinnati to Cairo, and from St. Louis to the Gulf:

"At noon we were in the blackness of despair — the whole village in the power of the demon of waters — hemmed in by sleet and ice, without fire enough to cook its little food. When the bell struck nine that night, there were seventy-five families on their knees before their blazing grates, thanking God for fire and light, and praying blessings on the phantom ship with the unknown device that had come as silently as the snow, they knew not whence, and gone, they knew not whither." . . .

"We finished our voyages of relief," Miss Barton concluded. "We had covered the Ohio River from Cincinnati to Cairo and back twice, and the Mississippi from St. Louis to New Orleans, and return — four months on the rivers — traveled over eight thousand miles, distributed relief in money and estimated material, one hundred and seventy-five thousand dollars — gathered as we used it."

With the need of personal service over, there came to Miss Barton the usual physical reaction. Fearing a collapse, she returned to Washington. Here she found notifications from Switzerland acquainting her that the 1884 International Conference was to convene in September at Geneva. When she asked Secretary of State Frelinghuysen to appoint a delegate, he said:

"I appoint you."

"I cannot go, I have just returned from field work. I am tired and ill," she replied.

"There is no one else who sufficiently understands the Red Cross — we cannot make a mistake in the matter of delegates to this first conference in which our Government shall participate," he answered. She argued that she should make further reports on the flood.

. . "Our Government relief boats have reported you officially and all the country knows what you have done and is more than satisfied. Regarding your illness — you have had too much fresh water, Miss Barton. I recommend salt — and shall appoint you."

Upon this, regathering her spent energies, the President of the Red Cross of America decided to go.

The government thereupon appropriated her expenses for the entire trip — also for two others — Judge Joseph Sheldon and Mr. A. S. Solomon, the vice-president of the American Red Cross.

Writing of the August voyage across, Dr. Hubbell, who accompanied the party, says:[1]

"Miss Barton reached Liverpool, 26th (August) — not an un-

[1] In a letter of September 6, 1884, to Mrs. Mamie (Barton) Stafford.

pleasant day, did not miss a single meal and was not ill an hour. She spent most of her time in the stateroom writing, preparing her paper for the Convention.

"On the way there was a general request from the passengers to have Miss Barton say something to them; so near the close of the voyage she met them in the saloon and read her paper to them, which was highly appreciated and complimented by many enthusiastic speeches. Then Judge Sheldon displayed the decoration to the passengers, much to their gratification and pleasure. I presume that you have seen notices of the Congress, in the papers, although but brief reports have yet been made. All goes well. Kindest regards to all the family."

At Geneva her reception by the founders of the International Red Cross and by the four hundred distinguished delegates and representatives of the signatory powers to the Treaty was the most notable in her experience. As she sat in the councils and took part in the deliberations accorded to titled and honored rulers, lords, nobles, military and scientific leaders of the human race, the fact that she was a woman among the most celebrated men of Christendom but marked her the more. Chief among the royal personages to introduce her and to surround her with equal honors was the Grand Duke of Baden, the Grand Duchess and her Imperial father, the Emperor of Germany.

The International Congress recognized Miss Barton's introduction of the Red Cross into disasters in times of peace as well as of war in that it had not only proved one of her main arguments for the conversion of American minds to the Convention, but it did much more, because it put in force the new Amendment in the International organization and therefore became known as the "American Amendment."

International interest was immediately focused upon it, and her presence greatly reënforced the resolution — "that the Red Cross societies engage in time of peace in humanitarian work analogous to the duties devolving upon them in periods of war, such as taking care of the sick and rendering relief in extraordinary calamities, where, as in war, prompt and organized relief is demanded."

It was evident that while Miss Barton had already gained recognition throughout the courts and chancellories of Europe for her success in founding the American Red Cross it was not till now that the pent-up admiration burst forth, touched off by the amendment incident, till she dominated the convention, which rendered an ovation never before accorded by so distinguished an assemblage to a woman.[1]

On returning in 1885 Miss Barton found her place in American influence also greatly magnified! "I had thought," she said, "all those little days of river work gone from memory." "But I found myself January, 1885, in the upper gallery of the New Orleans Exposition, and stepping in at a restaurant at the end of the hall was met by Colonel Lewis, the noted colored caterer of the South. He had been on the relief committee of New Orleans appointed to meet our steamer at the time of our visit in May. He came with cordial recognition, seated me and was telling me of his success in the restaurant when all his waiters, men and women, seemed to forget their work and stood gazing at us. The Colonel smiled and said, 'They have caught sight of the Red Cross brooch at your neck and recognize you by it. They will come themselves in a few minutes.'

"Next day I went in again for my lunch, when Colonel Lewis brought me a little, thin, white-haired mulatto man of seventy-three years, but still able to take charge of and direct the help at the tables, saying, 'This, Miss Barton, is Uncle Amos, whom I promised yesterday to introduce to you when you came again. Uncle Amos is my most true and faithful man.'

"I reached out for the withered, hard, dark bony hand he gave me as he said, 'Yes, Miss Barton, I wants to see and speak to you, to tell you in de name of our people how grateful dey is for what your society has done for dem. Dat is never forgot. You come to us when we had nothing. You saved what was never saved befo' in a flood — our cattle, — so dey could go on and help derselves to raise something to eat. Dey has all heard of it; all talk about it in the churches and de meetings. Our people is singular in some tings; dey never forgets a kindness. Dey hab notions. Dey hab a way of nailing up a hoss-shoe ober de do' for luck. I want to tell you dat in a thousand little cabins all up and down der river, dey has put up a little Red Cross ober de do' and every night before dey goes to bed

[1] See "Clara Barton as an Internationalist and Publicist," p. 9, where Miss Barton's reception by Europe's leading Internationalists is graphically described by Antoinette Margot.

dey names your name and prays God to bless you and de Red Cross dat he sent to dem in time of trouble and distress.' Uncle Amos looked straight in my face the while. Colonel Lewis wiped his eyes, — and I got away as fast as I could."

Thus in the New South as well as in the North her name was becoming endeared as no other woman's in America.

The year 1886 was to occupy Miss Barton with a transcontinental trip to California. The Charleston, South Carolina, earthquake occurred before her return. She remained west till early in December, but she came home by way of Charleston. With her usual sympathy and willingness she carried relief even at that late hour which however needed but $800 more of expenditure.

Her sympathy, however, meant much more.

The white people of Charleston received her to a South reunited with the North, which fact was typified by an incident before she left the stricken city. In her study of the wreckage she was guided about by an officer who at the siege of Sumter, when she was with the Northern army and navy before Charleston in 1863, had unconsciously trained upon her position the confederate guns, and had rained shot and shell over her head. This very officer climbed with her the shattered cupola of the Charleston orphan home and together in a moment of tearful silence they looked over the bay to Morris Island. Then they clasped hands, the battle-scarred veteran of the Confederates and the Angel of the Northern battle field, and in a sacramental moment they felt the reblending of sympathies sealed by this evidence of Northern relief which she brought to the old Southern citadel of the Confederacy.

Before this year ended in 1886, the South again drew her eye of sympathy and her hand of relief. A condition approaching famine began in the Pan Handle of Texas to which a speculative railroad had beguiled thousands of farmers from Mississippi, Alabama and Georgia.

Two years of drought faced them almost with starvation and their cattle were already dead. The press at first was muzzled by the railroad corporation and hushed up the scandal from the State. But through the report of a faithful clergyman, Rev. John Brown, of Albany, Texas, the tale broke through that ten thousand were found nearly starving in North West Texas. The Red Cross, already awake to the situation, was appealed to in the middle of January, 1887, by Dr. Brown. At the end of January, Miss Barton established head-quarters at Albany, Texas. With her General Field Agent, Dr. Hubbell, she started systematic and broadcast relief. Her methods and personal feelings are betrayed in this letter to her niece:

"ALBANY, TEXAS, Feb. 3rd, '87.

"DEAR FANNIE:

"I have not time to tell you how it is, but you may be sure it is bad enough. The Dr. and I left Washington the last of the month, have been here some days traveling, met the people, learned their necessities in their own homes and have done what we could in so short a time to make ourselves acquainted with the needs that lie upon them. The sum of one hundred thousand dollars has just been appropriated by the Legislature of this State for food which will do something toward providing for their present wants. Much more will be needed for seed, grain, clothing and household comforts before another crop could possibly be raised even if the rains make a good season which is still questionable. I am glad to tell you that we are both well and hope to be home before long and the still further hope lies in my heart that I may see you all in Massachusetts before another summer passes. Tell Ber that this is just such a field as I should like to see him busy in. I want to write to Annie, but fearing I may not be able to, will you please send her this when you have read it unless she chances to be with you. You will please give great love to all friends and believe me,

"Your loving sister,
"CLARA B."

"Feb. 17th.

"Did you notice in to-day's papers that the President had vetoed the bill concerning sending seed grain to Texas? I think he gave good reasons why he did it. He does not object to Congressmen giving their share."

By appearing at the editorial office of the 'Dallas and Galveston News,' Miss Barton had unmasked the terrible situation with the flood of informing facts. The paper at once changed its front and opened a broadside of truth, revealing in its next issue such appalling statements as to the multitudes of hungry, cheated people, that the Texas Legislature appropriated forthwith for food the one hundred thousand dollars which Miss Barton mentions in the above letter. This done, she returned to Washington headquarters, where she occupied herself in the administrative affairs of the fast growing National Red Cross.

In September of this year (1887) the International Committee at Geneva were invited to hold the next International conference at Carlsruhe, Germany. Grover Cleveland, President of the United States, appointed Miss Barton as the chief representative and delegate of the United States, Congress having appropriated expenses for two other delegates also.

As to her sailing she wrote her niece, Mrs. Stafford:

"August 29, 1887. Monday Morning.
"DEAREST MAMIE:

"I am going to write you to come to New York and see me off when I sail. It will be somewhere between the 6th and 10th, or rather say between the 5th and 9th. The boat is not selected, but I incline to think about the 7th will be the day — We are likely to go to Brooklyn for the three last days — to be with my friend Dr. Lucy M. Hall, who will go with us as a Delegate to the Conference and I should like to have you come on for one or two nights and days — and see us on to the boat. I'll then have some one whom I will find to see you back, and all safe on your own boat or train for home. G—— can take care of the babies, you can take a satchel, or trunk as you choose. Perhaps the latter but not many things will be needed for so short a time and not a very elegant time either — the rush of getting off on a voyage. I should like to see you, and think it will do you good to make the trip."

Just before leaving the Capital for New York whence she was to sail the Monday following, she again wrote Mrs. Stafford:

"WASHINGTON, Thursday Afternoon, Sept., 1887.
"DEAREST MAMIE:

"We may have the delay of September weather, and be too late for the conference.

"There will be all day in New York, when we arrive early Monday morning.

"Better take —— with you. He will be helpful and enjoy going to New York, I am sure, and see a big ship."

Carlsruhe being the Ducal Capital of Alsace and the home of the Grand Duchess Louise, she met again the Grand Duke and Duchess of Baden and the Emperor of Germany, the Empress Augusta, Bismarck and Von Moltke. Besides her important part in the International deliberations in the great Council Chamber, where she met delegates from thirty-two nations, Miss Barton spent many notable days with the Grand Duchess of Baden at the palace. From Baden-Baden, Miss Barton wrote at length describing one of her visitations with the Emperor, who again conferred upon her distinguished honors.

"BADEN BADEN, GERMANY, Oct. 28, 1887.

"The International Red Cross Conference had closed. Most of the delegates had left Carlsruhe, unless like ourselves, remaining for after work. The Grand Duke and Grand Duchess with their Court, had retired to Baden Baden for the customary birthday festivities of Her Majesty the Empress, and the Emperor and his suite would, as also customary, make his yearly visit in honor of the occasion, thus making that lovely and historic old town for the moment, the centre of interest for the Empire.

"Dr. H. and myself were at breakfast, when the hotel porter laid a telegraphic dispatch on my plate. It will be remembered, at least by personal friends, that three years ago, while in attendance at a similar International conference, the honored pleasure of a meeting with His Majesty the Emperor of Germany had been given me. This dispatch informed me that a like honor again awaited my presence in Baden Baden. Trunks were packed, adieus made, and the midday train of the following day took us in time for the appointed hour. Whoever has visited the interior of the 'New Castle,' the Baden Baden palace of the Grand Duke, and been shown through its tasteful apartments, rich in elegance, tradition and history, will require no further reminder of the *place* where the interview would be given.

"This was as well the birthday of the Crown Prince; and in tender paternal sympathy, for the painful affliction resting upon a life so treasured, and for the great anxiety of the German people, his

Majesty the Emperor would pass a portion of the day with the beloved daughter and sister, the Grand Duchess, at the castle; and in
honoring memory of the occasion, its halls were thronged with visitors
who came to manifest both respect and sympathy.

"At half past one o'clock, we were ushered in at the great castle
doors, by their attendants in livery of 'Scarlet and gold,' the national
colors of Baden; our damp wraps removed — for it was a pouring
rain, and after a half hour sitting by a cheerful fire, among pictures
which quite called one out of personal consciousness, we were escorted
to the grand reception and drawing room, to the centre of a magnificent
apartment with no occupant but ourselves. By another door one
saw the Emperor surrounded by guests, who paid formal respects.
Scores of visitors with coachmen in richest livery had entered while
we waited and registered titled names on the open pages.

"At length his Majesty turned from the group about him, and
taking the arm of the Grand Duchess, entered our apartment. It
was difficult to realize all the ninety years, as he stepped towards us
with even, and steady, if no longer elastic tread. He approached with
cordially extended hand, and in his excellent French, expressed satisfaction for the meeting. 'In the name of humanity, he was glad to
meet and welcome those who labored for it.'

"In recalling the earlier days of our acquaintance, Her Royal Highness, the Grand Duchess, alluded tenderly to the winter in Strassburg
of '70 & '71 — which I had passed among its poor and wounded people
after the siege — and selecting two from a cluster of decorations
which I had worn in honor of the present occasion, drew the attention
of the Emperor to them. The one he knew; it was his own, presented
upon his seventy fifth birthday. The other he had never seen. It
was the beautiful decoration of the German society, — The 'Warrior
Brothers in arms' of Milwaukee.

"It was puzzlingly familiar, and yet it was not familiar. There
was again the Iron cross of Germany, but it was on the American
shield. The 'American Eagle' surmounting the arms for defence;
and the colors of Germany, the Red White and Black of the empire,
uniting the two. His Majesty gazed upon the expressive emblem,
which, with no words, said so much, and turned inquiringly to the
Grand Duchess, as if to ask, 'Does my daughter understand this?'

"The explanation was made, that it was from His Majesty's own soldiers, who, after the 'German-Franco war,' had gone to the United States and become citizens; and this device was designed to express, that, as by its shield they were American Citizens, and true to the land of their adoption, so by its 'Iron Cross,' they were still German; and by the colors of the native land for which every man had offered his life, and risked it, they bound the old home to the new; and by the American Eagle and arms, surmounting all, they were ready to offer their lives again, if need be, in defence of either land.

"The smile of the grand old Emperor, as he listened, had in it the 'Well done' of the benignant father to a dutiful and successful son. 'And they make good citizens?' he would ask. 'The best that could be desired,' I said, 'industrious, honest and prosperous, and sire, they are still yours in heart, still true to the Fatherland and its Emperor.'

"'I am glad to hear this; they were good soldiers, and, thank God, true men everywhere,' was the earnest and royal response.

"His Majesty continued, speaking of America, its growth, its progress, its advancement in science and humanity, its adoption and work of the Red Cross, which meant so much for mankind; and when assured that its people revered and loved the Emperor of Germany, that his life was precious to them, and that thousands of prayers went up for him in that distant land he had never seen, the touching and characteristic response betrayed the first tremor of the voice the ear had caught in its kindly tones.

"'God be praised for this; for it is all from Him. I am only His. Of myself I am nothing. He made us what we are. God is over all.'"

"We stood with bowed heads while those slowly spoken earnest holy words from that most revered of earthly monarchs fell upon us like a benediction.

"At length His Majesty gave a hand to both Dr. H—— and myself in a parting adieu, and walked a few steps away, when turning back, and again extending a hand, said in French, 'It is probably the last time,' and in pleasant English 'Good Bye.' And again taking the arm of the Grand Duchess walked from the room, leaving his Highness, the Grand Duke, one of the kindest and noblest types of manhood to say the last words, and close the interview, one of the most impressive and memorable of a life time.

"CLARA BARTON."

In a card to Mrs. Stafford of which portions are indistinct, her final parting with the imperial party is described:

"BADEN BADEN, Oct. 24, 1887.

"I do not know if I have written since coming here or if my last was from Carlsruhe.   We were here for the 'Baden season.'   We were invited by the Duke and Duchess to spend a few weeks at Baden Baden and of course all the court proper would come.   The Empress came also; and the Emperor.   They will be here till next Friday, when she goes to Berlin.   The Crown Prince's health is very poor. The Emperor is better than ever, — bright and cheerful like a young man.   We went the other evening to see him take the train for Berlin. The station reserve rooms were like a drawing room and all the court and royal persons were in them, to wait the coming of the Emperor, and the town —   The Emperor shook hands with all — saying good bye, made pretty gifts to some special persons, then entered the royal train, to ride all night.   The day before yesterday the Empress sent for me to come to her.   I spent a most delightful hour. She had a great deal to say, and made me a lovely parting gift of a ruby brooch.   She insisted that we should meet again, that I should come to Europe again, and she should see me.   In the P.M. the Grand Duchess sent for us to go to her and we went and spent two lovely hours.   She is charming as ever.   Then next evening (last evening) she sent for us to come to dine.   We went and had a beautiful time. We are to go again to-morrow for a visit.   After the end of this week we go to Strassburg to spend a little time.   Shall most likely go to Berlin and back to Strassburg and down the French side of the Rhine to Basle, Bern, Geneva, Paris, London, Liverpool, and then we shall be on our direct way home, but it is some little time yet before we can go home."

The next letter from Miss Barton is written from Paris, December 2, 1887, also to Mrs. Stafford:

"While I wait for my cup of tea at the breakfast table, I can tell you how far we are on our way.   We spent nearly a week in Geneva, and it rained so much we could not do the things we would have been glad to have done.   It is foggy here but has not rained.   We came to the Hotel Louvre as being first-class, in the hope of finding a warm house, which we do.   It is very delightful.   I am rejoiced for once to be in Paris when I have the strength to walk, and to see it.   I

never could do this when here before. As I think of it, I do not suppose any one ever mistrusted how weak and miserable I was when I
tried to 'do' Europe — so much was expected of me, and I had so
little to give that I wonder I did not entirely 'give out'; and 'go
under.' But now, I can do what I want to. I suppose I walked
eight miles yesterday and did hosts of business, official things. We
shall stay a week or so, before going to London."

Then follows a letter which shows Miss Barton's inability ever to
forget a friend, whether as in the past autumn a German Lord or
Lady, or as in this instance, her humble one-time landlady and her
husband. Her sketch of typical English plain people and their
homespun struggles and habits breathes the air of Charles Dickens's
stories:

"196 EASTERN ROAD
"LONDON, Dec. 18, 1887.

"DEAREST MAMIE:

"If the above date recalls something to you I shall not be surprised.
I must have sent a card from Paris to mark our leaving there. We
had a good calm evening, and came into —— Station Saturday evening 5 o'clock. The large Grosvenor Hotel is in the Station, which
covers acres of ground. We stopped there to let the English Sunday
have its holy rest, but rode out in carriage Sunday morning to find
Mrs. H—— who, I saw, had left the old place at number 20. I
could not find her, but on Monday I started in earnest, to see if any
one near the old place knew anything of the H——s.

"The old house is all run down, and a female confronted me. She
knew nothing and could tell less. I went next door. The H——s
had moved away 2 years before, didn't know where; but the people
at 196 might know; went to 196. A Mrs. —— could find her; she,
Mrs. ——, was herself in lodging. They had been unfortunate, and
had gotten old, and could do no more work, etc. But Mrs. —— had
two rooms; looked at them and dumped ourselves down. In half a
minute Dr. went for the trunks. I brushed away the traditional
London dust. Meanwhile, the coal fire was set up in the shiny
grate, the curtains put back. The trunks came. The table was
spread while Dr. and I went down to 'Hampshire Market' — you
remember, end of Tottenham Court, — and came home with such a
basket of goodies — bacon, hot roasted potatoes as big as half grown

kittens, bread, sally lunds, Madeira cakes, strawberry jam, tea, sugar, grapes, apples, raisins, dates, figs, and-and-and — till no more could get in basket.   The little teakettle sung on the grill, the fire blazing, and Crockseller, the Landlord, broiled the bacon.   And how I did wish you were there to sit down to our first meal in lodgings on the old Road which is just as it was, — not a stone turned nor changed. So here we are, it rains and shines at least twenty times a day — and we dodge in and out between.   On Tuesday and Wednesday, after a terrible day's tramp, we took the Camden Road 'tram' to Beacon Hill.   All well as usual.   Mr. Noddington can no more walk, but sits on his lounge, full of intelligence and life.   The daughters both home, very pretty young ladies; Mrs. Noddington looks better than usual.   All possible inquiries were made for you and the children — are to go to dine to-morrow (Sunday) — But as to Mrs. ——.   I wrote a line on a postal card for Mrs. —— to send to her the first morning we were here.   The next day, in a pouring rain came the good jolly woman, only some older and a little lame.   The 'rent' had been changed —.   Some persons who owed them did not pay. And they became discouraged, had to give up the home, took another, got ill, had to leave that, kept furniture for one room or two, and took little lodgings at $8.00 per week, which her sister pays for the present. I don't know if they have a little bit of their own or not.   Mr. —— cannot get work at his trade any more — the new improvements have cut him off.   I am going to write them some day — and see if I can 'cheer them up a bit.'"

Then as to her sailing for home she added:

"The regular day was the 24 Dec. for the Alaska, that fine large boat — but she is suddenly drawn off for the winter repairs — and nothing took her place, so there is a vacancy in the sailing dates, from the 17th to the 31st and then an ordinary and rather slow boat — the Wyoming.   This, then, will probably be our day of sailing, which will bring us home a little before the middle of January.

"The Dr. is tolerably well — a little London sore throat, sends great love to Johnny, and so to all.   He is most tired of sight seeing — and will be glad to get home as I shall.   You must manage to keep well, all of you, for I want only good reports when I come home. Kindness to the children.

"Yours lovingly,
"BYAS."

Upon Miss Barton's return from the 1887 International Red Cross conference in Germany and from her Paris and London visits, only for a short time could she remain at Headquarters at Washington.

On February 19, 1888, a cyclone swept through Southern Illinois, leveling half of Mt. Vernon, the county seat, and leaving death and destruction along its wide swath through the surrounding parts of the state. Fire added to the terrors, burning to death a number of victims, pinned down by the fallen timbers. Effective communication with the outside world was cut off for several days. At once upon the news of the catastrophe Miss Barton headed the Red Cross relief and appeared at Mt. Vernon in the night. In the morning she sent throughout the United States the following telegram:

"The pitiless snow is falling on the heads of three thousand people who are without homes, without food or clothing, and without money."

This message, vibrating on the wires from Illinois, was enough to accumulate almost instantly ninety thousand dollars' worth of supplies. Two weeks were necessary for her to superintend the distribution.

At the finish of the task she wrote Mrs. Stafford ·

"DEAREST MAMIE:

"Our work in Mt. Vernon is accomplished. *Well done.*

"We have started home *via* Chicago, remain here till Tuesday, go directly home then. Dr. has gone to Iowa to see his people, will join me here and go home with me.

"Are all very well, both of us, and glad we came.

"I hope all are well.

"Lovingly,
"BYAS."

Exhibiting Miss Barton's manifold activities in periods of "rest" from relief work and between relief fields we have the following letter written April 20, 1888, from the Limited Express "below Philadelphia" to Mrs. Stafford:

"DEAREST MAMIE:

"This will be a shaky letter to tell you I am on my way home from Montclair, New Jersey — a pretty town 45 minutes from New York. I was invited there to make an address at the convention (State) of

s

the Congregational church including most of the Congregationalists from N. Y. to Washington. Wednesday, or rather Tuesday night — 11 P.M. into N. Y. City, but direct from Jersey City — attended committee sessions — Wednesday all day yesterday — spoke in the afternoon at —— church, probably 100 clergymen —. 'Women in Charities and Philanthropies,' selected by the convention. I believe it gave general satisfaction; I was entertained by Mrs. Dike, who was daughter of Dr. Miller, formerly dentist of Worcester. — A delightful home on the mountain. I attended the convention till its close last night, then took the train this morning, and came on towards home as fast as possible. I have not been into N. Y. City at all, and shall be home at four this afternoon. I will read you my address when I am home. I have another to write on a different subject to deliver in Philadelphia next Thursday, where I shall be with Dr. Hubbell until Saturday. I am very well and not tired out as you fear. I do not get tired, and I rest and sleep splendidly, and all the world is so full of kindness for me, that it keeps me up for all the things I need to do.

"'Byas.'"

After her Philadelphia Lecture, she wrote from Washington, May 5, 1888:

"Dearest Mamie ·

"I had intended to write you just a line on the train to and from Philadelphia, but one was in the night — the other so full of other things and the trip so short, I did not get to it.

"I can't think it was a week ago, but so it seems. The first day I met the Society in its Annual Meeting, and spoke to them a little. I attended a lunch party before the meeting and a reception after the opera at the elegant residence of Dr. ——, president of the Philadelphia Red Cross. That made four things after 12 o'clock.

"The next day we had informal meetings with officers of the society until 2 o'clock P.M. Then attended a lecture given in the regular course of the Red Cross Society. Then I gave a lecture. Then home to dress for the Reception to commence at 8.

"This was given in Union League Hall, very large, with a band of music. The dignitaries of the city attended in bodies. The physicians — the clergymen — the lawyers — the judges — the military army and navy in uniform. I received and shook hands with all. They left after 11. It was a splendid reception. There was still a meeting at the hotel (The Colonade) after our return, so we are only in bed by two o'clock next morning, got a hasty breakfast and hastened to the 9 o'clock train for home, found a large mail and I was very sleepy. I did sleep a day or two mainly, and that is what makes the week seem so short, I think.

"Then just think what a washing there was on hand, had never had time to have a full wash done since our return from Mt. Vernon. The Woman's council came directly on that, and an address to write for it. Then the conference of churches at Montclair, and another address to write. Then Philadelphia and another address to write with all that came between. The wash went to the wall till this week, when it was taken up in its turn and put through in one day, and all ironed yesterday, and clothes put away this very minute, and I haven't left the ware house yet, but am just dropped down at the table in front of the window, near the store. (Gaby will know all about it) while Alfred brings compost from the stable alongside ready to make up some flower beds, etc., and I direct him from the window as I scribble, to lose no time. It is just as lovely as it can be. Tell Gaby we have moved the rose bushes all down to the front of the yard, and they didn't mind it a bit, and went right on putting out buds, and he will appreciate how much better chance we had with a washing of 20 sheets, 30 pillow slips, and other things in proportion, and he knows how quickly and easily it all went out of the way, and no one got much tired, and not any sick."

The last paragraph of this letter marks the interesting intrusion of Clara Barton, the domestic New Englander, into the affairs of Clara Barton, the Red Cross leader. The same mixture of matters of State and homely interests are seen again in a second letter written to Mrs. Stafford May 8, 1888:

"I haven't time for more than a word. We are making out our foreign conference accounts for the government and I have the report to make out directly and a bill to draw up for Congress this next week and a host of correspondence, and we are having Alfred make up our garden, in front of the ware house and a pretty little plot it is too. I found time one night by moon light to plant lettuce and peppergrass and radishes, and in two days they came up and are green and pretty.

Yesterday we set out 2 doz. tomato plants a foot high, and all of our doz. grape vines are growing; splendid varieties, and when Alfred makes up the flower beds to-day, we shall find time to plant all the seeds I have. I have no bulbs to set, but I have a dozen nice holly-hocks, fifteen inches high, and all the rose bushes and fleur de lis in bloom and bud. I can't get time to hunt over the house for the little seeds we want to plant. I have nice seeds for kitchen garden things from Dansville but can't remember where to look for them. I want a pinch of caraway seed and 12 great sage roots and I want some catnip seed for Tommy. There is not a stalk of catnip anywhere about, and I can't get any seed. Have you some in your catnip herb bag? I like saffron, and red balm such as Julia raises. I can get plenty of elegant plants but the old, old things are hard to find — and I have not time to look, but should so like to stick a few out in my nice beds. So here is a place for small contributions. I do hope Johnny is all better. Please give him all the love I can send, and try to, all of you, keep well. We are well, the Saturday work is all done up, and every thing is lovely as spring can make it."

"The great 'Council of Women' is now over," she writes a little later, "the meetings are ended, the people are mainly leaving the city, and this hour my house has had its last visitor. Every day till now my space, and my table, has been filled to the utmost, and in addition to my full part in the 'Council,' its meeting, committees and speeches.

"The next morning (yesterday) I had to meet a senate committee at the Capitol and address them at 10 o'clock. Then I go with Mrs. Gen. Logan and others to the War Dept. to manage business there. And now it is 8½ the next morning, and at 10 I must be at the War Dept. with another committee."

Before the month ended the other Convention called her to Boston, where after an address and reception she goes to Wellesley to address 500 Wellesley girls.

All has gone well, she writes to Mrs. Stafford from Boston, where she had gone later that same month (May, 1888) to deliver the address. "My cold entirely left me, and I have had no trouble with it. So much for right living, and good cool blood. This is the last day of the convention. I am to speak to-night. I did say a little yester-day, and they all laughed at me; I wish you could have been here. There is to be a reception given me next Friday evening. Steve and

The General Grant Mansion, 17th and F Streets, Washington, D.C. — Red Cross Headquarters and Home (1892–1897)

Lizzie and Myrtie are invited. I go to the Wellesley College to take tea and speak to the 500 girls there on Saturday evening. Some things I must miss. I get back as soon as I can, so as to go on home. I am so glad of Sunday, — it was a glorious day, so good to see so many together again. I hope the children are well, that you don't wrestle too much with imaginary dirt, and are getting a little real strength, and that you believe me

"Your lovingly,
"BYAS."

In Florida, in September, yellow fever became epidemic. Working with the New Orleans Red Cross Branch through Colonel F. R. Southmayd, its local head, Miss Barton advised the sending of some twenty immune old "Howard Nurses," whom Dr. Southmayd had trained and drilled in many years of service.

The Red Cross found that the mayor of Jacksonville, the seat of the epidemic, with other agencies had risen to the emergency. By September 8th, all well people in Jacksonville were asked to leave. The flight was almost universal. For the poorer folk, unable to go, camps were established outside the city. It remained for the Red Cross to coöperate in stamping out the epidemic which had spread to many surrounding towns. Not Jacksonville alone but the State of Florida, became their charge. Through Dr. Gill, a Norwegian specialist, and other physicians and the immune nurses, the Red Cross hastened from plague spot to plague spot until the disease was stamped out, losing by death but three of the Red Cross band, who gave their lives to stay the march of disease.

Thus the Red Cross was in action in many towns and hamlets other than Jacksonville.

"The little company of eighteen," explained Miss Barton, "steaming on to Jacksonville, heard that the town of Macclenny, thirty-eight miles from Jacksonville, Fla. was in a fearful state of distress; no nurses — quarantined on all sides, no food, medicine, nor comforts for sick or well.

"The train slowed up a mile from the infected town and hand to hand, that none go astray in the darkness, they hobbled back over a mile of slippery cross-ties to the stricken town. At midnight, the sick had been parceled out, each nurse had his or her quota of patients, and were in for the issue, be it life or death." As the disease gradually succumbed to their watchful care, experience and skill, "they reached out to other freshly attacked towns and hamlets. They saw the dying through," and sped in a special train from place to place till the epidemic had died out with thousands saved as the happy result of their labors.

After seventy-nine days of such work when it was thought yellow fever was at last eradicated, it broke out again. All had planned to return to camp, be paid and go home for the holidays. . . . "But," interjected Miss Barton, "Enterprise, a hundred miles below, just stricken down amongst its flowers and fruits, reached out its hand with one accord. After two days in camp, all turned back from the coveted home and needed rest, and added another month of toil to their already weary record. At length this was ended, and word came again to us that they would go into quarantine."

Frost had now put the final check upon a recurrence of the disease and November 22nd, with Dr. Julian B. Hubbell, Miss Barton, who not being an immune nurse had not gone to the plague ridden State, set out for the quarantine camp. "Two days and one night of rail, a few miles across country by wagon where trains were forbidden to stop, and another mile or so over the trestles of St. Mary's on a dirt car with the workmen, brought us into camp," she concluded in the "Story of the Red Cross," as the evening fires were lighted and the bugle sounded supper."

"Surgeon Hutton's headquarter tent was politely tendered for the first meeting, and as one could never, while memory lasts, forget this scene, so no words can ever adequately describe it. The ample tent was filled. Here on the right, the Mayor, broad shouldered, kind faced and efficient, officers of camp and many visitors, wondering what it all meant; in the center the tall doctor and his faithful band — Eliza Lanier, Lena Seymour (mother and daughter), Elizabeth Eastman, Harriet Schmidt, Lizzie Louis, Rebecca Vidal, Annie Evans, Arthur Duteil, Frederick Wilson and Edward Holyland.

"Our little part of the relief of that misfortune was estimated at fifteen thousand dollars, and only those relieved were more grateful than we."

After the Florida Yellow fever campaign, intervening months were spent at her home and headquarters at Washington until Sunday morning, the 30th of May, 1889, when the country was shocked by the breaking in Pennsylvania of a dam above Johnstown, leaving four thousand dead and twenty thousand unfed and homeless in the gutted bed of the reservoir's spent current!

Miss Barton was now sixty-eight years old. But in the afternoon of this same day (May 30th), with Dr. Hubbell, a stenographer, a lady companion and one workman, she left Washington and arrived at Johnstown, Wednesday morning on the first train through from the east.

"I shall never lose the memory of my first walk on the first day," she declared; "the wading in mud, the climbing over broken engines, cars, heaps of iron rollers, broken timbers, wrecks of houses; bent railway tracks tangled with piles of iron wire; bands of workmen, squads of militia and getting around the bodies of dead animals, and often people being borne away; the smouldering fires and drizzling rain. . . ."

General Hastings, in command, was skeptical, and in his military chivalry at first wondered what "a poor lone woman could do." But he saw Miss Barton fall to work, and for five months remain at the stricken center of industry. She always worked in harmony with the State relief appointed by the Governor and distributed money and material. For immediate wants, food was provided by Pittsburg and other cities, who sent troops while provisions poured in from everywhere.

"I had already notified the Red Cross of Philadelphia, composed mainly of medical men, that their services might be needed," Miss Barton explains. A party of thirty or forty joined us by the following train. Some of our most valuable members who worked with us in other fields came at once. We settled ourselves in tents, the Philadelphia Society having been asked to bring camp equipments. Some cars were also retained on a side track. Our party soon increased to about fifty in number.

"Our stenographer commenced to rescue the first dispatches of any description that entered the desolate city. The disturbed rivers lapped wearily back and forth, the people, dazed and dumb, dug in the muddy banks for their dead. Hastings with his little army of militia kept order. Soon supplies commenced to pour in from everywhere, to be received, sheltered as best they could from the incessant

264 THE LIFE OF CLARA BARTON

rain, and distributed by human hands, for it was three weeks before even a cart could pass the streets."

Six buildings of one hundred feet by fifty, later known as "Red Cross Hotels," were quickly put up to shelter the people, furnish supplies and kept like hotels, free of all cost to them, while others were built by the general committee. When the latter were erected, the Red Cross furnished every one with substantial, newly purchased furniture, ready for occupancy.

Another structure was soon erected by Miss Barton known as the "Locust Street Red Cross Hotel." As described, "it stood some fifty rods from our warehouse, and was fifty by one hundred and sixteen feet in dimensions, two stories in height, with lantern roof, built of hemlock, single siding, papered inside with heavy building paper, and heated by natural gas, as all our buildings were. It consisted of thirty-four rooms, besides kitchen, laundry, bath-rooms with hot and cold water, and one main dining hall and sitting room through the center, sixteen feet in width by one hundred in length. In the six huge and hastily erected Red Cross 'hotels,' twenty-five thousand persons were received. Two hundred and eleven thousand dollars was in all distributed in supplies, and thirty-nine thousand dollars in money, leaving no single case of unrelieved suffering.

"I remained five months with these people," relates Miss Barton, "without once visiting my own home, only returning to it when the frost had killed the green I had left in May. In that time it was estimated, we had housed, handled, and distributed $211,000 worth of supplies — new and old — for, by request of the weary chairman of the general committee at the last, we took up the close of its distribution."

The gratitude of the sufferers was beyond description. On the eve of her departure the people's voice, the *Johnstown Daily Tribune*,[1] said: "How shall we thank Miss Barton and The Red Cross for the help they have given us? We cannot thank Miss Barton in words. Hunt the dictionaries of all languages through and you will not find the signs to express our appreciation of her and her work. Words fail, and in dumbness and silence, we bow to the idea which brought her here — God and humanity! Never were they more closely linked than in stricken Johnstown.

"Men are brothers, yes, and sisters too, if Miss Barton pleased.

[1] October 25, 1889.

The first to come, the last to go, she has indeed been an elder sister to us, nursing, soothing, tending, caring for the stricken ones through a season of distress, such as no other people ever knew — such as God grant, no other people may know. The idea crystallized, put into practice, 'Do unto others as you would have others do unto you.' 'Even as ye have done it unto the least of these, so also have ye done it unto Me.' — Christianity applied, nature appeased, and satisfied! This has been Miss Barton's work, and nobly has she done it.

"Picture the sunlight or starlight, and then try to say good-bye to Miss Barton. As well try to escape from yourself by running to the mountains. 'I go, but I return' is as true of her as of Him who said it. There is really no parting. She is with us, she will be with us always — the spirit of her work even after she has passed away.

"But we can say God bless you, and we do say it, Miss Barton, from the bottom of our hearts, one and all."

In similar vein is the editorial from the *Johnstown Democrat* of October 17, 1889:

"MISS CLARA BARTON — In view of her many benevolent acts and scrupulous devotion to her life work, too much cannot be said in praise of this lady. The flood sufferers of Johnstown have abundant reason to always hold her in grateful remembrance, as she has been 'instant in season and out of season' in relieving their distress and in ministering to their wants. Among the many noble, generous-hearted men and women that came to our relief on wings of love and sympathy, she stands to-day conspicuous among the foremost. Her advent was with the first eastern train that reached Johnstown, and was greeted as an angel of mercy. . . .

"With an ardor born of the noblest impulses, and with an energy that knew no respite she went everywhere on her great mission of love, gladdening the hearts of our destitute and suffering, asking no questions about nationalities, creeds, social standing or color. The one great controlling, inspiring bond of universal brotherhood made us all akin in her estimation.

"Never did an organization select so wisely and elect so judiciously as did the National Red Cross Association when it chose her to preside over its benevolent work. Such is her national reputation that the generous donors of money and goods had no hesitancy in putting all in her hands. . . .

"Appreciating her character, ability and work as Johnstown people now do, we do not wonder that Charles Sumner's estimate of her was so high. In ascribing to her the highest attributes of exalted womanhood, and in saying that she possessed in a marked degree the highest grade of both statesmanship and soldiership, he gave utterance to a truth that has been verified in all our great National disasters.

"To her timely and heroic work, more than to that of any other human being, are the people of the Conemaugh Valley indebted for whatever may be their favorable condition of to-day."

Still further commendation for Miss Barton's work came from the Governor of the State, Governor Beaver, who said that "In this matter of sheltering the people as in others of like importance, Miss Barton, president of the Red Cross Association, was most helpful."

The Flood Finance Committee in its official report stated that "At a time when there was a doubt if the Flood Commission could furnish houses of suitable character and with the requisite promptness, Miss Barton offered to assume charge, and she erected with the funds of the Association large apartment houses which afforded comfortable lodgings for many homeless people. She was among the first to arrive on the scene of calamity, bringing with her Dr. Hubbell, the field officer of the Red Cross Association and a staff of skilled assistants. She made her own organization of relief work in every form, disposing of the large resources under her control with such wisdom and tenderness that the charity of the Red Cross had no sting, and its recipients are not Miss Barton's dependents, but her friends.

"She was also the last of the ministering spirits to leave the scene of her labors, and she left her apartment houses for use during the winter, and turned over her warehouse, with its stores of furniture, bedding and clothing and a well-equipped infirmary, to the Union Benevolent Association of Conemaugh Valley, the organization of which she advised and helped to form, and its lady visitors have so well performed their work that the dreaded winter has no terrors, mendicancy has been repressed, and not a single case of unrelieved suffering is known to have occurred in all the flooded district."

At the Red Cross House on Locust Street at the close of her labors, the organization of the Union Benevolent Association presented Miss

Barton with a gold pin and locket both set with diamonds and an amethyst.

After her return from Johnstown in 1889, administration affairs occupied her time for the rest of 1889–1890. The last of March, 1890, a cyclone occurred in Kentucky and Southern Illinois. Miss Barton left for the field to bring ready relief which to this scene of disaster was carried by Dr. J. B. Hubbell and his search party from her local headquarters near the cyclone's path. April 3, 1890, she wrote Mrs. Marion Bullock — "Despatches each day from the Dr. and his search party down in Southern Illinois and Kentucky."

Late in 1891, she made a trip across the continent with her nephew, Mr. Stephen E. Barton, who was planning a camp for the sake of his health in the lofty Cascade Range in the State of Washington. This unusual experience of a trip away from Red Cross work she describes in the following letter. Even here it will be seen she could not forget her administration of the cause of The National Red Cross.

LAKE CHELAN, STATE OF WASHINGTON.
Sept. 5, 1891. In camp.

"MY DEAR FANNY AND BER:

"I believe I am indebted to you both for letters. I was so occupied before setting out on this trip that I could not answer anybody and had to take along my indebtedness and my unanswered letter to hunt a spot of more time if not leisure. I am getting a wee bit of it up here among the peaks of the Cascade range of mountains, on the shore of Lake Chelan where we have pitched a tent, and made a camp, living out of doors and eating fish and game. We took in the Yellowstone Park on the way, which is too large to be written about in a letter — it is a voulme in itself — and then came on to this point near the Columbia River for the hunting and fishing that Steve hoped to find. That he is not entirely disappointed would appear from the fact of his having the day before yesterday, caught and brought into camp ninety-three brook trout, one of them weighing nearly three pounds. He has gone up rowing to the head of the lake to-day with Myrtis and some young company for companions. They may remain over night. They look for game on this trip. The rest of the party stay in camp — Lizzie because she does not enjoy boating and climbing — Dr. Hubbell and I to work. Our table under the trees is cleared of all appearance of breakfast and spread like a mammoth desk — letters, papers, satchels, pens, ink, pencils. The camp fire gone down, the sun clear and bright, temperature 70 degrees — steady — no rain, dew or wind, the lake blue and clear as crystal a mile wide in front of us, and the mountain cliffs rising up from both banks, and all about us from 2000 to 6000 feet stunted pines and fir. Bare, jagged rocks, and patches of snow, about eighteen miles above, the glaciers are met, and the railroad Creek which pours into the lake at this point, white and turbid —

"The jays, woodpeckers and chewinks twitter over my head, a couple of chipmunks are tugging away at the bread bag, having succeeded in rifling a box of gingersnaps. Now all this seems very trifling and wasteful for grown people. But after all there is more of real time and opportunity in it than in keeping up the formalities of home in hot weather, entertaining friends, and keeping well, — for we are all that. Steve has never had an ache nor pain since we left, scarcely since he left Boston. For he was well all his stay in Washington and is hearty as an Indian here — no more sitting up in bed at night. He camps down on a bed of fir branches with a blanket under and over, and sleeps from nine at night till nine in the morning if not called to breakfast.

"The mountains are so high about us the sun scarcely gets down to us at $8\frac{1}{2}$. Nothing has been said about the termination of this camp — our first was in Yellowstone for eight days, but we were sightseeing. We had to make a new one nearly every night for the eight days we were there. This is continuous and commodious. We are within seven miles of the head of the lake which is 70 miles long by a little over a mile wide, like a great river, only with no current and said to be 500 to 700 feet in depth. It is a terrible gorge from the top of the mountains to the bottom of the lake. Only for one Catholic settlement of Indians, there is no settlement on the shores of the lake. A Mr. Moore of New York has made a landing at this point, put up a shanty and with his family resides there. There are two or three small steamers plying up and down the lake for the miners at the head, and tourists who visit the lake for its beauty. Thus we communicate as often as needed. I wish you were both here. I think it would be a healthful change, if any change is needed, but it is a great way, isn't it? I don't know how I get into such distances!!

"I hope you are both well and that the world is good and kind as I wish it to be to you.

"Yours aff.

"CLARA."

"Love to the other house and to all friends."

After the journey to the Pacific and the camp in the mountains, Miss Barton, stopping in the meanwhile at cities of the interior, returned in the latter part of 1891 and once more settled down at Headquarters.

The winter of 1891-1892 in the Red Cross Headquarters was spent in the large Grant Mansion near the army and navy building. It was a hard one as appears from the following letter to Mrs. Marion B. Bullock:

"17 E. F., WASHINGTON, D. C.

"Jan. 7, 1892.

"MY DEAR LITTLE GIRL:

"I have been so long trying for a time to write you as I should. It doesn't come, and I must pencil this scrap at midnight while I warm my feet for bed.

"I have wanted to talk with you about coming to see us but when I think how cold it is here, and how far from nice and cozy it is, I feel reluctant to invite one from a small, snug, pretty home, to this, so large and it seems to me, less inviting one. If you did not know it I should not dare to say you might try it, for we are having an exceptionally cold, hard winter. The ground is covered with snow, and the winds have blown an old 'North Easter' these last days, and you will know this is not an easy house to heat.

"My expenses have been so heavy, and receipts so 'nothing' that I cannot afford to take on more 'help.' I am obliged to have a woman for the work and the house, a man for the fires and walks, — shoveling snow and all the cold, rough work, and an amanuensis as my clerk and typewriter. They're all drawing steadily every month, — then my rent is high and no one to help share that, and then all the world expects me to give it something every time it can get through the door and get a letter to me. I have had to economize on myself." . . .

In March, 1892, ten years of Presidency of the Red Cross, the sole expense of whose headquarters she struggled to bear, found her working harder than ever. It was to be the year of the Russian Famine Relief. Her staff as indicated on the letter head of the Red Cross at this time was as follows:

Board of Consultation:
    President of the U. S. and Members of the Cabinet.
Executive Officers:
    Clara Barton, President and Acting Treasurer.
    Wm. Lawrence, 1st Vice-President.
    A. S. Solomons, 2d Vice-President.
    Walter P. Phillips, Gen'l Sec'y.
    Dr. J. B. Hubbell, Gen'l Field Agent.
Trustees:
    Secretary of the Treasury.
    Secretary of the Interior.
    Secretary of War.

She was working at highest pressure. Of the winter of this year (1892) with its desperate, sad, hard toil, she wrote, on March 16th, to Mrs. Riccius, her brother David's daughter in Worcester:

"My dearest Dida:
"I *will* take the time for *one* letter, for myself, and it shall be to you. I have so wanted to write. I thought I should have seen you long ago, and now it does not seem any nearer than at first. I have had a desperately hard working winter, and only slept a few hours at night, and it has not been pleasant. I mean the work, sad, and full of perplexities and no one knows when it will end. I mailed you a *Star* to-day which tells a little about it but not much. I am glad of all the little news you tell me.
"I am always glad you have a home. Since I left my home with all it had in it, except a half dozen pieces of furniture and what I could take in a hand bag, I have never been back till last Sunday, for a few hours. I have almost no clothing to wear, but I shouldn't have time to attend to it if I did. How much of the sweet of life one leaves in the rush of it."

One reason for the high tension to the strain of which she refers was that her watchful mind had long been noting the failure of crops in Russia. By 1892, repeated failures of harvest resulted in a worse drought with thirty-nine million people famine stricken. Even at this news the House of Representatives defeated a bill which the Senate had passed for an appropriation to transfer food. It fell, therefore, to Clara Barton and the Red Cross to take up the Russian cause. Societies everywhere responded. The Elks initiated the work of giving. The spirit of relief swept the Minnesota Country. Pennsylvania sent a large ship from Philadelphia. Iowa, led by Hon. B. F. Tillinghast of Davenport, prepared to ship one hundred and seventeen thousand bushels of corn and one hundred thousand pounds of flour to Riga in a British steamer *The Tynehead*, chartered by the Red Cross at an expense of $12,500. Dr. Julian B. Hubbell, the always ready Red Cross Field Officer, had charge of the distribution of these argosies of grain to 82 famine districts, some of them 3000 miles farther, even as far as the Ural Mountains. Before undertaking that, however, he took Miss Barton's place as representative of the Republic of the United States at Rome, Italy, where the International Red Cross Conference for 1892 had convened. But by the first week in May he arrived at Riga, the port of distribution, and was in full charge of American Red Cross relief.

The value of the total contributions from America was estimated at about $800,000. These supported 700,000 people, according to Ambassador Smith, for a month. Besides other tonnages of corn and flour, in the *Missouri* were sent 250 carloads, approximately $200,000 in value. The Conemaugh Valley from the Red Cross at Johnstown expressed its undying gratitude by sending to the relief cargo, and in the *Indiana* went 187 carloads.

Many cities sent thousands of dollars in cash to the minister of the United States, Charles Emory Smith at St. Petersburg. Dr. Hubbell found that all worked with the Czar of Russia, who pierced the wall of the bureaucracy and who, discovering the extent of the famine, provided ten million dollars of his own and obtained 45 millions from the Government. The nobility followed. Relief corps and philanthropists sprang up all over the empire. Soup kitchens and bread lines were everywhere and were supervised by the oldest and most aristocratic families. The upwards of thirty-five millions of people saved from starvation felt unspeakable and especial gratitude to the United States and to the Red Cross for coming to its aid in this time of need.

The Mayor of St. Petersburg, in an address on behalf of that city to American donors, declared:

"The Russian people know how to be grateful. If up to this day these two countries, Russia and the United States, have not only never quarreled, but on the contrary wished each other prosperity and strength always, these feelings of sympathy can only grow stronger in the future, both countries being conscious that in the season of trial for either, it will find in the other cordial succor and support. And can true friendship be tested if not in the hour of misfortune."

In an address to the people of the United States from the nobility, the American Minister at St. Petersburg received like assurances of the deep impression made on the heart of the Russian Empire. From Tolstoi and the peasants came also touching acknowledgments and blessings.

Therefore it was not surprising as the Committee looked back that when the Red Cross ships first arrived they found an Empire with open arms, many peasants lining the dock and offering themselves free as dockmen and stevedores. Since the beginning, when as special representative of the Red Cross Dr. J. B. Hubbell had arrived at Riga he had found the warmest reception everywhere from Czar to poorest peasant.

Amid these cares, Miss Barton spent her time in the Red Cross in America at Washington, making it her base of communication and supplies.

The opening of the summer of the next year, 1893, found her at Bedford, Indiana, where Dr. Gardner had proffered his many acres for Red Cross Headquarters. Years later the proffered estate was found impracticable and returned to Dr. Gardner. At this time Miss Barton, however, visited it with enthusiasm, as appears in a note to Mrs. Balcom:

"RED CROSS PARK, June 3, 1893.

"MY DEAR LITTLE GIRL:

"Your letter came to Mrs. Gardner and myself yesterday morning just as we were leaving Bedford for a drive to Mr. Morlan's, where we have spent the day (yesterday), and last night. I needn't tell you how grieved we are at your misfortune.

"All are well here, Mr. Morlan is hard at work building a big barn, for his stock. Drs. Gardner and Hubbell are in Chicago for a few days. Enola and I return to Bedford to-day."

Returning to Washington from Indiana before the end of July, she wrote Mrs. Marion Balcom Bullock again from Washington, D.C., July 28, 1893. "I have been home a few days, but very busy, no help — much cleaning up to do. But all has gone well."

August 28, a hurricane and tidal wave submerged the Port Royal Islands off South Carolina.

From Washington, September 13, 1893, a personal note to Mrs. Bullock indicates Miss Barton's sudden leap to action. It stated — "A despatch from the Governor of South Carolina calls the Red Cross to relief work among the islands, and it is probable that Dr. Gardner and another assistant whom you have not met will start with me to-night for Beaufort, S.C.

"It is 11 A.M. not an article packed and much to look after. Have no idea what clothing I shall take, but at the last minute something will go in, and on."

When the Governor of South Carolina called the Red Cross, Miss Barton at once left for the field and for almost a year, endeared to the stricken natives as "Miss Clare," she presided over operations in the field. Beginning at the first hour of departure, she summed it up in a paragraph in this way:

"The next night, following the tidal wave of August 28th, in a dark cheerless September mist, I closed my door behind me for ten months, and with three assistants went to the station to meet Senator Butler. At Columbia we were joined by Governor Tillman, and thus reinforced proceeded to Beaufort. After due examination the work which had been officially placed with us by the Governor was accepted October 1st, and carried on till the following July."

Five thousand negroes were drowned and thirty thousand left without homes which as they moaned were "done gone" or "ractified."

From the seventy odd islands fifteen to twenty thousand refugees had flocked to one place. These Miss Barton had to redistribute in homes again. Immediately the crying need for food and clothes was relieved. To reconstruct society she obtained lumber, seed and thirty thousand dollars. Altogether Miss Barton rehoused and rehabilitated thirty thousand survivors. She well understood the nature of the negroes, having been so long in their vicinity during the eight months' siege of Charleston in the Civil War.

"These seventy islands," said Miss Barton at the time, "are cut and crossed by rivers, sounds and creeks, often too narrow and shallow to navigate, too wide and deep to ford and again sweeping swift and dangerous, to the open sea. The boats were nearly all lost, bridges gone, and neither lumber, nails nor tools to make others. Whatever we have to give must largely be carried to them. But let me talk 'closen' and comforters and bed sacks. I pray you don't forget that all is fish that comes to my net, and nothing comes amiss here. I could use 15,000 cheap bed sacks to-day, if we could place them so soon. They could be filled with moss. And I could use as many comforters and blankets, or bedding of any kind, and as many little pillow sacks and any clothing worn by man and womankind.

"I am besought for it all day long — never clothing, but 'closen, please marm, I hasn't got nossing' — poor simple children!"

The submerged lands were drained, three hundred miles of ditches made, a million of feet of lumber purchased and houses built, fields and gardens planted with the best seed in the United States, and the work all done by the people themselves.

Of the scarcity of funds and the need of more workers, Miss Barton, unconsciously penning in the third sentence the deepest motive to explain her career, wrote to to Mrs. Bullock October 26, 1893, as follows:

"It is probable that the winter is to be spent in our present field. The scarcity of money and food for relief will compel this. *We cannot desert our great poor charge of humanity and must stay and suffer with them if needs be.*[1]

"There was never such a time for relief work. I am calling to our help the friends that can feel like giving their time to the service that holds us here. We find transportation and no more. We have not over 12¢ apiece in hand for our 30,000 to be in part fed, sheltered, clothed, directed and nursed and boats provided to get their supplies across the river to them. Our nurses come in that way.

"On the other hand, if Mrs. Bullock would like a winter on a Southern relief field and can join me in Washington in time to return with me to Beaufort, inside of eight days, I think I shall take her right on with me to my Southern home. I shall telegraph from Washington, to let you have time to make ready."

Mrs. Bullock spent, as a result, the entire campaign at Miss Barton's right hand.

[1] Italicized by the author.

Joel Chandler Harris said that when he set out on his tour of investigation of this Sea Island catastrophe, he had no enthusiasm for the Red Cross Society and its kind of work. But after observing the Red Cross and Miss Barton in person he changed his mind and declared he would hasten to announce his error based on preconceived judgment. He proceeded to pay a hearty [1] tribute to the noble work which Miss Barton was conducting from her headquarters at Beaufort.

"Miss Barton and her assistants," he declared, "had faced a good many emergencies, but I have their word for it that the conditions they were compelled to deal with in relieving the population of the Sea Islands have never been paralleled in all their experience. The problem they had before them was new. But they had the capacity for organization, the gift of promptness, the quality of decision; they had tact, energy, and enterprise. They knew what was to be done at once and there was no delay nor yet undue haste in setting the machinery of relief in motion. The local committees turned over everything to the Red Cross and immediately the work of relief as distinguished from indiscriminate charity took form and became substantial.

"Miss Barton had some experience with the negroes in this section the first months of the war and therefore had nothing to learn or unlearn in dealing with them. Her name was known to the older ones and one old negro woman — Aunt Jane — who had cooked for her when freedom came 'bout' came thirty miles to see her."

It will be recalled that the first of September, 1893, Miss Barton had left Washington for the scene of the inundation. But it was not until the middle of the summer of 1894 that she returned from her labors as social reconstructor of thousands of black people in the Port Royal Islands.

The *Charleston News and Courier* of July 30th, paid this parting tribute to the Red Cross Workers:

"Miss Clara Barton, President of the Red Cross Association and her staff left Charleston yesterday afternoon for Washington, having finished their work in South Carolina. The story of their undertaking in its broader features is known throughout the country and throughout Christendom. The disaster was too appalling in proportion for local relief, and even the State was paralyzed by the demand so suddenly made on its charitable resources. It was truly a work

[1] *Scribner's Magazine*, February, 1894.

for the State government, or for the General Government, with all the energies and resources either could command.

"It was undertaken and performed by a gentlewoman and a handful of devoted men, her companions in spirit and associated in purpose and endeavor. They performed it so well, not to extend their deserved praise further, that they have left the storm-swept islands and their inhabitants in better condition in all respects than before the flood."

Her return to Washington is described by a contemporary writer thus:

"About two o'clock Sunday morning, after several hours' delay en route by an accident to a preceding train, Miss Barton with her little party stood quietly unlocking the street door, as if their absence had been but for an hour, and these tired workers passed into the broad quaint hall, under the rich draping of the flags of our own and sister nations of the Red Cross League, an impressive reminder of the International character of her home and her work. It is as she herself has said, 'I know no section. In the labors that have come to me the nations of the world and their strange tongues have become my own. For thirty-five years I have known no home in this country, but its capital, which its 65,000,000 may all claim as home.'"

The remainder of the autumn and winter was "occupied with details unavoidable and overlooked," while the following summer for the first time in years she spends in part at her old New England home in Oxford. Returning to Glen Echo in the fall, she finds the pressure of work so great, that to relieve it in a measure she moves to the capital, for though she had previously been located only six miles out, she found it difficult, even at that distance, to transact official business.

She had hardly finished the details of the year's work in the South Carolina Islands when letters came to her concerning the Armenian massacres.

Political fear of collusion between the growing young Turk party and the missionaries prevented the latter from giving aid to the orphans, widowed and homeless.

The Missionary Boards unanimously fell back on Miss Barton and the Red Cross to effect the work of aid and rescue and distribution of food and supplies which England as well as the United States was rapidly accumulating, but had no means of distributing in Turkey.

"Human beings were starving," explained Miss Barton, "and could not be reached. Thousands of towns and villages had not been heard from since the massacres, and only the Red Cross could have any hope of reaching them. No one else was prepared for field work; it had its force of trained field workers, and Turkey was one of the signatory powers to the Red Cross Treaty."

Such was the force of the plea of Mission Board leaders like Rev. Judson Smith, D.D. of Boston and Mr. Spencer Trask of New York of the National and American Relief Committee, that a large fund was forthcoming and ready to be distributed from England and America.

But how and by whom?

All eyes turned to the Red Cross.

The butchered could not be brought back to life. But in the regions burnt and raided by the Kurds, thousands of human beings were starving and tens of thousands orphaned and helpless.

They could go to these. It was conclusively seen that the International Red Cross alone could reach a zone so jealous of interference of other nations. Non-political, non-sectarian, it could enter where no army could pass. So it was thought by all. Yet because Turkey was suspicious of political intrigue and interference, word came from the authorities in Turkey, that "not even so reputable an organization as the Red Cross" would be allowed to enter. But trusting in the strength of the International Treaty, Miss Barton determined to face the Sublime Porte in person. Therefore, at seventy-five years of age she departed for the Orient.

Arriving in London, February 6, 1897, she set out promptly for Turkey by way of Vienna. She paused to secure certain permission to enter the Ottoman Empire. This finally received, she proceeded to Constantinople.

"The first step," she narrates in the "Story of the Red Cross," "was to secure an introduction to the Turkish Government, "which had in one sense refused to see me." Accompanied by the American Minister, A. W. Terrill, and his premier interpreter, Gargiulo, one of the most experienced diplomatic officers in Constantinople, I called by appointment upon Tewfik Pasha, the Turkish Minister of Foreign Affairs, or Minister of State. To those conversant with the personages connected with Turkish affairs, I need not say that Tewfik Pasha is probably the foremost man of the government — a manly man, with a kind, fine face, and genial, polished manners. Educated abroad with advanced views on general subjects, he impresses one as a man who would sanction no wrong it was in his power to avert.

"Mr. Terrill's introduction was most appropriate and well expressed, bearing with strong emphasis upon the suffering condition of the people of the interior, in consequence of the massacres, the great sympathy of the people of America, and giving assurance that our objects were purely humanitarian, having neither political, racial, nor religious significance.

"The Pasha listened most attentively to Mr. Terrell, thanked him and said that this was well understood, that they knew the Red Cross and its president. Turning to me, he said: 'We know you, Miss Barton, have long known you and your work. We would like to hear from you, your plans for relief and what you desire.'"

If her agents were permitted to go, Miss Barton replied, such need as they found they would be prompt to relieve. On the other hand if they did not find the need existing there, none would leave the field more gladly than they. They would be no respectors of persons — humanity alone would be their guide. "We have," she added, "brought only ourselves; no correspondent has accompanied us, and we shall have none, and shall not go home to write a book on Turkey. We are not here for that. Nothing shall be done in a concealed manner. All dispatches which we send will go openly through your own telegraph, and I should be glad if all that we shall write could be seen by your government. I cannot, of course, say what its character will be, but can vouch for its truth, fairness, and integrity, and for the conduct of every leading man who shall be sent. I shall never counsel or permit a sly or underhand action with your government, and you will pardon me, Pasha, if I say I shall expect the same treatment in return — such as I give, I shall expect to receive."

Almost without a breath he replied, "And you shall have it. We honor your position and your work."

By June the Irade of the Sultan granting the freedom of the Empire was duly received. By the 10th of March, so energetic was Dr. J. B. Hubbell, Field Agent of the Red Cross, that even before the Irade was received, he left Constantinople, Miss Barton's headquarters, and on the 18th at Alexandretta began making up the caravans to

DR. JULIAN B. HUBBELL

General Field Officer American National Red Cross, 1881–1904.

Aintab central station for the southern field. They proceeded thence to points eastward, north to Harpoot and the Euphrates districts, and through rain, snow and mire to Marash, among the thousands of refugees packing the cities. The massacres had been followed by the deadly typhus, dysentery and smallpox. For the Zeitoun field of disease, plans were completed for calling Dr. Ira Harris, the hero master of plagues and epidemics in the East, to again stamp out the scourge.

Four great expeditions in all, the Red Cross sent through Armenian Turkey, from sea to sea, distributing, repairing, replanting, and resettling survivors in homes.

When the fugitives were once reinstated in their houses and villages, food and clothes, seeds, sickles, knives, looms and wheels were provided. Even the cattle driven off by the Kurds into the mountain passes were bought or reclaimed. To these two thousand plow-oxen were added.

The financial secretary was directed to send a draft for five thousand liras (twenty-two thousand dollars) to the care of the Rev. Dr. Gates, to be divided among the expeditions for the purchase of cattle and harvesting of the crops of 1897.

"Unheard of toil, care, hard riding day and night, with the risk of life, were all involved," explained Miss Barton, "in order to carry out that order. Among the uncivilized and robber bands of Kurds, the cattle that had been stolen and driven off must be picked up, purchased, and brought back to the waiting farmer's field. There were routes so dangerous that a brigand chief was selected by those understanding the situation as the safest escort for our men. Perhaps the greatest danger encountered was in the region of Farkin, beyond Diarbekir, where the official escort had not been waited for, and the leveled musket of the faithful guide told the difference.

"At length the task was accomplished. One by one the expeditions closed and withdrew, returning to Sivas and Samsoun, and coming out by the Black Sea. With the return of the expeditions we closed the field."

Still another dispatch had plead for an expedition of relief to Arabkir, north of Harpoot. Here according to the message of the famous American doctor and missionary, Dr. Shepard, of Aintab, virulent fevers were raging. To stay the pestilence doctors' aid was imperative. Dr. Hubbell at once diverted Red Cross relief and stayed the pestilence in five weeks. His little band of workers returned to Constantinople July 16. "I need not attempt to say with what gratitude," Miss Barton concluded, "I welcomed back these weary, brown-faced men and officers from a field at once so difficult and perilous, and none the less did the gratitude of my heart go out to my faithful and capable secretary, who had toiled early and late, never leaving for a day, till the face grew thin and the eyes hollow, striving with tender heart that all should go well, and 'the children might be fed.'

"The appearance of our men on their arrival at Constantinople confirmed the impression that they had not been recalled too soon. They had gone out through the snows and ice of winter, and without change or rest had come back through the scorching suns of midsummer — five months of rough, uncivilized life, faring and sharing with their beasts of burden, well-nigh out of communication with the civilized world, but never out of danger. It seemed but just to themselves and to others who might need them, that change and rest be given them.

"It would scarcely be permissible to express in words, the obligation to our American Minister, Hon. A. W. Terrill, at Constantinople, without whose unremitting care and generous aid our work could not have been accomplished. And, indeed, so many were the duties of that difficult and delicate field that it seemed the help of no one hand or heart could be spared. We felt that we had them all; from the palace of the Sultan to beloved Robert College, from the American Legation to the busy rooms of the American Board, with its masterly treasurer, Peet, were the same outstretched hands of protection and care for our little band.

"They knew we had taken our lives in our hands to come to them with no thought of ourselves." It was thus she analyzed the reasons for the peaceful reception for her expeditions into the wilds of Turkey. Then and there this conviction proved that there could be no more winning way for diplomats to devise nor for Internationalists to codify. It gave her entrance everywhere, where even International embassies failed.

After three months of campaign and expedition in Turkey, Miss Barton returned to London September 2, to leave it October 8, 1896.

Her homecoming to Washington was celebrated by a great banquet of citizens, an honor not unfrequently paid to her at the successful consummation of some difficult relief expedition.

After this she remained in her own country till appointed by the President to attend in September the International Red Cross conference of 1897 at Vienna, Austria.

CHAPTER XXXIII

CLARA BARTON IN CUBA AND THE SPANISH WAR

"IT was as far back as November, 1897," [1] Miss Barton recalled in 1898, speaking of Cuba, "that I was made aware of the intention of our President to address a personal appeal to the people of the United States. It is perhaps not too much to say that my own thoughts, and such little influence as I might possess, have been directed to the same object [2] since our return from Armenia, fourteen months before."

Spain's war with Cuba had been going on for over a year. Already in the summer of 1897, the cry had gone up from the reconcentrados who had been taken in droves from their homes in the rich fields about them and had then been stockaded in enclosed limits to suffer and to starve. Reports of their concentration in sea coast towns had long since reached the ears of sympathetic Americans. Thousands in Cuba were known to be perishing and Miss Barton exposed to view the masked truth of the horror of the situation. But in 1897, the press was full of paragraphs "to the effect," as she said, "that it would be useless to send relief, especially by the Red Cross."

[1] In a prophetic letter of twenty-four years previous (February 8, 1874, written from Washington to a relative) Miss Barton notes: "Spain is still fighting her only or almost sole remaining colony, Cuba. Spain had once immense colonies, but she has been so tyrannical, and careless of their welfare that she has lost nearly all. And Cuba you know has an "Insurgent Army" of socalled Rebels fighting for their freedom. If she ever gets free she must come to the U. S. as she is too small to stand alone against the greed of great nations which will try to gobble her up for her riches in soil and products.

"The Spanish Authorities have just published a new list of orders very stringent, and hope to crush out the Cuban Insurrection in six months. You must keep watch of that too and see how it ends. It will be history by and by to whom Cuba belongs, and while one has to study so hard to learn *past* history it is not worth the while to let slip that which is all the time making in our own day and generation. Comprenez vous?"

[2] Miss Barton's Red Cross Campaign in Cuba and the Spanish War has been detailed in reports in her books, "The Story of the Red Cross" and "The Red Cross." In this chapter I am much indebted to these compilations and quote them freely at times. But many original personal letters exist and add an amount of unpublished material.

"First, it would not be permitted to land."

"Next, whatever it took would be either seized outright, or wheedled out of hand by the Spanish authorities in Havana."

"The Spaniards would be only too glad to have the United States send food and money for the use of Havana."

"Again the Red Cross being International, would affiliate with Spain, and ignore the 'Cuban Red Cross' already working there and here."

"And finally poor Cuba, with no national government or treaty-making power, could not have a legitimate Red Cross that other nations could recognize or work with."

These were but some of the arguments that were used to discourage a campaign of relief work.

"However, societies of women were formed," Miss Barton explains, "to raise money; among these the most notable, influential and worthy ladies in American society; they labored incessantly in season and out of season, with small results; perfectly unable to comprehend their want of success.

"This state of things continued," Miss Barton goes on to say, through the year of 1897. "But with the new year the reports of suffering that came were not to be borne quietly, and I decided to confer with our government and learn if it had objections to the Red Cross taking steps of its own in direct touch with the people of the country, and proposing their coöperation in the work of relief.

"Deciding to refer my inquiry to the Secretary of State, I went to his department to see him, but learned that he was with the President. This suiting my purpose, I followed to the Executive Mansion, was kindly informed that the President and Secretary were engaged on a very important matter and had given orders not to be interrupted. As I turned to leave, I was recalled with, 'Wait a moment, Miss Barton, and let me present your card.' Returning immediately, I entered the President's room to find these two men in a perplexed study over the very matter which had called me. Distressed by the reports of the terrible conditions of things so near us, they were seeking some remedy, and, producing their notes just taken, revealed the fact that they had decided to call me into conference."

In January, 1898, the Red Cross was organized as follows: President, Clara Barton; Vice President, George Kennan; Executive

Committeeman, Stephen E. Barton; Counsel, David L. Cobb, Executive Surgeon, Dr. A. Monae-Lesser; Chief of Hospital Work, Bettina H. Monae-Lesser.

Acting for the Red Cross, January 2, Miss Barton sent out through the press a call for money and provisions, announcing that General Fitzhugh Lee would oversee the distribution of supplies. January 13, a second appeal was issued to be read in every church in the country. All during this time President McKinley's interest and coöperation were invaluable in the direction of the affairs of the society.

At his suggestion a committee was appointed consisting of Stephen E. Barton, the second-vice-president of the Red Cross, Mr. Louis Klopsch of the Christian Herald and the Hon. Chas. A. Schieren, representing the New York Chamber of Commerce. This committee, known as the "President's Committee of Cuban Relief" and later as the "Central Cuban Relief Committee," was to have its headquarters in New York and to act as the receiver of funds and supplies. Miss Barton was asked to go to Cuba and see to the distribution of the shipments as they arrived. She answered the call with her old-time enthusiasm, and left Washington for Cuba February 6. Her party included Mr. J. K. Elwell (nephew of her old Civil War friend, Colonel Elwell at Morris Island). He spoke Spanish fluently and had been six years in business at Santiago de Cuba. With letters from the President of the United States, the Secretary of State and the Spanish Minister at Washington, they reached Havana February 9, and at once were confronted with the hollow-eyed, famishing people who were "sharing crusts in dens of woe." At the hotel Inglaterra, met with letters of welcome, they were personally received by the committees of distribution. The S.S. Vigilancia, with fifty tons of supplies, had just arrived, and after inspecting her cargo and its discharge, Miss Barton began the round of the several hospitals in Havana, all of which had a pile of rude black coffins at their doors. Within these hospitals were hundreds of living skeletons, amongst whom many death-pallid mothers were lying, with glaring eyes and a famishing babe "clutching at a milkless breast." To prevent such deaths as far as possible, Miss Barton organized places of distribution, where thousands at each center thronged the station. She visited outlying towns and organized in them similar systems of relief.

As a permanent home Miss Barton was tendered one of Havana's beautiful villas, where amid flowers, fountains, and gardens, she made her headquarters. In these, however, she seldom could remain to rest. Starving towns and villages pleaded for her to come, and she traveled constantly among them, distributing supplies and relieving suffering and death.

Senator Redfield Proctor of Vermont, in a speech in the Senate, after describing the actual conditions in Cuba and the widespread suffering, noted the efficacy of Miss Barton's work. He said:

"Miss Barton and her work need no indorsement from me. I had known and esteemed her for many years, but had not half appreciated her capability and devotion. I especially looked into her business methods in Cuba, fearing there would be the greatest danger of mistake, and that there might be want of system, waste, and extravagance, but found she could teach me on these points. In short, I saw nothing to criticize, but everything to commend."

When Mr. Louis Klopsch, of the Christian Herald, the third member of the Cuban Relief Committee arrived and relieved Miss Barton of personal distribution, she had time to enter at once into conference with the Spanish authorities, with whom she pleaded to release the reconcentrados and allow them to work the land and so grow vegetables around their stockades of concentration.

"In some long and earnest interviews with General Blanco I laid this matter before him," she recounted, "and begged his interference and commands on behalf of the safety of the poor people who might desire to cultivate this land. The Captain-General said they had the matter already under consideration, and desired me to meet his board of education, who would be glad to coöperate. I met this body of gentlemen — middle-aged, thoughtful, intelligent men. They had already taken some important steps, but were perplexed on both sides; first by the Spanish soldiery, liable to attack the workers, likewise the Cuban guerillas, who were equally as dangerous. And yet, despite all this, some important steps had really been taken and some little commencement made. I need not say that the exciting news which followed in less than a month put an end to all thoughts of steps in that direction. A new enemy would appear and the ground was likely to be plowed by shells from the monster ships that would line the bay."

Miss Barton's ability as an Internationalist and diplomatist was evinced, however, in her conference with the Spanish Captain-General.

"I met the Spanish authorities, not merely as a bearer of relief, but as President of the American National Red Cross, with all the principles of neutrality which that implied, and received in return the unfailing courtesy which the conditions demanded. From our first interview to the last sad day when we decided it was better to withdraw, giving up all efforts at relief, and leave those thousands of poor, dying wretches to their fate, there was never any change in the attitude of the Spanish authorities, General Blanco or his staff, toward myself or any member of my staff. One of my last visits before the blockade was to the palace. The same kindly spirit prevailed; I was begged not to leave the island through fear of them; every protection in their power would be given, but there was no guarantee for what might occur in the exigencies of war. I recall an incident of that day; General Blanco led me to the large salon, the walls of which were covered with the portraits of the Spanish officials for generations past, and pointing to the Spanish authorities under date of 1776, said with a look of sadness, 'When your country was in trouble, Spain was the friend of America. Now Spain is in trouble, America is her enemy.' I knew no answer for this but silence, and we passed out through the corridor of guards, he handing me to my carriage with a farewell and a blessing. I could but recall my experience with the Turkish officials and government where I entered with such apprehension and left with such marks of cordiality."

Shortly after Miss Barton's arrival in Havana, she visited the battleship *Maine*. "Captain Sigsbee's launch courteously came for us," she writes in her journal, "his officers received us; his crew, strong, ruddy and bright, went through their drill for our entertainment, and the lunch at those polished tables, the glittering china and cut glass, with the social guests around, will remain ever in my memory as a vision of the 'Last Supper'!"

A few days later came the double explosion and the terrible destruction of the battleship.

"The heavy clerical work of that 15th day of February held not only myself," she says in "The Red Cross," "but Mr. Elwell as well, busy at our writing tables until late at night. The house had grown still; the noises on the streets were dying away, when suddenly the table shook from under our hands, the great glass door opening on to the veranda, facing the sea, flew open; everything in the room was in motion or out of place. The deafening roar was such a burst of thunder as perhaps one never heard before. And off to the right, out over the bay, the air was filled with a blaze of light, and this in turn filled with black specks like huge specters flying in all directions. Then it faded away, the bells rang, the whistles blew, and voices in the street were heard for a moment; then all was quiet again. I supposed it to be the bursting of some mammoth mortar, or explosion of some magazine. A few hours later, came the terrible news of the disaster."

"Mr. Elwell was early among the wreckage, and returned to give me the news."

The diary goes on: "She is destroyed. There is no room for comment, only who is lost, who has escaped, and what can be done for them. They tell us that most of the officers were dining out, and thus were saved; that Captain Sigsbee is saved. It is thought that 250 men are lost, that one hundred are wounded, but still living, some in hospitals, some on small boats picked up. The Chief Engineer, a quiet, resolute man, and the second officer met me as I passed out of the hotel for the hospital. The latter stopped me saying, 'Miss Barton, do you remember you told me on board the Maine that the Red Cross was at our service; for whenever anything took place with that ship, either in naval action or otherwise, *someone* would be hurt; that she was not of a structure to take misfortune lightly'? I recalled the conversation and the impression which led to it. — Such strength would never go out easily.

"We proceeded to the Spanish hospital, San Ambrosia, to find thirty to forty wounded, bruised, cut, burned; they had been crushed by timbers, cut by iron, scorched by fire, and blown sometimes high in the air, sometimes driven down through the red hot furnace room and out into the water, senseless, to be picked up by some boat and gotten ashore. Their wounds were all over them — heads and faces terribly cut, internal wounds, arms, legs, feet and hands burned to the live flesh. The hair and beards singed, showing that the burns were from fire and not steam; besides, further evidence shows that the burns are where the parts were uncovered. If burned by steam, the clothing would have held the steam and burned all the deeper.

As it is, it protected from the heat and the fire and saved their limbs, whilst the faces, hands and arms are terribly burned. Both men and officers are very reticent as to the cause, but all declare it could not have been the result of an internal explosion. That the boilers were at the two ends of the ship, and these were the places from which all escaped, who did escape.

"The trouble was evidently from the center of the ship, where no explosive machinery was located.

"I thought to take the names as I passed among them, and drawing near to the first in the long line, I asked his name. He gave it with his address; then peering out from among the bandages and cotton about his breast and face, he looked earnestly at me and asked: 'Isn't this Miss Barton?' 'Yes.' 'I thought it must be. I knew you were here, and thought you would come to us. I am so thankful for us all.'

"I passed on from one to another, till twelve had been spoken to and the names taken. There were only two of the number who did not recognize me. Their expressions of grateful thanks, spoken under such conditions, were too much. I passed the pencil to another hand and stepped aside."

"Suspend judgment," wired Captain Sigsbee to the American Republic.

But as February and March passed conditions became so acute that it seemed wise for the Red Cross Staff, with Miss Barton at its head, to withdraw for a time in order to avoid possible loss of life and property, although she had completely disarmed the Spanish authorities of suspicion against the American Red Cross. But gradually and irrepressibly the verdict veered to war, and war was declared by Congress, April 25th, though in a way hostilities had existed from April 21st. The blockade would soon be on, and a wall of fire about Cuba. The government cabled to Miss Barton — "Take no chances!" With all other American citizens, she obeyed the order to leave Havana. The 9th of April she set sail for Florida, making her headquarters temporarily at Tampa.

Availing herself of the enforced cessation from relief work, Miss Barton made a trip to Washington and New York to confer with the government officials and the Red Cross and Central Cuban Relief Committees. Just preceding the declaration of war, President

McKinley had requested the Central Cuban Relief Committee to charter a steamer, load it with relief supplies, and start it for Key West. In one week from this request the Committee had the *State of Texas* chartered from the Mallory Line, loaded with some 1400 tons of food, donated largely from the great West, principally Kansas City, Mo., and in charge of Dr. J. B. Hubbell, field agent of the Red Cross, she steamed for Key West, April 27th.

In a letter to Mrs. J. Sewall Reed, her constant correspondent and a most intimate woman friend of this era, Miss Barton describes her return to Tampa from Washington and her voyage to Key West where she joined the relief party on the *State of Texas*, as follows:

"KEY WEST, April 30, 1898.

"MRS. HARRIETTE L. REED,

"GLEN ECHO, MD.

"MY DEAR SISTER:

"I want to say that our journey has been all pleasant. We have had no accident, no seasickness, no sickness of any kind and no trouble.

"We reached Tampa about six o'clock Wednesday afternoon, found Dr. and Mrs. Gardner waiting for us, and all the others in good order and very happy. — Found Tampa a fine little military camp, with several regiments, or nearly amounting to divisions, of regular troops under command of Brigadier General Wade, the son of my old-time friends, Benj. and Mrs. Wade of the old army days. We made acquaintance at once, and our hostess made a fine reception of the church and military combined, and we had one of the most brilliant affairs you would ever wish to see from four to six Thursday evening, and at seven we were packed and away on the steamer for Key West.

"Our voyage was delightful, and on Friday afternoon at five we landed, meeting Dr. Hubbell, Mr. Duncan, Captain Young of the steamer 'State of Texas' and other persons, all waiting to receive us. We delivered our papers — the official orders from the Secretary not yet having arrived. Mr. Cobb, in charge of Red Cross at U. S. Camps, had taken the precaution to have three or four other copies made and we were ready to leave a copy with each officer we met. A copy has gone to Admiral Sampson in front of Havana, and we are expecting his reply shortly.

U

"The 'State of Texas' is an admirable boat for our purpose. It is fitted up for an ocean steamer, lacking only the size and newness of the steamers of to-day. The crew consists of some thirty or thirty-five men, and the discipline and the table are excellent.

"The memories of pitiful Cuba would not leave us, and knowing that under our decks were fourteen hundred tons of food, for the want of which people were dying, the impulse to reach them grew very strong and a letter was addressed to Admiral Sampson.

"Nothing could have exceeded the courtesy of the Admiral, but we two were acting from entirely opposite standpoints. I had been requested to take a ship, and by every means in my power get food into Cuba. He, on the other hand, had been commanded to take a fleet, and by every means in his power, keep food out of Cuba."

A week later she adds this postscript:

"May 4, 1898.

"MY PRECIOUS SISTER:

"How you have been neglected in all these days, but we got shut off from all typewriting in moving from point to point, and so much was coming in every hour that I have only now gotten down to stenographic work. I am afraid that in all that time nothing has gone to you, and yet every hour in the day I am thinking of something that ought to go. We are in the same good health and condition as when I commenced this letter, and I do not know that we are any nearer our point of destination. I have conferred with all authorities, visited Admiral Sampson at his flagship, and made known to the Committee in New York the purport of our interview. The blockade is firm in front of the northeast coast of Cuba, and he feels it his duty to keep all food out. The result of this must be apparent to every thinking mind. We wait day by day to see if anything opens which will let us in with something for the starving.

"The weather is beautiful to the eye, sun bright and on the water not too hot. On the land I suppose it is getting to be almost unbearable. The sands are deep and hot, and the wells dry, no water in Key West, the cisterns all giving out, and we are warned that, if the water fails on our ship, we will have to get it somewhere else, perhaps steam into Tampa for it. At present, we have a supply."

May 9th Miss Barton received her first request for aid. It was from U. S. Marshall John F. Horr, who wrote:

"On board the captured vessels we find quite a number of aliens among the crews, mostly Cubans, and some American citizens, and their detention here and inability to get away for want of funds has exhausted their supply of food, and some of them will be entirely out. As there is no appropriation available from which food could be purchased, would you kindly provide for them until I can get definite instructions from the Department at Washington?"

This opened up an opportunity for service and all the ships in need were supplied with food and medicine for ten days and renewed every ten days for some weeks.

Writing of her band of workers Miss Barton says: "Our company numbers seventeen, all in perfect accord, not a shadow that I know of between any of them. Our young ladies are patterns of modest decorum, and stand very high with the people on shore. Our ship being reckoned among the government ships, cannot be run on to by every person who desires to, or any reporter who desires to pick up news. They can only enter by permission which is not copiously granted. I learn that the reporters of the press, generally from New York, are very desirous of getting interviews with me, but they cannot reach me, which is certainly a comfort.

"If we remain here a time, as quiet as we now are, I shall have time to bring up all the correspondence and get ourselves in better shape than we have been for some time. It is impossible for us to buy a typewriting machine, but the *use* of one on shore is secured, and Miss Graves and Mr. Cobb take everything that is prepared, man their little boat, and go over and use the typewriter, bringing home the results which we are putting through an improvised press, which is very excellent. Thus, little by little, we are surmounting the difficulties that at first confronted us very stoutly. We have telegraphed to New York for a typewriter to be sent, which we trust will be here in a few days.

"I find a few checks here which I shall take the liberty of sending you endorsed, and let you draw them and place them with the fund. Our address for the present will be 'Key West, S.S. State of Texas.'

"Please give greatest love to all members of the family, always including our modest niece, and always remembering how hard it was for me to come away and leave you, and how longingly my thoughts turn back to you.   This life is all well, everything about it is pleasant as it could be, but still there is another I would rather live, and some day look forward to it.   I shall not allow these long delays in your letters any more, for we are getting ourselves better in hand, and will not allow interruptions unless the sea and the army get between us in some way.

"You will be glad to know what a comfort Dr. and Mrs. Gardner are to me.   It carries one back to old days, and I have such implicit trust and feel the same comfort there that I feel with you in my home. Accept my loving good-bye, with dearest memories.

"Yours,
"CLARA BARTON."

May 12th, Miss Barton is still on the *State of Texas* in the Harbor of Key West, as is shown by letters written at that time.

There was a strong tendency in New York, owing to the abundance of money and supplies that were coming to the "American National Red Cross Relief Committee," to ignore the national organization and send supplies direct to the various military camps at Tampa, Chattanooga, and elsewhere.

Miss Barton fully realized this situation, as will be seen from the latter part of a letter to Mrs. Reed at Washington.

"WEDNESDAY NIGHT, May 18, 1898.
" from KEY WEST.

"To

"DEAREST SISTER HARRIETTE:

"There are a good many rumors of war afloat, and the censorship is very close, to the great annoyance of the scores of newspaper men who hang around like vultures.   I wonder if you sent all the Davis articles you saw; and are there more Golden Rules?

"There is a tremendous call for R. C. literature.   I wish I could get into my own shanty for twenty-four hours, but it is so mixed and packed up that no one can be directed how to get it.   I think I wrote asking for paper and envelopes to be sent.   Did I, and can they be sent or shall I supply with plain paper from here?

"It will seem very lonesome when I feel you no longer in touch, and that the home is hollow and empty and as much out of my reach as any one else. I hardly think my good country people take this in, when they think of me at the field. They think only of the field end, the home end never enters into their calculations.

"In fact they think I have only a satchel, and carry the American R. C. about in my pocket.

"What do you think of the great new society in N. Y. They are having it all their own way. I hope they will be guided aright, but I feel no concern. I have done my part as well as I could. I was to bring the Red Cross into the U. S. and it is done. It is surely here and none too great to do it honor. What more do we little old workers want? We only have to stand still and see the work of God.

"Good-bye, dearie, good-bye.

"CLARA BARTON."

"At length, the fleet moved on, and we prepared to move with, or rather after it," Miss Barton continues in her diary. "The quest on which it had gone and the route it had taken bordered something on the mystery shrouding the days when Sherman marched to the sea. Where was the Spanish fleet? And what would be the result when found and met? And where were we to break that Cuban wall and be let in? Always present in our minds were the food we carried, the willing hands that waited, and the perishing thousands that needed. We knew the great hospital ships were fitting for the care of the men of both army and navy. Surely they could have no need of us, and the knowledge that our cargo was not adapted to army hospital use brought no regret to us."

June 20th came orders to report at Santiago to Admiral Sampson, who, as fighting had begun, had advised Miss Barton to proceed to Guantanamo.

On the way she dropped alongside of a returning ship this explanatory note:

"S. S. STATE OF TEXAS, June 24, 1898.

"MY DEAR SISTER HARRIETTE:

"It is only a line I can write to-day just to tell you that we still live and wander and love you all the same. We left Key West on Monday; it is now Friday. We will reach the fleet to-morrow. Until an hour ago we have not seen a sail or mast, but just then an armed ship bore down upon us and hailed. We ran up our double colors. She dipped hers, and bore off as rapidly as she came, evidently disappointed that she had lost a prize.

"I was home a few days. All as usual. I left things with Mr. Briggs, who will take the correspondence and help. The war department offers through our neighbor, Mr. Pierson, to take all our telegraphing. This I hope will put us in communication with home and the world.

"The great committees seem to me quite uncertain. We have placed R. C. representatives at the principal large camps. We hope to find a way open for our food when we reach Santiago de Cuba, but know nothing now. Our P. O. address remains for the present, Key West, Box 548, but this may change later. Miss Graves has about fifty dictations to put in type for first mail we can catch.

"In great haste,

"Lovingly,

"CLARA BARTON."

June 25 they arrived at Santiago. Thence they sailed to Guantanamo, where there had been fighting. Fifty wounded had been brought aboard the *Solace*, the first Naval Relief ship.

Miss Barton explains in "A Story of the Red Cross," that "at six o'clock our anchor sank in the deep still waters, and we had time to look about and see the beginning of the war. The marines were camped along the brow of a hill. On our right a camp of Cubans, and all about us the great warships with their guns, which told of forthcoming trouble."

From her own Red Cross ship Miss Barton stated that day after day, in its weary, waiting cruise, it watched out for an opening to that closed-in suffering island, till at length to the thunder of guns, Siboney and San Juan "opened the track, and the wounded troops of our army, hungering on their own fields, were the reconcentrados of the hour."

Towards the close of June 26, Miss Barton exclaims in "The Red Cross"

"Before the day closed news came to us of a more serious character than we had before learned. The daring Rough Riders had been harshly dealt with. Hamilton Fish and Capron had been killed, and the wounded needed help. Wherever they might be, it must be possible to reach them, and it was decided that no time should be lost. Our men commenced work in the hold of the ship to get at medical supplies and dressings, and the captain took his orders."

Her diary for that day records that: "It is the Rough Riders we go to, and the relief may be also rough; but it will be ready. A better body of helpers could scarcely be gotten together."

"Nine o'clock, June 26th, found us in Siboney and anchored in its waters, which can scarcely be called a harbor. It seems to be rather an indenture in the coast.

"We were wakened at daybreak to see the soldiers filing up over the hill in heavy marching order, forming in lines by ones and twos, winding up, in and out among the hills, higher and higher, like a great anaconda. As we watched them through a glass, they became a moving line trailing on toward the clouds, till lost in the mist, and we can only think as we look at them, on how many or on which is set the mark of death. He knows no more than we, poor fellow, and unthinkingly, perhaps, with his swinging, careless gait, toils up and up and waits for — he knows not what.

"It seemed at last that through Captain McCalla at least 20,000 rations might be gotten behind his camp at Guantanamo for Cuban refugees. General Garcia supervised a pontoon landing. Immediately while this plan was being prepared, Louis De Garde, Major and Surgeon, U.S.A. in view of the care of the wounded in an engagement about to take place, dispatched a request from the Commanding hospital to come for patients at the landing in view of the inadequate preparation on the part of the army for transferring her wounded."

Miss Barton at once replied with assurance of ready aid and service and Dr. and Mrs. Monae-Lesser and their assistants, went ashore to both United States and Cuban hospitals.

"When we returned to Siboney," Miss Barton tells us, "we learned that our troops had been fighting all day, and that large numbers of wounded were walking or being brought in for treatment. The Red Cross had been requested to take entire charge of a fever hospital of United States troops, which it did. Dr. and Mrs. Monae-Lesser and two of the sisters were assisting in the operating tent. All of us worked nearly through the night — the nurses and physicians as above stated; the others taking out supplies for wounded — one hundred cots, bedding, hospital utensils, medicine, food, etc. The reports were that we had taken and held all commanding positions around Santiago, but that it had cost us four hundred men."

Miss Barton's diary of July 2 says: "The day opened cool and fresh, and although having worked steadily until three o'clock the night previous, when they had been brought back to the ship for a little rest, the Sisters were ready for work at half-past six. Sisters Anna and Isabel had been on duty all night, and must now be relieved. Dr. Egan and Mr. Kennan made ready for the front, the former to have a field hospital.

"With a portion of my assistants I go ashore to visit the hospitals in the early part of the day to learn if anything further can be done for them. We find the wounded coming in rapidly, long rows of hospital tents being filled with them, and many waiting their turn on the operating tables. We learned that the officers had suffered very severely, having been picked off by Spanish sharp-shooters."

It was that Saturday evening, the second day of the San Juan battle, that at the door of her hospital, Miss Barton was handed a message from the front. This was from Mr. Kennan at the firing line saying that by order from General Shafter's headquarters, Miss Barton was directed to seize any empty wagons coming in and send by them hospital supplies and medical stores which were badly needed at the front.

In her diary Miss Barton records her departure with two six mule wagon loads of hospital supplies.

"It seemed very strange," she says in "The Red Cross," referring to this entry, — "passing strange — that after all this more than a quarter of a century, I should be again taking supplies to the front of an army of the United States of America; that after all these years of Red Cross instruction and endeavor, it was still necessary to promiscuously seize an army wagon to get food to wounded men."

"An ambulance had been spoken of," her description of the trip continues, "but could not be had. We walked out a little way to wait for it. Dr. Hubbell left our party and went again in search of an ambulance, notwithstanding the assurance an army wagon would answer our purpose quite as well. These were going line by line up the front, mainly with ammunition. We waited a little by the road-side. The doctor did not return; our own wagons had gone on, and stopping another, loaded with bales of hay, we made our way once more to the front.

"The road was simply terrific — clayey, muddy, wet and cut to the hub. A ride of about four hours brought us to the First Division Hospital of the Fifth Army Corps, General Shafter's headquarters. This was properly the second day of the fight. Two fearful nights had passed.

"The sight that greeted us on going into the so-called hospital grounds was something indescribable. The land was perfectly level — no drainage whatever, covered with long, tangled grass, skirted by trees, brush and shrubbery—a few little dog tents, not much larger than an ordinary tablecloth thrown over a short rail would have made, and under these lay huddled together the men fresh from the field or from the operating tables, with no covering over them save such as had clung to them through their troubles, and in the majority of cases no blanket under them. Those who had come from the tables, having been compelled to leave all clothing they had, as having been too wet, muddy and bloody to be retained by them, were entirely nude, lying on the stubble grass, the sun fitfully dealing with them, sometimes clouding over and again streaming out in a blaze above them. As we passed, we drew our hats over our eyes, turning our faces away as much as possible for the delicacy of the poor fellows who lay there with no shelter either from the elements or the eyes of the passers-by.

"The rain, that had been drizzling more or less all day, increased. Our supplies were taken from the wagon, a piece of tarpaulin found to protect them, and as the fire began to blaze and the water to heat, Mrs. Gardner and I found the way into the bags and boxes of flour, salt, milk and meal, and got material for the first gallons of gruel. I had not thought ever to make gruel again over a camp-fire; I cannot say how far it carried me back in the lapse of time, or really where or who I felt that I was. I did not seem to be me, and still I seemed to know how to do it, and when the bubbling contents of our kettles thickened and grew white with the condensed milk, and we began to give it out, putting it in the hands of the men detailed as nurses and of our own to take it around to the poor sufferers shivering and naked in the rain, I felt again that perhaps it was not in vain that history had repeated itself. And when the nurses came back and told us of the surprise with which it was received, and the tears that rolled down the sun-burned, often bloody, face into the cup as the poor fellow drank his

hot gruel and asked where it came from, who sent it, and said it was
the first food he had tasted in three, sometimes in four, days (for
they had gone into the fight hungry), I felt again it was the same old
story, and wondered what gain there had been in the last thirty years.
Had anything been worse than this? But still, as we moralized, the
fires burned and the gruel steamed and boiled and bucket after bucket
went out, until those eight hundred men had each his cup of gruel
and knew that he could have another and as many as he wanted. The
day waned and the darkness came and still the men were unsheltered,
uncovered, naked and wet — scarcely a groan, no word of complaint;
no man said he was not well treated.

"The operating tables were full of the wounded. Man after man
was taken off and brought on his litter and laid beside other men and
something given him to keep the little life in his body that seemed
fast oozing out. All night it went on. It grew cold — for naked men,
bitter cold before morning. We had no blankets, nothing to cover
them, only as we tore them off from a cut of cotton cloth, which by
some means had gotten in with us, strips six or seven feet long, and
giving them to our men asked them to go and give to each uncovered
man a piece that should shield his nakedness. This made it possible for
him to permit us to pass by him if we needed to go in that direction.

"Early in the morning ambulances started, and such as could be
loaded in were taken to be carried back over that rough, pitiless road
down to Siboney to the hospitals there (that we had done the best
we could toward fitting up) where our hundred cots and our hundred
and fifty blankets had gone, and our cups and spoons and the delicacies
that would help to strengthen these poor fainting men if once they
could get there, and where also were the Sisters under Dr. Monae-Lesser.
and Dr. Le Garde to attend them.

"They brought out man after man, stretcher after stretcher, to
the waiting ambulances, and they took out seventeen who had died
in the night, unattended, save by the nurse, uncomplaining, no last
word, no dying message, quiet and speechless, — life had ceased and
the soul had fled.

"By this time Dr. Hubbell had returned, for he had missed our
wagons the day before and gone at night for supplies. This time came
large tarpaulins, more utensils, more food, more things to make it a
little comfortable, another contribution from the surf of Siboney. We

removed our first kitchens across the road, up alongside the head-quarters tent of Major Wood in charge of the camp. The major is a regular army officer, brusque, thickset, abrupt, but so full of kind-hearted generosity that words cannot do justice to him. He strove in every way to do all that could be done. He had given us the night before a little officer's tent into which we had huddled from the pour-ing rain for a few hours in the middle of the night. The next day, although no tent as spacious as that could be had, a little baby tent, it seemed of about seven feet, was found, pitched alongside the other, the tarpaulins put over, a new fireplace made near us, magnificent in its dimensions, shelter given for the boxes, bags and barrels of sup-plies that by this time had accumulated about us. There was even something that looked like tables on which Mrs. Gardner prepared her delicacies.

"The gruel still remained the staple, but malted milk, chocolate and rice had come in, and tea, and little by little various things were added by which our ménage became something quite resembling a hotel. The wounded were still being taken away by ambulance and wagon, assorted and picked over like fruit in a barrel. Those who would bear transportation were taken away, the others left where they were. The number grew a little less that day.

"Six Red Cross nurses met each arrival. These were the Sister Bettina, wife of the Red Cross Surgeon, Dr. Monae-Lesser, the noted head of the Red Cross Hospital in New York City, Sister Minna, Sister Isabel, Sister Anna and Sister Blanche. For a sleepless stretch of forty hours, one by one the wounded and sick and shelterless were taken into their care."

Early in the dawn of the first day after the engagement, a rough figure in brown khaki appeared at the Little Red Cross hospital. Before him stood Clara Barton. His clothes showed hard service, and a red bandanna hung from his hat to protect the back of his neck from the already broiling sun rays.

"I have some sick men with the regiment who refuse to leave it. They need delicacies such as you have here for which I am ready to pay out of my own pocket. Can I buy them?"

"Not for a million dollars!" said Miss Barton.

"But my men need these things," he said, his face and tone express-ing anxiety. "I think a great deal of my men, I am proud of them."

"And we know we are proud of you, Colonel, but we can't sell hospital supplies."

"Then how can I get them?"

"Just ask for them, Colonel."

"Oh," he said, his face suddenly lighting up with a bright smile. "Lend me a sack and I'll take them right along."

Slinging the ponderous sack over his shoulder, the last they saw was the rough figure in khaki, overtopped by the red bandanna, swinging off out of sight through the jungle. It was Theodore Roosevelt.

"By the third day our patients," continues Miss Barton, "seemed strong enough to risk food as solid as rice, and the great kettles were filled with that, cooked soft, mixed with condensed and malted milk, and their cups were filled with this. It was gratifying to hear the nurses come up and say: 'I have sixteen men in my ward — so many of them would like rice; so many would like chocolate and a few would like a cup of tea; and another who is feverish, would like only some apple or prune juice,' and taking for each what he called for, go back to his patients as if he had given his order to the waiter at a hotel; and the food that he took was all well cooked, as delicate and as nice as he could have gotten there. The numbers were now getting considerably less —-perhaps not over three hundred — and better care could be taken of them."

A vivid description of the field of relief at Siboney is found in the *Chicago Times Herald* (later the *Record-Herald*). It was written by Miss Janet Jennings, one of Miss Barton's most valued colleagues and an eyewitness.

"SIBONEY, July 8, 1898.

"Above hospital tents Red Cross flags are flying, and here is the real life — the suffering and heroism. Everybody who can do even so little as carry a cup of water lends willing hands to help the wounded. Most of the wounded are from the first day's engagement, when the infantry was ordered to lead the attack on Santiago, instead of using the artillery.

"And it all came at once — a quick blow — with little or no preparation on the part of the army to care for the sick. There was then almost nothing — no cots, bedding or proper food, for less than one hundred sick men.

"Two days later, when the wounded came in, the needs of the hour were overwhelming. The situation cannot be described. Thousands of our men had hurried to the front to fight. It was well understood that it would be a hard fight. The dead would need only burial, but the wounded would need care. And yet, with the exception of a limited number of stretchers, a medicine-chest and a few bandages, no preparation had been made — neither cots nor food — practically no hospital supplies.

"It is not strange that surgeons were desperate and nurses distressed. The force of each was wholly inadequate. The exact number of wounded may never be known. But the estimate at this time is about 1000 wounded, some 1500 killed and wounded.

"Wounded men who made their way down on foot eight miles over the rough, hilly road will never know just how their strength held out. Others were brought down in army wagons by the load, as few ambulances were at hand. Fortunately, there were some tents here that had been used by troops before going to the front. Under these hay was spread and covered with blankets, and the improvised hospital was ready. One tent was taken for operating tables, and the work of surgeons and nurses began. They worked night and day for forty-eight hours, with only brief intervals for coffee and hard-tack.

"Wounded men had to wait for hours before bullets could be extracted and wounds dressed. But there was no word of complaint — only silent, patient suffering, borne with a courage that was sublime. As the wounded continued to come in, tent-room gave out, and hay with blankets were placed outside, and to those 'beds' the less severely wounded were assigned. It was evident that the medical department of the army had failed absolutely to send hospital supplies, or by this time they would have been landed. As it was, the surgeons turned to the Red Cross ship 'State of Texas' for the help, and the supplies originally intended for the starving Cubans were sent ashore for our wounded.

"Miss Barton had been urged and advised to wait until the army opened and made the way safe to land supplies for reconcentrados and refugees. But she had forseen the situation to a certain degree and followed the army as quickly as possible — to wait for the emergency, rather than have the emergency wait for her. The 'State of Texas' was here a week before the attack on Santiago.

"While surgeons and nurses were probing for bullets and dressing wounds, a force of men on the Red Cross ship worked half the night getting out cots and blankets, food and bandages, and at daylight next morning the supplies were landed, taking advantage of the smooth sea between four and nine o'clock, as later in the day the high surf makes it extremely difficult for landings. There were six tables in the operating tent and eight surgeons. In twenty-four hours the surgeons had operated upon and dressed the wounds of 475 men. Four Red Cross sisters, trained nurses, assisted the surgeons. They were Sister Bettina, wife of Dr. Monae-Lesser, surgeon in chief of the Red Cross; Sister Minna, Sister Isabel, and Sister Blanche. Their knowledge of surgery, skill and nerve was a revelation to the army surgeons. These young women, all under thirty, went from one operating table to another, and whatever was the nature of the wound or complication, proved equal to the emergency.

"In the Red Cross Hospital, across the way, Sister Anna was in charge of the sick men turned over to the Red Cross two days before, when army surgeons with troops were all ordered to the front. With 475 wounded men to feed, there was not a camp-kettle to be found in which gruel could be prepared, coffee made, or anything cooked, not a kettle of any sort to be furnished by the army. The whole camp outfit at Tampa in the way of cooking utensils must have been left behind.

"But there was an overruling Providence when the 'State of Texas' was loaded for Cuba. So far everything needed has been found in the hold of this old ship, which deserves to have and will have a credit page in the history of the war in Cuba. There were kettles, charcoal braziers, and cooking utensils carried over to the Red Cross Hospital. To prepare gruel, rice, coffee and various other proper and palatable dishes for forty or fifty sick men by the slow process of a charcoal brazier, tea-kettle, and boiler is by no means easy cooking. But to prepare food for 475 wounded men, some of whom had had nothing to eat for twenty-four hours, cooking over a little charcoal pot is something that one must take a 'hand in' to appreciate.

"There was the feeling as if one were dazed and unnatural to hear American soldiers, men from comfortable homes, literally begging for 'just a spoonful of gruel.' The charcoal pot burned night and day, gallons of gruel were made and quantities of rice cooked until the greatest stress had passed. It was no time to stand on trained ser-vice, and everybody, man or woman, was ready to lend a hand.

"A striking feature of the first day's engagement was the number of men wounded in the head, arm, and upper part of the body. Some of these cases, the most serious, were taken into the Red Cross Hospital, where they received the most skillful and gentle nursing.

"Two days' steady strain began to show on the Sisters.

"The strain had been greater because there were no facilities for anything like a regular meal short of the ship, reached by a long, hard tramp in the sand, then a row over the tossing waves. But nobody thought of meals. The one thing was to feed and nurse 500 sick and wounded men. Human endurance, however, has its limit, and unless the Sisters could get a little rest they would give out. I went on duty for twenty-four hours, at night, with the assistance of one man, taking care of forty patients, fever, measles and dysentery cases, and half a dozen badly wounded men. Among the latter was Captain Mills, of the First Cavalry, and William Clark, a colored private in the Twenty-fifth Infantry, regulars. They were brought over from the hospital tents and placed on cots out on the little porch, where there was just room to pass between the cots.

"Their wounds were very similar — in the head — and of such a character as to require cool applications to the eyes constantly. Ice was scarce and worth its weight in gold, for the lives of these men as well as others depended chiefly on cool applications to the eyes, with as uniform temperature as possible. We had one small piece of ice, carefully wrapped in a blanket. There never was a small piece of ice that went so far. If I were to tell the truth about it nobody would believe me.

"Never in my whole life, I think, have I wished for anything so much as I wished for plenty of ice that night. It was applied by chipping in small bits, laid in thin, dry cotton cloth, folded over in just the right size and flat, to place across the eyes and forehead, enough of it to be cold, but not heavy, on the wounds.

"The ears of the sick are strangely acute. Whenever the sick men heard the sound of chipping ice they begged for ice-water; even the smallest bit of ice in a cup of water was begged with an eagerness that was pitiful. I felt conscience-smitten. But it was a question of saving the eyes of the wounded men, and there was no other way.

To make the ice last till morning, I stealthily chipped it off so the sick men would not hear the sound.

"At midnight a surgeon came over from his tent ward with a little piece of ice not larger than his hand. I do not know his name, but it does not matter, it is inscribed above. 'This is all we can spare,' he said. 'Take it. You must keep those wounds cool at all hazards. I have another case very like these — a man wounded in the head. I want to bring him over here, where he will be sure of exactly the same nursing. His life depends on the care he gets in the next twenty-four hours. Have you a vacant cot?'

"There was not a vacant cot, but we could make room for one on the porch if he could find the cot. He thought he could, and went back, taking the precious piece of ice that he really needed more than we did. In the course of a half hour the surgeon returned to say it was impossible to get a cot anywhere, and the wounded man must be left where he was in the tent, at least until morning.

"And so it went on through the long night — the patient suffering of the men, the heroism of the wounded, all fearing to give any trouble, desiring not to do so, and grateful for the smallest attention.

"The courage that faces death on the battlefield or calmly awaits it in the hospital is not a courage of race or color. Two of the bravest men I ever saw were here, almost side by side on the little porch — Captain Mills and Private Clark — one white, the other black. They were wounded almost at the same time, and in the same way. The patient suffering and heroism of the black soldier was fully equal to that of the Anglo-Saxon. It was quite the same, the gentleness and appreciation. They were a study, these men so widely apart in life, but here strangely close and alike on the common ground of duty and sacrifice. They received precisely the same care, each fed like a child, for with their bandaged eyes they were as helpless as blind men. When the ice-pads were renewed on Captain Mill's eyes the same change was made on Private Clark's eyes. There was no difference in their beds or food. Neither uttered a word of complaint. The nearest to a regret expressed by Captain Mills was a heavy sigh, followed by the words: 'Oh, we were not ready. Our army was not prepared.'

"Of himself he talked cheerfully, strong and hopeful. 'I think I shall go home with the sight of one eye,' he said. That was all.

"In the early part of the night he was restless, his brain was active, cool, and brave as he might be. The moonlight was very bright, a flood of silver, seen only in the tropics. Hoping to divert him I said: 'The moonlight is too bright, captain. I will put up a paper screen so you can get to sleep.'

"He realized at once the absurdity and the ludicrous side, and with an amused smile replied: 'But you know I can't see the moonlight.' I said it was time to get more ice for his head and half stumbled across the porch blinded by tears. When told who his nearest neighbor was, Captain Mills expressed great sympathy for Private Clark and paid a high tribute to the bravery of the colored troops and their faithful performance of duty.

"Private Clark talked but little. He would lie, apparently asleep, until the pain in his head became unbearable. Then he would try to sit up, always careful to keep the ice-pad on his eyes over the bandage.

"'What can I do for you, Clark?' I would ask, anxious to relieve his pain.

"'Nothing, thank you,' he would answer. 'It's very nice and comfortable here. But it's only the misery in my head — the misery is awful.'

"Poor fellow! There was never a moan, merely a little sigh now and then, but always that wonderful patience that seemed to me not without a touch of divine philosophy, complete acceptance.

"I have mentioned these two men, not as exceptional in bravery, but to illustrate the rule of heroism, and because they were among the patients under my immediate care that night. It was a strange night picture — a picture that could never be dimmed by time but live through all the years of one's life.

"After midnight a restful atmosphere pervaded the hospital and the blessing of sleep fell upon the suffering men, one by one. In the little interval of repose I dropped into an old chair on the porch, looked away to the beautiful mountains sharply outlined in the moonlight, and the sea like waves of silver, the camp on the shore, near-by thirty or forty horses standing motionless. Then the hospital tents, with now and then the flickering light of a candle; in the backgrounds the cliffs, with here and there a Spanish blockhouse. Over all the tragedy of life and death, the pain and sorrow, there was the stillness

x

of a peaceful night — a stillness broken only by the sound of the surf brought back on the cool breeze, the cool refreshing breeze, for which we all thanked God."

Three times Miss Barton made her way between these hospitals at Siboney and the Santiago front in the first seven days. Toward the end, as General Shafter's land forces had finished the attack, yellow fever fell upon Siboney. Miss Barton narrowly escaped being infected by refusing to enter a proffered room in the post office.

In her Red Cross narrative she describes one of these visits and the circumstance leading up to this refusal:

"A dispatch on Thursday informed me that Mrs. J. Addison Porter would be on the hospital ship 'Relief' coming into Siboney that day. I would of course go to meet her. It was a great joy to know that she would return to us. We at once decided that an army wagon should be asked for from headquarters and a party of us go to Siboney, both for Mrs. Porter and more supplies. The roads were getting even worse — so bad, in fact, that I dared not risk an ambulance, an army wagon being the only vehicle strong enough to travel over them.

"We had blankets and pillows and the ride was fairly comfortable, but it was late, nine o'clock, before we reached Siboney. The 'State of Texas,' which in the last three days had made a trip to Port Antonio for ice, we thought must be back by this time, and on reaching Siboney, found that she had arrived that evening at five o'clock and was lying at her old anchorage. But there was no way of communicating with her in order that a boat might be sent for us. Everything was tried. We had no signals; there was no system of signaling on the shore by which we could reach her, or, in fact any other boat. There was no way but to remain where we were until morning. It was proposed that I go to the rooms assigned for the hospital attendants. I decidedly refused this, for every reason. I knew the buildings were not to be trusted, and persons nursing night and day among all kinds of patients were not the people to room with. I asked to be allowed to remain in an army wagon. This was not thought proper. I suggested that it might be drawn out anywhere, the mules taken off, and I be left with blankets and pillows. I thought it, in fact, a good place for any one to sleep, and ventured to commend it as an old-time method — a refuge which once would have been palatial for me on the war swept fields of old Virginia, or in the drifting sands of Morris

Island — What would that have been the night after Antietam or old Fredericksburg, Chantilly or the Wilderness? But the newer generation could not see it so; a building must be had somewhere, and as I refused the hospital appendage *in toto*, it was proposed that I enter the post office, a room there being offered to me."

Refusing the room, Miss Barton (a woman, it must be remembered, in her 78th year) sat crouched under the stars and dew all night, feeling instinctively that danger lurked within, a fact proved by the subsequent death of the postmaster in the very cot she would have occupied.

At last the Spanish wall of ships was broken, Cervera's fleet was forced out of the bottled-up harbor, and the siege of Santiago was a thing of the past.

Miss Barton's heart was, however, behind the lines with thousands of reconcentrados she knew were famishing and without shelter. For these a demand for thirty thousand rations came at one call. To meet it she had ready the black-hulled supply ship, *State of Texas.*

The yellow fever, which she feared, had attacked all Siboney which had to be burned. Red tape orders due to fear of fever contagion stood between the Red Cross and the landing of supplies.

The surrender of Santiago was arranged to take place at 10 o'clock July 17. Knowing the terrible conditions there she preferred to have *The State of Texas* steam down from Siboney to Santiago bay.

Friday, the 15th, she addressed to Admiral Sampson a note in which she said:

"There seems to be nothing in the way of our getting this 1400 tons of food into a Santiago warehouse and giving it intelligently to the thousands who need and own it. I have twenty good helpers with me. The New York Committee is clamoring for the discharge of the 'State of Texas,' which has been raised in price to $400 a day.

"If there is still more explanation needed, I pray you, Admiral, let me see you.

"Respectfully and cordially,
"CLARA BARTON."

"This was immediately responded to by Captain Chadwick," says Miss Barton, "who came on board, assuring me that our place was at Santiago — as quickly as we could be gotten there."

On Saturday, the sixteenth, feeling that it might still be possible to take the supplies to Guantanamo, requested by Captain McCalla, a letter was addressed as follows:

"Steamship 'State of Texas,' July 16, 1898.

"Captain Chadwick, Flagship 'New York' off Santiago:

"Captain:

"If there is a possibility of going into Santiago before to-morrow morning, please let me know, and we will hold just where we are and wait.

"If there is no possibility of this, we could run down to Guantanamo and land Captain McCalla's 100,000 rations in the evening and be back here to-morrow morning.

"Will you please direct me?

"Yours faithfully,
"Clara Barton."

In reply to the above came this answer:

'U. S. Flagship "New York,'
"Off Santiago de Cuba, July 17, 1898.

"Dear Miss Barton:

"We are now engaged in taking up mines. Just as soon as it is safe to go in, your ship will go. If you wish, you can anchor near us, and send anything up by boats, or, if we could get lighters, drawing less than eight feet, food may be sent by the lighters, but it is not yet possible for the ship to go in.

"There are four 'contact' mines, and four what are known as 'observation' mines, still down.

"Yours very truly,
"F. E. Chadwick."

"These were anxious days," exclaims Miss Barton. "While the world outside was making up war history, we thought of little beyond the terrible needs about us. If Santiago had any people left, they must be in sore distress, and El Caney — terrible El Caney — with its thirty thousand homeless, perishing sufferers, how could they be reached?"

But at last entry into Santiago was possible. The diary describes it thus:

"On returning from our fruitless journey to Guantanamo we stopped at Siboney only long enough to get out dispatches, then ran down directly in front of Santiago and lay with the fleet. A personal call from Admiral Schley, Captain Cook and other officers served to show the interest and good will of those about us. Between three and four o'clock in the afternoon a small Spanish steamer — which had been among the captures of Santiago — ran alongside and informed us that an officer wished to come aboard. It proved to be Lieutenant Capehart, of the flagship, who brought word from Admiral Sampson that if we would come alongside the 'New York,' he would put a pilot on board. This was done and we moved on through waters we had never traversed — past Morro Castle, long, low, silent and grim — past the Spanish wrecks on the right — past the 'Merrimac' in the channel, which Hobson had left. We began to realize that we were alone, — of all the ships about the harbor there was none with us. The stillness of the Sabbath was over all. The gulls sailed and flapped and dipped about us. The lowering summer sun shot long golden rays athwart the green hills on either side, and tinged the waters calm and still.

"The silence grew oppressive as we glided along with scarce a ripple. We saw on the right, as the only moving thing, a long slim boat or yacht dart out from among the bushes and steal its way up half hidden in the shadows. Suddenly it was overtaken by either message or messenger, and like a collared hound glided back as if it had never been. Leaning on the rail half lost in reverie over the strange, quiet beauty of the scene, the thought suddenly burst upon me: 'Are we really going into Santiago — and alone?' Are we not to be run out and wait aside and salute with dipping colors while the great battle-ships come up with music and banners and lead the way. As far as the eye could reach no ship was in sight. Was this to remain so? Could it be possible that the commander who had captured a city declined to be the first to enter — that he would hold back his flag-ship and himself and send forward, and first, a cargo of food on a plain ship, under the direction of a woman? Did our commands, military or naval, hold men great enough of soul for such action? It must be true — for the spires of Santiago rise before us, and turning to the score of companions beside me I asked, 'Is there any one here who will lead the doxology?' In an instant the full voice of Enola Gardner rang out : 'Praise God, from whom all blessings flow.' By that time the chorus was full, and the tears on many a face told more plainly than words how genuine was that praise, and when in response to a second suggestion 'My Country, 'tis of Thee' swelled out on the evening air in the farewell rays of the setting sun, the 'State of Texas' was nearing the dock, and quietly dropping her anchors, she lay there in undisputed possession of the city of Santiago.

"A message from the headquarters of General Shafter, telegraphed to us even after leaving Siboney, said :

"'The death rate at El Caney [1] is terrible.   Can you send food?'

"Word went back to send the thirty thousand refugees at El Caney at once back to Santiago; we were there and could feed them — that the 'State of Texas' still had on board twelve hundred tons of supplies. — If there were any that night who had not received food, no one knew it."

When the officers at General Shafter's headquarters notified Miss Barton of the conditions at El Caney, she immediately sent Mr. Elwell there according to the staff report, to form a citizens' committee to assist in distributing the food that was to follow as quickly as transportation could be got to carry it.   Every horse, mule, vehicle of any kind that could be borrowed, begged, or hired, was impressed into the service, and tons of supplies were taken there at the earliest possible moment.   For about two weeks the Red Cross force worked night and day in relieving this place.

Miss Barton's campaign was now to center at Santiago.

"Returning to our first day in Santiago," she said of her work there, "it is remembered that this narration has thus far left the navy, its flagship, and commander at the entrance of the harbor in obscurity.   It would seem but just that it reproduce them.

---

[1] According to the Red Cross records during the siege of Santiago, General Shafter sent word to General Toral, the Spanish Commander, that unless the city was surrendered within twenty-four hours, he should bombard it.   Notice was given to the citizens of that place, and the surrender was refused.   An exodus of non-combatants, men, women, and children, hurriedly took place; it was said there were thirty thousand of them, and they fled to the country to the north and east, some twenty thousand crowded into the little village of El Caney which normally has not over five hundred inhabitants.

The city of Santiago at that time was in a destitute condition, several people having already starved to death, and there was consequently little or no provisions for the people to take away.   So this Vaste horde of hungry wretches oVerwhelmed the little country places that they came to, and the suffering that ensued was something frightful.

"Until ten o'clock on Monday the eighteenth we saw no sign of life on the waters of the bay — neither sail, steam nor boat — but suddenly word passed down from the watch on deck that a ship was sighted. Slowly it came in view — large, fine, full masted — and orders went to salute when it should pass. At length here was something to which we could pay deference. The whistles were held, the flag was ready for action, ropes straight and without a tangle — all stood breathless — but she does not pass, and seems to be standing in. In a minute more a stout sailor voice calls out: 'throw us a rope,' and there, without salute, whistle or bell, came and fastened to the stern of our boat this glittering and masted steamship from whose decks below, Admirals Sampson and Schley and their respective staffs shouted up their familiar greetings to us."

No signs of reprisal or resentment existed in the American treatment of the captured. While Shafter had negotiated with Santiago, Miss Barton had noted how the Spanish wounded were tenderly sent back on American stretchers, General Shafter demonstrating to the letter, the Geneva Treaty of equal care to the enemy's wounded. During this, General Toral's troops stood at present-arms, suffering a mental revolution at the sight, for they had been filled with a mediæval fear of butchery. This attitude may account for the peaceful reception which Miss Barton's entry was accorded.

The discharge of the cargo of the *State of Texas* commenced at six o'clock Monday morning, July 18. One hundred and twenty-five stevedores were employed and paid in food issued as rations. Four days later the discharge was completed. Miss Barton remained over a month before and in Santiago.

"Although the army had entered the city," Miss Barton writes, "there had been no confusion, no groups of disorderly persons seen, no hunger in the city more than in ordinary times. We had done all that could be done to advantage at that time in Santiago. The United States troops had mainly left. The Spanish soldiers were coming into their waiting ships, bringing with them all the diseases that unprovided and uncleanly camps would be expected to hold in store. Five weeks before we had brought into Santiago all the cargo of the 'State of Texas' excepting the hospital supplies, which had been used the month previous among our own troops at Siboney, General Shafter's front, and El Caney during the days of fighting.

"These were the last days of General Shafter in Santiago, who was, as he had at all times been, the kind and courteous officer and gentleman. General Wood, who was made Governor of the Province of Santiago, upon the day of surrender — alert, wise and untiring, with an eye single to the good of all — toiled day and night."

"General Shafter, General Wheeler, General McKibben, General Wood, General Bates and Colonel Roosevelt, Admiral Sampson, Admiral Schley, Captain Chadwick, and in fact, almost every military and naval officer with whom we had any business relations did everything they could for the Red Cross, and it is our proud satisfaction to feel that we met their wishes to the extent of our ability."

At the end Miss Barton telegraphed President McKinley, asking for the use of a transport that she and her workers might go to Havana with aid and supplies. He promptly placed at her disposal the Morgan Line steamer *Clinton* which was then in the government service. "Within the following four days," Miss Barton says, "we loaded the 'Clinton,' with thirty-four mules that had been sent to us by one of the Red Cross auxiliary committees of New York, and about three hundred tons of general stores which we hoped would serve as a starter in the distribution at Havana, other supplies having been promised to meet us at that place."

In the following unpublished letter from aboard ship Miss Barton tells of the exhausted staff, almost all but herself, be it noted, being disabled through sickness or exhaustion, and one lost by death.

"EN ROUTE SANTIAGO DE CUBA TO HAVANA,
"August 24, 1898.

"DEAREST SISTER HARRIETTE:

"I know it has been a great while since I spoke, and even yet I can say but a few words. I am bringing up in this day or two on shipboard the great accumulations of mail on the field of Santiago, and trying to get a clean slate for the opening of the newer field of Havana, where we arrive to-morrow noon. Santiago has not been a long field — five weeks to an hour — still a busy field — more commotion for the same number of troops than I have ever seen at a field, because the order has been less and more defective.

"I am not going to try to describe to you at all what it has been, what Siboney was before it in the days of battle, for one day, God willing, we will sit down together, and I will tell it all to you. We have gone through it apparently unscathed, and yet when we made out a little list the other day of those with whom we started and those we had now, we found that of the twenty in the beginning, eight were on their feet, eleven had sickened, been nursed and gone home, and one had gone to heaven. And yet I do not suppose any one thinks that anything has happened to the National Red Cross at the field. We have added other numbers until our staff at the table is still twenty. Dr. and Mrs. Gardner, who were with us until a few days ago, finally gave in with hard work and the hard climate, and left us. The Lessers and all their nurses went among the first in the height of the yellow fever scare — for scare it was; Mr. Kennan went a few days ago, unable to regain strength in the climate where he had lost it, and so on, one after another, quietly down and out, and somebody else has stepped into the place, and still we are pushing on.

"They tell me poor Barker has gone; died at the old home he loved so much — that home changed, Harriette; among all its losses I wonder if I shall know it, or if it will seem like mine.

"If any one tells you that we have been badly treated; that either the Navy or the Army or any Officer thereof has been otherwise than kind, helpful, courteous, respectful and brotherly, do not believe him. Not more than one instance perhaps of rare ignorance could be cited, and even that atoned for in penitence a few days after. But of all the general officers, from General Shafter and Admiral Sampson down, nothing could have been finer, nothing more respectful, nothing more attentive, and we are not afraid of the testimony which your soldiers will give when they come home. The Red Cross has worked, and I believe it has won.

"Good-bye, dearest sister. Write me sometimes, and be sure to tell me you are well and happy.

"Lovingly,
"CLARA BARTON."

On her arrival in Havana, a warm welcome was extended Miss Barton, proving the hold upon the people of the International Red Cross friendships, which not even war had been able to sever. Hundreds of the best people of that city, including Spaniards as well as

Cubans, came aboard the *Clinton* and assured Miss Barton of their warmest regard and heartiest welcome. It is believed that they did their utmost to persuade the officials to allow her to undertake her work in Havana. They told the most harrowing stories of the suffering in and about the city, and they said that with the exception of some "soup-houses," which the government was ostentatiously supporting, and which gave out to the poor, miserable sufferers who called for it, a small quantity of an alleged soup, in which there was not enough nourishment to keep a chicken alive, there was no other distribution of food, and that people were daily dying in the streets. "We knew that this was true, as we had seen scores of these people every time we had gone ashore," is Miss Barton's comment on this.

Miss Barton returned to Washington in November, 1898. The official end of the Cuban war left her mind as in all other wars wandering amid the wreckage and deep in reconstruction measures. Great inspirations pervaded painful regrets at what she had left undone, as well as the exhaustion because of what she had done. "The reconcentrados were never reached" she says with a pang of regret. "To those who could not withstand, Heaven came; to those who could, 'Cuba Libre.'"

"Cuba was a hard field," is her verdict, "full of heart-breaking memories. It gave the first opportunity to test the coöperation between the government and its supplemental handmaiden, the Red Cross. Through all our discouragements the steady hand and calm approval of our great head of the army and navy was our solace and our strength. And when at length it was all over, his hand could trace for his message to his people the following testimonial, what need had one even to remember past discouragements, however great? It was as if the hand of the martyr had set its undying seal upon the brow of the American Red Cross. What greater justification could it have? What greater riches could it crave?"

This points to the message to Congress of December 6, 1898, in which President McKinley cordially commended the work of the Red Cross and its founder in America. He said:

"It is a pleasure for me to mention, in terms of cordial appreciation, the timely and useful work of the American Red Cross, both in relief measures preparatory to the campaigns, in sanitary assistance at several of the camps of the assemblage, and later, under the able and experienced leadership of the president of the society, Miss Clara Barton, on the fields of battle and in the hospitals at the front in Cuba. Working in conjunction with the governmental authorities and under their sanction and approval, and with the enthusiastic coöperation of many patriotic women and societies in the various states, the Red Cross has fully maintained its already high reputation for intense earnestness and ability to exercise the noble purpose of its International organization, thus justifying the confidence and support which it has received at the hands of the American people."

Naturally the toil during and following the Cuban Campaign brought a reaction. She paid the usual toll in secret — a toll of suffering the world seldom if ever knew. Of this she wrote Mrs. J. Sewall Reed:

"GLEN ECHO, Dec. 26, '98·

"DEAREST SISTER HARRIETTE:

"The heavy illness has passed. I am over my apartment, just a few times below stairs, but we are mainly (Dr. and I) on the second floor. Not once out of doors. The cough is still here in part; some sleep comes but not sure. I have tried to be equal to all my correspondence but when fifteen to twenty letters a day persist in coming, it is a strife to keep the snow away from the doors, especially if I have no clerk. I could not dictate to a typewriter, nor speak direct to a clerk and the fear that the effort I would make, too, would retard my recovery, has held me as I was — with no change until I could feel it prudent to make it. Our winter, so far, has been a marvel; so clear, so fine, so uniform, some of the days have been October, some April, but none December. The sun lies the length of all my rooms."

But the Cuban field was not quickly dismissed from her mind. Its wreckage lay heavy upon her heart for over a year and a half during which she and the Red Cross Staff made more than one trip in the interests of the reconcentrados.

The hardest, most unrealized and least appreciated work of Miss Barton came as always after the limelight of excitement, after the headlines and war news, after the booming of guns and the fighting of battles. When these were over and the world forgot the neglected sufferers on the devastated fields, she as always, devoted herself to the afflicted people and the war-wrecked and diseased society. Heavy-hearted and lonely as the task was she could not lay it down. Her reception by the people of the United States did much however to lighten her burden of woe.

The burial of the Santiago dead took place at Arlington, Va., opposite Washington, D.C., April 7, 1899. Miss Barton describes the occasion in a letter to Mrs. Reed:

"In the rain of this Friday morning, I am at the office and find your prompt and dear letter. You did all that one could have expected to be done, and it was quite enough.

"Yesterday morning soon after my arrival at the office, I received a telephonic message from Mr. Howland of the 'Outlook,' who had arrived in the city and called, desiring to know if I would accompany him in a ride to Arlington to witness the great burial of the Santiago dead. At twelve o'clock, I replied affirmatively; he came in his carriage with three seats, and we drove around to Bell Mansion, took in Mrs. Graham Bell, Mrs. George Kennan, a girl friend of theirs and J. Stanley Browne, who with Mr. Howland and myself filled the three seated carriage.

"We drove to Arlington in the dust, intercepted every step, but finally reached the place, left our carriage, walked up to the stand, and before I knew it, I was taken up on it. I then sent back for the others and we all stood on the President's stand and witnessed the ceremonies. Then after a continued reception all the way down and off the grounds, we got our carriage again and came home. There was an immense crowd of people—everybody that you did know and everybody that you did not. I kept getting into little squads of people, both ladies and military officers who recognized me, and thereupon made an impromptu reception. Then Mr. Howland would draw me out, and when we got a little further away the same thing would happen again, until finally, after a long distance he drew a long breath and said he had seen a great many affairs of that kind and a great many receptions, but he never saw the bows so low as they were made there. I thought on the whole, it did not hurt that New Yorker to see somebody at home; and indeed, it did not appear to hurt him. He said a great many nice things.

"There is very little beside this to tell you. The world at Glen Echo moves on in its own way. The chicks thrive; Jersey is happy; and General Bennett, who arrived the day after you left and who is a splendid horseman, took Baba (one of the two horses presented Miss Barton in Cuba) out for a little excursion. But just think how mortified I was that Baba could not keep his feet on the ground for the General to get on, and had to be held for him, and pranced himself all over the grounds, sometimes fore feet up and sometimes hind feet up and the remarks of the General were all the time: 'Baba, you are a splendid fellow. You are splendid. I like this.' And finally he got on him and went away like the wind of winds, and when he came back he declared him one of the best horses he had ever seen. So, after all, our mortification subsided.

"I have just heard to-day for the first time of the arrival of nurses in Havana. They are not yet disposed of, but I think they are all getting on well. Mrs. Kennan is spending some time with Mrs. Bell and will try to come out to Glen Echo if she can, before she goes to Baddeck, if she does not go too soon. Mr. Kennan is in the West lecturing; is not very well.

"Everything at home remains in *statu quo*, and yet you must not think for a moment that there is not a great, wide gap here and there that nothing fills. I miss my schoolmate, and cling very close to Mr. (Edward) Balcom, who carries the dinner basket. I know how glad they were to see you at home, and I give up my selfishness and congratulate them and you too. A little spell of settled life will be helpful. Let me hear often, dearie, and believe me always,

"Yours lovingly,
"CLARA BARTON."

In April, though a year after the war, the Cuban reconstruction work which she could never let go, impelled Miss Barton to go to Cuba herself, as appears from the following:

"WASHINGTON, D.C., April 25, 1899.
"Mrs. HARRIETTE REED,
"DORCHESTER, MASS.
"MY DEAR SISTER HARRIETTE:
"After all the waiting I have decided to run over to Havana for a couple of weeks. Affairs seem to have shaped themselves in a way to make this possible, and Mr. Cobb and I will leave together Tuesday, May 2nd, via Miami for Florida.

"I think they are doing well in Cuba, and for that reason, I feel that I owe it to them to pay the little visit that is proposed. We see no reason why we cannot leave here very well."

Thus in her 79th year she still worked on, declaring that while her burden for Cuba was heavy, she could not lay it down. More than a year after the conclusion of the war she was still, however, suffering a hard reaction from its strain.

CHAPTER XXXIV

LAST YEARS IN OFFICE

THE GALVESTON FLOOD, 1900 — RETIREMENT, 1904 — MEXICO — PRESIDENT FIRST AID TO THE INJURED, 1904–1910

ON September 8, 1900, a tidal wave and tornado of terrific force swept over the sea and submerged Galveston, the metropolis of Texas, — a city of some forty thousand souls. The island on which it stood and the adjoining mainland were engulfed in the ripping fury of the waves. Lives to the number of from eight to ten thousand were suddenly lost in the cataclysm of flood and cyclone, which crushed like eggshells four thousand homes and drowned their occupants.

Thousands of survivors, so the news came to Miss Barton, "through a terrible day of storm and a night of terror floated and swam and struggled, amid the storm-beaten waves, with the broken slate roofs of all these homes hurled like cannon-shot against them, cutting, breaking, crushing; meeting in the waves obstacles of every sort — from a crazed cow fighting for its life to a mad moccasin-snake — perhaps to come out at last on some beach some miles away, among people as stunned and bewildered as themselves. Some of them struggled back to find possibly a few members of the family left, the rest among the several thousands of whom nothing is known."

September the 10th, two days after, as soon as the interrupted wires could give news, Miss Barton dropped everything else at Headquarters and with her Red Cross circle and some ten helpers at once set off for the distant field of flood and death. The New York *World* stood behind her and acquired a large subscription list with which it had started the appeal to the country.

September 13th Texas City, opposite Galveston, was reached by Clara Barton and her committee, five days after the first news of the disaster at Washington. The trip was long because travel was interrupted. While waiting twenty-four hours for a boat across the bay,

Miss Barton had to sleep on boards thrown across the tops of car seats. But she felt this was nothing compared with the fact that she was compelled to wait a whole day and night while thousands in almost plain sight were in agony beyond the bar. Her party was met by the local caretakers of the many injured who were being accommodated in crowded quarters in Texas City itself, although it mostly, too, lay stricken level to the ground. Across the bay the doomed city of Galveston appeared lighted, — but not by electric lights! The jets of flame came from vast funeral pyres on the coast. Twenty-three such funeral pyres Miss Barton counted at one time. Everywhere the air reeked, as it was to reek for months, with the acrid smoke of burnt human flesh, frequently thirty bodies or more being in one of the awful conflagrations. At once the President of the Red Cross and her committee were confronted by hosts of refugees whom the little harbor-boat kept landing on the beach of Texas City. All were sufferers, whether maimed or dazed. With the rest, arrived lunatics and unnumbered cases of nervous prostration caused by the terror of the days preceding.

Thus warned of the catastrophe's extent, next morning Miss Barton's committee took the boat to Galveston.

When the waters subsided, more than eight thousand people were destitute, wandering about in the sand which coated everything, but which was not sufficiently deep to permit of the fixing of tent stakes for the erection of even canvas shelter from the elements.

Confronting these refugees and victims as they opened their eyes, shook off their stupor and became conscious of the catastrophe (to use Miss Barton's words) were "the débris of broken houses, crushed to splinters and piled twenty feet high, along miles of sea coast, where a space, six blocks wide, of the city itself was gone, and seas rolled over populated avenues; heaps of splintered wood were filled with furniture of once beautiful habitations, — beds, pianos, chairs, tables, — all that made up happy homes. Worse than that the bodies of the owners were rotting therein, twenty or thirty of them being taken out every day as workmen removed the rubbish and laid it in great piles of ever-burning fire, covering the corpses with mattresses, doors, boards, anything that was found near them, and then left them to burn out or go away in impregnated smoke, while the weary workmen 'toiled' on the next."

Almost every family in the city had all or part of its members among the dead, while the living, for the most part without roof, remained to suffer in the blasts of the retreating hurricane and coming " nor'easters." To shelter and succor the thirty thousand people left, one third of whom at least were huddling in the wreckage like cattle in a pen, the Red Cross proceeded to work. Meeting the Red Cross officers the city officials at first declared that they "needed no nurses." The quick reply of Miss Barton's spokesman was that she "was glad" as they had none to give. The look of surprise which followed upon the face of the high-keyed local head of medical relief was countered by the Red Cross representative's rebuttal: "What *are* you most in need of?"

"Surgical dressings and medical supplies!"

Telegraphing the huge order it was filled and received by the Red Cross in twenty-four hours.

Thus the Galveston local committee of relief learned that the Red Cross had come with the country behind its back. They saw that a nation was subject to the Red Cross's beck and call.

"What do *you* most need?" the chief of police was asked.

"Homes," was the reply.

Estimating the material needed for homes, Miss Barton sent at once over the whole United States a plea to all lumber, hardware, and furniture dealers.

This demonstration by action was proof enough to Galveston of the Red Cross and its President, and Miss Barton was asked to assume charge of the administration of relief.

Preferring to coöperate, joined by Vice President Stephen E. Barton and Fred L. Ward, together they faced the actual needs, and the Red Cross went to work, each group with a separate department of investigation empowered to meet the discovered want, whether it be for stoves, heaters, food, clothing, bedding, blankets, or for other necessities of life.

In answer to these needs, from constantly arriving carloads and shiploads centralized at the Red Cross warehouses, came huge boxes, branded with a flaring Red Cross, their contents ready to be handed out at every place where clustered a group of the needy.

The task was tremendous. Miss Barton, who herself remained over two months, thus sketched the condition:

Y

"Dead citizens lay in thousands amid the wreck of their homes, and raving maniacs searched the débris for their loved ones, with the organized gangs of workers. Corpses, dumped by barge loads into the Gulf, came floating back to menace the living; and the nights were lurid with incinerations of putrefying bodies, piled like cordwood, black and white together, irrespective of age, sex, or previous condition. At least four thousand dwellings had been swept away, with all their contents, and fully half of the population of the city was without shelter, food, clothes, or any necessities of life. Of these, some were living in tents, others crowded in with friends hardly less fortunate; many half-crazed, wandering aimlessly around the streets, and the story of their sufferings, mental and physical, past the telling. Every house that remained was a house of mourning. Fires yet burned continuously, fed not only by human bodies but with thousands of carcasses of domestic animals.

"By that time, in the hot, moist atmosphere of the latitude, decomposition had so far advanced that the corpses — which at first were decently carried in carts or on stretchers, then shoveled upon boards or blankets — had finally to be scooped up with pitchforks in the hands of negroes, kept at their awful task by the soldiers' bayonets. And still the 'finds' continued, and at the average rate of seventy a day. The once beautiful driving-beach was strewn by mounds and trenches, holding unrecognized and uncoffined victims of the flood; and between this improvised cemetery and ridge of débris three miles long and in places higher than the houses had been, a line of cremation fires poisoned the air."

Even during the sixth week in Galveston, happening to pass one of these primitive crematories, a party of Red Cross workers stopped to interview the man in charge. Boards, watersoaked mattresses, rags of blankets and curtains, part of a piano and the framework of sewing machines piled on top, gave it the appearance of a festive bonfire, and only the familiar odor betrayed its purpose.

"Have you burned any bodies here?" they inquired. The custodian regarded them with a stare that plainly said, "Do you think I am doing this for amusement?" He shifted his quid from cheek to cheek before replying:

"Ma'am," said he, "this here fire's been going on more'n a month. To my knowledge, upwards of sixty bodies have been burned in it."

One department of the Red Cross took care of all surviving children orphaned by the loss of parents. This was a group especially appealing to the country, and for it in New York alone was raised fifty thousand dollars.

Miss Barton not only continued to aid the island of Galveston but planned to reach the suffering mainland across the gulf where nearly twenty counties, for forty miles inland, were inundated. There were one thousand square miles and sixty different towns and villages in need. At Houston she therefore established another center for relief. Besides supplies and aid, Miss Barton arranged for the replanting of a portion of the devastated fields with strawberries, furnishing a million and a half plants for this purpose.

It is little wonder that a woman in her eightieth year in the midst of such distress should for a moment succumb. The weak spot in Miss Barton's physique was her chest and the trouble as formerly centered here and soon developed into double pneumonia. But Miss Barton's wonderful recuperative powers came to her aid, and to the surprise of every one she was soon her usual self again.

She rose from her sick bed to prosecute the campaign of relief with greater ardor than ever, actually conducting work on the field for two more months, and expanding it to thirty counties. Besides the incessant toil in the wreckage, at Headquarters she found her tired nerves met by nights of clerical detail. "My stenographer," she said, "Miss Mary Agnes Coombs, found her post by me, and sixty to eighty letters a day, taken from dictation, made up the clerical round of the office of the president. This duty fell in between attending the daily meetings of the relief committee and receiving constant calls both in and out of the city.

"Our men made up their living room at the warehouse. The few women remained at the hotel, the only respectable house in the town.

"All this time, the stench of burning flesh penetrated every part of the city. Who could long withstand this? Before the end of three months there was scarcely a well person in Galveston. My helpers grew pale and ill, and even I, who have resisted the effect of so many climes, needed the help of a steadying hand as I walked to the waiting Pullman on the track, courteously tendered free of charge to take us away."

In a letter to Miss Barton Governor Sayres refers to the success of her mission in relieving the thousands of Galveston sufferers and homeless, and concluded:

"I beg to assure you of my high appreciation of your services; their value cannot be computed in dollars and cents. Your very presence amongst us at this trying time, even without the substantial aid which you have rendered, would be indeed a benediction, and it has served to inspire our people with energy, self-determination and self-confidence. Nothing that I could say or do would adequately compensate you and the Red Cross for your and its kindly and substantial offices at this time. I can only pray that God be with you and with it, and prosper all your undertakings."

In addition, the State of Texas, which had already known Miss Barton through the Pan Handle famine, adopted the following resolutions, February 1, 1901 (H. C. R. No. 8) ·

"In behalf of the people of Texas, the Legislature extends to the American National Red Cross Society, the most grateful acknowledgment for the relief extended through the Society to the sufferers in Texas by the storm of September 8th, 1900, and especially does the Legislature thank Miss Clara Barton, President of the Society, for her visit to the State and her personal supervision and direction of relief to those who were in need and in distress.

"That the Governor be and he is hereby requested to transmit a copy of this resolution to Miss Clara Barton."

Engrossed Resolutions were drawn up by the Central Relief Committee as follows:

"Resolved, That we especially thank and render homage to the woman who is the life and spirit of the Red Cross — who is the embodiment of the saving principle of laying down one's life for one's friend, whose friend is the friendless and whose charge is the stricken, and should be exalted above Queens, and whose achievements are greater than the conquests of nations or the inventions of genius and who is justly crowned in the evening of her life with the love and admiration of all humanity — MISS CLARA BARTON."

In the summer of 1902 occurred the International Convention at St. Petersburg, Russia. Miss Barton was appointed by the President to represent the United States, Congress voting appropriations.

In May, at the age of eighty-one, but judging from her photograph at the time, a woman more nearly in the prime of life, Clara Barton set forth on her journey over halfway round the world.

The remembrance of her in 1892 when she aroused America, through the Red Cross, to send food to aid the thirty-five million starving Russians was fresh in the mind of all in the Russian Empire.

When she arrived where the International Convention of the Signatory Powers to the Treaty of Geneva was to meet in St. Petersburg, she was tendered a warm and significant reception, the depth of which her country men and women little realized. Her address before the convention was received with the usual acclaim.

As a further and official mark of Russian esteem, the Emperor conferred upon Miss Barton the Russian Decoration of the Order of the Red Cross.

HER RETIREMENT FROM THE PRESIDENCY OF THE AMERICAN NATIONAL RED CROSS

June 6, 1900, the American National Red Cross was reincorporated by Congress — it being the wish of Miss Barton to make the organization more representative and also on the other hand to limit the scope of its insignia to legitimate Red Cross uses. From this time more power was assumed by the Board and its executive committee. Between Miss Barton and a member of the board of control and its executive committee, a slight shadow of misunderstanding increased as time went on, and led to misconstruction, misinterpretation and conflict of authority.

Though unhappily it sank at times to a matter of personalities and comparative unessentials, in the large it was a contest between two systems, the one that had fitted the creative twenty-two years when the Red Cross centered about Clara Barton, to whom it owed its life — the other the system of the future, struggling to fit itself to the time when the founder should be no more, and when therefore, a different system would be necessary, — a system centering around not a single person who could never be reproduced — but about a board of control and executive committee.

Miss Barton was at first inclined to be resigned to the new system. Had the atmosphere remained clear and not become clouded with

factionalism and discolored by these personal charges she would undoubtedly have seen the wisdom of a change both in leadership and
in plan. But these unfortunate characteristics aroused at first her
antagonism.

The conflict of authority between Miss Barton and the new Board
and its representative, was manifested slightly at Galveston, when a
representative of the Board and Miss Barton differed; Miss Barton,
notwithstanding her severe illness, reassumed control, however, and the
representative departed from the field.

Miss Barton returned to Headquarters in the fall of 1900, after
three months at Galveston, and occupied herself in recuperation and
in administrative affairs.

When in the spring of 1902 the terrible Mount Pelee earthquake
occurred, astounding the world with its unheard-of destruction of
human life, Miss Barton was on her way to St. Petersburg. She felt
that a second test of the Board of Control and Executive Committee
which remained in power, was here presented. But upon her return
she declared that the Red Cross in her absence had failed to do as
she had always done successfully, take the initiative in an appeal to
the country to spring to the relief at once, in this the most terrible
earthquake in human history. When Congress finally appropriated
money, she felt that the part the Red Cross played was insignificant
and a poor proof of the ability of the Board of Control. With the
aged President this weighed deeply as proving that the divided authority the by-laws made possible was bad and the cause of inaction.
Strong central authority for immediate action was, she thought,
absolutely essential. To make this possible she felt it necessary to
resume actual control, and to this end led a movement to amend the
by-laws. At the annual meeting of the American National Red Cross
in Washington, D.C., December 9, 1902, these amendments providing
for the increase and consolidation of power and the election of Miss
Barton as President for life were offered for adoption.

Objection to the new by-laws grew rapidly into a remonstrance —
the chief charge being an over-centralization of authority in Miss
Barton as President.

" Shortly after the adoption of such by-laws," explained Miss
Barton in 1904, "and because of certain objections made by the
remonstrants, and to satisfy their every complaint, if possible, the

President of this Society appointed a committee consisting of Hon. Richard Olney, Hon. George F. Hoar, Hon. John G. Carlisle, the Honorable Chairman of this Committee, and Lieut. General Nelson A. Miles, to draft a set of by-laws for this Society; that the Committee met and drafted a set of by-laws, and copies of the same were mailed to members a month in advance of the last Annual Meeting, and at such last Annual Meeting such by-laws were presented for consideration and unanimously adopted; that such by-laws so adopted were in all essential respects the same as the by-laws complained of and adopted in 1902, except that such new by-laws provided for the establishment of a First Aid Department, and provided for a Board of Trustees of 13 members, of which the President shall be a member ex officio. .

"This course is taken," Miss Barton declared later, as to this 1903 action, "the new code of by-laws proposed and circulated, and the annual meeting called with the sole purpose of doing everything in my power to harmonize existing differences between members of the corporation and to make the Red Cross an efficient instrument of the beneficent objects it is designed to serve. If in initiating these measures for the conciliation of opposing interests and views, it may seem to some of my friends that I overlooked just grounds of personal offense in imputations wantonly made upon my honor and integrity, I do so knowingly and willingly, and because the cause that the American Red Cross is meant to promote stands first in my affections and my desires. It would be strange if it did not — if the cause for which I have devoted myself for half a century were not deemed by me worthy of any possible sacrifice of personal pride or personal interest. It would be equally strange if, after so many years of earnest effort for the relief of human suffering, during which I have always lived and moved in the full glare of the public gaze, I could not now safely trust my character and good name to the care of the American people. I am sure that I can and that I risk nothing in doing so, and if those now at variance with me will meet me in the same spirit by which I am animated, we cannot fail to adjust all differences to our mutual satisfaction and to the great advantage of the cause all should have at heart." [1]

[1] These paragraphs are from p. 72 of " Clara Barton and The Red Cross," "Reply to Remonstrants," issued March 30th, 1904.

However, the minority dissatisfied at the annual meeting of 1903 were not content. They protested to President Roosevelt and succeeded in securing his aid. Through Secretary Cortelyou on January 2, 1904, he stated that the President and the Cabinet could not serve under the conditions of the Board of Consultation.

January 29, the minority's memorial, headed by John M. Wilson, vice president, was introduced to Congress as embodying the protest, and printed as House Document No. 340. This memorial charged in the large that the amended by-laws centralized in Miss Barton, as President, too much authority, pointing out in this connection that she was allowed to select her own executive committee.

Had it confined itself to this, the memorial would have been a fair protest against Clara Barton's Red Cross system as a whole from 1881 to 1904, as being unfit for the future, when Miss Barton's régime should have been finished. But in that it led them to criticize the past of the Red Cross, as it had been directed by Miss Barton, it generated heat instead of light, confused unessentials with essentials and degenerated into a contest of personalities in place of principles.

The Investigation Committee, equally sought by Miss Barton and the remonstrants, was appointed by the Red Cross with Senator Redfield Proctor as Chairman. Under its direction a treasury official went over the Red Cross books and records Miss Barton had laid open.

The result was that the charges pending in 1904 were dropped. The report was never made public and cannot now be found. They dropped the investigation, and in this way exonerated Miss Barton of the petty charges of misappropriating funds, and did not incriminate her past administration.

Miss Barton presented her resignation June 16, 1904.[1] By this, for the sake of harmony in the Red Cross, whose welfare she put above her own, she yielded to the new system, clearing the decks for it in its

---

[1] "In the month of December a public call was issued by the burgess of Butler, Pa., for aid in the relief of the epidemic of typhoid, which was raging at that place with great severity, reaching nearly 2000 cases — over a hundred deaths having occurred. This call was answered at once by the president, accompanied by Dr. J. B. Hubbell, general field agent of the Red Cross, and Gen. William H. Sears, an experienced worker, going in person to Butler and assisting in organizing the committees, and associating with them such outside Red Cross bodies of relief as were adjacent, remaining until the relief was fully and satisfactorily organized. This service was most gratefully received by the central committee, as expressed by public vote of thanks."

entirety by removing herself from power and thus doing away with the centralized authority about which the Red Cross had in the past swung. This put the Society under the Board of Control with the Executive Committee, and the President of the United States as nominal President.

The Committee of the opposition had evidenced the lack of any real belief of serious fault on Miss Barton's part by having prepared to propose her as Honorary President with a salary for life.

The serious charges made were against the system, and at that, so far as it had its deepest grounds, against the system not necessarily as operated in the past, but against it as adapted for the future.

Time has not only already exonerated Miss Barton's character and career, but has seen the Red Cross which she feared would suffer, come out of the controversy unscathed — the Red Cross winning its new system, ready to meet the future, but leaving Clara Barton also secure in her achievement as founder and successful administrator for nearly a quarter of a century of its affairs.

One reason for Miss Barton's inability to turn the Red Cross over earlier to the new system was her individualism. She had always, except in the Franco-Prussian war, worked as an individualist, on her own initiative, her only referendum being the people of the country or the world. Temperamentally impossible to her was the new system demanding that she work under the direction of a Board of Control. To one trained for thirty-three years to proceed on her own initiative on the occasion of disaster — it was beyond possibility to accept the new plan. Differences and the divorce of the two systems, her own and the new one, were on this account inevitable, when

" the old order changeth, giving place to new."

Miss Barton's mistake was in wishing the Red Cross President to combine both field work and the work of administration. No human could do both — and she could not keep away from the field of action. Therefore that which suffered, if any, would be the business details.

Grant that receipts or accounts of certain details did fail to reach Headquarters when she left them to risk her life in Mississippi floods, or in Cuba, or with the wounded at Siboney or Santiago! That is no wonder! The only wonder is that she could keep accounts at all. When General Shafter sent word to seize wagons — anything — only to come, she could hardly sit down and foot up accounts. Such times, when men are dying by the hundred in the night, are not times for systematizing a commercial institution. When the magnificent government of the United States suffered its commissariat, even in the camps at home, to fail so miserably, and when after engagements with the Spanish the army department confessed its terrible unpreparedness and called on seventy-seven-year-old Clara Barton to unload her Red Cross ships and rush their supplies to the battlefield to meet the mortal emergency — who can wonder that she could not stop to supervise items of bookkeeping.

Supplies and gifts always were receipted direct to the senders. Never was this fact denied. For example, as to not filing complete reports as in the Mississippi floods, she was told not to by the Government and Secretary of State Frelinghuysen. As to diversions of funds, — there were cases when she had to divert funds, as, when asked by the army commanders at Santiago to seize supplies, she then diverted supplies meant for reconcentrados. Such diversion does not incriminate. Refusal to divert would have been, instead, her real incrimination.

If the country were asked to-day — would it have preferred that in the Civil War, in the Franco-Prussian War, in the Spanish War, at Galveston and in twenty odd national catastrophes that Clara Barton, head of the Red Cross, had stayed at home and kept the ledger perfect or have acted as the nation's arm of mercy and the mainspring of relief at the front, what would it say?

It would say, give us Clara Barton, the nation's heroine, on the field. Give us the woman herself actuating all America to the relief of suffering.

We can grow hundreds of thousands of bookkeepers, but of such national heroines, there is but one. In the perspective of history, where little things grow small and big things large, the national verdict for Clara Barton will be one of endless love and pride.

Her system had done its work; nevertheless this was in the past. Soon she must leave it. The opposition was planning for the time when no such figure as Clara Barton in her vigor would exist.

It was hard for her to understand this because the air was beclouded with personal charges on her own side and on the other which made her feel that it was necessary in defending herself to defend the old system of centralized authority and action in the President.

Her modesty and natural simplicity never let her once feel but what some new Clara Barton could arise to embody the spirit of the Red Cross and swing the country as she did. Those behind the new system knew this succession was impossible.

Another thing Miss Barton did not see was that the Red Cross was old enough to stand alone upon its feet. Had she realized the permanency of its foundation she would not have feared so its transfer to the new system of administration. She could not see that it was unnecessary now for her to keep the Presidency, and full power, in order to insure the stability of the Society. She did not understand that her work had been so built into its blessed system that the Red Cross was regarded by the American people not as a changeable organization, but as an indestructible organism, which no change of names could overthrow.

Had Miss Barton seen all this it would not have been so hard for her to let others hold the reins and conduct the detailed administration while she remained the animating initial genius — and President at large — an honorary position from which the heart of America would never have dislodged her. Had she been able to get away from petty fears on the one hand and petty charges on the other, she would have seen that the new system institutionalized the Red Cross where she had once individualized it.

In December, 1904, came the new bill reincorporating the Red Cross. By this Act of Congress the American Red Cross was newly organized and reincorporated, and brought under Government supervision, the charter providing that the President of the United States be President and that among other members of the Board, five should be chosen from the Department of State, Treasury and Justice and that a disbursing officer of the War Department should audit the accounts.

The association is the officially recognized Volunteer Relief Society of the United States and is not under any one of the Executive Departments. In time of war its personnel would coöperate with the medical departments of the Army and Navy.

In 1915 the organized directorate was as follows: Hon. Woodrow Wilson, President; Mr. Robert W. De Forest, Vice President; Mr. Ernest P. Bicknell, National Director; Hon. John Skelton Williams, Treasurer; Hon. John W. Davis, Counselor; Mr. Charles L. Magee,

Secretary; Maj.-Gen. George W. Davis, U.S.A., Chairman Central Committee; Brig.-Gen. C. A. Devol, U.S.A., General Manager; Miss Mabel T. Boardman, Chairman National Relief Board; Hon. Robert Lansing, Chairman International Relief Board; Maj.-Gen. William C. Gorgas, Surg.-Gen. U.S.A., Chairman War Relief Board; Maj. Robert U. Patterson, Medical Corps U.S.A., Chief Bureau of Medical Service; Miss Jane A. Delano, Chairman National Committee, Red Cross Nursing Service; Miss Fannie F. Clement, Superintendent Town and Country Nursing Service; Mr. Lewis E. Stein, Chief Bureau of Membership; Austin Cunningham, Chief Bureau of Information and Editor of Magazine.

Executive committee: Miss Mabel T. Boardman, Washington, D. C.; Hon. Robert Lansing, Secretary of State; Mr. Robert W. de Forest, New York, N. Y.; Hon. Franklin K. Lane, Secretary of the Interior; Major-Gen. William C. Gorgas, Surgeon-General, U. S. Army; Surgeon-General William C. Braisted, U. S. Navy; Mr. Charles D. Norton, New York, N. Y.

Referring to the last days of her connection with the Society Miss Barton says in a letter written August 1, 1904, from Washington:

"It is very important that I be here until the changes of the Red Cross organization are made. I have to turn things over to new hands and really ought not to be away at all till it is finished." Of the great work of the Society she adds: "When the Government accepted the Red Cross, perhaps a bit arrogantly, I felt that my end was accomplished, and that I was ready to give it up."

Clara Barton might retire from the actual Presidency of the Red Cross — but in the minds of the people and in the hearts of the soldiers of the Grand Army of the Republic nothing could remove the lasting impression she had made as the mother of the greatest organ of mercy this land has known.

To-day the Governmental estimate and the place in American public opinion Clara Barton holds is thus expressed in "the last word" of the able and pointed speech of acting Secretary of War, Henry Breckenridge, at the laying of the corner-stone of the American Red Cross Building, March 27, 1915.

In a portion of the address he concluded ·

"The War Department of necessity feels a very close connection with the Red Cross. Out of the suffering of the wounded soldiers at the battle of Solferino first came Dunant's idea of the Red Cross. America's participation in the Red Cross Treaty of Geneva was agitated and induced by a noble woman whose sympathies had drawn her to the battlefields of the Civil War. To every soldier who fought in the Union Army and survived the War, the name of Clara Barton was known. And as long as the American Red Cross endures or its name is remembered the memory of Clara Barton will be cherished. Her sympathies were universal, her zeal unflagging. She nursed the wounded of two wars on two continents, in our Civil War and in the Franco-Prussian War. She directed the work of her association to the calamities of peace as well as the stricken fields of war. She was in Cuba before the Spanish War — was on the *Maine* the day before it was blown up and tended the wounded survivors in the hospital ashore. Wherever humanity called for help — in the Balkans or in Strassburg — in Cuba or in Galveston — in Paris or on the American battlefields of the sixties — there came the ministering hand of Clara Barton."

He added as to the Red Cross which she founded

"The meaning and significance that underlie the development of the Red Cross movement are fully symbolized in its emblem. The Red Cross banner symbolizes to America those qualities that must be found in our nation if the nation is to endure. The Red Cross banner spells for humanity the qualifications that are prerequisite to a sustained onward and upward march of the human race. The white field of purity and in it set the cross of self-sacrifice blazoned with the deep red of courage and bravery — this is the banner that the Red Cross unfurls in the van of marching humanity. And to the degree that America approximates the realization of the ideals spread upon that banner, to that degree will the nation endure and persist in righteousness and in strength. In honoring the self-sacrifice and consecration of its women and in rearing a useful monument to the spirit of humanity, as exemplified in the Red Cross, the nation not only honors itself but gives hopeful pledge and assurance of the sound ideals that lie at the basis of American national life."

To take an historical perspective, disfavor with a temporary and passing administration means nothing in the end to a name as great and a career as long as Clara Barton's, as this estimate shows.

For a while it may mean on both sides much misconstruction and suffering. But in the end this is forgotten and the fame remains undimmed.

It has been true of all the great humanitarian relievers of war. Henri Dunant, the founder of the European and the International Red Cross, was called at first a humanitarian crank and suffered many rebuffs. To-day this fact, however much pain it caused him then, is obsolete and unremembered amid the world tributes to his name.

Dr. Henry Bellows, who headed the great Ambulance system and Sanitary Commission of the Civil War, which finally developed into the greatest then known in the world, faced untold opposition and lack of sympathy from even the Civil War cabinet, who, when he sought to introduce the Red Cross, called it " the fifth wheel to the coach." Succeeding administrations for ten years rebuffed him, till by 1877 he gave up in despair trying either to make permanent or to graft the old Ambulance system and Sanitary Commission into the Treaty of Geneva.

Florence Nightingale, at the Crimea, England's great introducer into the world of the system of women hospital nurses, was actually so ignored by a subsequent English ministry that, though a poor invalid, she was ousted from her minor position in a Governmental office. It caused her intense pain, and although a chronic sufferer from her many labors, she saw herself ignominiously thrown out by new political leaders who, great as they were, could not understand her.

But when she became an octogenarian, all this became a buried incident, and all England but a few years ago bent to do her homage, when the Lord Mayor of London granted her the freedom of the city, and the Golden Casket, England's highest of honors. Now, since her death a monument is being erected and nothing is considered too good to let Great Britain make her memory green in the British Isles.

Thus will perish the temporary unhappy misunderstanding and misconstruction of 1902–1904 which Clara Barton suffered. In the atoning stream that swallows time's ticking seconds of little troubles its unessentials will be dissolved.

Indeed, as demonstrated in nearly 3000 American newspapers in 1912, they have already been dissolved, leaving her character and career eternally crystallized at the base of an enduring national foundation and an immortal American destiny — the greatest an American woman has yet produced.

Nevertheless, that Miss Barton felt her severance of relations at the time deeply is shown in the following letters to Professor Charles Sumner Young:

"My dear Mr. Young: —

"I wonder if I have ever said a word in reply to your comforting letter of May. If I have or have not said anything on paper I have in my heart answered it many times and bless both you and Mrs. Logan for your kindliness and trust. I have never in my life a moment's doubt of the loyalty of Mrs. Logan. She stood the brunt of the battle while she could and longer than I wished her to.

"She foresaw what was coming with her keen knowledge of human nature and thorough political training. She read the actors like a book. I well remember one night when she made this remark, and it was comparatively early in the game. Looking at me, she said, calling me by name: 'At first I called this prosecution, then I called it persecution, but now I name it crucifixion, and that is what they mean.' I knew it too, but there was no redress, no course but to wait the resurrection if it came.

"The trust, even of one's best friends, under the circumstances, and knowing nothing of the facts, could not be expected to withstand it. That it was physically withstood was beyond either the expectation or the intention. But my good friend, that is all passed. The press no longer turns its arrows upon me. The harvest was not what the reapers expected, and I suspected if it were all to be done over again in the light of their newly gained experience it would not be done.

"I would like to tell you some day of the newer work that occupies, and will take pleasure in sending you a report issued at our second annual meeting when it leaves the press. I am writing from Boston, where I am spending a few days at headquarters, but return soon to Glen Echo, where I hope to see you whenever circumstances call you to the east.

"Again thanking you most warmly for your letter, which brought me so much satisfaction, and wishing the best of all good things for you, I am, dear Mr. Young,
                                        "Most cordially yours,
                                              "Clara Barton."

Again she writes, proposing Mexico as a field:

"GLEN ECHO, MD., January 13, 1904.
"MY DEAR MR. YOUNG, —
"It is a blessing to your friends that you have a good memory. Otherwise, how should you have carried the recollection of poor me, all these weary months, running into years, and, through friends all unknown to me, sent such tribute of respect.

"I waited, after receiving the notices from you, to be sure of the arrival. I have directed the acknowledgment to be made to Mr. and Mrs. Canfield, but words tell so little; you will, I am sure, thank them for me. You will never know how many times I have thought of you, in this last, hard and dreadful year to me. I cannot tell you, I *must* not, and yet I *must*. So much of the time, under all the persecution, it has seemed to me I *could not* remain in *this* country, and have sought the range of the world for some place among strangers, and out of the way of people and mails, — and longed for some one to point out a quiet place in some other land; my thoughts have fled to you, who could, at least, tell me a road to take outside of America, and who would ask the authorities of Mexico if a woman who could not live in her own country might find a home, or a resting place in theirs.

"This will all sound very strange to you — you will wonder if I am 'out of my mind.' Let me answer — no. And if you had only a glimpse of what is put upon me to endure, you would not wonder, and in the goodness of your heart, would hold open the gate to show me a mule track to some little mountain nook, where I might escape, and wait in peace. Don't think this is *common* talk with me. I have never said it to others; and yet, I think they who know me best *mistrust* that I cannot bear *everything*, and will try in some way to relieve myself.

"To think of sitting here through an 'investigation' by the country I have tried to serve, — 'in the interest of harmony' they say, when I have never spoken a discordant word in my life, meaningly, but have worked on in *silence* under the fire of the entire press of the U.S. for twelve months, — forgiven all, offered friendship, — and still am to be 'investigated' for 'inharmony,' 'unbusinesslike methods,' and 'too many years' — all of these I cannot help. I am still unani-

LAST YEARS IN OFFICE

337

mously bidden to work on for 'life,' bear the burden of an organization
— meet its costs myself, — and am now threatened with the expense
of the 'investigation.'

"Can you wonder that I ask a bridle track? And that some other
country might look inviting to me?

"Mr. Young, this unhappy letter is a poor return to make for your
friendly courtesy, but *so long* my dark thoughts have turned to you,
that I cannot find myself with the privilege of communicating with
you, without expressing them. I cannot think where I have found
the courage to do it, but I *have*.

"I know how unwise a thing it seems, but if the pressure is too
great the bands may break, that may be my case, and fearing that
my better judgment might bid me put these sheets in the fire — I
send them without once glancing over. You need not forget, but
kindly *remember*, rather, that they are the wail of an aching heart and
that is all. Nature has provided a sure and final rest for all the heartaches that mortals are called to endure.

"If you are in the East again, and I am here, I pray you to come to me.

"Receive again my thanks and permit me to remain,

"Your friend,
"CLARA BARTON."

Later came, among others, this answer from Mr. Young.

"MY DEAR MISS BARTON

"Now, Miss Barton, why you have confided in obscure me is a
mystery I cannot solve; such a compliment is more than I can hope
to deserve. Having written the above, General W. R. Shafter came
into the library and sat beside me at the table. I stopped writing
and we entered into a discussion of you and your affairs. He is
exceedingly complimentary of you and your work. He especially
requested me to extend to you his greetings and sincerest wishes.

"My Uncle, General Ross, never told me of any event of his military career with so much pride as that of offering his services and acting as your lieutenant in the ware-house of the Red Cross at Havana.
Likewise would I be proud of the distinction to serve you in the most
humble capacity, either for the cause you represent or for yourself
personally.

z

"While I do not, and cannot, take seriously even the remotest suggestion that you might seek retirement and seclusion, I would gladly volunteer to be your Kit Carson over any mountain trail to happiness. I don't think the American people will ever permit your forced retirement, but in the event you should voluntarily withdraw from public service, I would indeed be glad to suggest to some of my friends, who I am sure would esteem it an honor and privilege, to offer you a home in Los Angeles, and a competence the rest of your life.

"If in my humble way I can be of any service to you, you will please remember that you have but to command me.

"Believe me,

"Sincerely your friend,

"C. S. YOUNG."

And yet even in her grief Clara Barton is planning the extension of the Red Cross. The vision of helping humanity in pain was still one on which she fed. Studying the situation carefully, she saw but two fields where there was no Red Cross — China and Mexico. She did not want to go as far as China to found a field. Mexico became her passion, and at 83 she even packed her things actually to go. But her friends stood in the way and at the last moment dissuaded her.

To Mexico, however, had she gone, conditions of barbarism might have been overturned and the sad pages of the late warfare have been reversed. There is no doubt Clara Barton's little figure, bringing its lessons of International Mercy, would have won the warm Mexican heart and established a real Red Cross. As it was, when the revolution broke out, no Red Cross existed worthy of the name. According to ambassador Wilson, who told it to me personally at the commencement of the Mexican trouble, no system of any sort was ready to care for the wounded, teach modern civilized treatment to the "shot on the spot" prisoners, or to prevent the other horrible cruelties of guerilla warfare.

In April, 1909, writing from Glen Echo to Professor Young, she refers to this desire of hers to go to Mexico:

"Does Mexico recall to your mind a request that I once made of you, that you should see me across the border line of that strange country? However much I needed it, and whether well or ill, I never knew. I only know I did not go. But my own country seemed to me so hard that I thought I should not live it through.

"The government which I thought I loved, and loyally tried to serve, had shut every door in my face and stared at me insultingly through its windows.   What wonder I want to leave?"

In a later conversation with Mr. Young about this letter Miss Barton said:

"Referring to that letter I wrote you in which I expressed a desire to go to Mexico, I meant it.   For several months I have been gathering together my belongings and adjusting my affairs so that I could go.

"There were but two countries where the Red Cross Society did not exist — one in China, and the other in Mexico.   I did not want to go to China, but did want to go to Mexico, and fully intended to go.

"My friends finally dissuaded me and perhaps it was for the best, for if I had gone I probably would not have been alive now."

Concerning her abandoned purpose to seek a refuge in Mexico, she wrote:

"I can never understand why I failed to go.   A greater power and a wiser mind were guiding, no doubt.

> " ' To God my life was an open page.
>   He knew what I would be;
>   He knew how the tyrant passions rage,
>   How wind-swept was all my anchorage,
>   And how I would drift out to sea.' "

Yet, as we see it now, was not her first intuition the divine one, to found a Red Cross south of the Rio Grande?   In the light of events in Mexico, it was an inspired intuition.   In the light of her death, as a preventive of decline, it would have been also the truer plan, as it would have fanned to life the embers of the nonogenarian and she, who at 77 sat on a gun carriage at Siboney, as in five other collapses just as severe, would probably have risen again in Mexico to the occasion of suffering and to the task of mercy.

Contrary to what seemed best in the light of what we know now, the wiser plan, the divine plan, would have been for her to go.   It would have added another great chapter to her victories — the operation of the International Red Cross in Mexico whose benighted war-torn regions remain unenlightened and unhealed and know not mercy and civilization.   And also it might have prolonged her own life by granting as in the past new reservoirs of power on which to draw.

But if she could not go to Mexico she could do something else. Since her retirement from the leadership of the Red Cross Society at a time when most people in her position would feel that they were entitled to rest, Miss Barton was not idle. April 18, 1905, the National First Aid of America was organized and she became its President. Faithfully she attended the official board meetings occurring in June during her summer vacation period at Oxford.

Miss Barton had been molded by her past work into a perpetual statue of watchfulness. As for individuals she was always on guard, so also she watched out for masses of people collectively. "As the result of my work among the injured and sick both in wars and calamities, my mind," she said during a Boston convention in 1906, "has been trained to look for trouble, for accidents and disorder wherever great masses of people were assembled."

"Years ago, when it was my privilege," she said to her new Society, "to bring the Red Cross to this country, and after years of untold labor, gain for it a foothold, I thought that I had done my country and its people the most humane service it would ever be in my power to offer. But, as originated, it reached only a certain class. All the accidents incident to family life, the great manufactories and railroads, with their hundred thousand[1] victims a year, were not within its province. Hence, the necessity and the opportunity for this broader work covering all.

"A wise providence has permitted me to leave the one, that I might stand with the other in its beginning.

"You will carry to its consummation what I only commence.

"To you, my faithful officers, the welcome I give is from a heart tried as by fire; as to the results of the hard field you have chosen to make warfare between knowledge and ignorance, to walk beside the toiling man, to reach under the grimy shirt to find the rough, untaught heart of the wearer, and to teach it the uses of pity and the ways of mercy — the love of man for man, born of the sufferings he is heir to.

"Your joy will be the joy of those you serve, and minister to; your reward the success you achieve. It is a search for the Holy Grail; in God's mercy may you find it."

[1] Now many more.

CHAPTER XXXV

CLARA BARTON AS INTERNATIONALIST AND PUBLICIST

AMONG the great spirits of Worcester County with whom Clara grew up, and as a young teacher labored seventeen years from 1836–1853 in North Oxford, were the master minds of the Free Soil Era, who gave birth to the Antislavery movement and the party of freedom. In the decade preceding 1853, it is recalled that to colonize the new state of Kansas with free settlers instead of slavery sympathizers, representatives were in session in Buffalo to organize the National Aid Society, with headquarters in Chicago. At that time, as noted by the Reverend Calvin Stebbins, Edward Everett Hale said of the steady helpful spirit of Worcester women : "The women of Worcester meet every afternoon to make up flannel clothing (and woolen in general) for Kansas. It is a permanent sewing committee and enlists people of all sorts. Not long after this comes you will get an installment of this sort of comfort for your soldiers from your state clothing committee, which expects to forward one thousand suits of clothing into Kansas by October 1st; I say expect rather than hope as I think the hope will come true."

In view of her leadership in aid of the soldiers later, this early lesson of the women under Clara Barton's eye must have indeed sunk deep. Besides Edward Everett Hale, Worcester's circle of coming abolitionists numbered among its able workers such pioneers of Antislavery as Thomas Wentworth Higginson, Eli Thayer, George Frisbie Hoar, and his father, Samuel Hoar. Coöperating with them were Sumner, Adams, Andrew, Palfrey, Garrison, Burlingame, Howe, and Dana of Boston, and Henry Wilson, who had left his shoemaker's bench at Natick. But none were more active in the movement to colonize Kansas and make it a free state with a majority voting for Antislavery than Edward Everett Hale.

Edward Everett Hale, as Pastor of the Church of the Unity, lived

in Worcester in the years 1846–1856.   June 28, 1848, in a great
mass meeting, Worcester cradled The Free Soil Party, that afterwards
became the party of Emancipation and Union.   Only 10 miles away,
Clara Barton, at 27 years of age, in the acme of her school era at North
Oxford, was captivated by the rising cause.   Strongly, in November,
1854, Mr. Hale bespoke this sentiment in an address "An Essay to
Enquire into The Most Rapid Means for Removing American Slavery."   It is confirmed by his successor, the Rev. Calvin Stebbins,
that he was then minister of the Church of the Unity in Worcester
and was in copartnership with George F. Hoar and his father and Eli
Thayer, a leading spirit, in getting up the Kansas colony.   Mr.
Thayer introduced a bill to charter the Emigration Aid Society, which
he presented to the Massachusetts Legislature.   But Mr. Hale had
been interested from the time of the Texas agitation, even in 1845,
publishing then a pamphlet "How to Conquer Texas before Texas
Conquers Us."   That plan fell through.   But now he planned to
project it into the State of Kansas, writing to his father that his aim
was to get twenty thousand of the two hundred thousand Irish and
German people going West to settle in Kansas, be provided with saw
mills, grist mills and temporary barracks, and so secure a free state
constitution.   The Kansas charter threw the entire South into great
excitement, and fiercely fought verbal encounters took place in Congress and in New England.

Of all this, Clara Barton, in the prime of her young intellect, was
an intensely interested spectator and hearer.   First Worcester, and
in 1855 the Capital, became generators not only of coming passions,
but of the white light of clear convictions which were to burst full
orbed in the battles for freedom.

As a member of the younger circles of society in Worcester she had
been electrified after the manner of George Frisbie Hoar, who said:
"There was something in that struggle with slavery which exalted
the hearts of those who had a part in it, however terrible, as no other
political battle in history.   I became of age at just about the time
the Free Soil party was born.   It awakened in my heart all the enthusiasm which my nature was capable of holding, an enthusiasm
which from that day has never grown cold.   It was a pretty good
education, better than that of any university, to be a young Free-
soiler in Massachusetts."

Into this enthusiasm and into this education Clara Barton came between the ages of twenty and thirty-two. As she often thus met the Hoars, Edward Everett Hale, Henry Wilson, Thomas Wentworth Higginson, and their colaborers and imbibed with them the political principles of antislavery, she shared socially their democratic nature and republican simplicity. It so stamped itself upon her that her plain living and high thinking can hardly be understood without it.

This simplicity of personality and democratization of manners persisted with all these men and women of Worcester to the end of their days. Hale especially was throughout his life an incarnation of democracy and equality, of which the following homespun incident was told the author but the other day.

The narrator was the head of a stall in an up-town Boston market where Dr. Hale appeared one day in Spartan simplicity, with market basket on his arm. It was up near Roxbury, and fashionable women were alighting from liveried carriages.

The proprietor of the stall before which Dr. Hale stopped was a little boot-lick of a man with curled mustache. He ran to the curb and bowed and scraped to his customers as their coachmen drove them to market. The flunky proprietor eyed Hale, however, suspiciously as he stood there with his basket, and when he was civilly approached by the author of "The Man Without a Country," he snubbed him.

Regally turning his back upon the tradesman, Hale strode on as if nothing had happened till he reached the narrator's counter. "*Do you deal in courtesy here?*" he thundered in a voice as deep as an organ fugue that could be heard up and down the entire market. "*Because if you do,*" he went on, "*I will deal with you in other things.*"

"You may send the rest," he continued a little later when he had given his order and secured some of his purchases, "but as I want these soon, I will carry them myself." He unconcernedly piled his basket full to the brim and then departed with a pleasant, "Good morning, Madam."

His Homeric head, overtopping the overdressed crowd who everywhere had begun to bow to him, had at length disappeared in the direction of his home when the boot-lick market man came up to the tradeswoman. "Who was that old tramp?" he sputtered forth. But he said it half apprehensively, for he had seen men and women go out of their way to recognize Hale and to be recognized by him.

"It was at that moment," said the marketwoman, "that I straightened up to my full height, looked the pocket edition of a man in the eye and piling in all the titles I had ever heard, replied, 'That, *that* sir, That was the Reverend Edward Everett Hale, D.D., Ph.D., LL.D., the greatest man in Boston !' "

Of such was the greatness in simplicity, the equality in manners and the old fashioned democracy in the Worcester zone of leaders of which Clara Barton was never ashamed. It never left Hale or his circle. It never left her.

But democratic as her rearing and bearing — at gatherings of Kings, Emperors, Dukes, Imperial Chancellors and European diplomats and reformers of first rank, like Benjamin Franklin in the French Court, Miss Barton never felt embarrassment, but was received as one of them and talked as their equal, even as she did with the Presidents and the statesmen of America.

Never did this appear in greater relief than at the first International Red Cross Conference at Geneva which she attended in September, 1884. Great as the position accorded her as a representative of this Republic by appointment of the President of the United States, with her usual democracy, she chose as her closest companion little Antoinette Margot, the Swiss French maid who had been so faithful at her side through the Franco-Prussian War. She took this girl by the hand right through the midst of this International convention of crowned heads, princes, and ambassadors. Little did she know when she did this democratic act that the one to immortalize her position in this convention, would be this same Antoinette Margot, who thus describes Miss Barton's triumph, in a letter happily preserved

"The Government of the United States has done itself no greater credit than in selecting Clara Barton to represent it among the nations abroad. During the last week I have looked on as she sat day by day in one of the greatest and grandest assemblies of men that could be gathered — men representing the highest rank among the civilized nations of the earth; men of thought, of wisdom, of power, called together from over the world to deliberate on great questions, of nautical import, military power, the neutrality of nations, humanity in war, wisdom in peace. In the midst of this assemblage of stately gray-haired men, glittering with military decorations with national honors, won and conferred, sat this one woman, — calm, thoughtful, self-possessed, recognized and acknowledged as possessing every right and privilege belonging to any member of that conference; not merely permitted to be there, but there by the sovereign right of nations; not merely allowed to sit there by the courtesy accorded to a lady but by the right due a nation's representative, her vote not merely accepted as a matter of form, but expected and watched for; grave questions referred to her as the representative of a great nation and all deference paid to her judgment: her demeanor so unobtrusive, her actions so wise, that it could not otherwise than reflect merited credit upon her and her country.

"But the crowning recognition of her philanthropic labors at home and abroad was given when one of the Italian delegates, springing upon the platform, proposed to the assemblage to vote by acclamation that '*Mademoiselle Barton bien merite de l'humanite.*'

"Even Miss Barton was moved from her usual composure by the thunders of applause. I do not know whether you in America are familiar with the peculiar significance of that phrase. It is an expression of the highest approbation, honor, and esteem that the French language can convey. It is probable that Miss Barton is the first woman in the world who has ever received such a tribute; and that from the official representative of all the Governments of Europe and from seven different countries, which gave these votes a very great importance."

It was here that the Grand Duchess of Baden arose and presented Miss Barton with a Court Jewel, an amethyst an inch and a half square in the shape of a pansy. This was afterward a favorite brooch.

If we except the Civil War period and the era of Presidents Lincoln, Grant, Arthur, Garfield, and McKinley, Clara Barton's International friendships number greater acquaintances abroad than at home. In fact European Internationalists in many ways appreciated her more, especially as to her work for the Red Cross.

In America we find that one of Miss Barton's greatest allies was the press; she could not have been oblivious to the fact that the Associated Press and other syndicates, as well as all the great dailies, had thrown themselves at her feet in her relief activities. In its power as king of public opinion she knew full well that it was the press that vibrated her will to every State in the Republic and to almost every country in the world.

The cause of the sympathy between Miss Barton and the press was not mere sentiment, nor just the love of a national heroine. Underlying this was an underground reason based on identity of interest. It was that Clara Barton and the press stood for the same thing. Each bravely swept into the fire zone and into the sphere of suffering, not to fight, neither to paint war glories nor to laud generals, but amid common masses of humanity, to expose suffering and pain and to conduct society to its immediate relief.

Miss Barton performed many of her deeds of heroism by forcing publication of truths that had been masked by militarism. When, for instance, in the battle of the Wilderness, at the deadlock at Fredericksburg in 1864 in the blackness of the night, she forced a way over swamps and waters from Aquia Creek and appeared like a prophetess out of the darkness before the Chairman of military affairs and exposed the fate of thousands of bleeding, dying soldiers lying in the mud, — it was an act of a great reporter. And in almost every appeal in war or disaster, she employed the agency of the press, casting her success or failure into an appeal to the people through publicity. This plan of coöperation with the papers that dominated her remarkable victories, which began at her request for supplies when she wrote the Worcester papers after the April 19th attack on Massachusetts troops at Baltimore, did not cease to be her plan through all the Red Cross eras later, till her death. The wonderful oneness between the Press of America and Miss Barton never was broken.

Momentarily discolored by variant reports of her retirement in 1904, the press returned again before 1912 to the unanimous championing of Clara Barton as the greatest national heroine. At her death over two thousand leading newspapers the length and breadth of the land, in their editorials and news articles outvied one another in words of honor, love, and esteem. Not an article that press clipping agencies could bring before the eye retained an iota of less esteem for her because of her break with the incorporators who changed the Red Cross to more of a Government institution.

This power of the press in blazing the pathway for such leaders in mercy as Clara Barton and the Red Cross, and the identity of their interests in exposing and relieving suffering, have not always been seen clearly. But a fine recognition of it has occasionally been framed, of which I recall the following:

"Christianity was a thousand years old before anybody seemed to care a straw what became of the wounded after a battle. As a whole, armies paid no heed to the wounded. At last, the newspaper reporter invaded the battlefield. He cared nothing for glory and saw the wounded. Then it was that people really began to understand what a fight meant. It was the reporter who sent Florence Nightingale to the Crimea.

"Henri Dunant, a Swiss gentleman, played the part of a reporter and pointed out to the people of Europe the truth about a battle. His paper 'A Souvenir of Solferino' was the inspiration of a wholly new method of treating battles. The reporter told the truth, left out the glory, and described the misery and suffering. The moment the people knew the facts, they invented the greatest charity organization the world had then known.

"'The Reporter at Solferino,' — Henri Dunant deserves this title as he did a good reporter's work and set all Europe to consider whether glory was not another name for barbarism, inhumanity, neglect and cruelty."

Militarism knows the truth of this fact. The searchlight by which the press flashes war's horrors, militarism fears more than all the aeroplane searchlights of opposing armies. Militarism welcomes hostile hosts. But it flees the newspaper.

Europe has muzzled the press in this International warfare begun in 1914. And there was a reason. There is always a reason. It is that once exposed to the people at home, the horrible realities of war that militarism masks, would cause rebellion against warcraft and institute revolution against the system that gave it birth.

While an Internationalist, Clara Barton was not a diplomat. She was greater than a diplomat. She did what diplomats failed to do, and succeeded where ministers plenipotentiary were utterly stampeded.

For example, we recall that in 1864–1867 the United States minister to Switzerland and his successors, and from 1867–1877 Dr. Bellows, the famous head of the United States Civil War Sanitary Commission, failed to bring the United States into the International Red Cross treaty of Geneva. But in 1882, when men failed, she, a woman of 61, succeeded.

In Russia in 1896, when Congress failed to grant ships to carry grain to the Czar's starving Empire, Clara Barton also succeeded. By this act, which she shared with the aroused country, she conquered as a friend the ruler of all the Russias. Nicholas never forgot it. When, presented at court in 1902, she knelt and bent to kiss the Emperor's hand according to court custom, the Czar lifted her up, refusing her tribute, exclaiming, "Not you, Miss Barton."

During the Armenian massacres in Turkey in 1892, when diplomacy failed, missionaries were muzzled and Internationalists deadlocked, it was Miss Barton alone, through her impression upon the Sublime Porte, who made the way for five International Expeditions of relief.

In Germany, above almost any American, she understood the new Empire and was received by its rulers as no other American, before or since.

In Cuba she alone maintained diplomatic harmony with the Spanish Governor-general and won Spain's rulers over to the International Red Cross.

Her rank as an Internationalist was well expressed in Washington, where a great diplomat once approached her as she admired the medals on his breast.

"Oh yes," he said, "but all mine are from my own country, while yours are *from the world.*"

The list of the objects of humanity's affection proves the truth of his remark, as we recall the following decorations and honors bestowed upon Miss Barton:

1870. The Gold Cross of Remembrance, Grand Duke and Grand Duchess of Baden.
1871. The Iron Cross of Prussia, Emperor William I, and Empress Augusta.
1882. The Medal of International Committee of the Red Cross of Geneva, Switzerland.
1884. The Red Cross by Queen of Servia.
1884. The Silver Medal by Empress Augusta of Germany.
1884. The Flag voted by Congress of Berne, Switzerland.
1884-1887. Jewels by Grand Duchess of Baden.
1885. The Diploma of Honor from German War Veterans, Franco-Prussian.
1887. The Jewels by Queen of Prussia.
1888. The Diploma of Honor from Red Cross of Austria.
1896. The Diploma and Decoration by Prince of Armenia.
1899. The Diploma and Decoration by Spain.
1899. Vote of Thanks by the Cortez of Spain.
1900. The Vote of Thanks by the Portuguese Red Cross.
1900. The Resolutions of the Central Relief Committee of Galveston, Texas.
1901. The Vote of Thanks from the Legislature of the State of Texas.

INTERNATIONALIST AND PUBLICIST 349

1902. The Decoration of the Order of the Red Cross by the Czar of Russia.
1911. Decorations from Supreme Assembly of the National Society of the Red Cross of Cuba, and Diploma of Honor.
1912. Engrossed resolutions of the Michigan Legislature in special session of appreciation for her work in the Civil and Spanish-American Wars, and extending sympathy in affliction and hopes for recovery.
The representative of America under appointment of the President of the United States, she has represented the Government at four International Red Cross Conferences —
1884. At Geneva, Switzerland ;
1887. At Carlsruhe, Germany ;
1892. At Rome, Italy (appointed, but could not leave the Russian Famine Relief, then in progress) ;
1897. At Vienna, Austria ;
1900. At St. Petersburg, Russia.

Clara Barton underestimated these world honors and refused to let them artificialize her naturalness and democracy or in any way stiffen her to false pride — of which she had none. Her priceless jewels and diamond crosses could not overcome her simplicity. Once she took the brooch presented by the Grand Duchess of Baden to a jeweler. It is said that the clerk to whom she handed it asked permission to go for another clerk, who in turn departed to get still another to look at the jewel. The manager of the store was finally summoned, and he asked Miss Barton if she knew of the value of the pin. "Each of these jewels," said he, "is almost priceless. They represent almost a king's ransom!"

"Miss Barton," the narrator goes on to say, "mentioned her name, and told him the story of the pin. In accordance with a promise made to the Grand Duchess, she wore it constantly, to show that she held the giver in her thoughts."

Clara Barton's other treasures included many pieces of old and rare lace, the gifts of foreign potentates. But these she accepted as she did most presents — as impersonal acknowledgments of her work, and as marks of esteem for the Red Cross.

In the hearts of American soldiers she held a place deepest of all. As late as September 13th, 1910, when she was too ill to come to the reunion of the 21st as in the past, tear-blinded eyes in Worcester greeted her message through her nephew Stephen, for they felt the force of her frequent remark: "In all the world none are so dear to me as the Old Guard who toiled by my side years ago."

Always the ones to whom she naturally was dearest and to whom her presence was a love-feast, were the soldiers of the Civil War. Again and again each year during the fifty years that passed after the war, she came before them to become, more and more, a sweetener of hearts and bodies scarred by past conflicts.

For instance, at a meeting in Boston in 1909 she purposely sought to avoid an ovation by remaining on the platform until she supposed that the audience had all turned to go. Then she started to walk down the aisle with General Shafter, with whom she was chatting. Suddenly she paused while resting on his arm to become conscious of a great audience still sitting, an audience of old soldiers, who refused. to stir. As she turned towards them they rose, choking their emotions. Then the tumult broke.

"Three cheers for Miss Barton!" Voices hoarse with feeling rang out on every side.

"Tiger," shouted one.

"No, not tiger," interrupted another, "Sweetheart!"

At this they collapsed, and the cheers broke into sobs.

All nations shared this soldierly affection. The flags of Germany, France, Italy, Switzerland, the Papal States, Russia, Turkey, and other countries were presented to Miss Barton by officials of those nations. And these flags long hung in the house in Glen Echo as mementos of the many battles and campaigns and disasters which she had served.

They were of every hue and form and country and time.

Thus the world as well as her own country, buried with marks of love and appreciation the single mark of Governmental forgetfulness shown in the Congressional investigation which was promptly dropped, the charges being dismissed by Senator Redfield Proctor as unfounded.

But if the Government gave no words of tribute at her resignation or later at her death, its act in taking over the Red Cross in 1904 was a signal honor. It was an act done not in effort of praise; yet when to succeed her as President of the Red Cross it could find but one — the President of the United States — it conveyed an honor unprecedented. He only was great enough to fill the place she created and for twenty-two years filled.

However discordant may have been the way in which it was done, it yet fulfilled her original plan. For she had first plead with President Garfield, with succeeding Chief Executors, to be President of the Red Cross.

In other ways has the Red Cross evolved according to her plan. The great central Red Cross Headquarters, for instance, is the culmination of what in the large she had always hoped for and planned.

But perhaps greatest of all, the Internationalization of the United States was begun and brought forward out of a certain national jealousy and suspicion engendered for many eras, by the medium of the Red Cross, America's first and greatest teacher of the new Internationalism.

Naturally fearful of the abuses of monarchical systems in the old world from which our Republic had been freed, an intense national individualism made America fearful of any International coöperation, such as the Red Cross proposed.

When in 1882 she won her country to it, Miss Barton broke this almost insuperable barrier. She did it by just one cry — humanity. Neither before nor since, until President Woodrow Wilson's stand for International humanity, has any such step toward Internationalism been attempted or achieved. Other types of Internationalism have been proven scraps of paper or idle dreams. The Red Cross alone survives as an International organ of unshakeable power. Whatever new International movements in the name of humanity our country may initiate, she will be known as the mother and first parent.

Such is the opinion of the public mind in America. To express this, the Boston (Mass.) *Herald* of April 15, 1912, condensed as an epitome of thousands of similar opinions this verdict of the whole press of America.

"The rulers of many nations have done her honor, while her great work for humanity must ever be her best monument, there are many who feel that no other American woman has a better right to have her memory perpetuated in our American Hall of Fame.

"As an object of National and International affection, Clara Barton presents, within the era of a hundred years, America's most remarkable woman."

CHAPTER XXXVI

Clara Barton in her Homes

"I became a notable housekeeper," declared Miss Barton in a retrospect of Civil War campaigns, "if that might be said of one who had no house to keep, but lived in fields and woods and tents and wagons with all out of doors for a cooking range, mother earth for a kitchen hearth, and the winds of heaven for a chimney." This paragraph leads us to understand Clara Barton aright. It exposes her home, not as one of brick and stone, but as a place of pain, and her domicile — the cross. Locate her where you will, it reveals her as choosing no dwelling but that. Pathetic as is the above description of her as housekeeper and as the childless mother of a race, it is literally true, and remained literally true until her death.

Her home, in so far as she had one at all, was something like the heart itself, a central service station from which she could pump life blood to surrounding members and recede only to be refreshed in order to return and lift life again with her power.

The first place of return of this kind was Oxford, the heart of the Commonwealth of Massachusetts, the region she first called *"home"* and never ceased to pine for as she wandered under sorrowful skies among earth's homeless. Thousands of times amid life's shifting terrors it came back to anchor her heart and soothe it. To be true to its trust was a chief concern.

In the murky awfulness of Morris Island, under the sulphurous belching of five forts, from her station behind the Union "swamp angel" she wrote in a letter of October 27, 1863: "Oftener than I could wish, my heart sinks heavily, oppressed with fear, that I am falling far short of the fulfillment of life's duties. But if ever there be a time when I come nearly up to the measure, no one, not even myself knows, how much of it is due the kind hearts that never forget and the willing hands that never weary. If with all this to sustain me, I fall, I am doubly culpable.

"A long way off seems the dear old New England home — its sheltering loves, and quiet hills, — Amid the clustering memories, my tears are falling thick and silently like the autumn leaves in forest dells."

Not often, for she was no chimney corner hero, but as often as she could, for inspiration and rest, she came back to Oxford.

"Yes, my dear friend it is even true," she wrote the author in 1909, "when dear New England put out its roses, and the skies grew clear and bright, I came with the birds of the Southland to old Worcester County, so brimming with grand, dear and tender memories for me, as indeed for every other of its straying wanderers, who once tasted its unconventional childhood.[1]

"Here trod the 'little Barefoot Boy,' its Maud Mullers raked the hay, and its Louisa M. Alcotts swung on the gates. And somewhere not far away, it was talked that a man was building a mill for the sawing of straight strips with a round saw, and they laughed at him.

"But how has the old county kept pace with the world? How about its people so slow of comprehension? Quiet and modest they have always been; manly and womanly, for they can be no other.

"Those spindles without hands. The example of that one Slater factory has turned more spindles without hands in its goodly state, than all the country combined.

"From the first click of one little sewing machine has come help to the overburdened, and rest to the 'fingers weary and worn' the world over.

"It has sent commerce and skill through the whitened, toiling cotton fields of the Southland. And in the West the patient skill of a Burbank bids fair to rival in value to the nation, the wealth of California's richest mine. It has robbed the surgeon's knife of terror and pain has died at its behest. It has opened the dens of Bedlam, and taught a misled, superstitious world to be merciful to those 'possessed of devils.'

"And over all towers the venerable and venerated form so long gracing the Legislative Halls of the Nation, watching its welfare, advising on its perplexities, presiding in its councils, revered and loved by all — Senator Hoar.

---

[1] Later published as a "Greeting to Worcester County," by the Secretary of the Chamber of Commerce, Herbert F. DaVison.

2 A

"With all these memories, is it strange, my good friend, that I too honor the old county and have sought a little foothold in the town of my birth with its classic name? Here lie the ashes of all the world held dearest to me, and from here I send out my greeting to the people of this grand county of Worcester, asking only that they kindly hold me as one of them."

It is plain she partook of the atmosphere of this countryside in which she was born. It was the atmosphere sentient with inventive genius — more so in proportion to its size than any region of the world.

It is the impression of this upon her mind that she gives us in her letter. All the creators and geniuses she describes lived in her county, mostly within a zone of ten or fifteen miles of Worcester. To her own home they were very near. Blanchard, the discoverer of a new principle in mechanics, the lathe for turning irregular forms, lived at Sutton, six miles away. Slater revolutionized the mills of the world by the invention and construction of his spindles and by building the first loom works in America. He worked this out at Webster only seven and one half miles away. Elias Howe, inventor of the sewing machine, sprang from the old homestead at Spencer eight and three quarter miles distant. Eli Whitney, who had invented the cotton gin, causing an industrial change that fed the mills of England, made a new South, and politically through developing the demand for slave labor till it overleaped itself, so brought on the Civil War, came from Westboro, twenty miles to the east. William T. G. Morton, who conquered pain by the discovery of ether, which she saw used everywhere for the first time to still the suffering of thousands in the Civil War, came from Charlton, five miles across the hills to the West.

Dorothea Dix had gone from Worcester to found the modern system of insane asylums of America, Great Britain, and the world. Luther Burbank, discoverer of a new plant world, came from Lancaster, some fifteen miles distant from Worcester. From Worcester itself came her contemporaries, George Bancroft, the historian, Edward Everett Hale, and John B. Gough, the great temperance orator. Senator George Frisbie Hoar was with his father at the birth of the Free Soil party in Worcester, June 28, 1848, when was generated the movement of freedom that gave birth to the Republican party of Lincoln.

These were all living forces in the hilltop county of Worcester, and but typify the thinkers that were around her. They were not writers such as followed the Renaissance in America after the revolution. They were founders in a zone of deeds and a sphere of creation, discovery and reform unlike any other in the world. They all had to break through a crust of prejudice, ignorance, and abuse in order to appear in rôles unknown to humanity.

The result of this association with these great original minds was the birth in Clara Barton of an overpowering desire — almost amounting to a passion — to do hitherto unheard-of things herself for the good of mankind. "The influences that prepared and made or finished the character suitable for the work she accomplished could not have been done without the early preparation, training, and association, coupled with the inherited traits and character peculiar to early New England life," stated one who of two people in the world knew her best of all, — the Field Officer of the Red Cross, Dr. J. B. Hubbell, a man who for thirty years served with her and for the Red Cross.

But to return to our consideration of Miss Barton's home, we find that memories still about Clara Barton's birthplace show her first thought-molds forming there. Some baby experiences stirred her imagination in ways most amusing to her sisters. It is related that when her sister once asked her how she supposed a vice president looked she replied: " I suppose he is about as big as our barn and green."

On another occasion a gay bobolink, the first one she had ever seen, came and perched himself on a tall flag. Swinging back and forth, he burst into one of his rich, rare, willowy songs. When the melody ceased he flew up into the chestnut tree. The little girl ran to the house and called in great haste to her sister that " an angel had been singing on a cat-tail in the swamp, and he was up in the chestnut tree. . "

Leaving the birthplace at the age of eleven, she went with her parents to the Learned homestead, of which, of all her homes, she is said to have been the most fond. It was for those days a commodious building set at the base of surrounding hills on the turnpike with the French river mills two hundred yards to the north and Oxford center over a mile to the south. Here, and later in a newer house across the road to the south, from 1831 till 1853, Clara Barton spent her young womanhood. Her life radiated from this center to all her schools during the seventeen years of teaching.

North Oxford needed a school to educate the mill town. None existed. But there was the old picker room of the mill. She fitted it up till soon it became packed with pupils — her raw material. No other building ready to receive them, she with her brother designed and built one complete — from the steps to the bell whose tones summoned to her hundreds of boys and girls whom she taught for years.

In the days of Clara's youth neccessity impelled invention and self-help. Did she want a straw hat? She must make it, even to the straw.

There were the green rye fields. Into the rye above her head she went out and there cut it green as it waved on the tilting stalk. Then she carried an armful to the house and scalded it. Out in the yard she laid it carefully in the sun till it was bleached. Then she cut it into lengths. With her teeth she split it into strands and thus flattening it, braided it into eleven strands and fashioned the first straw bonnet she ever had.

Of such a creative mind were all her associates. A neighbor wanted something beside flint to start a fire with. He invented the sulphur match — the first " Portland matches." " He tried new things and was an enterprising man," said Miss Barton to Mrs. M. E. Bullock. From 1832–1834 he made these matches as they are made now. " Again he wanted thread. Therefore he made it in skeins which the people took home to separate and put in boxes. Wanting the boxes, he made them also." At the first spooling of thread in Oxford Clara Barton for awhile posted numbers on these same spools of thread.[1]

The big "Learned House" was the nucleus for clergy, lecturers, and visiting literary men in the old-time lyceums. Its atmosphere was alive with the central forward movements of the day, to all of which the formative, supersensitive mind and imagination of Clara Barton were keenly alive and receptive. Opposite, two minutes walk southward, was the smaller house her father built for a residence — a house she never liked but lived in awhile in her Oxford teaching period. Her brother David later made it his homestead. On the left, opposite also, was the homestead of her brother Stephen. Both stand to-day. Stephen's is across from the large upper mill

[1] As told M. E. Bullock by Clara Barton in the Charlton Street House in Oxford, June, 1908. " She began to talk and on bits of paper aVailable at the moment I jotted it down," explains Mrs. Bullock.

pond and David's southwards on the street corner. By the chimney and blazing hearth in winter, and about the expansive four hundred acre New England farm in summer, her father and her mother with this close-knit circle about them, heartened life and endeared it with affection, sympathy, advice, and confidence. The home was an ideal one for two decades of her young womanhood. Filling it with in_ spiration, it held her nature back under the finest of New England reserves, — physical, mental, spiritual, and patriotic, — until the tide of time was at the flood and ready for her career.

When this time came — 1855–1861 — she was in the ante-bellum days and at the opening of the war, in Washington. "A sister and family followed me there," she explained, "that I should not be quite alone in that slave city, for up to '60 they bought and sold slaves at the capital."

In 1855 she had rented in Washington at 1013 T Street her own lodgings — a large room with several small ones.

"She was a law unto herself," says Mrs. Fannie Vassall, who was with her much of this time. "She did not care for the bother of conventionalities. Many people could not get along with the few conveniences she had."

To this center she came and from it she went during the Civil War. It was this she first used as a storehouse for her supplies which she accumulated for the soldiers. "She kept these lodgings alone," explains Mrs. Vassall, "if one could be said to be alone who always had some one to whom shelter and help and sympathy were a direct necessity, and it is needless to say all such were made happy and welcome and often put in a way of self-helpfulness." To many a sick soldier coming back disheartened, her lodgings offered a bit of New England cheer and uplift. To the seclusive New England mind this was quite incomprehensible. But Clara Barton was a Christian cosmopolite and, if any one sick or in need appeared she opened her rooms as a free hospital and place of refuge. Further on in the Civil War she used her quarters as a warehouse for the relief of the wounded, — making them more and more a central dispensary, where she decided once for all to be "as poor, yet making many rich — as having nothing, yet possessing all things."

During the war little did she use her rooms for herself, however much she needed them. One who could say, "I spent the winter of

1862 at Falmouth before Fredericksburg in a wagon," found them not often accessible as chambers of comfort. Miss Barton though not able to be much in them had insisted upon establishing them. She had similar private lodgings in the European wars from 1870–1872, especially at Carlsruhe.

As to one of Clara Barton's homes at Carlsruhe in the Duchy of Baden we have it preserved in a letter that King William's daughter, the Grand Duchess of Baden, sent to the Sheldon family at Berne. It was at 3 Blumen Strasse. This was the manse of Pastor Zimmerman. Here Miss Barton found lodgings part of the time. Hence radiated many of her sudden forced marches through the field. And hence she was accompanied on many of these marches of mercy by the pastor's daughter Anna, who became devotedly attached to her, and who, with Miss Margot and Miss Minnie Kupfer, became her inseparable companions at the sieges and on the field.

In a letter to Mrs. Vassall, during the French Commune, she says that even there, between those twenty-four months on European battlefields, in the place of hotels she always preferred to create her own independent home.

Many, used to the luxurious furnishings of to-day, remarked up to the time of her death upon the plainness in her rooms, a plainness so bleak as to be unusual for a woman, but Clara Barton had no time for fancy work.

Her rooms seemed only plain until she entered them with her regally furnished mind and her peerless contributions of experience. Such richness at once made up for lack of appointments — till at length every hearer felt a pauper at her feet, confessing that the moment she entered, high thinking transfigured plain living.

During the war, for four years thereafter and even when Miss Barton went abroad, her letters show that she still kept her apartments in Washington. In 1867 she left her two nieces, Ida (Barton) Riccius and Mrs. Mamie (Barton) Stafford, in these rooms she called "home," and rejoiced to see that they liked her cozy little Washington home, always feeling glad when she thought of them there in her house. Any one, believing Clara Barton gave up a woman's love of home, will find that when almost every one would have been compelled to give it up, she anchored to a local habitation. She never could endure the feeling of not having a home of her own and often owned two or three at the same time to preserve the home feeling and conserve her love of a domestic hearth.

She not only felt the importance of the home influence in her own life — she regarded it as essential to the welfare of her sex generally.

In May, 1874, upon the death of her sister Sally, she went to Worcester for six months, with relatives. She spent most of the time at the home of her cousin, Jere Learned, in North Grafton, then New England Village. At this time Vice President Henry Wilson died. What he had meant to Miss Barton as senator, chairman of military affairs in the Civil War, as Vice President in the reconstruction era with Grant, no one in this country ever knew. There was a deep understanding between them. At any crisis either as Senator or as head of the military committee of the Senate or as Vice President, he would rise up and do her will. He understood her perfectly and she him. They were two minds that thought as one and she felt his death deeply.

As early as the middle of 1877 Clara Barton's ambition to found the Red Cross in America which she had nursed since 1870, forced her from convalescence to the Capital. Toward the end of 1877, when these activities began to call her to Washington frequently, she centered her home life in the house on Leonard Street in Dansville, N.Y., returning there from the Capital. She lived in Dansville off and on from 1876–1886. But she had all along, as we have seen, owned her T Street house in Washington. "About the house in N. E. Village," she said, "I gave it up having no need of it, and no one to keep it who could make any use of it further than to be hired to stay in it. You know I only went there at all as a means of escape from a city, which gave me no liberties from a house too large and burdensome for my strength, and a rent too heavy for my means. I was too weak to move far and that little home of Jerry's was all that opened to me and I took it till I could get to a more serviceable one. You remember asking me last winter when we were reading Dr. Jackson, 'Why Byas! why don't you go to Dansville,' and I replied that only want of power to get there kept me away. I was not strong enough to make the journey. I meant to come sometime, but I did not think it would be possible to come so soon. The few things I had, I took with me of course, as with the exception of a few pieces of chamber furniture they are all personal things which I need constant access to, in my present small strength and large needs.   I remember all too keenly the trouble I made other persons when I first came back to Worcester separated from my things and had to have them sent on, ever to let myself get far from them again, until I am much more secure and independent in physical strength and health than I am at present and have any reasonable hope that I ever shall be.   I cannot dispense with the *facilities* of making me an immediate home of my own much better or more sagely than a turtle can with his shell.   Of course I do not need a home just now, as I am able to bear the usual and necessary routine of the Institute, but I have seen many poor pitiful months when I could not have borne it, and I am liable to again, so for the present and future I carry my tent.

"Everything is pleasant here.   I meet very *many* old acquaintances, and this makes it seem like one large home family to me.   We are some hundreds in the dining hall now and the utmost good social humor prevails, a chatty, jolly family, with the best possible good food. The Institute grounds are lovely, the landscape fine, the view large, taking in an expanse of at least 10 miles, spread out like a beautiful landscape garden to meet your eye.   It lies as fully under the eye as viewed from the windows and piazza of the Institute and its cottages as does Paris from the piazza of our sweet little Hotel of Madelain Sq.; only imagine the view a hundred times broader, and made up of village plots, meadows, gardens, fields, orchards, forests, fountains, brooks and shade trees of the most beautiful willows, majestic elms and sturdy maples, one could hope to see.   The town lies between two long hills so that facing us two miles or more distant is a hillside as high, and much finer in prospect than our own when the sun lies down to rest at the close of his day's journey with a magnificent ease, and quiet rest that holds the eye fixed and the heart still, till the nestling notes of the birds, and the purple shadows warn us to follow an example so glorious and so beautifully given, and so with the daystreaks still lingering, every step is stilled, every voice hushed, and no farmer's home in New England's most primitive nook, was ever more quiet when the last rays of its summer days went out than is this broad hillside with its camping armies, for there are many here whom nothing but a pelting rain ever drives under a roof at night. Their stretchers stand under the trees and their hammocks swing from the boughs, and the night winds sing their lullabys.   'Byas' can't do this yet, but she remembers so well when she used to, and enjoys having the others do it."

In 1886 Miss Barton felt sufficiently strong to give up her Dansville home altogether. "I have long owned my residence in Washington," she told the people of Dansville in 1886. "From time to time I add to its dimensions and now its importance seems to call for my personal care and oversight and it is to this I go. For this I say good-bye to you, and such thanks as I can speak. Your pretty town has given me back my strength. You have all helped to this — every kind word spoken to me, every friendly smile and clinch of hand, has helped me. To the loving smile of your merry children, I am grateful. They have helped me. To your soft breezes and your beautiful sunsets, winning me back to quiet sleep, I am grateful. To the rest of your valleys and the strength of your hills, I am grateful."

By 1882 Miss Barton had moved from T Street, Washington, to 1915 Vermont Avenue. Here she was established in a small two-story building near by the first Red Cross National Headquarters.

"I recently sought Clara Barton in her dwelling, on Vermont Avenue," writes a contemporary. "She lives in a modest two-story frame house, standing in a large yard. Several shade-trees surround it, and roses in bloom and beds of flowers add to the prettiness of the house. In an adjoining lot is a small white, two-story building, bearing the Red Cross symbol above its roof. It is the store-house of the National Association. Entering the dwelling from its vestibule, I was shown into a room on the right. There are double parlors, separated by lace portières. Over the mantel, in the front room, is a large portrait of Miss Barton, bearing the signature of the Emperor and Empress of Germany. Under it is a framed certificate of membership in the Austrian Association. Between the windows hangs a framed and finely emblazoned engraving of the 'Red Cross Tree' with its numerous shields hung on the branches, including that of America, bearing the date of 1882. The shield of each adhering nation is accompanied by the date of its formal acceptance of the Geneva Convention. In one corner stands a pretty cabinet, containing bric-a-brac and valuable collections. Cases of books line the walls, rich rugs cover the floor, and rare tapestry drapes the lounges, gifts from the late Empress Augusta of Germany. In a niche at one side of the fireplace is an earlier portrait of Miss Barton. It represents her at the age of twenty, and presents a strikingly beautiful face and form. Large, soulful eyes, which seem to see with prophetic vision the days to come; white shoulders and bust, with a stray curl from her luxuriant, dark, glossy hair; a lofty brow; and a firm and strong mouth give promise of the large personality and grand womanhood which since has developed into the Clara Barton of to-day. While musing over this portrait, I heard a slight rustle, and looking up, Miss Barton stood greeting me tenderly. Telling her that I had come to learn a little of her own life, at first she hesitated, but finally she yielded, and talked freely. Clara Barton is of medium height, slender and very active, although slow and dignified in movement. In repose, her face is pale and worn-looking, showing lines of care and thought. Her complexion is exquisitely delicate; her hair is worn short in front, and in soft natural curls. Her eyes — it is in her eyes this woman lives. They change, and are iridescent. Now they are softly, dreamily tender; again they are dark, acute and piercing, reading your inmost thoughts; again, coldly calm and intellectual, or, again, they flash with light as if in command. Chatting awhile by her invitation, I soon found myself seated in Miss Barton's special sanctum upstairs. It is in a sunny room, with light streaming from broad windows on two sides that look out on trees, grass and flowers. Around us were the evidence of her busy life — shelves, tables and desks covered with papers, letters, manuscripts — some very artistic pictures, the work of Clara Barton's earlier years. A wide, comfortable couch, a few chairs, the floor covered with matting — these make the simple furniture of a room in which this American woman, a true republican queen, conducts her correspondence with Old World princes and potentates." [1]

In 1892, from this Washington home she moved to the former spacious mansion of General Grant on 17th and F Streets. From here Grant had gone to the White House as President of the United States. He occupied this home at the height of his career in the Civil War. Here she remained near the Army and Navy building, administering the growing activities and receiving many National and International committees, Red Cross leaders and her growing number of associates until just previous to 1897.

The Red Cross building and Miss Barton's home at the corner of

[1] "Observations of Isabella B. Hinton."

17th and F Streets, N. W. Washington, was described as standing on a terrace high above the pavement. A broad hall intersected the mansion. On the side walls were the flags of all nations to whose suffering people Miss Barton was going. The hall opened into long parlors whose walls were dignified by the Red Cross whose bars incarnadined the white square flag at one end, — while a large blue and white flag from Greece added an International background to the other end of the hall.

Shortly after the Johnstown relief campaign, she planned to leave this handsome residence and selected a site at Glen Echo.

While Miss Barton did not permanently settle there till 1897, as early as 1890 with her accustomed foresight she had noted this suburban spot across the line in Maryland, seven miles away. Her usual homing instinct centered upon it both as a future "nesting place" and as a foothold for new crises that should later confront the Red Cross. It would remove her from the excessive expense of city headquarters at the capitol, indulge her love of close communion with the soil and allow her, in her shut-in days, sunshine and better warmth than her cold Washington home, as she was, after 1892, to find the Grant mansion to be. Here she could gratify her old Oxford longing for domestic pets and have her horses and cows about her as a diversion. Here she could walk amid green trees and on the soft turf receive undisturbed the renovation of nature after unnatural and abnormal trials to which she was sure to be subjected. The relative seclusion of Glen Echo was from now on to afford welcome relief to one who, save at Dansville, had found little shelter for sensitive nerves and a bleeding heart for thirty-eight years.

The building which Miss Barton in time proceeded to erect and which was to serve as a home for herself and the Red Cross, was a large one fashioned after the design of one of the half dozen huge houses which she constructed at Johnstown, Pa., immediately following the terrible flood. In fact, a part of the lumber donated to Miss Barton for those houses, was used in the construction of this Glen Echo home, which was built with an eye to usefulness and intended as a central warehouse for the accumulation of supplies for future emergencies that might call for the aid of the Red Cross. After leaving the Headquarters on 17th and F Streets, Miss Barton practically camped here, as a Red Cross general, with the United States, and at times the whole world, before her as the field of action. Up to the time of her death, Glen Echo was a trysting place for her distinguished as well as her humblest friends. All knew that they would find her here, for, besides being a Red Cross center, Glen Echo was a friendly lodging, "a rest for her old age, a place to die in." Removed from the red tape of officialdom she could here receive her own personal friends, and give and take confidences.

Glen Echo had been a Chautauqua meeting ground before Miss Barton bought it, and afterwards it was within sound of all the noise of a suburban summer resort for the masses. In her letters she even sometimes speaks of a summer evening of the environing noises of the "loop the loop" and the "merry-go-rounds." The building itself was an enigma to strangers. It was a long edifice of many windows, many chimneys, many towers. The neighbors noticed its architectural questionability and whispered: "She is more for comfort than looks."

Within, one would have said he were entering a steamboat. A skylight above a hollow center and a balcony around the second story chambers added to the effect. A salon-like open space lay before him on the ground floor.

Flags and Red Cross testimonials from the kings and queens and rulers of all nations fluttered from the walls. The towers on either side were to hold vaults for valuable Red Cross papers and cor respondence. All through the house were built-in pockets for similar purposes.

Only two small crosses of red glass gleamed in the front windows above the balcony. But above the house the Red Cross banner floated from the peak as if to tell the world, "His banner over us is love." Before it and all it stood for, even the roistering Camp Alger soldiers who at the time of the Spanish war passed by in hundreds and thousands, were never too boisterous to sober up and respectfully stand at salute.

Notwithstanding the "ocean liner" effect of the interior — once within, one saw that sunlight and comfort were attained to an unusual degree through many windows, while in winter ubiquitous fireplaces sent their gleam everywhere.

Her first Red Cross building at Glen Echo was architecturally an ideal of picturesqueness. It was like a small cathedral. It was built of gray stone with arched roof and a huge red cross over the doors. However, as the effect on health was bad, the stone walls making it a clammy and cold structure, Miss Barton with characteristic aggressiveness had it torn down.

At times, in the display of strength of character in contrast to a mistaken charity people wanted her to assume, she had manifested great insight. For instance, while at home at Glen Echo it was noted that there were great supplies and deposits of emergency material. Naturally it would have been easy to regard the place as a free dispensary. Miss Barton regarded these supplies, however, as sacred for national Red Cross uses. She refused to let them leak out for neighborhood and county uses as though the Red Cross was a county infirmary. Yet, individually she still had to be herself, which meant she could not view local suffering and not help. Night after night, at her own expense, she took in some homesick soul and sat up with her charge till he or she got well before she let them go. Even at eighty-seven she was engaged in such a case which at the time was to her a joy that she would not yield to any one else.

In doing this, her methods were not those of a regular trained nurse. "She just mothered you, and made you well in spite of yourself," was the testimony of one of her patients.

A nurse by instinct and genius, Miss Barton was never a registered army nurse. This was why, technically, she could not, had she desired to, be buried at Arlington, a cemetery with whose founding she had much to do. Had it been Miss Barton's wish, however, to be buried at Arlington, her appointment as Superintendent of Nurses at City Point in the last years of the war would no doubt have done much to cover the technical lack.

Her home was a warehouse for supplies, and before it were car tracks leading to and from the capital. On these when 1898 came she started for the fever-stricken camps and the malarial battlefields and swamps of Cuba and Porto Rico. Hence she sent her supplies and her associates scattered also to the camps of sick and dying soldiers everywhere.

The impression of Glen Echo upon those who knew Miss Barton was much deeper than upon those who could not understand how it came to be thrown together as a home. The ramshackle effect was dissipated when one entered it with the understanding of B. F. Tillinghast, of Davenport, Iowa, who described it thus in 1900:

"Eight miles from Capitol hill, just outside the District of Columbia, up the historic Potomac, may be found the picturesque and altogether delightful spot known as Glen Echo. It is the sylvan retreat of the weary in Washington, the resort of those who must get away from the heated, monotonous brick rows to find a touch of nature. The river which below Washington's monument is deep enough for sea ships, is here almost too shallow for canoes. The rocky bottom rises above the water's surface; in places, there are falls, and so the ceaseless music of the flow goes on, placid at times, but dashing not far away. The banks are high; for a spur of the Blue Ridge mountains, quite well wooded. Cutting through these are frequent ravines that point the way for other mountain streams to flow. The most rustic of these is known as Glen Echo. The old Chesapeake and Ohio Canal, which did a great business before the railroads came, follows the Potomac's side, almost as primitive as when first built. Higher up the surface rolls ruggedly and the outlooks are dotted with homes of high and low degree. Flowing springs abound, and the views as the sun rises and sinks are subjects for the artist's canvas.

"The Red Cross cottage is the one first pointed out to the visitor. From its staff two flags are always flying, the Stars and Stripes, and the white field with its deep red Swiss cross, which soldiers cheer after the battle and which all civilized nations honor as the emblem of neutrality and defend with their guns, though it be unfurled between hostile armies. The Red Cross is never a belligerent. Its aim is to save not to destroy. The emblem makes a saint of the woman who wears it on the battlefield or any other field of duty.

"This cottage faces the east with sloping lawn in front and the heights not far away. On the west the Potomac's bank is high and precipitous, with the canal between the river and the house. A wide hall runs from front to rear with living rooms to right and left. The office is in the west end. Upstairs are the library and sleeping apartments. The records are all preserved in fire proof vaults on each floor. Every room in the house bears the red cross on its walls or furniture. There are gifts, trophies, books, souvenirs, paintings and pictures all around. The main halls and principal rooms are hung

with a profusion of flags from all the countries of the earth; all
the colors of the rainbow worked into indescribable and rarely seen
designs.   In brief, the Red Cross cottage is a flag museum of historic
achievement."

"Miss Barton will talk by the hour," concluded Mr. Tillinghast,
"about others and the work they have done.   She is confidential
among friends about her plans; but she is reticent on the subject of
most personal interest.

"Miss Barton could, if she cared to do so, write a book on 'The
Presidents I have known.'   They include Lincoln, Johnson, Grant,
Hayes, Garfield, Arthur, Cleveland, Harrison and McKinley.   Every
one of them she has known well, some of them intimately, having
business affairs with all.   'They have been familiarly, helpfully
kind,' she said.   And individualizing, she added: 'Arthur was
always gentlemanly, indulgent, pleasant and encouraging.   No
President has been more so.   Cleveland was generally kind.   Many
times has Mr. McKinley remarked as if he meant it, "Don't hesitate
when you want to speak to me." '"

From 1899 to 1904, Glen Echo was properly Miss Barton's winter
quarters.   Her description for one winter is true of almost all of them.
"All winter, I was home in Glen Echo because it was home, and because
it was winter and having a temporary amanuensis, made the most of
my time in things long neglected, and long needed."

To Clara Barton the long summers and late falls were particularly
delightful.   A spring letter [1] reads: '

"My errands in New York were all easily done, and I arrived
home at 8 P.M. Tuesday, found all well, and happy.   Several broods
of chickens, some going up to roost already. — The house plants all
in bloom.   The rooms look so bright, sunny and flowery that I don't
see how I can ever go away from them again."

Again in April, 1910, she writes:

"The season is pretty now — a part of the trees are in full leaf —
and the flowers lovely.   I have been to the city to-day with Doctor
and the parks are ravishing and the overhanging maples and lindens
are shading the side-walks like summer.

"We are having almost summer weather now.   The trees are
passing out of bloom, and the strawberry bed and quince bushes are

[1] March 31, 1905.

nearly white with blossoms.   We are expecting strawberries in about three weeks.

"I do wish there were some way to avoid sickness — and I do believe there is to a greater degree than is generally reached.   Let us try to find it, and be happier than we are.

"Dr. is getting his bees into shape for summer business.   He will have some eight or ten hives, and several hundred pounds of honey."

But by June and July in these later years she found Washington too warm.

"We are having very hot weather, like everyone else," she wrote June 1, 1911, "but it has not disturbed me very much only to make me weak — of course.

"Now there is just a wee bit of a thought in my head that it would be well for me to go to Oxford — as, here, I have to face the same as three months of almost tropical weather, i.e. half of June, — July — August and half of September, with probably little change from 80° to 95° — or even 100° of heat, continually."

In 1898 Glen Echo seemed more of a camp than ever.   A barbed wire fence inclosed an acre and a half of house lot.   Chicken houses were on the right and flower gardens on the left.   Apparently Miss Barton cared nothing for artistic effects or appearances.   Health and comfort and utility were what she sought, and it was this she offered her friends when they came.   In every respect the "Red Cross" kept true to its resemblance to a camp whence she could fly to her score and more of campaigns and use it as a base of communication.   Because of this she loved it.   Another reason she loved it was because in the distance across the river lay the hills and mountains of Virginia through which she had been on the marches to the most tragic crises of her career in the sixties.

To this building she returned at the end of her campaigns, and after the Spanish War under the crimson Red Cross banner she lived and set out for further National and International disasters up to 1904.   Thence she retained it as a home eight years till her death in 1912.

To many of the thousands who came to visit her home as one of the great humane centers of the world — she became known as the "Beautiful Lady of the Potomac," and as such she has been charmingly described by a writer who visited her in 1910.

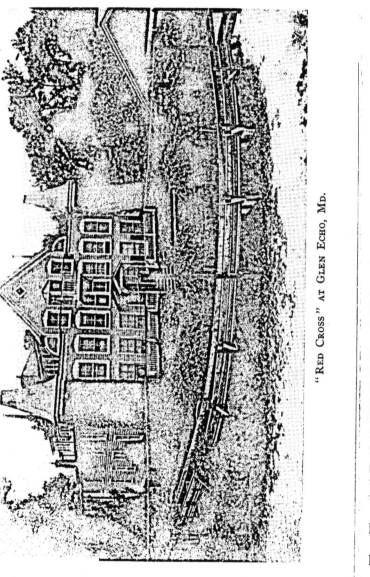

"RED CROSS" AT GLEN ECHO, MD.

"A few ▮▮▮
Potomac River ▮
lighteth to ▮▮

"On looking ▮
to-day, it is ▮▮
spent upon the
among the ▮ ▮
she moves slowly
her home at Glen
that it is hard to
She seems ▮▮▮
rather than the
country air ▮▮
ness which fills ▮
drawn about her
and death.

"Miss Barton
every way belied
shoulders, which
over sick beds ▮▮
One observer ▮
Because of her ▮
time till long ▮
the Lamp." "Im
paring ▮▮▮▮▮
busy ▮▮▮▮ of ▮
a mission ▮▮▮ ▮▮
more work ▮▮▮ ▮
get it out of the ▮
who went at ▮▮▮
wounded ▮▮▮▮

Such was ▮▮▮ ▮
hero loving ▮▮▮
Another ▮▮▮▮
Pilgrims to her ▮
"When I ▮▮▮
presence. Mrs
charter-memi ▮▮ ▮

"A few miles out of Washington, on a slope overlooking the Potomac lives a woman," he said, "whom the whole world 'de_ lighteth to honor.' "

"On looking into the serene eyes and placid face of Clara Barton of to-day, it is difficult to realize that the greater part of her life has been spent upon the battlefields, at scenes of sorrow and suffering, and among the wounded, starving and homeless men and women. As she moves slowly about the roomy house and old fashioned garden of her home at Glen Echo, she seems to be such an embodiment of peace that it is hard to associate her with the thought of war and bloodshed. She seems always to have looked upon the woods and meadows, rather than the face of dying soldiers, and to have smelled fresh country air instead of smoke and battle. And yet the pitying sweet_ ness which fills her eyes and the sympathetic lines which have been drawn about her mouth bear witness to a long intimacy with suffering and death.

"Miss Barton is now nearly ninety years old, a fact which is in every way belied by her appearance, except for a slight droop in the shoulders, which seems some way to have come more from bending over sick beds than from the weight of years."

One observer of her here was not from our country, but from Canada. Because of her devotion to her countless correspondents, who took her time till long after midnight, he styled her, "*The American Lady with the Lamp.*" "Interviewers who went to see her with the idea of pre- paring obituary notices in advance generally," he says, "found her busy ironing or preserving. Once when some one spoke to her about a mission, she said, 'I have never had a mission but I have always had more work than I could do lying around my feet, and I try hard to get it out of the way so I can go on to the next.' This is the woman who went at seventy-seven to Cuba and did field work among the wounded soldiers at the personal request of President McKinley."

Such was the impression Miss Barton made upon people from the hero loving, chivalrous British Empire.

Another impression of one of the thousands of coming and going Pilgrims to her Glen Echo home comes from her circle of neighbors:

"When I visited the place it seemed to be still vibrant with her presence. Mrs. Hinton, widow of Colonel Richard J. Hinton, a charter-member of the Red Cross, and for fifty years an associate of

2 B

Miss Barton, and Mrs. Sarah E. Canada, her most intimate friend and neighbor in Glen Echo, told me many incidents of her old age.

"Physically frail as she was and quietly as she had to live in the later years, she never gave herself up to invalidism. Indeed she was a soldier to the last — systematic, industrious, severely simple in her tastes. It was a rule of the household that every day's duties should be disposed of before turning in for the night. To do this she would stay at her desk until late at night, and at five o'clock the next morning she would be rolling a carpet sweeper over her floor. She always observed military order, and took a soldier's pride in being able to keep her quarters straight.

"Hung on the wall between her bedroom and private sitting room is a small mirror into which her mother looked when she came home as a bride.

"Clara Barton's bed is small and hard. Near it are the books that meant so much to her — the Bible, 'Pilgrim's Progress,' the stories of Sarah Orne Jewett, Lucy Larcom's Poems, Barrie's Stories, 'Jane Eyre,' all of Miss Austen's novels and the works of the Brownings. Near her desk hang framed copies of John Burroughs' 'My Own Will Come to Me,' and Virginia Woodward Cloud's 'Leisurely Lane.' Probably best of all says one who knows, she loved Eugene Field's 'Little Boy Blue,' which always brought tears to her eyes.

"There are few pictures in the house except those relating to Miss Barton, or to the Red Cross. On the walls hang certificates and testimonials from every country to which her mission took her. One of the most beautiful of these memorials is from the Sultan of Turkey. Many decorations and jewels were given her, but among them all there were only two she kept as personal souvenirs.

"Red Cross was a kind of private sanitarium presided over by this wonderful little woman. When a neighbor looked worn out or ill, Miss Barton would take her in charge and invite her for a visit. Once at the Red Cross, the patient had an opportunity to testify to Clara Barton's powers in the rôle of a ministering angel.

"On state occasions when she was strong enough to receive visitors she used to wear very beautiful costumes. Though very slight she was fond of trained gowns. To the last she would never put on black. Her dresses ran through lavender and royal purple shades to a peculiar wine color of which she was very fond.

"Even when very weak and when all excitement had been for-bidden, she still kept open house at Red Cross for the 'soldier boys.' The place is full of mementos and gifts from the men whom she nursed."

While Miss Barton could never cease to be humanity's nurse, man-kind's mother and the soldier's sister, she never posed for this rôle.

"I never even wear a Red Cross chevron," she declared to the author. "Please have the cross badge taken off the brooch," she said to me in relation to a picture of herself on which the photographer had inserted prominently a large cross on the brooch at her neck. It was not because she had lost her love of the insignia that she did not wear it. It was simply her dislike of parade. And again Miss Barton never wanted to become a skeleton in the closet, nor a death's head at the feast. From her dress one would never have guessed she was what she was, although the Red Cross always flew over the head-quarters. When away she was the same Miss Barton. She never "struck a picture," as the actors say.

Eleanor Ames, visiting her in New Haven, like all her observers, was equally impressed with this simplicity.

"When I reached the Sheldon home, the family and their guests were gathered around a big open fire in the library," she says. "Every-body was laughing heartily at one of 'Aunt Clara's' jokes.

"It never occurred to me that a really famous person would tell a joke and I recall the idea of Miss Barton having a sense of humor was a bit of shock.

"A woman of medium size in a brown gown, which was in the latest mode, rose and shook my hand."

Miss Barton's life at Glen Echo was wholly democratic. She was the most democratic woman America has produced. She always appealed to the laboring man in overalls and jumpers. She seemed to understand him and he understood her. This was, it must be said, after the first introduction, for he was somewhat surprised to find when he came into her neighborhood that the most celebrated woman around Washington was the first one up in the morning. He saw her weeding her garden or feeding the chickens before the earliest sun had kissed away the dew. By these things he soon learned to know that she too believed in winning her way by the sweat of her brow. He soon learned by this sign to recognize a fellow laborer.

Two thoroughbred Jersey heifers lent a further rustic touch of life to existence at Glen Echo and Miss Barton took interest in superintending the milking, and overlooking the other household affairs. It was true that she who had been bred in military discipline where word was law, wanted things done in her own way and in her own time. But her servants had been with her for years and understood her peculiar methods of work while she in turn treated them not as things, or cattle, but as human beings. This evoked from them a sense of pride and trust.

They knew that her old Yankee punctiliousness about little things around the place at times struck a very human chord, and if things went wrong, that she felt upset till she righted them. Thus it became pretty generally understood that her home was to her a camp and martial order was the rule.

She was fond of travel, and up to the eighty-ninth year of her life made her journeys of thousands of miles. In the year 1906, in mid-March, she traveled from Worcester to Glen Echo in a blinding snowstorm without ill effects, making a shopping journey through New York. In the summer of 1906, being eighty-five years old, she continued her habit of transcontinental journeys when a G. A. R. encampment occurred at Minneapolis. On her return she found the help sick and gone and the table so high with accumulated correspondence that she could not look over the top of it. Yet as usual, she said, "it is nothing," and pushed on. In the meantime she communicated the same spirit of conquest to her friends in trouble, whose letters littered her desk. On her two thousand mile journey alone to Chicago and back at ninety, in 1910, she demonstrated even more her wonderful continuation of strength.

In the West Miss Barton had friends in every city. Detroit, Minneapolis, Chicago, and all the great western cities vied with one another in their reception to her. At Detroit in the procession through the streets, it was declared the ovations given her were more telling than even the applause rendered President Theodore Roosevelt in the same line of march.

Miss Barton enjoyed these trips because she loved humanity and wanted to be with people in a life of action.

Her eyes were full of expression and great kindliness. Indeed this friendly attitude toward the world was one of her dominant char-

CLARA BARTON'S SUMMER HOME IN OXFORD, 1884–1911

acteristics. The same impression of personal friendliness, Miss
Barton left upon her neighbors in her New England home in Oxford.
In later life the birthplace was in other hands. So was the other
old roof tree. In 1884, therefore, she bought a stately home with
colonial pillars in Oxford Center on Charlton Street. Here, as in
Washington, though she went to keep house for herself, she actually
kept "open house" to the neighborhood, the county and the world.
The latch string was always out to humanity, to each of whom she
spoke as if he or she were the only one. Each of the human procession went away confessing that in her God had sent a friend unequaled
in the human list of great-hearts.

Then at nightfall till midnight, when the last footstep died away, or
even till two o'clock in the summer morning, when it grew light again,
she bent over the letters that had poured in to her as if each one that
she took up was the only one.

Though to bed at daylight, or at the best, midnight, yet she never
slept very late. "You must get up with the birds or miss the best
part of the day," she would say as she spoke of the early summer
mornings which she spent in her garden. Her love of the farmyard
and its animal pets never left her. Her affection for dumb creatures
showed itself in almost every letter. At Glen Echo the good milch
cows were always in the stable, and she watched the little chickens pick their way out into the world through the shell with childlike
wonder every spring. After the Cuban war, among the horses that
she loved best was "Baba," an intelligent saddle horse, half
Arabian and half English, presented at Santiago by the war correspondent of the New York *World.* "Baba" was later sent to Glen
Echo and finally to Worcester and Oxford, in all of which homes Miss
Barton was never tired of petting him.

Here in her homes in the country side she was the acme of New
England thrift, but never even in her garden was it for herself. Looking out of the windows at a grass plot in the back yard, she exclaimed
one day, "There goes my conscience again! That land now a grass
plot will support enough to keep a family and next year I think I'll
have to have it plowed up."

Her Oxford neighbors, even the milk man, said they could not go
late enough or early enough not to see her up. In 1909, I quoted to
a Red Cross companion, "her working hours in Oxford are fourteen

out of twenty-four." Giving a surprised laugh, the companion said correctly, "fourteen out of twenty-four — eighteen, you mean."

She received, as was her custom for years, several hundred of her friends, from the countryside and the little town of Oxford. They came with their children and their grandchildren and she gave to each a kindly smile and cheering word.

After one of these receptions, as the sun sank behind her dear old Oxford hills, she said:

"I am never weary when meeting my friends and particularly friends whose mothers were my very dear friends in the years gone by. Their coming to-day brings back to memory, our very delightful days.

"Many a night I attend to my correspondence, which is very large, long after the rest of my neighbors are asleep, and seeing my light some of them have asked, 'When does Miss Barton retire?' I never think of weariness. One is as old only as his strength and I feel equal to and do work twelve hours a day. I am blessed with good health and intend to work as long as my strength lasts.

"This day has been full of sunshine to me and I have been exceedingly happy. Not a cloud has marred it; it has been a home day to me, that I will remember with a great deal of pleasure."

Some summers she could hardly more than open the house — but with her garden and suggestions of old New England, she could not forbear at least a few weeks in the atmosphere of the long ago.

She wrote of it October 30th, 1909, from Oxford to Mrs. Schoppe in Worcester.

"I was so sorry when I saw what a delightful day we were having for our friends gathering on Wednesday, that you were not with us. I wanted you both all day to meet the people and if you knew how many times you were kindly referred to and asked about, you would see how I regretted that you were not here to speak for yourself. I do not at all understand your reference to me in the *Monitor*. I do not see my *Monitor* here. It goes to Glen Echo for Dr. H. and is preserved for me. Thus do I not get its refreshing daily visits as I ought to.

"I have never spoken openly about going to Glen Echo, but it is probable that a combination of home interests and climate may draw me there a few months. It is not settled just how soon. I shall hope for a Sunday in Worcester."

As an example of her usual procedure of yielding to the cold, closing her Charlton Street home and retreating southward, we find her writing to a Los Angeles friend in 1909 as follows:

"I am just in the little turmoil of closing my house in Oxford, and going to Glen Echo. Six months of New England winter seems a little too much to face without a stronger motive than I can picture to myself. I am to leave for New York on the fifteenth, where I remain a few days before going to Washington. You in balmy Los Angeles, would not consider that much of an improvement, still 'every little counts,' and the snows will not be so deep and lasting, and the skies will smile oftener. I have some nephews, or rather grand nephews on your side, who think it 'barbarous' for me to remain in the east. Clarence B. of the 'Riverside Enterprise,' writes me imploringly, to come to him — argues that there are more Bartons in California than in the East and why do I stay? Bright boy! full of life and good heart."

We have seen enough to know that Clara Barton believed "homekeeping hearts are happiest," and that she loved a home and was instinctively a woman. Thus while her place on the firing line and amid disaster and sudden death was always in company with brute force and masculine surroundings, she herself was never masculine. She kept sacred a woman's privacy. What she proffered was always a woman's gift. It was the woman's side she gave. If mothering the race, being sister to the suffering and relieving the crushed be womanly — Clara Barton played only the part of a woman.

Like Florence Nightingale, Dorothea Dix, Julia Ward Howe, and most women heroines, she was a lifelong advocate of equal rights for women. In an address given at a May Festival of the New England Woman's Suffrage Association, she said:

"I believe I must have been born believing in the full right of woman to all the privileges and positions which nature and justice accord to her in common with other human beings. Perfectly equal rights — human rights. There was never any question in my mind in regard to this. I did not purchase my freedom with a price. I was born free; and when, as a young woman I heard the subject discussed it seemed simply ridiculous that any sensible, rational person should question it. And when, later, the phase of woman's rights to suffrage came up, it was to me only part of the whole, just as right, just as certain to take place.

"And whenever I have been urged, as a petitioner, to ask for this privilege for woman, a kind of dazed, bewildered feeling has come over me.

"Of whom should I ask this privilege? Who possessed the right to confer it? Who had greater right than woman herself? Was it man, and if so, how did he get it? Who conferred it upon him? He depended upon woman for his being, his very existence, nurture and rearing. More fitting that she should have conferred it upon him. What are governments? What were they but the voice of the people? What gave them their power? Was it divinely conferred? Alas! no, or they would have been better, purer, more just and stable.

"Was it force of arms — war? Who furnished the warriors; who but the mothers? Who reared the sons and taught them that liberty and their country were worth their blood? Who gave them up and wept their fall, nursed them in suffering, and mourned them, dead?

"Was it labor? Women have always as a rule, worked harder than men. Was it capital? Woman has furnished her share. Who, then, can give her right and on what basis? Who can withhold it?

"There is, once in a while, a monarch who denies the right of man to place a crown upon his head. Only the great Jehovah can crown and anoint him for his work, and he reaches out, takes the crown and places it upon his head with his own hand. I suspect that this is in effect what woman is doing to-day. Virtually, there is no one to give her the right to govern herself, as men govern themselves, by self-made and self-approved laws of the land. But in one way or another sooner or later she is coming to it. And the number of thoughtful and right-minded men who will oppose will be much smaller than we think, and when it is really an accomplished fact, all will wonder, as I have done, what the objection ever was."

CHAPTER XXXVII

SOCIAL TRAITS

EVERY victory in her campaigns at the front or diplomatically as an Internationalist, Clara Barton accomplished by sheer initiative. This personal initiative, and the aggressiveness which it required, were seemingly at cross purposes with her painfully retiring disposition. Sensitiveness and a fearsome timidity were deep pitted in her system. By force of these, we would have expected her to be, instead of a great original, the clinging vine type of woman, always leaning upon her friends. The opposite was the case. It was said that even during the Civil War, when Miss Barton had no organization of any kind, nor indeed any connection with the other nurses, she could yet get anything she wanted for her work, due no doubt in part at least to her friendship with General Rucker (Commissary-general). President Lincoln, Senator Henry Wilson, Chairman of the Committee of Military Affairs, and General Butler were also in hearty sympathy with her endeavors, as in fact were other officers. Nevertheless it was her putting her own foot forward that in each case gained her the *entrée* to the Civil War leaders. Be that as it was, neither of these two characteristics — her first-born timidity and her reborn aggressiveness — betokened a social nature. Each presented the two cold poles of individualism, very far from the social gulfstream.

Yet to the student of human nature, the two traits of timidity and aggressiveness are not antagonistic to each other but action and reaction. They often go together — for a timid person smarting from backwardness is stung with the impulse to dash ahead. Thus, they are found far beyond the critical circle of ordinary folks who cannot understand them and from whom they have haply been kept in brooding reserve.

But when they break this long-kept silence — something happens! This is exactly what occurred after Clara Barton reached forty. She

377

sprang into the public eye in the company of generals, vice presidents, and presidents, senators and military chairmen as well as later into the company of Emperors, diplomats, and Internationalists. At first, while her timidity had kept her from frittering her life away in trifles — her aggressiveness now kept her from being held down by mechanical subalterns. Thus she pressed her way past lesser leaders to friendships with those in seats of power.

In very little things Miss Barton was apt to be as insistent as she was when larger matters were at stake. In fact some of her friends maintain that she reminded them in the ordinary walks of life of a general conducting a campaign.

She was an individualist — even in dress. She would set out on a shopping trip with as much determination to carry her point as if she were going through a bombarded town. So familiar a household name had hers become and so well known her face that she preferred to shop *incognito*, and would stray into the less known stores, where she could do what she wanted and be unobserved.

She once made her way with her niece into a ten cent store to gratify her weakness for gaily colored ribbons. Her eyes fixed on vivid reds and pinks.

"Oh! lady! A person of your age should have lavenders and violets," interrupted the girl behind the counter. "I guess she doesn't know I wear what I want to!" exclaimed Miss Barton, setting her teeth as though to face a charge and executing a flank movement.

So it was in all her habits of dress. Style and age made no difference to her. She was absolutely independent. But she never dressed, strange to say, out of place. You might say she was ageless and universal even in her attire. She was always well and neatly dressed, but in types to which one could not fix a label or attach a date. Her dark hair did not change with the years, and her complexion, that of a brunette, was apt to be becomingly set off by a dash of red in her dress.

For her first public appearance after her fame was made in the Civil War when she appeared on platforms with Harriet Beecher Stowe, Henry Ward Beecher, Wendell Phillips, Horace Greeley, and the nation's greatest voices, she had a modiste make for herself very handsome gowns with trains. One, her friends recall, was a dark velvet and one a delicate steel gray.

A friend in Worcester once called attention to the stately effect. "How stunning!" she exclaimed. "What did you say?" parried Miss Barton, turning to her, and giving her a look that was a damper upon further remarks on clothes.

Indeed Miss Barton was never pleased by the attention centering on attire, and she certainly was not in other ways vain as to her appearance. Of her strong features and her small body, Miss Barton made light with her most intimate friends.

"How many letters you will have to write before you can lay your eyes on mine," she wrote a friend. "I wish it would not be too many — but if that cannot be, the letters are the next best thing, aren't they? And besides, it wouldn't be much to see me after all. I am only an ugly old Auntie, and am just as well not seen as seen. I was never nice and am less so than ever now, so if you never see me you must not feel that you have lost anything."

As to the deeper things, Miss Barton was indeed extremely sensitive at times and felt cuts and impositions intensely. For instance she never felt as though her literary ventures were as financially successful as they should be. I can never forget her return from New York on one of her dark days when it seemed to her that all the world was against her — even the taxicabs she said exorbitantly overcharging her. It was while she was looking up certain sales of a book she had issued, and whose plates she sought for in vain, while all the time she felt the book was being sold and all the proceeds taken from her.

Indeed, such a nature as hers could be imposed upon in a business way. In this she was much like her grandfather, Dr. Stephen Barton, the good physician, who healed everybody but too seldom was paid. That occasionally she was sensitive about it is evident in the following letter to the author concerning her book, which she feared was being pirated by the publisher.

"GLEN ECHO, MARYLAND,
"February 14, 1910.

"Your roses came fresh with the dew still on them, and I hasten to speak before they are dry. I have just sent a line to Miss Knapp, all inadequate of course, but it will at least speak my thanks, however poor.

"Yes, a rose to the living is sweet, but my dear friend, I am being well made to feel that the rose could be dispensed with, if only the little nuts that had been so laboriously gathered and stowed away for future use, could be suffered to remain. It is when these are brought temptingly out to the eyes of an admiring public as one's own pickings, and the little squirrels that have worked so hard to gather them sit chattering unfed by the empty hole, that one asks for grace and patience.

"Yes, the roses are sweet, and blessed be they who bring them into one's life. With love to Mrs. Epler and the children.

"Always gratefully yours,
"CLARA BARTON."

Sometimes little things annoyed Miss Barton too often. These she had to battle with and triumph over with an intensity as real as when she faced battle fields and calamities and was past-master of a crisis. She was so jealous of the Red Cross that opposing views as to detail she was too inclined to believe were born of enemies of the Red Cross. She exaggerated small criticisms. This was due partly to the overmastering power of loyalty. When she had to fight so long to bring it into being and be always on her guard, it was no wonder the fussing over a detail bored her. It was very human it should when it interrupted the great essentials, such as packing ships to feed the starving in Russia or Cuba, or rushing aid to the drowned-out people of Johnstown or Galveston. To her it seemed absurd to insist on petty items of bookkeeping when she was giving up her nights and days to dying men or to piteous hosts of skeleton children with abdomens bloated by hunger.

In the midst of her splendid passion to guide the Red Cross to immediate help, little obstacles annoyed her. In the campaign to relieve the Russian famine in 1892, while held up by quiddities as to the ships from each state which were to carry the thousands of tons of corn and wheat and kiln-dried meat and flour to Russia, she wrote, May 19, 1892, to the head of the great Iowa Commission, Mr. B. F. Tillinghast: "It grows out of the old spite about the loading. It is a poor thing to do. But there is no doubt but Mr. —— intends to demoralize the little Red Cross when they get well home and can unite their strength. I thought it was best to let the friends know the condition of the patient that they will not be too greatly confused when bidden to the funeral. Of course we shall expect Iowa as chief mourner and expect her to sit with us in our woe. I should hope to get around to the writing up of some good things, reports, etc., — if they would cease throwing sticks at me."

Had she apprized her value to society more and so seen the un_ shakeable foundations of the Red Cross she had established, she would have been free from this annoyance.

Sharply as Miss Barton felt misunderstandings she had the cure always at hand. It was the cycle of the world's sufferers whose presence always drew out the poison sting and made her forget it. Or, if utterly exhausted, she could curl up and sleep in a most cramped angle and in fifteen minutes rise refreshed to take up her work where it was left off.

In all her camping in the path of pain, she practiced a constant withdrawal into the pavilion of peace away from the strife of tongues. To her grandniece, Myrtis Wilmot Barton, she appeared so quiet and calm "that she never wasted her strength." She practiced what she told her niece to practice. "Be calm, always calm my child. Keep yourself quiet and in restraint. Reserve your energies, doing those little things that be in your way, each one as well as you can so that when God shall call you to do something good and great, you will not have wasted your force and strength with useless strivings, but will be ready to do the work quickly and well. Go slowly, my child, and keep ready."

Miss Barton sought to avoid misunderstandings all she could. She sought to retain those whom she met by the silver cord and golden bowl of gratitude. To express this solicitude she wrote from a Civil War field to Miss Childs (Miss Annie Childs of Worcester):

"MY DEAR ANNIE:

"Again I am made a debtor to my friends, and as ever their delicacy leaves me at a loss whom to thank, and again I must commission you to act for me, — Perhaps I shall not award you sufficient credit for the labor I impose upon you, for I cannot fully realize how the performance of a duty which would afford me such unmixed and unqualified pleasure, can be other than a satisfaction to you. How gladly I would take by the hand every friend who remembers me so kindly in my absence, and tell them how their kindness strengthens and sustains and cheers me amid life's daily round of cares.

"Oh, be careful, my friends, be generous and noble still! Remember that of all anguish our Heavenly Father calls us to endure none pierces more keenly or wounds more deeply than the sting of ingratitude.

"And when at morning and evening repast — with folded hands and grateful hearts — you bless God for the bounties he has spread before you, let your thoughts wander a little — to find if there is not another.

"I am well and strong as ever but not so the faithful gifts, worn, faded, soiled, and blood stained. They are lying as they left the field, treasured relics of the war, but to supply their place, come others bright and beautiful from the same kind source, and again I can only renew my pledge, to sustain the honest confidence of those noble friends. Beg them for me, then dear Annie, to accept this as my report upon the disposition of their former gifts, and my pledge for the latter, and with love and gratitude to all, I remain as I ever have been,

"Your true friend,

"CLARA BARTON."

Such a nature, so intensely loyal, was naturally supersensitive of others' loyalty. She wanted to keep her friends, not lose them. Her force lay not in contention. She was not at her best there. It was an atmosphere in which she was not at home. The leadership Miss Barton displayed, whether as a public school teacher or as a war heroine or as a founder of the Red Cross, lay not in her driving power, but in her drawing power. Sooner or later it was a matter of friendship. No one could long be in her presence without feeling her magnetism, rightly called "The Magnetism of Mercy."

Dr. L. P. Brockett was one of the first and best observers of Miss Barton in the Civil War and after. He describes this magnetism by which she converted him as well as others to an enthusiasm to aid the wounded and injured:

"In form, Miss Barton is about medium height, a brunette in complexion, with dark but expressive eyes and a form and figure which though well rounded, indicate great powers of endurance. She is not technically beautiful but her features have much expression and she possesses unconsciously that magnetic power, which attracts others to her and makes them ready to do her bidding. Her executive ability is remarkable. As Dr. Bellows said of her: 'Had she belonged to the other sex she would have been a merchant prince, a great general, or a trusted political leader.'"

But disassociating her force of leadership from masculine brute strength, Dr. Brockett concluded, "There is nothing of the Amazon in her appearance. She is modest, retiring, and ladylike."

The qualities of independence and initiative offer a master key to Clara Barton's whole career and explain her nature and its defects. Without these qualities she never could have made her discoveries, instituted her reforms, or established her foundations. Without her intense individualism she never could have pierced precedents nor have achieved advances. Taking the situation in her own hands twenty-five years before America adopted the Red Cross Treaty, to the amazement of militarism she practiced whenever she could its principles of Neutrality in caring for the wounded of the enemy and preventing neglect of the disabled soldiers. She did this as often as she could in the Civil War.

Ida Tarbell intuitively sees in this a prophecy of Miss Barton's future career as mother of the Red Cross in America:

"Irregular and dangerous as the practice was, a large number of women did attach themselves to the armies quite independent of all authority and of all organization and did valiant service. Clara Barton, for instance, got the preliminary experience which led to the foundation of the Red Cross work in this country by her independent work on the battle field through the Civil War. She was practically a free lance, going where she would, furnishing her own supplies, doing unobstructed and unimpeded what she found to do. She dressed the wounded of both armies indiscriminately — a practice which first annoyed and sometimes angered the Union Officers — from whose headquarters she worked. But opposition never swayed her purpose, and before the war was over Miss Barton's individual efforts had established the right of the wounded or suffering, irrespective of uniforms, to all the aid which swayed her purpose. This was really Miss Barton's greatest service to the country of this period, though not the only one." [1]

Notwithstanding her breaking of precedents and unconventional leadership in camp and on battle fields, Clara Barton innately was a

[1] Ida Tarbell, 1909, *American Magazine*, p. 804.

cultured woman. Externally as the camp was her home, so her home
was the camp, and this is why dress and domestic delicacies played
no large part in her life. Her culture was shown not in these things
but in the well furnished inner life — and in a delicate graciousness of
manner and mind prompted by the passion of self-bestowal that
broke no law and offended no taste because its first instinct was concern for others. This was the secret of her power.

"How would you define Culture, Miss Addams?" Jane Addams, who
was Clara Barton's close friend, was recently asked at a Chicago dinner.

It was a gathering of distinguished leaders in civic uplift. One
well-known guest had followed another in describing true culture, and
their ideas differed.

In answer to the question put to her as a last resort, after a moment
of meditation, Miss Addams said: "That person is most cultivated
who is able to put himself in the place of the greatest number of
persons!"

Miss Barton could "put herself in the place of the greatest number
of persons" of any woman or man who has lived in America. Miss
Addams's definition expressed exactly the essence of Miss Barton's
culture. And this is why this camper on the trail of disaster, always
quite far afield from elegance and style, outmatched most folk in gen-
tility and was as much at ease in imperial palaces and court circles
as she was in an Oxford farmhouse of one story or in a herd of mule
drivers in the wilderness.

Since shrinking reserve was the constitutional characteristic of
Clara Barton's nature, to front society was the last thing she would
choose from a matter of personal taste. "Some critic has said of me,"
she once remarked — "that I was visibly agitated when I arose to
address my audience — the critic was right and why should I not be?

All speech-making terrifies me. First, I have no taste for it
and lastly, I hate it. I always did and always will. Nothing but
necessity drives me to it, and whenever a speech of any description
or length from an hour and a half down to three minutes is proposed to
me, the first incentive is straight rebellion, open defiance, positive
declination, and having delivered myself of these, tersely and promptly
I feel very comfortable and happy for a short space of time. And so
it would continue with me, I think, if no one appeared to care any more
about it than I did. But at length it gets to me that some one is sorry,

disappointed, had expected a little help, more accommodation, greater generosity, from me, is really very sorry. Then the various tenants of the upper story commence to wake up and express themselves; approbativeness says, 'Aren't you ashamed?' 'You didn't even try to oblige.' Benevolence says, 'Was that kind?' Conscience asks if it were quite right, if it were exactly what I would have liked myself? Then trail in that precious band, always sure to be found on the track of the wrong-doer, — conviction, contrition, repentance! One says, 'You have done very badly,' another, 'I know you are sorry for it' — another, 'If you are really sorry, it may not be too late to retrieve. If you will try, we will help you.' Then good-will and poor judgment get around and join the group, and all commence to batter down and weaken my fortifications. They level the little earthworks I had thrown up so vigorously in the beginning. They order away the sentinels I had set to guard them; with the greatest care they pull down my stars and leave the stripes, and the result is a perfect surrender, accompanied by a humble apology and a promise to do the best I can."

Even to close observers Clara Barton did not grow old — a fact well exemplified by a reporter's description of her in her eighty-fifth year as "a middle aged woman." When she was over seventy, another wrote: "Clara Barton is a woman of fifty or thereabouts, whose face corresponds with the ideal that one might form of her character. Her hair is that rare thing in nature — artists sometimes call it an impossible thing — raven black. It is thick, heavy hair, a burden to the comb, and she wears it after the simple fashion of our mothers and grandmothers, drawn in satiny waves over the ears and pinned up in loose curls behind. Her eyes are like her hair, very dark and very bright. Her features are regular, but one hardly notices them, for the rare beam of good-will that shines out from the soul through the countenance."

When she was eighty-nine and the guest in Chicago at the May festival of the Social Economic Club, she described her "duties" as consisting in "receiving and shaking hands with *two thousand persons*," and then "sitting down to the May breakfast at one o'clock with eleven hundred, leaving the table at four P.M."

This was the commencement of a stay of three weeks in Chicago, the events of each day deepening and brightening with lunches, dinners,

2 C

and receptions and the meeting with human souls, which was always
to her an inspiration.

The first Sunday of May, 1910, the eighty-nine-year-old heroine
occupied the pulpit of the Congregational Church at Oak Park, of
which her esteemed cousin, Reverend Wm. E. Barton, was pastor.
Notwithstanding Dr. Barton's eminent success, "I got my revenge by
having a larger audience than he did in the morning," she said.

All the time, old friends, and field workers from the Central West,
radiated around her, while she in turn stole off to see those Red Cross
field workers who could not come to her.   Among them were, for instance, the Gardners, in Southern Indiana, whither the octogenarian
went by express, to visit the family of the man who had tendered to the
Red Cross hundreds of acres of Indiana farm land in the early struggles
of the society but whose offer had ultimately to be declined, owing to
the inaccessibility of the estate.

From this two thousand mile trip to and from Chicago, Miss Barton
returned alone in June, 1910.   She was not at all tired out.   As a
proof she made a Boston visit to the First Aid, of which she was President and then took the street car for 40 miles from Boston to Worcester.
She was unaccompanied, and had telephoned her close friend and former
Oxford pastor, Dr. Schoppe, to meet her.

"I am at Park Square, Boston, returning from Chicago, and wish
you could meet me at the end of the line," she said over the phone.
Travel-worn as she was, the always victorious personal energy of
Miss Barton carried her through the two hours' trip without mishap,
but Dr. Schoppe, endeavoring to connect with the car, missed it as it
turned off into Salem Square, Worcester, before reaching City Hall,
where he waited.

Most women fifty years younger, in her predicament, and after a
two-thousand mile trip, would call a carriage or taxicab.   But she
started to walk across the square in the crowded street.   A few minutes
later, Dr. Schoppe looked up to see Clara Barton crossing at City
Hall, accompanied by a big policeman.

"I thank you," said he to the officer, "for turning over into my hands
so precious a friend of our country as Clara Barton."

The policeman, absolutely astounded, lifted his helmet and saluted,
amazed that in the grand old lady he should have been conducting so
famous a foot passenger.

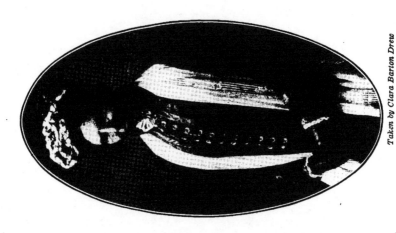

At 87

Taken by Clara Barton Drew

Always gracious to her opponents, Clara Barton was unerringly true to her friends, particularly those who perhaps had no other friend and occupied a humble corner. It was this type she took great joy in taking by the hand and presenting at the point of her supremest moments of achievement and recognition.

A literary character Miss Barton very much admired. She realized the public applause given a literary attainment and the idealization of a writer. Had she planned to be a creator of books instead of a performer of great deeds and a founder of a great arm of service for organized practical mercy in America, she would have succeeded. Her message, however, would not have been in the fields of imagination, although poetry appealed deeply to her and fed her vision always. Often, we even find her ordinary letters breaking into original verse. She had almost a hero worship of the poets, forgetting that the deepest themes of the poets sang of women like her. She consoled herself with books of verse from the age of eleven, while shut in with David, her brother, till her final years of illness eighty years after. When she died, books of poetry were lying all about her desk, and when she lived, they were quoted continually as her vehicles of expression, even of battle scenes.

Together with other of the Barton blood she herself flashed off impromptu poems which were the versifications, not of a great poet, but of a minute-man of fancy to point some immediate occasion with brilliant repartee and wit. Such were her verses "To the Women who went to the War." Such, also, was her tribute to the Congregational mission Treasurer, W. W. Peet, of the American Board of Missions in Turkey.

Yet she never took to making poetry seriously, and was not born a poet, taught to love the poets as she was by her sister Sally. With the rest of the family, for this, as for all the finer instincts of the scholar, she thanked her father's father, Dr. Stephen Barton, the good physician. This trait descended to his children's children. It reblossomed, not in the corn fields of material wealth, but in the flower gardens of the intellectual, the spiritual, the altruistic and the merciful.

As a writer of history, though her manuscript was too devoid of dates and without evidence of the love of the chronologist, she had great power. Her varied experience had taught her to see beneath the thunder and the show, the real significance of war, — and this she was able to realistically put on paper for others to see. Her war diaries and battle-field sketches are unsurpassed in trueness to the life they reproduced.

Clara Barton knew the art of letter-writing. Frequently in this mode of expression she almost reaches classic strength. Yet had she sat down to do a great piece of literary work, as such, she could not have done it. It had to be extracted from life. Her literary accomplishment came when she was unconscious of it. Her choicest thoughts, her most elegant conceptions fell into form when she unconsciously gave them as a literary prodigal, never thinking whether anyone would so much as look at them twice.

Year after year, even when there were no wars and disasters, plain human life with all its calls for sympathy absorbed her. With her own life she was not concerned, only with her friends. There was something great, something Christlike, in this absolute lack of anxiety about her own name, fame and deeds, especially as she might well have been thought anxious about them after the bitter hours of momentary misinterpretation and misunderstanding that floated over her in 1904 and 1905.

One would have thought Miss Barton would have written her life to vindicate herself if for no other purpose. But she felt no need of vindication, as she felt there was nothing to vindicate. So, while she was always writing, it was never about herself. No one can look at even a few stray letters of hers and not see her love of souls, North, South, East, West. And across the seas, "the leaves thereof were for the healing of the nations."

"I found her deep in her correspondence." This one phrase time and again from observers who went to see her, describes the most frequent attitude in which, ever since 1856, interviewers discovered her when not on fields of action.

' "Buried deep in her correspondence."— Such a phrase frequently as it was used did not convey the real situation — for in this as well as on the field was a ministry to earth's spheres of souls, dying for help. It was not a secretarial attitude. It was compassion for the multitude with which she was filled. If it was not one kind of multitude, it was another. When the day's procession went from her door the silent multitude stole in. Masses of letters from all parts of the world beclouded her desk. They looked at her in the dusk and seemed to say — "Come to me." Did she think of herself? She must stop it. Everything else but the need in these messages should be put aside. Their pleas were too human for her kind heart to resist.

"But, Miss Barton, the world wants your autobiography! A great thing like that must never be put aside for the multitude."

When this conviction was expressed it was a great test of the life of Clara Barton; for the point arose as to whether after three score and ten, she should retire from activity and write her life, or risking the perpetuation of her career, forget Clara Barton utterly and consume her remaining energies for the good of her fellow beings.

We know how she decided. Scores of times she sat down to try to write her autobiography, but she could not do it. Though her pen played with a glimpsing shadow of her childhood, she never wrote even the first chapter. There came a knock at the door — the knock of some one from a circle of trouble or a sphere of pain, or perhaps it was only the plea of just a crude letter from a soul humble and obscure. The call was irresistible. To heed it she must sacrifice her autobiography, though many of her closest friends continued to plead on with her to write it and let the incessant details of humane activities go. "'She' saved others, 'herself she' could not save." That was all. She had every reason to have surcease from service. Her public career, her Civil War career, her European career, her career as founder and her career as developer of the Red Cross into a permanent national institution — all were accomplished. She had nothing to gain by continuing such activities.

But as long as humanity was in pain, she could not close her ears. She could not fold her arms. She could not put her feet over the fender and crystallize her past career.

"As a correspondent," says one of her nearest friends, "for many years she accomplished the marvelous. She never wearied in letter writing, and refused to turn this self-imposed duty to a secretary except when sheer impossibility made it imperative. Thinking clearly, she composed rapidly, choosing the simple, telling word that could not be misunderstood. There is doubt if so many letters bearing the autograph of any other woman are in existence to-day. Her memory was a storehouse upon which she could draw at will with rare accuracy for names, dates and essential details."

She wrote a correspondent, Mrs. S. B. Vassall:

"Paris, France, Sept. 18, 1871.

"These letters are the sore spot — the worrying vein of my existence. That little package which I cannot put by, but which lies around and looks me in the face on the most impossible of occasions, and reproaches in silence, and comes late at night and early in the morning to haunt, — it may be to taunt me a little — that little package is the plague of my life and yet I prize it most of all and wouldn't have done without it, but I can never quite dispose of it."

Thousands of extracts of wisdom are in these fugitive letters, extracts classic in beauty and immortal in helpfulness. They are expressed unconsciously, not written for the press. She so created an atmosphere of sympathy in these communications that you could almost catch the falling tear, or vibrate with the passing emotion. Especially for anyone drugged by auto-intoxication and lying in a gutter of hopelessness, she believed in the "gold cure" of a lifting thought. She practiced it decades before the name Christian Science came to the lips of men.

She believed above all else that the "truth shall make you free." She believed in it for herself. I have before me many of her letters pleading — "Send me a great thought." — "Send me a beautiful truth and I shall be well again."

It was this that she longed for herself which she gave so overflowingly to others. Her confession of faith in the power of mind and truth over body, she practiced all through her life in tender, living touches that melted the heart and released the life strain.

In writing these letters, she haunted the house hours after the others were asleep, stealing around for some stored-away word or communication she wanted to answer. Then, on the wings of sympathy, she wrote like a nightingale in the still dark hours all through the night. "That is why she wanted the end of the house at Glen Echo to herself," her relatives have told me, "so that she could prowl around like a night-hawk and search for letters to answer and not disturb others."

Here, for example, is a characteristic beginning of one, as if all the good were on the other person's side,

"Oxford, July 12, 1910.

"My dear, dear Mrs. ——:

"How forgiving and how like you to face this tide of heat, to break a silence for which you were in no way accountable. Every one of these long, silent days, I have written you in my heart, if not alone for the love of you, because there were things concerning which I wanted to consult you, and have waited for the better days, when, face to face, I could speak   ”

In ordinary life, caught on a delayed trip or a storm, Miss Barton would occupy the moments by writing some friend even if she had to drop on the floor under a sputtering gas lamp.   Here is one such instance very early in her career.

"WORCESTER DEPOT,
"Wednesday Morning.

"DEAR IDA: (Mrs. Riccius)

"Thinking it must interest you, I seize the opportunity to sit down on the floor under the gas light and tell you that we are all here in the dark, and it rains as hard as it can pour — They tell us that they are having a 'change' of weather which consists of its having commenced to rain last Saturday and continued unabated until the present moment, with no prospect of interruption.   I said that beautiful last Sunday that I knew it was raining and blowing and drizzling in New England; so it was.

"Well, to leave that interesting topic.   Steve met us at Newark. We went to Central Park yesterday — cold and damp — and took the boat at four for this.   Stephen has issued a waker to Captain David to trot out one of his spans to meet the train, when we all expect to sail or 'wade in,' I don't know which, but sure it is we run by water some way.

"We had a nice journey.   May took us through N. Y. all straight, and didn't get her feet wet crossing the Sound.   She is fast asleep on the settee at present and Steve remains not far from the same comfortable condition.

"Don't talk about my taking 'bread and milk,' — next time I am going to take a cow — not a drop of milk for love or money since I left Washington.   The nearest approach has been a 'mess' of condensed milk reduced and boiled down — didn't partake — but 'stuck' to the bread — going to try my luck at 'Aunt Lucy's' next.

"Tell Sally that I think I am as well as when I left and hope to be a great deal better when I see her in a few weeks from this."

This independent and democratic trait of Miss Barton was marked by every friend:

"Of an ancestry noble, but unostentatious," declared Charles
Sumner Young, one of her closest friends in later life, "she is of the
purest New England and yet without the least tinge of the aristocracy that loves to reign; she merely 'went about doing good.' She
was in demeanor modest, — unpretentious as is the house in Oxford
where she was born over ninety years ago."

Characteristic of her modesty is this extract from a letter of November 14, 1909, to this same friend:

"May 31st the date runs, and I know I never answered that letter,
for I never could have in my life answered a letter like that, but still
more I never even tried to, discouraged at the onset and gave up the
encounter. A glimpse of the topics it handles were so far beyond any
reply from the 'likes of me.' 'Great services unnoticed.' 'Future
remembrances when others are forgotten.' 'To be told in story and
sung in other lands' — poor little me who has never seen the ruler of
her own."

Miss Barton carefully treasured her letters and relics of her battle
fields, but diaries of ordinary details she seldom kept, though she
did keep certain war diaries of the utmost value. She said to me,
speaking of diaries of unimportant things: "only two classes of
people can keep such diaries — those who never have time to do anything else, or those who have stopped. I have done neither."

One thing that saved so intense a nature as hers was a dissolving
quality of humor. Humor was the one trait productive of Miss
Barton's fine longevity. We remember it all through the campaigns
of the Civil War, we recall it at the gates of beleaguered Strassburg
as she laughed at the Consul's horse. Later we can see it in her humor-
ous account of the struggle with the publishers as to her age when they
made her birthday nine years later than the true date.

Strange to say, most of the biographical notices of Clara Barton,
even many standard encyclopedias, placed her birth in 1830, nine
years afterwards. In a letter of September 30th, 1909, Miss Barton
humorously wrote me, "That error in the date of my birth has been
traveling about for the last fifteen years or more, from one biographical sketch to another. I made strenuous efforts to correct and set
it right when my attention was first called to it, but it was too late;
it, like other falsehoods, had gone the world over. The publishers
could not call it off, and met me with polite, good-natured pleasant-

SOCIAL TRAITS393

ness, as the mistake was all in my favor; if other persons did not object,
I scarcely needed to; until I grew discouraged and gave it up, excepting to state the truth whenever the opportunity presented. December 25, 1821, according to the calendar is correct."

A later letter to me makes more fun out of this mistake in age and
then jokes about her being shut in for fear of the cold, wet days — a
fact she never took seriously.

"Concerning the foot note explaining the discrepancy in dates of
birth, I do most highly approve of it. Something surely is needed to
clear it up, and that statement ought to do it. Please make any use
or application of my homely speech that may seem best. It is like
the old Vicar's night gown, not elegant, but will wear well.

"I must confess that the Equinox hit us rather hard, and I drew in.
for repairs for a few days. I almost began to fear that the recent
developments (the Peary-Cook controversy) had gotten the pole so off
its base, and so loosened, — that it was swinging around. But these
few Indian Summer Days have calmed my apprehensions, and the
world seems to be in its orbit again."

Just before this, on a September Sunday in 1909 following dinner
after an address at the Adams Square Congregational Church of
Worcester, where she had shaken hands with hundreds, I urged her
to retire and rest, a suggestion to which she gave no quarter, turning
to me quizzically as if to say, "How can you insult one so young as I,
by asking them to rest in the middle of the afternoon?" At the
third attack, eighty-eight years old though she was, she aimed the
batteries at me straight, volleying, "Are you in your right mind to ask
me to rest?"

At the end of the day, after an auto ride through the rain with
Dr. Walter H. Richardson of Worcester, an esteemed comrade in the
militia with her cousin, Will Barton, we asked her if she were not
chilled, and she said to the rest of us huddled under the robes to keep
dry, "No, I should enjoy going farther, if *you* would."

It reminded me that I had ventured to say an hour before, as amid
the drizzle of that overcast Sabbath morning in September I went
to escort her to the church door from the touring car,

"I am sorry it's raining, Miss Barton."

And I recalled her answer.

"Is it?" she said with a laugh, "I hadn't noticed it."

This is a trivial incident. And yet it reveals her constant attitude, and is why the greatest woman of heroic action in the world, who had faced unflinchingly fields of carnage and had had shells tear the men she held in her arms to fragments, was a healthful and happy server of her race till ninety.

Indeed, one reason for her attaining such an age after going through hundreds of bloody and death-dealing crises in war and disaster, any one of which would turn a strong man's reason in a night or drive a woman into nervous prostration, was this ever-present unconcern for what you cannot help.

Like all the truly brave, especially war veterans, she was always ready and all afire for action, but she disliked display and hated parade. A newspaper man desiring to be kindly once wrote an advance account of a program in which Miss Barton was a figure, adding as an embellishment, a reception of an elaborateness we never planned and a triumphant ride in a touring car. Fearing that should Miss Barton see this notice she would be unnecessarily annoyed, I slipped in to her apartment and explained the situation.

The idea of a parade and show aroused in her a measured tone of dignity and command which had she been a cavalry colonel I would have said came from the bottom of his boots. It was a force-repressing tone which simply said, "I command" and which called the hearer into the attitude of, "I obey."

"I prefer to take a common car from Oxford like anyone else," she said, "and come without formality and parade, which I hate."

I was glad it happened, for it was her battle tone.

A soldier one can tell by his step, but Miss Barton as a battle field heroine, I could have detected by her voice. It was a wonderful voice, doing the opposite to what common humanity does when aroused. It, when aroused, raises its voice. She, when aroused, lowered it,—and the more affecting the circumstance, the deeper was the voice. Used to controlling herself from excitement, it told by its expression the story of a lifetime of repression. It was phonographic of the past. It revealed the heroine capable of being stirred to the depths but in absolute self-control.

Miss Barton's love of children was pitifully tense for one whose arms have held only the mangled of the battle field and whose ears had heard instead of the crooning of a babe, the moaning of the dying.

Children were her only masters. While she would hold a world at bay, she would do anything for them.

It was a habit of Miss Barton's to speak in public only when inspired by some compelling idea. If no such idea came she would merely remark that she had nothing to say. A regiment could not then move her. I knew this, and when I asked her to speak I always feared she might disappoint a great audience. On a particularly important occasion, what was my chagrin when with that decisive tone she pronounced in a low staccato, "I have nothing to say."

Open attack would not win the day, and I retreated to my chair behind the pulpit. But I noted that quite unconsciously as she sat in the church at the foot of an enormous flaming Red Cross of salvia, she bent over the bright faces of little children dressed in whites and pinks and banking the steps of the chancel. She became absorbed in watching the children's every move, and her face was aglow with joy.

"Ah, here is an opportunity," I said to myself, "for a master stroke of strategy.

"Miss Barton, see the children occupying even the pulpit steps all about you. They are waiting for a story. You won't disappoint them, will you?"

"I *will* speak to the children," she replied. When she closed she had beneath her sway every child of three and every octogenarian of eighty. Then followed a scene reproduced in hundreds of audiences year after year. The sea of faces became hidden by the Chautauqua salute, made by a field of fluttering white handkerchiefs that had all along wiped away teardrops. For all realized that the little figure standing so modestly before them was really the one who had been through the blood and fire that she recalled.

Besides her voice and her slight stoop, another evidence of the battlefield heroine lay in her eyes, deep-sunken like port holes under frowning battlements. They were not the eyes of one accustomed to retire, but accustomed to go on at any cost; not the eyes of one hunted, but of the hunter whose sharp gaze scans every part of the field of vision for its shot victim, shot, in this case, by others.

In searching for these victims Clara Barton's eyes had been bloodshot for weeks and months by the sulphurous cannon. Indeed, she never lost the smart and sting of the fumes through which she had gone for many months of weary campaigns.

And yet to one who knew Clara Barton, there was nothing forbidding in her glance. "Her eyes," said one who often looked into them, "are the sweetest in the world. They challenge you to tell what is absolutely true. They appeal to that which is best in you. They shine with a love-light that is all their own. They are dark eyes and have a questioning in them like those of a child seeking truth."[1]

CHAPTER XXXVIII

CLARA BARTON ON "WAR"

"NARRATIVES of battles," Miss Barton once said in a restrospect, "as they are found in histories and official reports, are all wonderfully alike. There is the same intricate and incomprehensible machinery of divisions — brigades — regiments — battalions and squadrons of right centers and left wings. There are some attempts to flank some other incomprehensible mechanism to prevent being flanked. The same advancing and falling back, extending and contracting — whirling — charging — deploying and enfilading. A perfect chaos — intelligible to few, and interesting to still fewer — where the natural eye can discern no human being — or scarce a sign of human presence."

She then asserted that her work and words were for the individual soldier, and what he does, sees or thinks, in those dread hours of leaden rain and iron hail, or in the reaction which follows.

"I shall not essay to enlighten you upon the subject of war," she explained with some feeling. "Were I to attempt it, I should doubtless miserably fail, for it has so long been said, as to amount to an adage, that 'women don't know anything about war.'

"I wish men didn't either. They have always known a great deal too much about it for the good of their kind. They have worshiped at Valkyria's shrine, and followed her siren lead, till it has cost a million times more than the whole world is worth, poured out the best blood and crushed the fairest forms the good God has ever created.

"General Sherman was right when addressing an assemblage of cadets he told them war was Hell! Deck it as you will, it is this, and whoever has looked active war full in the face has caught some glimpses of regions as infernal, as he may ever fear to see. If any listener of mine on this subject expects ever to hear me converse of the war side of it, he had best prepare early for a disappointment, because

that was not my side.   The war side of the war could never have
called me to the field — *Through and through — thought and act —
body and soul — I hate it !*"

"The side of the picture which history never shows," she speaks
of as "belonging to those who must follow the track of conquering
armies, faces bathed in tears and hands in blood, — the lees in the
wine, the dregs in the cups of military glory.   It would be out of such
as this that I must sketch the battle glimpses I could bring you, were
I to attempt it, for there was my lowly place in all wars I have known."

As to woman's voice against war and for peace, in the winter of
1870–1871, she writes from Germany : "Madame de Gasparin's appeal
for Peace has found a warm and strong advocate in Mrs. Howe.
I hope some good may come of it.   All that you say upon the subject is
true, and it is no small amount of picking up that women have to do in
consequence of the carelessness of their reckless fellows from boyhood
to manhood, and from manhood to age it is all the same.   I can never
see a poor mutilated wreck, blown to pieces with powder and lead,
without wondering if visions of such an end ever flitted before his
mother's mind when she washed and dressed her fair-skinned baby.
Woman should certainly have some voice in the matter of war, either
affirmative or negative, and the fact that she has not this should not be
made the ground on which to deprive her of other privileges.   "She
shan't say there shall be no war — and she shan't take any part in it
when there is one, and because she don't take part in war, she must not
vote, and because she can't vote, she has no voice in her government,
and because she has no voice in her government, she isn't a citizen, and
because she isn't a citizen, she has no rights, and because she has no
rights, she must submit to wrongs, and because she submits to wrongs,
she isn't anybody.

"And 'what does she know about war ' and because she doesn't
know anything about it, she mustn't say or do anything about it.

"I pray for peace . . ."

In her Red Cross Address in the year of the founding of the Red
Cross in America, Miss Barton spoke of women as an aid to the Red
Cross and the Red Cross as an aid to the peace quest of womanhood.
"Women as a rule," she quoted, are not war-makers.   For centuries
the caprices of men have plunged the world in strife, covered the
earth's surface with armies and enriched the soil with the best blood

that ever flowed in human veins. It is only right that at length, in the cycle of ages, something should touch man's heart and set him humbly down to find out some way of mending as much of his mischief as he could. Perhaps he "builded better than he knew," for in that one effort, the creation of the Red Cross, he touched the spring that sooner or later will mend it all. No grander or truer prophecy has ever been made than uttered in that first convention: "THE RED CROSS SHALL TEACH WAR TO MAKE WAR UPON ITSELF." It is the most practical and effective peace-maker and civilizer in the known world. It reaches where nothing else can. If proof of this be wanting, study the action of Japan in its late war.

"But is man doing this work alone? No — gladly, no! Scarcely had he made his first move, when the jeweled hands of royal woman glistened beside him, and right royally have they borne their part. Glance at the galaxy — the great leader and exemplar of them all — Empress Augusta of Germany, her illustrious daughter, the Grand Duchess of Baden, Eugenia, Empress Frederick, Victoria and Princess Louise of England, Margherita of Italy, Natalie of Servia and the entire Court of Russia, and to-day the present Empress of Germany, the hard-working Empress of Japan with her faithful, weary court, even now busy in the hospitals of convalescing Chinese. The various auxiliary societies of women of all the principal Red Cross nations are a pride and a glory to humanity."

Among the many women who followed Miss Barton's example and went to the Civil War is a legion of her friends, of whom she speaks in this animating original poem:

"The Women Who Went to the Field"

The women who went to the field, you say,
The women who went to the field; and pray,
What did they go for? — just to be in the way?
They'd not know the difference betwixt work and play.
And what did they know about war, anyway?
What could they do? of what use could they be?
They would scream at the sight of a gun, don't you see?,
Just fancy them round where the bugle-notes play,
And the long roll is bidding us on to the fray.
Imagine their skirts 'mong artillery wheels,
And watch for their flutter as they flee 'cross the fields

When the charge is rammed home and the fire belches hot;
They never will wait for the answering shot.
They would faint at the first drop of blood in their sight.
What fun for us boys, — (ere we enter the fight),
They might pick some lint, and tear up some sheets,
And make us some jellies, and send on their sweets,
And knit some soft socks for Uncle's Sam's shoes,
And write us some letters, and tell us the news.
And thus it was settled, by common consent,
By husbands, or brothers, or whoever went,
That the place for the women was in their homes,
There to patiently wait until victory comes.
But later it chanced — just how no one knew —
That the lines slipped a bit, and some 'gan to crowd through;
And they went, where did they go? — Ah! where did they not?
Show us the battle, — the field, — or the spot
Where the groans of the wounded rang out on the air
That her ear caught it not, and her hand was not there;
Who wiped the death sweat from the cold, clammy brow,
And sent home the message "'Tis well with him now"—?
Who watched in the tents whilst the fever fires burned,
And the pain-tossing limbs in agony turned,
And wet the parched tongue, calmed delirium's strife
Till the dying lips murmured, "My mother," "My wife?"
And who were they all? — They were many, my men;
Their records were kept by no tabular pen;
They exist in traditions from father to son,
Who recalls, in dim memory, now here and there one,
A few names were writ, and by chance live to-day;
But it's a perishing record, fast fading away.
Of those we recall, there are scarcely a score,
Dix, Dame, Bickerdyke, — Edson, Harvey and Moore,
Fales, Wittemeyer, Gilson, Safford and Lee,
And poor Cutter dead in the sands of the Sea;
And Frances D. Gage, our "Aunt Fanny" of old,
Whose voice rang for freedom when freedom was sold.
And Husband, and Etheridge, and Harlan and Case,
Livermore, Alcott, Hancock and Chase,
And Turner, and Hawley, and Potter and Hall,
Ah! the list grows apace, as they come at the call;
Did these women quail at the sight of a gun?
Will some soldier tell us of one he saw run?
Will he glance at the boats on the great western flood,
At Pittsburg and Shiloh, did they faint at the blood?
And the brave wife of Grant stood there with them then,
And her calm stately presence gave strength to his men.

And Marie of Logan; she went with them too,
A bride, scarcely more than a sweetheart, 'tis true.
Her young cheek grows pale when the bold troopers ride.
Where the "Black Eagle" soars she is close at his side,
She stanches his blood, cools the fever-burnt breath,
And the wave of her hand stays the Angel of Death;
She nurses him back, and restores once again
To both army and state the great Leader of men.
She has smoothed his black plumes and laid them to sleep
Whilst the angels above them their high vigils keep;
And she sits here alone, with the snow on her brow —
Your cheers for her, Comrades! Three cheers for her now.
And these were the women who went to the war.
The women of question; what did they go for?
Because in their hearts God had planted the seed
Of pity for woe, and help for its need;
They saw, in high purpose, a duty to do,
And the armor of right broke the barriers through.
Uninvited, unaided, unsanctioned ofttimes,
With pass, or without it, they pressed on the lines;
They pressed, they implored, 'till they ran the lines through,
And that was the 'running' the men saw them do.
'Twas a hampered work, it's worth largely lost;
'Twas hindrance, and pain, and effort, and cost;
But through these came knowledge, — knowledge is power, —
And never again in the deadliest hour
Of war or of peace shall we be so beset
To accomplish the purpose our spirits have met.
And what would they do if war came again?
The scarlet cross floats where all was blank then.
They would bind on their "brassards" and march to the fray.
And the man liveth not who could say them nay;
They would stand with you now, as they stood with you then
The nurses, consolers, and saviours of men.

This poem was read by Clara Barton in response to a toast, at the
farewell reception and Banquet given by the ladies of the Potomac
Corps, at Willard's Hotel, Washington, D.C., Friday evening, November 18, 1892. She later explained that returning home from a journey
she was notified in the afternoon that she would be expected to attend
the banquet and respond to the toast, "The Women Who Went to
the Field." As there was little or no time for preparation, the foregoing poem was hastily written, and may almost be considered as
impromptu.

2 D

The first name honored in the poem is Dorothea Dix, General Superintendent of war nurses.   Having founded the modern systems of insane institutions in America and Great Britain, and other countries, she was sixty years old when the Civil War broke out.   But three hours after the attack at Baltimore, April 19, she left the New Jersey Insane Hospital, where she made her home and was on the train for Washington.   Miss Dix was the last one to leave Baltimore. Hence it was that she became aware of the plot to waylay and kidnap or assassinate Lincoln.   She it was who led with others in giving the information that resulted in Lincoln's change of plans and his consequent trip in safety.   April 20th she offered herself for free service and became Superintending Head of all the war nurses of the war of the Rebellion, which post she held without a period of rest for the four years of war.   Before this, after a girlhood in Worcester, she founded the modern systems for the Insane in America, and other parts of the world.   Ill at each stage, by some new need or by the "tonic of opposition," as she called it, she made connection with what she was pleased to style "the Source of Power."

It was thus she resembled the other little sister to the soldier, Clara Barton.   She was like her in other ways.   As in Miss Barton's case her voice, it was said, "was low, not particularly sweet, but gentle."   "She is rather small," it was reported, "dresses indifferently, has good features, but indifferent eyes.   In her general interest for human suffering Miss Dix seems neglectful to the individual interest."   In this lay a great difference from Miss Barton — caused no doubt by Miss Dix's administrative position.   In her war service, like Florence Nightingale, Dorothea Dix spent her time in hospitals, while Miss Barton was largely on the field.

In a retrospect of the battles in the Civil War as if forecasting the present Red Cross Memorial Building at Washington, Miss Barton exclaimed: "Mothers — wives — and maidens, would there were some testimonials grand enough for you, — some tablet that could show to the world the sacrifice of American womanhood and American motherhood in that war!   Sacrifices so nobly and so firmly — but so gently and so beautifully made.

"If like the Spartan mother she did not send her son defiantly to the field, — bidding him return only with his shield, or on it, — if like the Roman matron she did not take him by the hand and lead him proudly to the standard of the Republic; like the true Anglo-Saxon, — loyal and loving, tender and brave, — she hid her tears with one hand while with the other wrung her fond farewell, and passed him to the state."

As Miss Barton grew older her opposition to war increased. In 1900, as England was confronted with the Transvaal, she wrote: "All this war business is very dreadful, and it seems unnecessary. It may be a great humanizer, but certainly it is not a harmonizer. I get so tired of what I try to do, that I wish I had never heard of war. What an excitable changing world this is, only a few weeks ago nothing was heard but Dreyfus; now one does not know where he is, or seem to care *if* he is, and we are plunging after the Transvaal. What next?"

The difficulties of preserving peace through arbitration she fully realizes, however, as is seen in this letter written from Europe in 1872

"If there be any power on earth which can right the wrongs for which the nations go to war, I pray that it may be made manifest, but when I think, I fear — How supreme an International court must it have been to be able to induce the Southerners to liberate their slaves or to convince them the 'mudsills,' and 'greasy mechanics,' and 'horned Yankees,' are a people entitled to sufficient respect to be treated on fair International ground? And how much legislation would it have taken to convince the world what a worthless bubble of assumption was France, so utterly unworthy the leadership she assumed and to have laid her in all respects so open before the world that it should with one voice repudiate her leadership, and refuse to follow her as heretofore in frivolity, immorality, folly, fashion, vice, and crime. It seems to me to have been only one great balloon and now that bayonets and bombs have pierced it full of holes, it sends out tens of thousands of little balloons in its collapse. It is bad for France, but I am not certain but the lesson will be beneficial to the rest of the world. I don't know if we may always trust councils. We had one at Rome not half a year ago that voted a dogma which turned backward the progress of enlightened thought two centuries; and how great a power of legislation would have been required to overthrow that decision? But I suspect the fear of Victor Emanuel's bayonets have seriously interfered with it. Ah, I don't know; it is such a mystery, and mankind the greatest mystery of all. I shall never get it right in this world, whatever may happen in the one 'that sets this right.'"

Miss Barton characterizes the Civil War soldiers as: "Men who marched and fought their way from the Black water and the Dismal Swamp up through the marshes of the Chickahominy, and the James, till they stood on the brow of the Cumberland — with Culpepper — Manassas — Spottsylvania — Todds Tavern — Meadow Bridge — Mechanicsville — and Cold Harbor — all among the past. Men who swept down the mountain sides with Sheridan, and the gallant Custer, till Strassburg — Gordonville — Trevillian Station — Five Forks — Cedar Creek — Winchester — and Appomattox were carved upon their scabbards."

"I have studied the massing of forces," she continues, "and scanned from point to point the old battle grounds of Marengo — and Jena — and Waterloo — Magenta and Solferino, — and it always seemed to me that these armies had fairer field, and better chance than ours."

No one sympathized or understood the soldier's suffering and sacrifice in later life more than did Miss Barton. The Grand Army of the Republic of America claimed her as its bosom friend — dearer than any other.

"Soldiers," she said in one of a hundred of characteristic addresses — "a word with you. From the old armies of the Union — representatives of every section, and every battle field you have met here to-night to commemorate the fall of Richmond, and to celebrate the new salvation.

"While accompanying our armies I of course passed much more among the rank and file, than among the officers of any grade. And while I would not disparage the many hundreds of noble men deservedly decorated with stars and eagles, my experience deepened a conviction, otherwise strong, that in peace or in war the fate of the Republic is mainly in the hands of the innumerable multitude of our citizens who wear no titles.

"What can be added to the glory of a Nation whose citizens are its soldiers? Whose warriors, armed and mighty, — spring from its bosom in the hour of need, and peacefully retire when the need is over?

"A nation, which from its civil walks of life furnished to its armies, — captains, — colonels, — brigadier and major generals, — and more than all, the great Captain, — the sainted soul, that marshaled and sped our conquering hosts, till they wore the victor's crown, and he the martyr's — Abraham Lincoln.

"When the civil North rises in her might — the shadows of her warriors darken the land, and the bristling of her steel brightens the heavens. And when the ground shakes under the tread of her marching armies well may rebellion and traitors tremble.

"How they came trooping from cottage and hearthstone, how they filed down your streets and crowded your cars and boats in their haste to meet the foe; — how the music of the fife and drum rolled over your heads — have you forgotten these days?"

While Clara Barton hated war, she loved the warrior. "The history of a country is mainly a history of its wars," she stated to the soldiers of the Grand Army, "and you are the men of history — from the first call of the bugle till its closing note died away in the cadence of peace you were a part of that great struggle.

"You were with Fremont and Lyon in the early west — with Dupont at Port Royal — with Burnside at Roanoke and Fredericksburg and with the gallant Ellsworth when he fell —

"You were with the glorious, but ill-fated Army of the Peninsula — with Banks at Cedar Mountain — with Pope at Manassas and with McClellan when he hurled back Lee from Maryland.

"You were with Grant at Vicksburg and Donaldson — Your shouts mingled in the thunders of Shiloh — Chattanooga — Kenesaw and Atlanta — and your hearts and your feet kept time with the glorious music when Sherman marched down to the sea.

"You were with Butler at New Orleans — and with the old Sea Lion, Farragut, when he slowed his engines and shouted his orders in the iron hail of Fort Jackson and St. Philip.

"You were with the lion-hearted Thomas and Rosecrans in Cumberland — with Hooker at Chancellorsville, with McPherson and Howard and Logan in Tennessee — with Meade at Gettysburg — with the noble Berry at Fair Oaks and Fredericksburg — with Chamberlain at Five Forks and Spottsylvania — with Kearney at Chantilly — with the invincible Sheridan in the Valley, and with Kilpatrick everywhere.

"You were with Gilmore at Charleston — and Olustee — with Foster at Newbern — with Butler and Terry at Bermuda Hundred — Petersburg and Fort Fisher — with Hancock in the charge — and with the immortal Sedgwick when he fell. With Grant at Cold Harbor — the Wilderness and Spottsylvania, and last of all you were with him in his death throttle upon Richmond.

"The long dreary winter of '64 passed as you lay out upon the snows of Virginia —

"Four years of ceaseless warfare —

"In the spring of 1865, the towering blaze of the Carolina pine streams out upon the swinging lines of Sherman's marching legions — bearing northward."

Memorial Day after Memorial Day, she stood with the "Boys in Blue" in the God's acre of the soldier. "Yes, Mr. President, mourners, soldiers! It is good to be here," she declared, on one of these occasions. "It is good that ye meet to build an altar, and deck it with your offerings, — and throughout our whole vast land, from zone to zone, from sea to sea, there rises not the question in any mind, To whom do ye build? — All the world knows to whom our nation builds its altar on the 30th of May, and all approve. Truly when she set apart and made holy this day, she did well, and builded better than she knew. It is well, that not only the nation pay this great tribute of respect and gratitude once every year to those who fell in defence of its liberties, — but that those who struggled in the same noble cause, and survived, should meet, and in some manner, live over again the scenes which make, and forever must make up, to them the most important era of their lives.

"For there is no true loyal soldier to-day, who served his term of enlistment in the war of the rebellion, who, if asked for some portion of his past life to be taken out of his record and remembrance, but would say — 'Take whatever three or four years of my existence you will, but leave the old army life untouched, — I did in those days what you never did, and I can never do again — leave *that* to me.'

"But time rolls rapidly, — and the events we meet to revive, are already history.

"Eighteen years ago, it was, — comrades! Can you realize it was so long, that the white blossoms of May fell on our young, untried armies, forming quickly to the call for 75,000 men?

"They fell unheeded, too, on the bowed heads, and tear dimmed eyes of the mothers, wives, and sisters, who gave up their bravest and their best to that new strange call.

"Terrible days of misgiving were these, still, — all were coming back, all would live, and all come home the same, with the glory of a soldier added.

"It was only a separation, and for only three months! Ah! bright days, — bright uniforms — bright eyes — bright hopes — and bright blossoms — and the May went bravely, and merrily on — and June! — and July! — Ah! that checked a little —

"Bull Run told us something we had not taken into our estimate — and the Peninsula — and the campaigns in the west; but the hopes grew and strengthened, under trials and adversity, and in answer to the second call, rolled back the mighty chorus, 'We're coming, Father Abraham, 300,000 more.'

"And the next May blossoms fell on uniforms less bright, but more soldierly and they fell, too, on the new-made graves, that by this time began to stud the distant lands.

"We had learned they would not all come back!

"Shall we follow our marches another year, and find where they led by field, and river, and shore and sea?

"Pittsburg Landing — Shiloh — Fort Pillow — Corinth — Grim Ben Butler in New Orleans — Bold Farragut lashed to the rigging

" ' And lay there, wood to wall,
When, scarce a cable's length from the fortress 'mid case shot, shell and ball,
Lo! the Hartford slowed her engines.'

"Williamsburg — Fair Oaks — seven days before Richmond Malvern Hill with its spiteful fire — Cedar Mountain — 2d Bull Run — Chantilly with its rain and darkness, its mingled artillery of Heaven and Earth — Webster and Kearney dead, South Mountain with its stubble hillside, burning September sun, and its gallant Reno!"

At another time, Miss Barton said, "Friends — had this our late contest been an ordinary war, by which we had merely acquired new territory, established a disputed boundary, settled a feud, retaliated an insult, or secured the uncertain claim of some aspiring ruler, tho' it had been waged at its own fearful cost, it were, perhaps, even now, before the graves are green, time to stop speaking of it, put the subject aside for a whistle so dearly bought — we could not afford to blow it — and to be forever laid away — as a memento of our inexperience and folly.

"But ours has been no ordinary war. We have no more territory. Our boundaries are not changed. All insults and injuries avenged have been the outgrowth, rather than the cause of war. And it is a great public question if the position of our chief ruler has been strengthened beyond that of his predecessors.

" Notwithstanding all this, and although it has cost three thousand millions of treasure and 300,000 noble lives still we can afford not only to blow whistles, but to sound golden trumpets from the four corners of our free land, till their notes ring out against the blue dome of Heaven.

"Europe makes war, and deluges her land in blood, and but for the morning and evening Bulletin, and the rise of a few articles of import, we, as a nation should never know it.

" But our recent contest — tho' but the struggle of an infant, as compared with hers — rattled the moss grown stones of her old ivied towers. She has looked well to her household since, added new space to her chariot of Liberty, and new speed to her car of progress.

"Still, it is not abroad, that the great work of our war was accomplished, but at home, among our own people, and it has been confined to no class, or condition, color, or sex. All have been touched and taught by it, and so far-reaching are its effects, so great must be the results, that as yet, it is scarcely possible to commence an estimate.

"Thus in speaking of the war, so far from regarding my subject as *old*, I feel that it is so *new*, so *crude* and *undeveloped*, that I am unable to grasp, and clearly comprehend even its first pages, much less to do it justice.

"As I reflect upon the mighty and endless changes which must grow out of its issues, the subject rises up before me like some far-away mountain summit, towering peak above peak — rock above rock — that human foot has never trod, and enveloped in a hazy mist, the eye has never penetrated.

"A hazy subject you may suggest — Ay! hazy, indeed, and please bear in mind that I do not attempt to make it clear.

"*That,* — time and the great breath of the Almighty, as he issues his mandates of power to coming generations — can alone accomplish.

"I said that the result of our late contest has been confined to no class, or condition, color or sex, — not only have all been touched and taught by it, but all have been strengthened and advanced.

"In the whole work, there has been no step backward, and there is to be none.

"We cannot always hold our great ship of state out of the storms and breakers. She must meet and buffet with them. Her timbers must creak in the gale. The waves must wash over her decks; she must lie in the trough of the sea as she does to-day. But the stars and stripes are above her. She is freighted with the hopes of the world. God holds the helm; and she's coming into port.

"The weak must fear, the timid tremble, but the brave and stout of heart will work, and hope and trust."

Miss Barton's hope grew with the years that America had seen its last war. Her ardent prayer was that her race might never have to go through again what she had seen it go through. In August, 1904, at the G.A.R. Convention after watching in Boston a living play of thousands of school children she passionately wrote: "Who could repress the hope that great as the record of martial glory that glorious banner bears, among that throng of child patriots there might be those who would live to see the last blood stain fade from its beautiful folds.

Peace to our land forevermore

Clara Barton

"All wars involve injustice," she concluded one day in 1909 after a conversation with us. "Wars are a gain to only a few, they're a drain upon the people."

As I spoke of the coming war, the old gleam filled her eyes again, till washed with tears.

"What of the increasing flotillas of battleships and dreadnoughts?" I inquired.

Her voice grew almost awful in its deep prophetic reproof. "Each one," she said, "is a menace to the peace of the world. With each new battleship every nation carries a chip on its shoulder. No! We've done with war. Let us struggle for peace. Peace is the question now, — no longer w-a-r-r!"

And in the deep rise and fall of her voice rolling out that last word — w-a-r-r, I saw the past rise before her like a dream. I felt the shrift of all the pleading pathos of her life.

CHAPTER XXXIX

The Religion of Clara Barton

"Inasmuch as ye have done it unto one of the least of these my brethren, ye have done it unto me."

"I never in my life," declared Miss Barton, "performed a day's work at the field that was not grounded on that one little sentence, and that it did not come to me hourly till kindly sleep brought relief to both body and mind."

While her religion was real, it was thus a thing expressed not in words or creeds, but almost wholly in deeds. Her creed fulfilled Tennyson's standard

"The creed of creeds, — the loveliness of perfect deeds."

This is well expressed in the midst of a camp of nurses and doctors of the Red Cross Campaign at the conclusion of the Yellow Fever epidemic in Florida when she exclaimed, — "Few camp meetings ever came nearer to the heart of Him who offered his life a ransom, and went about doing good."

Amid all branching out of her investigations into twilight zones of religious experiment, she never left the tap roots of her old faith which held her grounded. Perhaps the nearest she came to a statement of her belief in words is found in a letter to Judge A. W. Terrell of Austin, Texas, written from Glen Echo, April 2, 1911, only a year before her death.

"I suppose I am not what the world denominates a church woman. I lay no claim to it. I was born to liberal views, and have lived a liberal creed. I firmly believe in the divinity of Jesus Christ, the Jesus of Nazareth; in His life and death of suffering to save the world from sin, so far as in His power to do. But it would be difficult for me to stop there and believe that this spark of divinity was accorded

410

to none other of God's creation, who, like the Master, took on the living form, and, like Him, lived the human life."

Human as was her expression of Christianity, her measure was the divine one, and with Christ's standard alone she measured all ideals of mercy.

"Like the Master," was what she said of Julia Ward Howe. To be like the Master was the pattern for herself and for every life she tested. Born Christmas day, the Master's birthday, dying on Friday, the day He was crucified, her ninety years between birth and death partook of "the mind of Christ."

Not sentimentally but practically in unconscious outbursts of real religion, she often declared her Lord's approbation and good will were her one final reward.

What she concluded in an ascription to one of her campaigns of mercy, was felt by her at the end of all. "If also acceptable," she said, "to Him who gave us the courage, protection and strength to perform it, we need care for little more."

To countless people, and to the press of the United States, she herself incarnated a human measure of modern mercy. What one great paper concluded shares the verdict of all when it said:

"She was perhaps the most perfect incarnation of mercy the modern world has known. She became the founder of the most significant and wide-spread philanthropic movement of the age, a movement that already has become an intrinsic part of world civilization. The earth has little need for more religious doctrine or for new prophets. It already has enough sects and creeds to serve it until the conclusion of things. But the earth never can have enough women like Clara Barton, the embodiment of one vital principle of all religion, — love for humanity."

This paragraph from a representative journal in America could be paralleled in effect in two thousand that sought to give her life estimates when she died.

But in religion she never explained away organized effort. Believing in deeds instead of words as she did, she yet recognized the need of churches and the need of the place of organized religion in space and time.

Her conviction of the need of the church is shown in a letter to Mrs. Jennie S. M. Vinton at Oxford, and is thus expressed:

"I am glad to learn by your valued letter of September 5th that the old church of our fathers is about to be refitted and I thank you for the information. It is thoughtful of you to name the facts of the early history of the church which I am happy to corroborate, both by tradition and recollection. My father was present at the ordination sermon of Hosea Ballou (a white-headed boy he seemed). He was one of the pillars of the church. His family came over the hills of extreme North Oxford, five miles every Sunday, to sit in its high pews. When I was a grown young woman it was decided to build the present church, and no body of church people ever worked harder than we. We held fairs, public and home, begged, and gave all but the clothes we wore; we cleaned windows and scrubbed paint after workmen, bought and nailed down carpets, fitted up the parsonage, and received the bride of Rev. Albert Barnes, our first settled pastor. And I carried their first baby to the Christening.

"There are few people there who have memories of harder church work and better church love than I.

"Think this over, dear sister, and remember that I have never lost my love for the old church of my fathers, my family and my childhood.

"Yours fraternally,
"CLARA BARTON."

While her father rocked the cradle of Universalism in Oxford, and Universalists claim her, she was not simply a Universalist. She saw the best in Christian Science, but she was not out and out a Christian Scientist. In 1910 I asked her directly, "Are you a Christian Scientist?" and she replied, "No, I don't know enough to be one or to understand it."

"Do you really take in Christian Science spiritually?" asked a Christian Science friend. "I understand the letter. I cannot take it spiritually," was her answer. It was this friend's conclusion that Miss Barton never grasped the basic principles of Christian Science.

Two Congregational clergymen were asked by her request to voice her great life at the main memorial service at the end, together with Rev. Dr. Schoppe of Worcester, her former Universalist pastor at Oxford and at the time a Christian Science Reader. Yet Clara Barton was not a Congregationalist.

Though not originally a member of an Evangelical church, to individuals she was times innumerable an evangelist. Exemplifying this, Rev. A. B. Beresford of Hamilton, Ohio, in 1912, recalled the following:

"The last time I saw Clara Barton she stood beside an open grave. The grave had received the mortal body of a heart-broken mother. Clara Barton had come from a distant city, and in the midst of a tempest led a young man — that mother's son — to that grave-side. He had been a prodigal. He was maudlin with drink at that funeral hour. She stood holding his arm and refused to have the earth thrown upon the casket until that man had promised to mend his life. He promised; she led him away. He then and there began a new life."

Yet evangelist though she might be, she was very keen against cant, as appears in the following letter in the seventies to a niece:

"Thursday night.

"If one acts with good intentions, believing they are doing rightly, and later, concludes it was unwise or wrong — there is a mistake somewhere, or has been. It may have been in the act, or it may be in the later conclusion, but it is only a mistake, not a sin, you poor little chick.

"Another time when you are requested in prayer meeting to act on a double question, the putter of it mixing up your desire or willingness to stand up before an audience and be made a subject for public prayers, with an act of personal courtesy or discourtesy to himself as to whether you want to hear him or *not*, once leaves you free to vote as you like, and then comes and questions your decision, and asks your reason, — if you feel like answering him at all, — tell him to divide his questions, put one at a time and you will act on each separately. He put two questions together, as a dodge to get all up to be prayed for, thinking and knowing it put everyone in a hard place, as all would see that it was a little impolite not to hasten to accept his offer to come and preach. Oh, how tricky.

"You have done rightly in it all, my dear little girl. When he asked why you did not side with the Lord you answered that you did. That was right and all he could ask for. When he added, 'Then why did you not rise and kneel,' you might tell him you did not understand that request as coming from the Lord, or you should certainly have done so.

"I send you a Banner of Light today. You will find two articles bearing on your subject, — the one a lecture by a good sturdy Briton on Mr. Moody's Sermon on Hell. I think you will read it with interest just now, and every time you get assaulted in public prayer meeting, and followed by men, I should advise you to run home and calm your hysterical nerves by re-reading that lecture from end to end.

"The other longer marked article on 'Revivalism,' is a fine sermon by a sound Unitarian clergyman who does not believe in special Revivals of religion, as gotten up for the occasion, and to fill churches, but thinks religion as being the best part of man's nature will revive itself like all else in nature, and feels that God does not need to be implored to save from endless pain and loss the poor creatures he has made, but believes that if we do our best to enlighten and elevate those around us we do all we are called upon to do in the way of their salvation.

"But read it well and carefully for yourself, or read it again with Ida and 'reason together' about it and see if you can find in your own convictions some justification for the course you are taking with the S.S. There is much to be read, before you decide, much to learn and consider, take time and do it and don't either fall into a trap nor be driven into one. — Selah!

"OLD BYAS."

Notwithstanding such cool discrimination, the impression she created upon humanity was a religious one. At her death in 1912, over two thousand journals in America found human parallels to fail and could only measure her influence by using the spirit-level of religion.

"Has there been one who so truly followed the Divine example and precept?" This question, asked by one, was answered in but one way by all papers. Many other journals denominated her who never so much as professed it, because she was a bearer of the Red Cross to the four ends of the earth, "the world's greatest modern missionary. Her mission was to put great numbers of men and women on their feet and to nurse many hundreds of dying to the better land."

The press of America has ever jealously guarded her reputation from harm, refusing to allow the names of statesmen or warriors whose policy was to destroy, to precède the name of Clara Barton who saved. The Duluth *Herald* in April, 1912, happily voices this distinction:

"Put on one side of the balance the soul of Clara Barton, who gave her life to the relief of soldiers in the field, and who was the animating spirit of a movement that has spread over the battle fields of the world a message of mercy and helpfulness that has soothed the sick, healed the wounded, and cheered the last moments of the dying. Put on the other side of the balance the souls of a thousand statesmen who have coolly plotted wars or conquest and empire, calmly sending men to their death that commercial greed and the sinister ambitions of royal houses might be satisfied.

"Who can doubt how that balance will be judged in the just arbitration of Eternal Justice?

"That one unspotted woman's soul which reflects the glory of the gratitude of afflicted millions shall weigh more than the bloodstained souls of the thousand makers of war who shed the blood and spend the treasure of others — but never their own."

The passion to save was indeed the secret of the power that saved Miss Barton, for it was that which connected her with the Divine current that supplied to her after one crisis, strength to meet another.

One day a friend asked her about her first experiences as an army nurse. "You had done no nursing then, you were frail and unused to the sight of suffering. How could you bear all that you had to see on the battle field and in the hospitals?"

"By forgetting myself utterly," Miss Barton said quietly. "That is the only way. You must never so much as think whether you like it or not, whether it is bearable or not; you must never think of anything except the need and how to meet it. Then God gives the strength and the thing that seemed impossible is done."

Miss Barton never failed to give the glory to God. It was not unusual for her at the end of a relief campaign to hold a praise service. Such was the service held at the successful return of the first expeditions through Turkey after the massacres and famine, in Mohammedan Constantinople. The chorus of "Nearer, My God, to Thee," and "My Country, 'tis of Thee," rolled out through the open windows of the Red Cross Headquarters in Constantinople, and "fell," she said, "on the listening ears of Christians and Moslems alike, and though the tunes were new and strange, all felt that to some one somewhere they meant more than the mere notes of music."

From the first her influence was always indirectly, if not directly, a religious one. Only lately I talked to one of the boys whose life she once tied to the church before the Civil War. "At the time," he said, "Rev. Horace James was the pastor of the Old South Church in Worcester, and later the Çhaplain of the 25th Mass. Infantry. He was very anxious to organize a Band of Hope, an organization of young people then very popular in Scotland.

"George, youngest son of Judge Barton, as well as myself, were members of one of the classes of older boys in the Sunday School; we were given to understand that most of the school were waiting to see what that class would do, while the class was sitting, waiting to see where we stood. Miss Barton knew we were rather indifferent and undecided. She came to us; her talk decided our course. The fall of that year found us two boys members. The Old South Band of Hope was a very active organization when with my parents I left the city for a time."

Miss Barton's path crossed the path of this boy twice afterwards — once, following the battle of the Wilderness when she found him wounded and helped save his life, and later when she was eighty-eight years old and the boy a wounded veteran, when she helped him into the life of the church.

While a good man, religion as an organization had become an artificial thing to him and he had not been to church for years. Miss Barton was the magnet to draw him there. Bending over him from a pulpit where she had spoken she whispered words assuming his habits of churchmanship. This broke the veteran's heart, and from that day, though carrying a living wound, he became a devoted attendant at divine service and at weekly prayer.

Thus did her influence visibly follow a man through life.

Like Dorothea Dix and Florence Nightingale, Clara Barton was an instance of an invalid who conquered and forgot her invalidism. She did it by sensing first one great cause and then another. The world never knew the story of the relapses after a cause released her. In addition to all the outstanding collapses, I cannot find a single winter after 1854 when she left the North on account of chest trouble that she was not, even in Washington or Dansville, threat-ened with throat trouble, or at least attacked by chest pains and pleural symptoms.

Cheerfulness was a leading component of Miss Barton's faith, and it was this characteristic more than medicine that helped her to get well. Her friends and their mental attitude made a tremendous difference. "A merry heart doeth good like a medicine" was her constant insistence. If she saw that she was in any way making any one unhappy even through sympathy for her ills, she was made miserable. Concern for herself did not trouble her so much except when it troubled others, — then she felt that it would kill her.

To such a nature which, though in the midst of pain, preached and practised cheerfulness, the faith of Christian Science was naturally most appealing. But the tenets of Christian Science did not *create* her attitude. It was there, and because it was already in her, she welcomed the accent of the new cult.

An incident which increased Miss Barton's interest in Christian Science is narrated in a letter written from the 1906 Convention of the Scientists:

"What I had expected from that great crowd of twenty to thirty thousand people, was so conspicuous by its absence that it set me thinking. What does this quiet mean? Nothing out of the ordinary had occurred. Everything was so orderly — so much so that the policemen might all have gone to church themselves. But an accident did occur. An automobile — 'a sight-seeing Boston' — filled with visitors, Christian Scientists from different parts of the country, be-came unmanageable, the chauffeur lost control, the car and its living load was overturned at the bottom of an embankment.

"Ah, I reflected, now we will have a proof. I think that right then and there, although unconscious of it at the time, I accepted Christian Science as something better than I had known without having seen its textbook, without ever having heard an argument. But I saw the original in the attitude of those bruised and injured Christian Scien-tists who courteously refused surgical aid, — who, when the pain seemed so great that they must cry out, sang instead."

It was not long after this that Miss Barton sat up half the night to finish reading Mary Baker G. Eddy's "Science and Health." From

2 E

what she had heard from the Christian Science side she felt at first that the founder of the cult was the greatest of geniuses. Yet, while her heart admired, her head held her back from absolute and final commitment to Christian Science. Later, when she heard of Mrs. Eddy's illness and limitations, she was puzzled and could not at first believe the reports. These facts, together with her refusal to follow Christian Science philosophy, which denies the material and human, prohibited a complete going over to the church, as such.

Miss Barton's Oxford pastor, Dr. Schoppe, turned to the Christian Science faith, and it is he who, while he points out that Miss Barton never accepted the denials inherent in the system of the Christian Science philosophy, — yet asserts that she practised the positives.

Miss Barton was very friendly to the growth of Christian Science, as is testified by the following:

"OXFORD, August 26, 1908.

"MY DEAR SCHOPPE:

"So glad this only door has opened for you. I cannot see why more Universalists should not become Scientists. They have so little to change, nothing at all to give up, and the one lacking addition to make. I am so anxious to know how the practice comes to you. It seems to me that it is something that must all the time be getting stronger.

"I felt the loss of the privilege of seeing my pastor in his desk all that last Sunday and longed for the chance to come. I have had such a good summer and autumn, that I shall feel the strings draw early in spring time to taste them again. Oxford people have been lovely to me. I hope to see you.

"C. B."

As late as 1908, when a reporter asked her about Christian Science and told her of the report that she had gone over to its teachings, she said that she did not know enough about Christian Science, as she had only been looking into it about a year and would not dare as yet to give an opinion on so vast a subject.

As proof of this is the fact that she employed doctors up to the time of her death. She in this as elsewhere held to her unalterable conviction of allying herself nominally to no particular creed or denomination of Christians.

Dr. Schoppe, as we have noted, exerted great influence over Miss Barton. He was her pastor in the cradle of the denomination, the Universalist Church in Oxford, and Miss Barton felt much drawn towards his able preaching. He was a widely read man. He him_ self had studied Christian Science doctrines and soon became a healer and the First Reader in Worcester.

Miss Barton was much interested in the step, and being a close neighbor, listened attentively to Dr. Schoppe's mental observations as he felt himself turning to the Christian Science Church. After_ wards, she went to him again and again, sharing the deepest of spiritual confidences.

In a talk with Dr. Schoppe December 17, 1914, he made the fol_ lowing statement ·

"Clara Barton's connecting point with Christian Science was on the positives it accented — not from its negative philosophy. She welcomed its doctrine of the Divine presence of God working with us and in us and working upon her own life, — present to help. She was exceedingly grateful to Christian Science for bringing out this point of the Divine absoluteness.

"Further than that she could not understand it; she could not go. She did not deny but she believed (unlike the Christian Science negativism) in a perfectly vast realm of material and human progress. She traced it in the wonders of geological ages and historical evolution. She saw God's handiwork in a colossal complex material creation. She never could bring herself to believe the material or human creation a mortal error !"

Yet as to absent treatment and answer to prayer, she practiced the one and experienced the other. From Glen Echo December 2, 1909, she wrote the Schoppes — "I am most happy to tell you that I feel that I am restored. I was able to leave my bed and dress yesterday A.M. and am relieved of pain and the resulting soreness is fast disap_ pearing.

"I felt that when my letter could reach you it would be sufficient and that my pain would leave. There was comfort in the faith that was in me. I read 'Science and Health' very conscientiously at all times. To me that book is a great study, so well thought — so well written."

Yet she was absolutely honest, and she qualified the above thus ·

"Thursday morning.

"After writing yesterday evening I regret to say that the pain returned. We had a sudden change of weather! I had a hard night but hope it will, with your good help, pass off during the day."

"Isn't it blessed," she wrote to Mrs. Schoppe, August 26, 1909, "that the way is opening for the relief of the ills of the human race — poor suffering race, how many of our ills we make ourselves.

"There are many things I want to speak with you about. It seems to me I have been waiting for months to do it but I wanted more time than a call or a wee visit.

"I wonder if Mrs. Eddy is in her usual health — there are so many reports — I look upon them all as false, and rejoice to think they are, but what persistence. How worthy a better cause!"

It has sometimes been said that Miss Barton was a friend of the Spiritualists. She manifested, at times, a certain interest in the problem of communications with souls in the Great Beyond. "How often have I wondered, will they know us there," she queried even back in 1871. March 3, 1907, from Glen Echo she wrote to a friend: "They have begun to feel that they have established the fact of spiritual communications between the world of those still living here and those who had passed over. I only hope it is so. What a step between this and the old school Presbyterianism of 50 or 80 years ago."

Spiritualism as well as Christian Science was fully discussed by Miss Barton and Dr. Schoppe and on one occasion the conversation turned to Theodore Parker, who Miss Barton had frequently said was her guide. The nearness of his spirit, she maintained, was a great power to her. Referring to this, Dr. Schoppe said in reply to some question of Miss Barton: "As to the spiritual oneness between you and Theodore Parker there were never two souls braver for humanity's sake. For community of interest for human kind, I could easily yoke you up in the spirit with Theodore Parker. But who was Theodore Parker's guide? — God. Then why isn't it so that you too have him as your guide, direct?

"You believe that God is a Divine Immanence. You believe that God is now communicating Himself to humanity and that his loving Presence is here now as ever. Why, then, can't you call up a direct relationship rather than going around through the uncertain illusions of Theodore Parker?

"Moreover, you have admitted that you have found your little affairs sometimes troubled you and you had gotten mixed up. If you were relying on Theodore Parker, he could not have been a helpful guide."

At the end of Dr. Schoppe's narration to me of Miss Barton's questioning attitude and partial sympathy for spiritual communication, he turned to me and said, "So far as I know in all my conferences with her, she never had recourse to mediums."

But in one place in her private letters, I have found a beautiful consciousness of her father's nearness which it may be well to present as the kind of rational spiritualism upon which she verged, but to which, beyond this she never wholly gave herself. It is a letter written to her niece two years after the death of her father:

"WASHINGTON, D.C. Mar. 15, 1863.

"DEAR MAMIE: "Sunday night.

"My darling little girl:

"It was very kind in you to write me such a nice letter, and say such good things of poor 'Grandpa.' I am glad you remember him in his grave, and in Heaven, not that 'Grandpa' would be lonely if you came, because I think his spirit would be just as near you here as there, but it looks kind, and good to remember him where he is laid. I know that you place flowers on his grave for I have been told so, and I think 'Gramp' knows up in Heaven that his little Mamie loves and cares for him. Do you remember the night but one before he went and left us when you promised to 'remember and love him always.' Grandpa was happier for that promise, he was afraid his little girl would forget him, but she never will, I am sure, and she will always be the good girl she promised him she would be, and finally go to 'Gramp' in Heaven.

"I know poor 'Gramp' went out when it seemed to us that he would have been better in the house, but you must not reproach yourself for it, my dear little girl, because if God had not wanted and intended to take him up to Heaven then he would have spared him without our help. It was time to go and we could not save him, and I think he is far happier than he would have been here, and he has no pain, and no sickness, and nothing troubles him now, and if he knows anything of this cruel war, he knows better than we do what it is for, and when it will end. God takes care of 'Gramp' as he always did, so don't you trouble or grieve more about it now, darling, for it is all right.

"Sometime when your papa is here you must come and see him and me, and we will talk a great deal about poor 'Gramp.'"

While as to its extent this question of the twilight zone of inter-communication with the departed was a problem, the Beyond was no problem. It was to her a great certitude, a near fact. On the threshold of her Oxford home one of the last times we were talking together of immortality. Never did a soul so crave the meat of the thought, nor feed more upon its truth. In this she was indeed a "partaker of the Divine Nature." "O let us have more," she cried wistfully, before she closed the door, — "do let us have more."

"As the Leaves Fall"

CHAPTER XL

"*LET ME GO! LET ME GO!*"

APRIL 12, 1912

"As the leaves fall, how fast one's friends fall with them and the nations are called to give up their best. England has given up her Florence Nightingale, Switzerland her Dunant and her Moynier, the pillars of the Red Cross, and America our beloved Julia Ward Howe. Rich contributions these to that other world! They had made the most of this and take their gathered wealth of culture, intelligence, integrity, goodness, Christian fortitude, justice and faith to lay on the shrine of that other world, a tribute to the possibilities of this. Great souls they were. God's own children. I am lonesome when I think of them as gone out of my life, but glad when I feel how much richer and more ample that other field to which they must have gone. "CLARA BARTON."

IN the autumn of 1910, upon a crumpled postal card, two years before her own passing, Clara Barton wrote me these inspiring words. Before this year of 1910 her own illnesses she had not only conquered but spurned.

"Until that work is done," she said of one of the latest zones of service — "I cannot go to Heaven!" This was her reason for living. Of age itself she was apparently independent, never thinking herself, or letting others think of it, as a crutch to send her limping down the avenues of time.

As to the "eternal attack of the 90th birthday," she wrote me in 1911:

"Notwithstanding the much and more that is said of 'age' and all the stress laid upon it, I could never see and have never been able to understand how it comes to be any business of ours. We have surely no control over its beginning, and unless criminally, none over its ending. We can neither hasten or arrest it, and how it is a matter of individual commendation I have never been able to see. I have been able to see painfully that the persistent marking of dates and adding one milestone every year has a tendency to increase the burden of 'age' and encourages the feeling of helplessness and release from activities, which might still be a pleasure to the possessor. I have given the exact age as recorded, lest I be suspected of trying to conceal it, but I have never, since a child, kept a 'birthday' or thought of it only as a reminder by others.

"Somehow it has come to me to consider strength and activity aided so far as possible by right habits of life, as forming a more correct line of limitation than the mere passing of years."

We recall that almost every winter of her life she had conquered attacks of the cold upon her system.   From these she recovered, but during them she suffered much in chest and throat and voice.   Frequently in the winter season she had to stay shut in.   Occasionally we hear of these struggles, but where she could, she preferred to suffer in silence, as shown in the following:

" November 29, 1908.

"To Mrs. and Mr. Schoppe,:

"I have taken a cold that has settled itself on the nerves of the body and is giving me severe neuralgia pains.   There does not seem to be a nerve from the shoulders to the hips that has not been tried.

"It will, I presume, wear off in time, after a manner, but I do not want its dregs left, and I feel like telling you of it, if perchance your good thoughts could aid.

"Perhaps you can make out enough of this to get my meaning.   I am not very strong, nor steady, to-day.

"Yours affectionately,
"Clara Barton."

By the summer her energies had generally risen again to full tide. This rise of physical power continued as is proven by her 2000 mile trip to Chicago and back in the summer of 1910, a journey followed by her trip to Boston to officiate as President of the First Aid Society.

The five years devoted to the founding of the First Aid Society were to interest her much, but great as the interest, the spread of the work was a matter of instruction and secretarial work.   No fields were offered to arouse her peculiar latent energies.   Nevertheless she gave to it her advice and it was her loyal determination to do this in person in June, 1910, that brought on her fatal attacks.

Of this she wrote Mrs. Schoppe, July 12, 1910: "I reached here in the early June days, but alas, a cold storm of almost sleet, and an exposure which, as a traveler, I could not avoid, had met me in New York, and I reached Oxford unable to speak, and with these conditions to be gotten rid of, I went like a mummy, to Boston for six hours (officially). After that, it (the attack of sickness) had to come to me."

She left Oxford in August, 1910. As midwinter drew on at Glen Echo to which she returned, double pneumonia developed, which she bravely fought off.

"It is an attack of pneumonia and you have but one chance of recovery," said her physician. "Then I shall take that chance," she said.

A letter post-marked Glen Echo, Md., from Dr. J. B. Hubbell, February, 1911, also informs us that "She had been very ill. She had worked excessively — almost continuously since her return from Oxford — often declining one of her two meals a day because it made her sleepy and drowsy — thus interfering with desk work and her correspondence.

"Then came the news of the sudden death of a favorite niece in Worcester, Mrs. Riccius. The shock was too much for her weakened strength. Her heart fluttered and nearly stopped.

"An attack of bronchitis with lung congestion followed close on this bad news." Of this her nephew writes me in February, 1911:

"DEAR SIR:

"I am Miss Barton's nephew, and am endeavoring to respond to some of her most urgent correspondence that has lain unanswered for a fortnight, owing to her very serious illness, which occurred about ten days ago. There has been no public mention of it and I doubt if she would care to have it known, although for a week past we have almost despaired of her recovery. The ailment was Bronchitis and Pneumonia, but with the best of skill and nursing I am pleased to say that to-day she shows encouraging signs of recovery, although she is yet exceedingly weak.

"You might make such judicious use of the information as your judgment dictates with Miss Barton's friends.

"She will doubtless answer the two questions which you ask in your letter, when she is recovered sufficiently.

"As to the Memorial Day suggestion, I believe that if her health and the weather permit, she will go to Massachusetts in time to take part as you have proposed to honor her; I should certainly encourage her doing so, if her condition will allow, and I earnestly hope it will."

Recovering from this attack Miss Barton herself writes to Mrs. Reed in April:

"MY DEAREST SISTER HARRIETTE:

"To all others I send a mere card, for I have not yet arrived to the dignity of letters, but dear sister Harriette's troubled eyes are not to strain them over fine writing from me, and I must send a line to tell her that all is well, and that I am well. Not strong, but I must 'wait a wee' for that.

"Our warmer days are coming and I go out a little every day — all I spare the time for. You wonder what can occupy me? No wonder you do; you could not believe without seeing, but 'seeing is believing.' I lost two and a half months time, entire, but the time went on and spun its web each day. In the first days when I wasn't very sharp, I think, a bevy of reporters got access, and some word went out that I was ill. (You know, dear Harriette, how I would have withheld it, if I had been captain in charge) but it went and set the country, nay, the world, by the ears, and the letters came pouring in by the score, yes, and more. Two clerks could not have handled them, they say, and all the house, with doctor and trained nurses were busy with me; and what to do but for the poor doctor to open the drawers in my big mammoth desk and tumble them in unopened, each day as they came. Of course, he tried his hand at just a few that must be spoken of, and so it went on through the months. Day before yesterday (I had been card dealing with present mails, for a week or ten days) he unlocked the desk drawers and handed me the keys.

"You can imagine what met my gaze. Yesterday, I opened, read and registered or noted eighty and was tired.

"To-day I have not commenced, but will later. Such beautiful letters! I read them through the tears. What will I do with them? Lying there two months in mystic silence, you ask? The Lord knows, and alone can direct me. I have neither clerk, typewriter, nor reader; but this is what occupies me. I don't know what, now, how many, but they are far in the hundreds.

"I see almost no callers. I did see your lovely friend, Mrs. Gen. Pickett. Doctor is filling his houses with tenants, and getting more lots. Miss Bissell sees that we have something to eat; Mr. Lewis is here, as man about the house and stable.

"I still aristocratically eat by myself and look a little after chamber work. A good washer, ironer and sweeper every other week. How tired you must be of this humdrum recital."

At Easter in acknowledging a cluster of double violets, she announced that she was well again after this manner.

"Oh, the ravishing beauty of this great cluster of double violets; so purple, so royal; so full of kindly thoughtfulness never failing, never waning. What do they ask of me? That I send my heart's thanks and say that I am well again and my prayer is for the best of all blessings for the dear ones at Adams Square.

"As always,
"C. B."

The heat of Washington was soon to draw her north. She writes Mrs. Reed:

"DEAREST, DEAREST SISTER HARRIETTE:
"You see I am at my old trick — sending out *printed* letters — but I hope they are better than none.

"I can only add that I am getting stronger and will hope to see you some day — not yet. All is well here. We are all by ourselves. Mrs. Hinton was with us a few weeks, but has gone north. Our hot wave passed and no other has yet come to take its place.

"I do hope dear sister Mary is better.

"Doctor is sending off a few hundred of these printed circulars to acknowledge the unread letters of last spring, in my illness. I hope it will do.

"Don't mind answering this; keep cool and rest and we will meet some day.

"If it gets too hot here, I may have to flee north, if I can.
"Send love to all,
"CLARA."

In July, accompanied by her nephew, Mr. Stephen Barton, she came to Oxford, her last trip to her home town.

In September, 1911, to give rest to immediate rumors, Stephen Barton, hoping against hope, issued the following statement to the press:

"The recent newspaper accounts of Miss Clara Barton's condition have been inaccurately misleading and non-authorized. Because it is due to her legion of friends and to herself, I make this statement to reassure them. She is not at the point of death. She is not attended by two physicians and two nurses. Her most intimate friends know that such attendance would be more likely to prove fatal than of benefit. Her attending physician is a close family relation, Dr. Byron Stone, of Oxford. She has one faithful competent nurse, Miss Henrietta Eldridge, of Philadelphia.

"When one contemplates Miss Barton's eventful life, her mental attainments during one half century; her constant labor day after day, without rest or recreation, as we know it, the hardship and privation to which she has submitted herself during the long years since the first day of the Civil War, in her labor for the relief of human suffering, it is a remarkable thing in history that she still lives.

"Only her simple mode of life, free from all excesses, excepting labor, and supported by an unusually strong constitution and will power has sustained her.

"The nearly fatal sickness of last winter from pneumonia left her with some of its ill effects. Her appetite and digestion are normal. The former is simple, the latter good. All her organs are pronounced good by Dr. Stone of Oxford, and Dr. Pratt of Glen Echo, and are performing their functions properly.

"Long years of constant work and the sickness of last winter have caused a slight weakness in the muscular action of her heart, which she is inclined to aggravate in her desire to attend, as usual, to her great correspondence and numerous visitations of friends. Our aim and effort is to restrain her from these.

"Her intellect was never keener, clearer, more alert than now. She has the deepest appreciation and gratitude for the sympathy, affection and solicitude of her many friends and admirers, and has only Christian forgiveness for others.

"Six weeks ago Miss Barton made the journey with me from Glen Echo to Oxford in the ordinary way, with no ill effects. Since her arrival here she has somewhat overtaxed herself.

"Yesterday I spent two hours with her in our customary old time way in conversation, in the transaction of business, household, liter_ary, and personal affairs.

"At Galveston, in 1900, her physician told me that she could live only a few hours. She overheard him and whispered to me, 'I shall not die. Don't let them frighten you.'

"At Glen Echo last winter her physician told me she had but one chance of recovery. She replied, 'Then I will take that chance.'

"Yesterday she was considering with me whether she might take the risk of spending the winter with us at her Oxford home instead of returning to the less rigorous climate of Glen Echo.

"No report concerning Miss Barton's health should be credited unless authorized by Dr. Stone or myself in Massachusetts, or Dr. Hubbell, Dr. Pratt, or Dr. Underhill, in Glen Echo." — STEPHEN E. BARTON.

This fall of 1911 was her last autumn on earth and her good-by visit to her beloved Oxford. It was here that I met her for the last time. Her very close friend, Professor Charles Sumner Young, of Los Angeles, was at the time visiting her. By him she sent for me to come to see her. But my hopeful expectations suffered a disappointment, for in place of the great soul, expectant of years on earth, it fell upon me that I was holding with her an audience of death.

It was not that Miss Barton was not cordial. She was — but all was so different. It was more like a visitation with some one in eternity. She seemed already adjusted to a place beyond the mortal. Her playful, buoyant spirit was gone. The dignity of last things charged the atmosphere.

Miss Barton, I plainly saw, had not received the usual reinvigoration of former summers in New England. She remained sitting — a thing not like her custom at all. Her voice, always deep, was not merry and light hearted, but stately and measured — keyed to a solemnity not mortal. It was pitched low — It was her battle voice stirred to the depths.

Mr. Young had just returned from the burial knoll at North Oxford where he had gone at Miss Barton's request to attend to the details of the last resting place for her body. They had been talking it over together before I came. I could see little, hear little — so shocked and grieved was I at Miss Barton's evident will to go. An immortal

hope was in her gaze and in her soul. She looked over us, not at us.
Her mind was fixed beyond things of this earth and she was not
looking forward with dread. Once before, contemplatively, she had
said:

"Nature has provided a cure and final rest for all the heartaches
that mortals are called to endure."

She felt this rest very near.

We are told by Mr. Francis Atwater that some years before, the
monument had been placed as Miss Barton desired: "The family
lot was added to and the ground prepared with great forethought.
She attended to every detail of this herself. Hundreds of loads of
dirt and soil were carted in and underneath it was placed bushels of
salt, the moisture of which will keep the grass green when otherwise
it would dry up. In life she did everything thoroughly. What more
natural than she should want to know her last resting-place should be
in order when the Master called?"

At this last interview I realized with a shock that humanity's
merciful little mother, Clara Barton, had determined that it was her
time to go and that her soul was resigned soon to leave her body in
the burial place by the side of her father's.

She never had planned to rest at Arlington in which are buried so
many who, compared with her, are absolutely unknown. Like Florence Nightingale, who refused Westminster Abbey, Clara Barton
put this honor away from her. She never even had herself enrolled
as a registered army nurse, the necessary prerequisite to such a burial,
and so she never had planned to magnify the God's acre of soldiers
with her own grave.

Her plan was rather to be buried with her dear ones on the beautiful
hill crest near her old home close by the great pines of the Oxford
forest, alone in the heart of the old Commonwealth of her fathers.

Soon after this Miss Barton decided that instead of remaining for
the winter in Massachusetts it would be wiser to make the journey
back to Washington and Glen Echo. With her nephew she made
the trip.

Those of us who saw her go were convinced that she would never
return, for we saw that she did not plan to live.

As the months rolled on towards the last one she still called her
friends to her.

"I visited her at Christmas time on her ninetieth birthday," de_clared Francis Atwater. "We talked several hours of the things that had been done, the people who had passed away during our acquaintance and our own private affairs. She knew she had but a short time to live, but if her strength would not permit of further usefulness, she was ready to go. She was glad she was born at such a period when it seemed to her people were more honorable and there was more distinctive character. On this occasion she said she had regarded me as a younger brother, and it had been a source of great satisfaction to know that when she needed the counsel and advice of a confidential friend I had always left my business to serve her and she wanted me to know she could not have appreciated and thought more of me had I been her brother."

At Christmas she sent the world this message: "Please deliver for me a message of Peace and Good Will to all the world for Christmas. I am feeling much better to-day and have every hope of spending a pleasant and joyful Christmas when I shall celebrate my ninetieth birthday."

After Christmas hope alternated with fear and the old enemy — double pneumonia — again appeared.

In February her nephew telegraphed

"I am overjoyed to tell you that I found my aunt apparently much stronger than when I left her a week ago. Dr. Hubbell says she will recover. He expects her to be able to dictate some letters this sum-mer — of course he is hopeful and sanguine beyond what others might be. There is some little swelling in her feet but she seems more hope-ful herself and she certainly does sleep much better. Anyway, I am happy over her apparent improvement and I hope it is real and lasting. The whole household is filled with hope, whereas it was fear two weeks ago."

But in March she was sinking:

"I was with my aunt a week," Mr. Barton writes, "during which time she was very ill, except the last few days. I'm going there again to-night for the balance of this week. A card from Dr. Hubbell this morning says that her improvement has not continued since I left. I will write you from there."

On Palm Sunday, she was still living and very sensible of the deep concern of her legions of friends.

A large congregation of "the old guard," veterans of the 21st, and others, gathered in the Adams Square Congregational Church in Worcester. At a service in her honor they sent her this Palm Sunday telegram, read at the mass meeting by Commander Hubbard:

"To Miss Clara Barton,
    "Glen Echo, Maryland.

"On Palm Sunday, in the name of the great Cross Bearer who victoriously on this day ascended the heights of suffering and conquered, we send you Easter greetings from the G. A. R., Women's Relief Corps and citizens of Worcester.

"Their prayer is that you, who have borne the Red Cross for unestimated thousands in the United States and the world, may likewise conquer through the strength of the Everlasting Arms."

This brought from her bedside the following message through her nephew Stephen: —

"To Mr. George Booth,
    "Editor of the Gazette.

"Sir: Having just returned from one of my frequent visits to my aunt, Miss Clara Barton, at Glen Echo, Maryland, I beg to take this first opportunity to thank you in her name and for myself, also to extend our thanks to the members of the G. A. R. and the public, for the service in her honor on Palm Sunday, at the Adams Square church, and the excellent account of the same given in the Gazette.

"The telegram sent to Miss Barton by Commander Hubbard was exceedingly gratifying to her. I read the message to her and sent the original to her Royal Highness, Louise, Grand Duchess of Baden, to whom I was writing at the time, in my aunt's behalf. They have been most intimate and confidential friends for 42 years and it gave my aunt great pleasure to forward to the Grand Duchess such a beautiful message of respect and esteem.

"I am pleased to say while the condition of Miss Barton's health is very discouraging, her mental condition is as active and clear as at any time in her life, and her wonderful physical power of recuperation gives us hope of her possible recovery. She does not suffer physical pain. Her long confinement is very trying to her.

                                "Yours very truly,
                                    "Stephen E. Barton."

BURIAL PLACE OF CLARA BARTON AT NORTH OXFORD
The Red Cross and Flag mark her grave.

With her in her renewed fight for life vibrated the heart strings of hundreds of thousands of the American people. The veterans throughout the land suffered with her. Representative of all, is the tribute that was sent to her bedside from the Grand Army of the Republic of New York by General George B. Loud, Commander:

"From the hearts of 4000 Civil War Veterans in the great empire state goes up a prayer to the great white throne for the recovery of the woman — yourself — whose sublimest work for suffering humanity has never been paralleled anywhere in the civilized world to-day."

But her own thoughts these last days were seldom upon herself — As always, they were centered upon others' suffering and upon the field of their relief.

Toward the last she often spoke of dreaming that she was again on the battle field. April 10, two nights before she died, she opened her eyes and said:

"*I dreamed I was back in battle. I waded in blood up to my knees. I saw death as it is on the battle field. The poor boys with arms shot off and legs gone, were lying on the cold ground, with no nurses and no physicians to do anything for them. I saw the surgeons coming, too much needed by all to give special attention to any one. Once again I stood by them and witnessed those soldiers bearing their soldier pains, limbs being sawed off without opiates being taken, or even a bed to lie on. I crept around once more, trying to give them at least a drink of water to cool their parched lips, and I heard them at last speak of mother and wives and sweethearts, but never a murmur or complaint. Then I woke to hear myself groan because I have a stupid pain in my back, that's all. Here on a good bed, with every attention! I am ashamed that I murmur!*"

Two days after, at 9 o'clock in the morning, not as to end life but as if to fly to new fields of service, she breathed her *last* — crying out: "Let me go! — Let me go!"

2 F

INDEX

Alsops Ferry, engagement at, 91.
Amen, the, of the war, 102.
Ames, Miss Eleanor, 24.
Andersonville Prison, 113.
Antietam, Battle of, 54.
Antiquity, Worcester Society of, 5.
Appia, Dr. Lewis, 138, 139, 142.
Aquia Creek, Va., 92.
Armenian Massacres in 1892, 276, 348.
Atwater, Dorrance, at Andersonville, 116.

Baden, Grand Duchess of, 136, 137, 154, 251;
Grand Duke of, 157, 251.
Baker, Gen. Edward D., 33.
Ballou, Rev. Hosea, 7.
Baltimore, April 19, 1861, 29.
Bancroft, George, 7.
Barton, Clara, Birth and Birthrights, 1-4;
her father and mother, 5; her teachers,
9-11; "The Story of my Childhood," 11;
a nurse at eleven, 12, 13; her timid
sensitiveness, 14-17; teacher, eighteen
years a, 18-23; in Washington for five
years before the war, 24-27; Bull Run,
on the field of second, 39; "Harper's
Ferry, not a moment to be lost," 48;
a new call, "Please take the bullet out
for me," 57; "They will fight again, can
you go?" 60; Rappahannock, crosses
the river under fire, 69; "You saved my
life," 74; Charleston, S. C., near death at
siege of, 79; appointed Superintendent of
Nurses, Army of the James, 90; Petersburg Mine, her midnight ride to, 99;
a four-year search for missing men, 110-
121; appointed "official correspondent
of friends of Paroled Prisoners," 113;
is recognized by 37th Congress, 118;
"I want every one to hear her," — John
B. Gough, 121; at Geneva, Switzerland,
124; the Grand Duchess of Baden calls,
136; goes to Basle, Swiss Red Cross Hd.

Qrs., 138; "First time in my life was a
prisoner," 154; Paris, enters with her com-
panion afoot and alone, 164; advent and
Christmas with the war-torn poor, 176;
Strassburg, Christmas fête to her helpers
in, 182; tours in Italy and the Isle of
Wight, 190; sick in England, nervous
prostration, 203; her emblems and decorations, 218, 348; foundation of the Red
Cross in America, 226; Geneva (1884)
International Congress, a delegate to, 245;
Emperor and Empress of Germany, Bismarck and Von Moltke, she meets, 251;
Orient, January, 1897, starts for the, 277;
"We know you, Miss Barton," was her
greeting at Constantinople by the Turkish
Minister, 278; Cuba and the War with
Spain, she goes to, 282; Blanco, Gen., has
long interview with him, 285, 286; U.S.
battleship the Maine, she visits the, 286;
the U. S. S. Maine, her story of the
destruction of, 286, 287; "Take no
chances," the U. S. Government cables
her, 288; Santiago, she reaches, 294;
Siboney, her letter from, 300; "Her
retirement," 328; in her home, Oxford,
Mass., 352; Washington, D. C., 357, 358;
Dansville, N. Y., 359; Glen Echo, Md.,
363; straw bonnet, her first, made by
herself, 356; inventing first Portland
match, by neighbor, 356; spooling thread,
she assists at, 356; "Her social traits,"
377, 378; "Gen. Sherman was right,"
397; "Her Religion," 410-422; "Let
me go! Let me go!" 423-433.
Barton, David (her brother), 6, 10, 11, 86;
Dorothy (her sister), 6, 9, 212; Mathew,
1; Sarah Stone (her mother), 5; Sally
(her sister), 6, 9, 222; Samuel, 1; Stephen
(her grandfather), 2; Stephen (her father),
3; Stephen (her brother), his prayer,
104-108; Stephen E. (her nephew), at

435

age of 14 he entered the service, 86, 87; goes to Cuba on Supply Ship *Texas*, 284; assists at the 1900 Galveston Flood, 319; Rev. William E. (a cousin), 386.
Barton, Hartford County, N. C., 103.
Battle Hymn of the Republic, 33.
Battles, at Bennington, Vt., 8.

Civil War, 1861–1865

Antietam, 59; Ball's Bluff, 33; Bull Run, 1861, 33; Bull Run and Chantilly, 1862, 36–47; Cedar Mountain, 34; Charleston, the siege of, 77; South Mountain, 52; Crampton Gap, 52; Fair Oaks, 34; Fredericksburg, 66; Groveton, Va., 36; Harper's Ferry, 48, 60, 64; Manassas, 36; Peninsular, 31; Petersburg Mine, 99; Richmond, before, 109; Spottsylvania, 91; Wilderness, 91.

Franco-Prussian War, 1869–1870

Weissenburg and Saarbrücken, 142; Metz, Sedan and Strassburg surrender, 156, 157; siege of Paris and the Commune, 164.
Belle Plain, 92.
Bellows, Rev. Dr. Henry, 124, 227.
Bennington, Battle of, 8.
Berne, Switzerland, 132.
Blackwell, Elizabeth, 20.
Blanco, Gen., she has long interview with, 285, 286.
Bolton, Mrs. James R., *née* Sheldon, 136.
Breckenridge, Henry, Secretary of War, his address at laying of corner stone of Red Cross building, March 25, 1915, 332.
Brown, J. Stewart, 29.
Buchanan, President James, 26.
Bull Run, 1861, 33; and Chantilly, 36–47.
Burnside, Gen. Ambrose, 54, 91.
Butler, Gen. Benj. F., his brigade, 30; Department of the James, 90, 99; he appoints Miss Barton Superintendent Women's Prison, Sherburn, Mass., 240.

Cedar Mountain, 35.
Chantilly and Second Bull Run, 36–47.
Childs, Annie E., 84, 160, 165.
Childs, Miss Fannie, *née* Vassall, see "letter while abroad," 21.
Church, Oxford Congregational, 2; First Universalist, 7.

Cleveland, U. S. President Grover, he appoints her delegate to (1887) Conference at Carlsruhe, Germany, 250.
Clinton (N. Y.) Liberal Institution, 20.
Cometti, Lady Anna Pasteris, 89.
Commission, Christian, 94.
Convention of Geneva, 128.
Coolidge, Dr., Medical Inspector, 34.
Craven, Dr., Medical Purveyor, 83.

Dahlgren, Admiral James Adolf, replaces Admiral Du Pont, 77.
Dana, Jonathan, 18.
Davis, Mrs. Shumway, 18.
Devens, Gen. Charles, 33.
Dewitt, Alexander, 25.
Dix, Miss Dorothea, 90; hers the first name honored, 402.
Dolfus, Mons. August, President International Red Cross of Mülhausen, 145.
Dolfus, Madam, 145.
Dunant, Mons. Henri, a Swiss gentleman, 125; his paper, "A Souvenir of Solferino," 347.
Dunn, Dr., of Conneautville, Pa., 55.
Du Pont, Admiral Samuel Francis, at siege of Charleston, S. C., 77.
Dyson, Joseph M., 29.

Elwell, Col. J. S., Chief Q. M., Dept. of the South, 81, 82; J. K. (his nephew), goes to Cuba with Miss Barton, 284; his visits to the wreck of the U. S. S. *Maine*, 287.
Emancipation Proclamation, 75.

Fair Oaks, Battle of, 34.
Fales, Mrs., 38.
Falmouth, at the Lacy House, 65.
Ferguson, George, 21.
Florence Nightingale, 125, 208.
Fort Sumter, 28.
Franco-Prussian War, 123; the cause, 132.
Franklin, Gen. William Buel, 52.
Fredericksburg, a winter campaign at, 64.

Galveston, the 1900 flood — first aid to the injured, 319.
Geneva, the Convention of, 124; Treaty of, 126; International Congress at, 126; President of United States signs treaty of, 241.
Germany, King William of, 132.

Gillmore, Gen. Q. A., at siege of Charleston, 77.
Glen Echo, Md., her late home, 236.
Golay, Eliza, of Geneva, Switzerland, 102.
Gough, John B., "I want every one to hear her," 121.
Grand Duchess of Baden, 136, 137, 154; now Her Imperial Highness, 178, 252.
Grant, Gen. Ulysses S., "the great Captain," 90.
Gregg, the siege of Fort, 77.
Grout, Willie (The Vacant Chair), 33.
Groveton, Va., engagement at, 36.

Hale, Rev. Edward Everett, 9; "Who is that old tramp," 343.
Hall, J. Brainerd, at the Wilderness, 91, 97.
Hall, Dr. Lucy M., delegate (1887) International Congress, 250.
Hamilton, Charley, an old friend she finds wounded, 39.
Hamilton, Mrs. Margaret, President Association of Army Nurses, 74.
Hammond, Dr. William A., Surgeon General U. S. A., 34.
Hancock, Gen. Winfield S., U. S. Army, 91.
Harper's Ferry and South Mountain, 48, 60, 64.
Harrison, Wm. Henry, President U. S. (Old Tippecanoe), 3.
Heintzelman, Gen. Samuel P., U. S. Army, 43.
Hooker, Gen. Joseph (Fighting Joe), 36, 54.
Horr, U. S. Marshal John F., calls for aid, 290.
Howe, Mrs. Julia Ward (Battle Hymn of the Republic), 33.
Hubbell, Dr. Julian B., Red Cross Field officer, 237; is sent to International Conference at Rome, 272; goes to Riga, Turkey, 271; at Alexandretta, Turkey, 278; off for Key West with supplies, in War with Spain, 289.
Huguenot settlers, 2.
"Hungry? not very, but Annie is," 120.

Indians, the Nipmuc, 2.
Interior Department, the Patent Office and the Secretary of, 25.
International Congress of 1864, 125; Red Cross, 124.

Jennings, Miss Janet, receives descriptive letter from Cuba, 300.
Johnson, Hugh, Miss Barton answers his call for Mary, 40, 42.

Kearney, Gen. Philip, at second Bull Run, 36, 38.

Lacy House, at Falmouth, Va., 65.
Learned, Col. Ebenezer, 2.
Lee, Gen. Robert E., C. S. A., 90.
Letters Miss Barton wrote while abroad Lyons (1871) to Miss Annie Childs, 160, 166; Mrs. Fannie Childs Vassall, 163; Paris, 390; London (1872), 198; (1873), 203; Belfort (1871), to her sister, 176; Carlsruhe (1872), 181; touring Italy, 190; London, 200; Isle of Wight, 199; Baden-Baden (1887), 251; to Mrs. Mamie Stafford, London (1873), 206; (1887), 255; Paris, 254.
Lincoln, President Abraham, calls for troops, 29, 75, 111.

Maine, U. S. Battleship, her story of the blowing up of, 286, 287.
Malvern Hill, Battle of, 99.
Manassas (Bull Run), battles, 36.
Margot, Mdlle. Antoinette, a faithful friend, 143; painting by, 158, 174; at Geneva International Congress, 344.
Mason, Charles, Supt. of Patents, 26.
McClellan, Gen. George B., 34.
McClellan, Robert, Secretary of the Interior, 25.
McCormack, Dr., Chief Medical Director, Army of the James, 90.
McDowell, Gen. Irving, U. S. A., 36.
Meade, Gen. George G., U. S. A., 91, 99.
Medical Inspector, Dr. Coolidge, 34.
Memorial Day she stood with the boys in blue, 406.
Mills (Capt.), and (Private) Clark, in hospital, 303; one is white, the other black, 304.
Mississippi, the 1882 and 1883 floods, 237, 243.
Monae-Lesser, Dr., at Cuban hospitals, 295, 298, 299; Surgeon in Chief at Siboney, 302.
Moynier, Mons., of Geneva, 227.

Napoleon declares war, 132.
Nightingale, Florence, 125, 208.
Nipmuc Indians, 2.
Norton, Mary, 20.
Nourse, Rebecca, 2.

Paris, the siege and the Commune, 164.
Patent Office, Commissioner of, 25; Charles Mason, Supt. of, 26.

Petersburg, Va., siege of and the Mine, 99.
Picker Room at brother's mill she made into a schoolroom, 356.
Plunkett, armless Sergt. 21st Mass., 72.
Pope, Gen. John, 36.
Porter, Gen. FitzJohn, 54.
Presidents of the U. S.: Franklin Pierce, 25; James Buchanan, 26; Abraham Lincoln, 29; Rutherford B. Hayes, 227; James A. Garfield, 231, 234, 237; Chester A. Arthur, 241; Grover Cleveland, 250; William McKinley, 289; Theodore Roosevelt, 300; Woodrow Wilson, 351.
Proctor, U. S. Senator Redfield, 285, 328.
Putnam, Col. H. L., 78.

Quartermaster-general, Gen. Rucker, 34, 49.

Red Cross in America, 12; International, 124; Swiss Society of, 138; first planned in America, 211; foundation in America, 226; field of relief, 1881 to 1905, 236; Glen Echo, Headquarters of the Nation, 236; American Association organized, 238, 283; Storehouse of National Association, 361; in 1904 the R. C. Society is reincorporated by Congress, 331; 1915 Directorate, 331; on March 25, 1915, corner stone of R. C. building is laid, 332.
Reed, Mrs. J. Sewall, received descriptive letters from Cuba, 289–294, 312; from Glen Echo, 315; from Washington, 317.
Reno, Gen. Jesse L., 36, 52.
Reynolds, Gen. John F., 36.
Richie, Lieut. U. S. S. Pawnee, siege of Charleston, 83.
Roosevelt, Col. Theodore, finds money cannot buy her supplies, 300.
Rucker, a Quartermaster General, 34, 49.

Salem Witchcraft, 1.
Santiago, the surrender arranged, 307.
Sedgwick, Gen. John, 54.
Seward, William H., Secretary of State, 128
Seymour, Gen., at Charleston siege, 77.
Sharpsburg (Antietam), Battle of, 54.
Shaw, Col. Robert G., 54th Mass., Colored, 77.
Sheldon, Capt. L. F., Military Telegraph Dept., 87.
Shepherd, Dr., American Armenian doctor and missionary at Aintab, 279.

Sheridan, Gen. Phil., 91.
Sigel, Gen. Franz, 36.
Sigsbee, Capt. U. S. S. Maine, 286.
South Atlantic Squadron off Charleston, 77.
South Mountain and Harper's Ferry, 48, 60, 64.
Spottsylvania, Battle of, 91.
Spy, Worcester, 29.
Stanton, Mrs. Cady, 20, 122.
Stevens, Mrs. M., an angel of mercy, 92.
Stockings for dead men, 101.
Stone, Mrs. Lucy Blackwell, 20; Col. Richard C., 9.
Strong, Gen. George C., at siege of Charleston, 77.
Sumner, Charles, 27.
Sumner, Gen. Edwin V., 54.
Sumter, Fort, 28, 77.
Surgeon-general Wm. A. Hammond, 34.

Terrill, A. W., U. S. Minister at Constantinople, 277.
"Texas Village" (North Oxford), 18.
"The Vacant Chair," 33.
Treaty of Geneva, the nine articles of, 126; the President of U. S. signs the, 241.

Upton, the U. S. Consul at Geneva, 129.

Vassall, Mrs. Fannie C., 161 n.
Vassall, Mrs. Sally (Barton), 21 n., 28, 173.

Wagner, siege of Fort or Battery, 77.
War, the Franco-Prussian, 123–136; "Prepare for war," replies the King of Prussia to Napoleon, 134.
Ward, Fred L., faces actual need at Galveston flood, 321.
Warren, Gen. George K., 91.
Washburn, E. B., Minister to France, 123.
Washburn, Henry S., writes "The Vacant Chair," 33.
Wilderness, Va., Battle of the, 89.
Williams, Gen. A. S., 54.
Wilson, U. S. Senator Henry, 92, 93, 118.
Women, "The Women who went to the field," 399.

Young, Prof. Charles Sumner, letter to, 335–337; his reply, 337, 338.

Zimmerman, Anna, with Miss Barton, enters Paris afoot and alone, 164.

Printed in the United States of America.

THE following pages contain advertisements of a few new Macmillan books on History and Biography.

Henry Codman Potter

Seventh Bishop of New York

By GEORGE HODGES

Cloth, 8vo, Illustrated, $3.50

It will be a source of gratification to Bishop Potter's
many friends to learn that the preparation of the official
biography of Dr. Potter has been entrusted to Dean
Hodges of the Episcopal Theological School. Long conversant with the large essentials of Dr. Potter's life,
his training and sympathy have been such as to qualify
him to do the task well. The biography that he has
written describes Dr. Potter's career throughout his ministry, especially as rector of Grace Church and as Bishop
of New York. The great public services of Bishop
Potter are also dealt with at length.

THE MACMILLAN COMPANY

Publishers   64–66 Fifth Avenue   New York

A Reverie of Childhood and Youth

By WILLIAM BUTLER YEATS

Cloth, 12mo

Here the celebrated Irish writer gives us his reminiscences of his childhood and youth. Like most poets, Mr. Yeats was a nervous, impressionable, and sensitive boy. His childhood, as is shown in this volume, was passed with his grandfather in Ireland, and his youth mainly with his father, a painter. The memories are written, as is to be expected, in charming prose. They have the interest invariably attached to the account of a sensitive childhood. For those who have been interested in the author's work or in the Irish drama the reveries will be found valuable as supplying a sort of spiritual and emotional biography of Yeats's early years.

The Life of Benjamin Disraeli, Earl of Beaconsfield

VOLUME IV

By THE LATE W. F. MONYPENNY

AND

GEORGE EARL BUCKLE

Formerly Editor of the " London Times

With Portraits and Illustrations. Cloth, 8vo, $3.00

This volume well continues a remarkable biography, a work which is meeting with the favor of historians, students of government, and the general reader.

THE MACMILLAN COMPANY

Publishers   64–66 Fifth Avenue   New York

History of the Norwegian People

By KNUT GJERSET, Ph.D.

Professor of Norwegian Language, Literature, and History in Luther College

Cloth, 8vo, Illustrated. In two volumes. $8.00

This is a history of Norway from the earliest times to the present, in which the author shows the social and cultural growth of the nation as well as its economic and political development. In the first volume he traces the origin and early years of the race and its progress as a united and seafaring people. He describes in an interesting way the deep and permanent influence which the Norsemen exerted on Scotland through their extensive colonization there — their settlements in England, and the parts they have played in English commerce, their occupation of Ireland and the fate of their colonies on the adjacent islands. In the second volume he treats of the decline after the first period of national greatness, the rise of the Norwegian democracy and the new development under the national constitution after 1814. A brief chapter regarding Norwegian immigration to America and the life of the Norwegian people in this country is also included.

Economic Origins of Jeffersonian Democracy

By CHARLES A. BEARD

Author of " An Economic Interpretation of the United States," etc.

Cloth, 8vo, $2.50

The publication of Professor Beard's *Economic Interpretation of the Constitution* two years ago marked the beginning of a new period in historical writings on American politics. The fundamental conclusions of that volume have been accepted in the latest historical work covering the period of the formation of the Constitution.

The new volume on Jeffersonian democracy is a fresh treatment of the period from the formation of the Constitution to the establishment of Jeffersonian democracy in power. It brings together for the first time the economic elements in the party conflict and treats that conflict as growing, in the main, out of the antagonism between rising capitalism and agrarianism.

THE MACMILLAN COMPANY

Publishers   64–66 Fifth Avenue   New York

Made in the USA
Columbia, SC
29 August 2018